Lecture Notes in Computer Science 3443

Commenced Publication in 1973
Founding and Former Series Editors:
Gerhard Goos, Juris Hartmanis, and Jan van Leeuwen

Rastislav Bodik (Ed.)

Compiler Construction

14th International Conference, CC 2005
Held as Part of the Joint European Conferences
on Theory and Practice of Software, ETAPS 2005
Edinburgh, UK, April 4-8, 2005
Proceedings

Volume Editor

Rastislav Bodik
University of California
Computer Science Division, #1776
Berkeley, CA 94720-1776, USA
E-mail: bodik@cs.berkeley.edu

Library of Congress Control Number: 2005922868

CR Subject Classification (1998): D.3.4, D.3.1, F.4.2, D.2.6, F.3, I.2.2

ISSN 0302-9743
ISBN-10 3-540-25411-0 Springer Berlin Heidelberg New York
ISBN-13 978-3-540-25411-9 Springer Berlin Heidelberg New York

Springer is a part of Springer Science+Business Media

springeronline.com

Printed in Germany

Typesetting: Camera-ready by author, data conversion by Scientific Publishing Services, Chennai, India
Printed on acid-free paper SPIN: 11406921 06/3142 5 4 3 2 1 0

Foreword

ETAPS 2005 was the eighth instance of the European Joint Conferences on Theory and Practice of Software. ETAPS is an annual federated conference that was established in 1998 by combining a number of existing and new conferences. This year it comprised five conferences (CC, ESOP, FASE, FOSSACS, TACAS), 17 satellite workshops (AVIS, BYTECODE, CEES, CLASE, CMSB, COCV, FAC, FESCA, FINCO, GCW-DSE, GLPL, LDTA, QAPL, SC, SLAP, TGC, UITP), seven invited lectures (not including those that were specific to the satellite events), and several tutorials. We received over 550 submissions to the five conferences this year, giving acceptance rates below 30% for each one. Congratulations to all the authors who made it to the final program! I hope that most of the other authors still found a way of participating in this exciting event and I hope you will continue submitting.

The events that comprise ETAPS address various aspects of the system development process, including specification, design, implementation, analysis and improvement. The languages, methodologies and tools which support these activities are all well within its scope. Different blends of theory and practice are represented, with an inclination towards theory with a practical motivation on the one hand and soundly based practice on the other. Many of the issues involved in software design apply to systems in general, including hardware systems, and the emphasis on software is not intended to be exclusive.

ETAPS is a loose confederation in which each event retains its own identity, with a separate program committee and proceedings. Its format is open-ended, allowing it to grow and evolve as time goes by. Contributed talks and system demonstrations are in synchronized parallel sessions, with invited lectures in plenary sessions. Two of the invited lectures are reserved for "unifying" talks on topics of interest to the whole range of ETAPS attendees. The aim of cramming all this activity into a single one-week meeting is to create a strong magnet for academic and industrial researchers working on topics within its scope, giving them the opportunity to learn about research in related areas, and thereby to foster new and existing links between work in areas that were formerly addressed in separate meetings.

ETAPS 2005 was organized by the School of Informatics of the University of Edinburgh, in cooperation with

- European Association for Theoretical Computer Science (EATCS);
- European Association for Programming Languages and Systems (EAPLS);
- European Association of Software Science and Technology (EASST).

The organizing team comprised:

- Chair: Don Sannella
- Publicity: David Aspinall
- Satellite Events: Massimo Felici

- Secretariat: Dyane Goodchild
- Local Arrangements: Monika-Jeannette Lekuse
- Tutorials: Alberto Momigliano
- Finances: Ian Stark
- Website: Jennifer Tenzer, Daniel Winterstein
- Fundraising: Phil Wadler

ETAPS 2005 received support from the University of Edinburgh.

Overall planning for ETAPS conferences is the responsibility of its Steering Committee, whose current membership is:

> Perdita Stevens (Edinburgh, Chair), Luca Aceto (Aalborg and Reykjavík), Rastislav Bodik (Berkeley), Maura Cerioli (Genoa), Evelyn Duesterwald (IBM, USA), Hartmut Ehrig (Berlin), José Fiadeiro (Leicester), Marie-Claude Gaudel (Paris), Roberto Gorrieri (Bologna), Reiko Heckel (Paderborn), Holger Hermanns (Saarbrücken), Joost-Pieter Katoen (Aachen), Paul Klint (Amsterdam), Jens Knoop (Vienna), Kim Larsen (Aalborg), Tiziana Margaria (Dortmund), Ugo Montanari (Pisa), Hanne Riis Nielson (Copenhagen), Fernando Orejas (Barcelona), Mooly Sagiv (Tel Aviv), Don Sannella (Edinburgh), Vladimiro Sassone (Sussex), Peter Sestoft (Copenhagen), Michel Wermelinger (Lisbon), Igor Walukiewicz (Bordeaux), Andreas Zeller (Saarbrücken), Lenore Zuck (Chicago).

I would like to express my sincere gratitude to all of these people and organizations, the program committee chairs and PC members of the ETAPS conferences, the organizers of the satellite events, the speakers themselves, the many reviewers, and Springer for agreeing to publish the ETAPS proceedings. Finally, I would like to thank the organizer of ETAPS 2005, Don Sannella. He has been instrumental in the development of ETAPS since its beginning; it is quite beyond the limits of what might be expected that, in addition to all the work he has done as the original ETAPS Steering Committee Chairman and current ETAPS Treasurer, he has been prepared to take on the task of organizing this instance of ETAPS. It gives me particular pleasure to thank him for organizing ETAPS in this wonderful city of Edinburgh in this my first year as ETAPS Steering Committee Chair.

Edinburgh, January 2005

Perdita Stevens
ETAPS Steering Committee Chair

Preface

The program committee is pleased to present the proceedings of the 14th International Conference on Compiler Construction (CC 2005) held April 4–5, 2005, in Edinburgh, UK, as part of the Joint European Conferences on Theory and Practice of Software (ETAPS 2005).

Traditionally, CC had been a forum for research on compiler construction. Starting this year, CC has expanded its mission to a broader spectrum of programming tools, from refactoring editors to program checkers to compilers to virtual machines to debuggers. The submissions we received reflected the new scope of the conference.

The Program Committee received 91 submissions (one was later withdrawn), a significant increase from previous years. From the 90 submissions, the Program Committee selected 21 papers, for an acceptance rate of 23%. Four of the accepted papers were tool demonstrations; the submission pool included eight such papers. I believe this is the first CC conference that includes tool demos.

The Program Committee included 15 members representing 10 countries on three continents. Each committee member reviewed (or delegated) roughly 19 papers. Each paper received three reviews. Sixty-eight external reviewers participated in the review process. Committee members were allowed to submit papers, although no paper by a committee member was selected. The Program Committee met on December 4, 2004, in New York for a one-day meeting. All but one of the members participated in the meeting; three members attended via teleconference.

The work of many contributed to the success of this conference. First of all, I want to thank the authors for the care they put into their submissions. My gratitude also goes to Program Committee members and external reviewers for their insightful reviews. IBM generously provided the teleconference service for the Program Committee meeting; thanks to Kemal Ebcioglu for arranging this service. Special thanks go to Manu Sridharan for helping to prepare and run the Program Committee meeting. CC 2005 was made possible by the ETAPS Steering Committee, in particular by the hard work of Don Sannella, the ETAPS 2005 Organizing Committee chair, and José Luiz Fiadeiro and Perdita Stevens, ETAPS chairs. I would also like to thank Evelyn Duesterwald, Görel Hedin, Nigel Horspool and Reinhard Wilhelm, all recent CC chairs, for our many discussions on CC's future directions. Finally, we are grateful to Andreas Zeller for accepting the invitation to give a keynote talk.

Berkeley, January 2005 Rastislav Bodík

Conference Organization

Program Chair

Rastislav Bodík	*UC Berkeley, USA*

Program Committee

Charles Consel	*LABRI, France*
Grzegorz Czajkowski	*Sun Labs, USA*
Angela Demke-Brown	*University of Toronto, Canada*
Amy Felty	*University of Ottawa, Canada*
Antonio Gonzalez	*UPC, Spain*
Thomas Gross	*ETH, Switzerland*
Jan Heering	*CWI, Netherlands*
Roberto Ierusalimschy	*PUC-Rio, Brazil*
Chandra Krintz	*UC Santa Barbara, USA*
Rustan Leino	*Microsoft Research, USA*
Eduard Mehofer	*University of Vienna, Austria*
Michael Philippsen	*Universität Erlangen-Nürnberg, Germany*
G. Ramalingam	*IBM Research, USA*
Michael I. Schwartzbach	*University of Aarhus, Denmark*
Andreas Zeller	*Saarland University, Germany*

Referees

Ali Adl-Tabatabai, Alex Aleta, Erik Altman, Lars Bak, Siegfried Benkner, Claus Brabrand, Mark van der Brand, Joachim Buhmann, Vipin Chaudhary, Aske Christensen, Josep M. Codina, Jesus Corbal, Matteo Corti, Laurent Daynes, David Detlefs, Danny Dubé, Jan van Eijck, Robert van Engelen, Xiaobo Fan, Steve Fink, Ingrid Fischer, Kyle Gallivan, Enric Gibert, David Gregg, Dan Grossman, David Grove, Selim Gurun, Laurie Hendren, Michael Hind, Douglas Howe, Daniel Jackson, Timothy Jones, Mick Jordan, Wayne Kelly, Michael Klemm, Jens Knoop, Gabriella Kokai, Andreas Krall, Geoff Langdale, Julia Lawall, Sorin Lerner, Chuck Liang, Christian Lindig, Josep Llosa, Lukas Loehrer, Guei-Yuan Lueh, Carlos Madriles, Hidehiko Masuhara, Hussam Mousa, Priya Nagpurkar, Krzysztof Palacz, Carlos Garcia Quiñones, Ramshankar Ramanarayana, Jesus Sanchez, Dominic Schell, Florian Schneider, Bernhard Scholz, Christian Sigg, Glenn Skinner, Sunil Soman, Walid Taha, Mads Torgersen, David Ungar, Ronald Veldema, Xavier Vera, Jurgen Vinju, Phillip Yelland, Lingli Zhang

Table of Contents

Invited Talk

Compilation

Parallelism

Memory Management

Program Transformations

Tool Demonstrations

Pointer Analysis

When Abstraction Fails

Andreas Zeller

Saarland University, Saarbrücken, Germany
zeller@cs.uni-sb.de

Abstract. Reasoning about programs is mostly deduction: the reasoning from the abstract model to the concrete run. Deduction is useful because it allows us to predict properties of future runs—up to the point that a program will never fail its specification. However, even such a 100% correct program may still show a problem: the specification itself may be problematic, or deduction required us to abstract away some relevant property. To handle such problems, deduction is not the right answer—especially in a world where programs reach a complexity that makes them indistinguishable from natural phenomena. Instead, we should enrich our portfolio by methods proven in natural sciences, such as observation, induction, and in particular experimentation. In my talk, I will show how systematic experimentation automatically reveals the causes of program failures—in the input, in the program state, or in the program code.

1 Introduction

I do research on how to debug programs. It is not that I am particularly fond of bugs, or debugging. In fact, I hate bugs, and I have spent far too much time on chasing and eradicating them. People might say: So, why don't you spend your research time on improving your specification, model checker, software process, architecture, or whatever the latest and greatest advance in science is. I answer: All of these help *preventing* errors, which is fine. But none can prevent surprises. And I postulate that surprises are unavoidable, that we have to teach people how to deal with them and to set things straight after the fact.

As one of my favorite examples, consider the *sample* program in Fig. 1 on the following page. Ideally, the `sample` program sorts its arguments numerically and prints the sorted list, as in this run ($r_{\checkmark}$):

```
sample 9 8 7   ⇒   7 8 9
```

With certain arguments, `sample` fails (run $r_{\times}$):

```
sample 11 14   ⇒   0 11
```

Surprise! While the output of `sample` is still properly sorted, the output is not a permutation of the input—somehow, a zero value has sneaked in. What is the defect that causes this failure?

R. Bodik (Ed.): CC 2005, LNCS 3443, pp. 1–9, 2005.

```
/* sample.c -- Sample C program to be debugged */

#include <stdio.h>
#include <stdlib.h>

static void shell_sort(int a[], int size)
{
    int i, j;
    int h = 1;
    do {
        h = h * 3 + 1;
    } while (h <= size);
    do {
        h /= 3;
        for (i = h; i < size; i++)
        {
            int v = a[i];
            for (j = i; j >= h && a[j - h] > v; j -= h)
                a[j] = a[j - h];
            if (i != j)
                a[j] = v;
        }
    } while (h != 1);
}

int main(int argc, char *argv[])
{
    int  i = 0;
    int *a = NULL;

    a = (int *)malloc((argc - 1) * sizeof(int));
    for (i = 0; i < argc - 1; i++)
        a[i] = atoi(argv[i + 1]);

    shell_sort(a, argc);

    for (i = 0; i < argc - 1; i++)
        printf("%d ", a[i]);
    printf("\n");

    free(a);
    return 0;
}
```

Fig. 1. The *sample* program (almost) sorts its arguments

In principle, debugging a program like `sample` is easy. Initially, some programmer has created a *defect*—an error in the code. When executed, this defect causes an *infection*—an error in the program state. (Other people call this a *fault,* but I prefer the term *infection*, because the error propagates across later states, just like an infection.) When the infection finally reaches a point where it can be observed, it becomes a *failure*—in our case, the zero in the output. Given that a failure has already occurred, it is the duty of the programmer to trace back this cause-effect chain of infections back to the defect where it originated—the defect that caused the failure.

As an experienced programmer, you may be able to walk your way through the source code in Fig. 1 and spot the defect. When it comes to doing so in a general, systematic, maybe even automated way, we quickly run into trouble, though. The difficulty begins with the terms. What do we actually mean when we say "the defect that caused the failure"? What are we actually searching for?

2 Errors are Easy to Detect, But Generally Impossible to Locate

An *error* is a deviation from what is correct, right, or true. To tell that something is erroneous thus requires a specification of what is correct, right, or true. This can be applied to output, input, state, and code:

Errors in the output. An externally visible error in the program behavior is called a *failure.* Our investigation starts when we determine (or decide) that this is the case.

Errors in the input. For the program *input,* we typically know what is valid and what not, and therefore we can determine whether an input is erroneous or not. If the program shows a failure, and if the input was correct, we know the program as a whole is incorrect.

Errors in the program state. It is between input and output that things start to get difficult. When it comes to the program *state,* we frequently have specifications that allow us to catch infections—for instance, when a pre- or postcondition is violated. Types can be seen as specifications that detect and prevent illegal variable values. Common programming errors, such as buffer overflows or null pointer dereferences, can be specified and detected at compile time.

Errors in the code. Unfortunately, specifications apply only to *parts* of the program state: conditions apply to selected moments in time; types allow a wide range of values; tools can only check for common errors. Therefore, there will always be parts of the state for which correctness is not specified. But if we do not know whether a variable value is correct, we cannot tell whether the code that generated this value is correct. Therefore, we cannot exactly track down the moment the value got infected, and therefore, we cannot locate the defect that caused the failure.

Of course, we can catch errors by simply specifying more. A specification that covers each and every aspect of a program state would detect every single error. Unfortunately, such a specification would ne no less complex and error-prone than the program itself.

In practice, it is the programmer who *decides* what is right upon examining the program—and fixes the program according to this *implied* specification. In such a cases, deciding which part of a program is in error can only be told after the decision has been made and the error has been fixed. Once we know the correct, right, and true code, we can thus tell the defect as a deviation from the corrected code. In other words, *locating a defect is equivalent to writing a correct program.* And we know how hard this is.

3 Causes Need Not be Errors, But Can Easily be Located

While it may be hard to pinpoint an error, the concept of *causality* is far less ambiguous. In general, a *cause* is an event that precedes another event (the *effect*), such that the effect would not have occurred without the cause. For programs, this means that any aspect of an execution causes a failure if it can be altered such that the failure no longer occurs. This applies to input, state, and code:

Causes in the input. We can change the input of the `sample` program from `11 14` (run $r_{✗}$) to `7 8 9` (run $r_{✓}$), and the failure no longer occurs. Hence, we know that the input causes the failure.
One may argue that in any program, the input determines the behavior and thus eventually causes any failure. However, it may be only parts of the input that are relevant. For instance, if we run `sample` with `11`, we find that it is the additional `14` argument which causes the failure:

$$\texttt{sample 11} \quad \Rightarrow \quad \texttt{11}$$

Causes in program state. If we can change some variable during execution such that the failure no longer occurs, we know that the variable caused the failure.
Again, consider the failing `sample` run $r_{✗}$. We could use an interactive debugger and stop the program at `main()` (Line 28), change `argc` from 2 to 1, and resume execution. We would find an output of `11`, and thus find out that the value of `argc` caused the failure.
As we can see from this example, a cause does not imply an error: The value of `argc` probably is correct with respect to some implied specification; yet, it is tied to the failure.

Causes in the code. All variable values are created by some statement in the code; and thus, there are statements which cause values which again cause failures.
In the `sample` program, there is a statement which exactly does that, and which can (and should) be changed to make the failure no longer occur. The interesting aspect is that we can find that statement from the causes in the program state. If we can find a failure cause in the program state, we can trace it back to the statement which generated it.

Once again, it is important to note that causes and errors are two orthogonal concepts. We can tell an error without knowing whether it is a cause for the failure at hand, and we can tell a cause without knowing whether it is an error. In the absence of a detailed specification, though, we must rely on causality to narrow down those statements which caused the error—in the hope that the defect is among them.

4 Isolating Failure Causes with Automatic Experiments

Verifying that something is a cause cannot be done by deduction. We need at least two *experiments:* One with the cause, and one without; if the effect occurs only with the cause, we're set. This implies that we need two runs of the

Table 1. One of the state differences between $r_{\checkmark}$ and $r_{\times}$ causes *sample* to fail

Variable	Value in $r_{\checkmark}$	Value in $r_{\times}$
argc	**4**	**5**
argv[0]	"./sample"	"./sample"
argv[1]	**"9"**	**"11"**
argv[2]	**"8"**	**"14"**
argv[3]	**"7"**	**0x0 (NULL)**
i'	1073834752	1073834752
j	1074077312	1074077312
h	1961	1961
size	**4**	**3**

Variable	Value in $r_{\checkmark}$	Value in $r_{\times}$
i	**3**	**2**
a[0]	**9**	**11**
a[1]	**8**	**14**
a[2]	**7**	**0**
a[3]	1961	1961
a'[0]	**9**	**11**
a'[1]	**8**	**14**
a'[2]	**7**	**0**
a'[3]	1961	1961

program—one where the failure occurs, and one where the failure does not occur. In debugging, this second run comes at the very end after fixing the defect—if the failure no longer occurs, this verifies that the defect actually caused the original failure.

However, having a passing run $r_{\checkmark}$ and a failing run $r_{\times}$ initially is the key for finding causes. The initial difference in the program input causes differences in the program state, which propagate until we see the final difference in the program outcome. By comparing $r_{\checkmark}$ and $r_{\times}$, we can extract these differences, and compare them to get a first idea of what caused the failure.

Again, consider the `sample` program. Table 1 lists the `sample` program states, as well as the differences, as obtained from both $r_{\checkmark}$ and $r_{\times}$ when Line 9 was reached. (a and i occur in `shell_sort()` and in `main()`; the `shell_sort()` instances are denoted as a' and i'.)

Formally, this set of 12 differences is a failure cause: If we change the state of $r_{\checkmark}$ to the state in $r_{\times}$, we obtain the original failure. However, of all differences, only some may be *relevant* for the failure—that is, it may suffice to change only a *subset* of the variables to make the failure occur. For a precise diagnosis, we are interested in obtaining a subset of relevant variables that is as small as possible.

Delta Debugging [3] is a general procedure to obtain such a small subset. Given a set of differences (such as the differences between the program states in Fig. 1), Delta Debugging determines a *relevant subset* in which each remaining difference is relevant for the failure to occur. To do so, Delta Debugging systematically and automatically *tests* subsets and narrows down the difference depending on the test outcome, as sketched in Fig. 2. Overall, Delta Debugging behaves very much like a binary search.

Originally, Delta Debugging was designed for program inputs. However, one may consider a program state as an input to the remainder of the program execution; hence, it is pretty straight-forward to apply Delta Debugging on program states to isolate causes. Applied on the differences in Table 1, Delta Debugging would result in a first test that

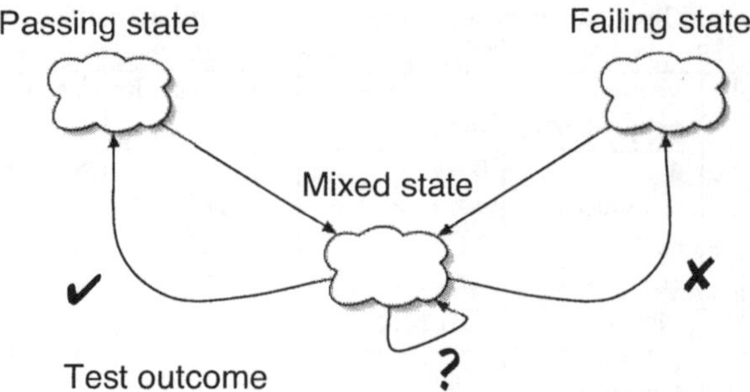

Fig. 2. Narrowing down state differences. By assessing whether a mixed state results in a passing (✔), a failing (✘), or an unresolved (?) outcome, Delta Debugging isolates a relevant difference

- runs $r_✔$ up to Line 9,
- applies *half* of the differences on $r_✔$—that is, it sets `argc`, `argv[1]`, `argv[2]`, `argv[3]`, `size`, and `i` to the values from $r_✘$—, and
- resumes execution and determines the outcome.

This test results in the same output as the original run; that is, the six differences applied were not relevant for the failure. With this experiment, Delta Debugging has narrowed down the failure-inducing difference to the remaining six differences. Repeating the search on this subset eventually reveals one single variable, `a[2]`, whose zero value is failure-inducing: If, in $r_✔$, we set `a[2]` from 7 to 0, the output is `0 8 9`—the failure occurs. We can thus conclude that the zero being printed is caused by `a[2]`—which we can confirm further by changing `a[2]` in $r_✘$ from 0 to 7, and obtaining the output `7 11`. Thus, in Line 9, `a[2]` being zero causes the `sample` failure.

The idea of determining causes by experimenting with mixed program states (rather than by analyzing the program or its run, for instance) may seem strange at first. Yet, the technique has been shown to produce useful diagnoses for programs as large as the GNU compiler (GCC). As detailed in [2], scaling up the general idea, as sketched here, requires capturing and comparing program states as *memory graphs* [4]. Also, Delta Debugging must do more than simple binary search; it needs to cope with interferences of multiple failure-inducing elements as well as with unresolved test outcomes [3].

5 Locating the Statements That Cause the Failure—Automatically

The tricky question is now: How do we get from failure-causing states to failure-causing statements? One straight-forward way might be to look at the statements which created the value. Alas, we won't find such a statement for `a[2]`; it is never assigned a value before Line 9.

However, it turns out that at the start of `main()`, in Line 28, it is not `a[2]` which causes the failure, but *argc*—if we change the value of `argc` from 4 (its value in $r_{\text{✗}}$) to 3 (its value in $r_{\checkmark}$), the failure no longer occurs. Since initially, `argc` caused the failure, and later, `a[2]`, there must have been some moment in time where this transition from `argc` to `a[2]` took place. This transition can be isolated using binary search over time: it takes place at Line 35, at the call

```
shell_sort(a, argc);
```

This is where `argc` stops to be a cause, and `a[2]` begins. This transition implies that Line 35 causes `a[2]` to cause the failure—or, in other words, that we can change Line 35 to make the failure no longer occur. Line 35 is a failure cause.

So, let us focus on Line 35 to see whether it is not only a cause, but in fact, erroneous. Let us assume that in the declaration `shell_sort(int a[], int size)`, the parameter `size` stands for the number of elements in `a[]`. Then, the call in Line 35 is wrong—simply because `argc` is not the number of elements in `a[]`, but off by one. The correct call would be

```
shell_sort(a, argc - 1);
```

By changing the statement, we can re-run the test to see whether the failure still occurs. It does not; hence, we have proven that the defect actually caused the failure—and successfully fixed the program.

In this example, the cause transition from `argc` to `a[2]` occurred right at the place of the defect. As a programmer, though, I may also have decided to change `shell_sort()` instead such that `size` is the number of elements in `a` plus one. I could also decrease the value of `argc` or introduce a new variable `arguments` initialized with `argc - 1`. This number of alternatives shows that it is difficult to *predict* an exact change, say, in an evaluation. Therefore, when evaluating whether cause transitions are effective in locating defects, one uses a measure of *closeness:* If we cannot predict the exact location of the defect, how close are we in locating it?

To evaluate a defect locator, one thus ranks the statements of the program according to their likelihood to be defective. In our case, we'd rank the locations of cause transitions at the top, followed by "close" locations—that is, those related by one control or data dependency—and followed by less close locations by doing an exhaustive breadth-first search along the system dependency graph. The assumption is that a programmer starts with the most likely locations (at the top) and then walks down the list until he or she finds the defect. In a case study [1], it turned out that cause transitions are the best defect locators available—they locate the failure-inducing defect twice as well as the best methods known so far. The technique is implemented as part of the ASKIGOR debugging server (Fig. 3).

Yet, we have just begun to explore the idea of making experimenting a part of program analysis. There is still a long way to go before these techniques can become part of the mainstream: in particular, extracting and mixing program states becomes a challenge if the program is deeply interwoven with its environment. On the other hand, having automated diagnoses is not only convenient

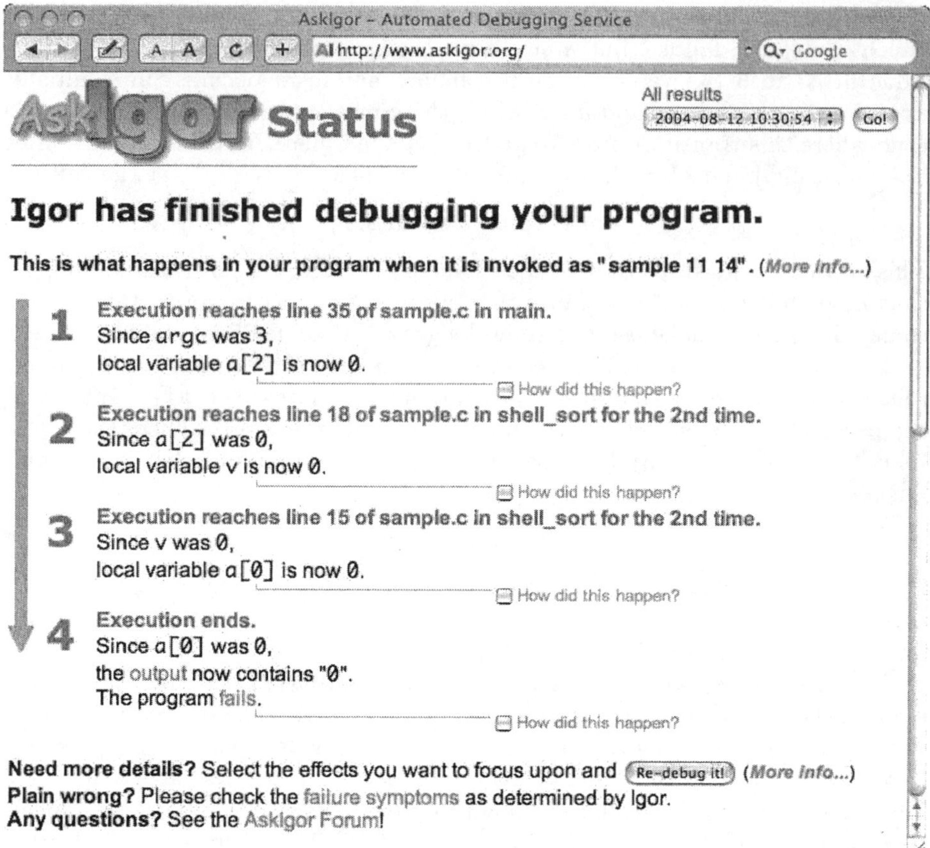

Fig. 3. ASKIGOR with a diagnosis for *sample*

for the programmer, but also may enable new generations of self-aware systems: Think of a Web server, for instance, that automatically determines a failure cause in its own code, and thus disables the appropriate configuration module—at least as a temporary fix until the code is corrected.

6 Conclusion: Prevent Errors *and* Prepare for Surprises

Why focus on cure, when prevention is so much better? Of course, we should continue to strive for systems that have as few defects as possible. But this must not mean to neglect the cure altogether. In a world where software systems become more and more complex, we must be prepared for surprises. And a surprise is exactly what happens when the given abstraction fails, or where there simply is no abstraction that could tell what's right and what's wrong.

Program analysis has long been based on abstraction alone—deducing predictions from the program code that hold for future program runs. To analyze *past* program runs, though, requires a much wider portfolio of techniques—simply because there is much more data to take into account: Besides program code, we can look at actual runs, test outcomes, version histories—any artifact created during development is welcome. And if *induction* to derive common patterns from all these instances is not enough, we can use *experimentation* to generate even more. Fortunately for us, we now have the computational power available to apply all these techniques. What we need is a confluence of static and dynamic analysis, of deduction and induction techniques—to foster the understanding of today's programs, and to bring surprises and their damage to a minimum.

Acknowledgments. Thanks to all who gave me feedback on earlier instances of this talk. Christian Lindig and Stephan Neuhaus gave valuable comments on this paper.

References

1. Holger Cleve and Andreas Zeller. Locating causes of program failures. In *Proc. International Conference on Software Engineering (ICSE)*, St. Louis, Missouri, May 2005.
2. Andreas Zeller. Isolating cause-effect chains from computer programs. In William G. Griswold, editor, *Proc. Tenth ACM SIGSOFT Symposium on the Foundations of Software Engineering (FSE-10)*, pages 1–10, Charleston, South Carolina, November 2002. ACM Press.
3. Andreas Zeller and Ralf Hildebrandt. Simplifying and isolating failure-inducing input. *IEEE Transactions on Software Engineering*, 28(2):183–200, February 2002.
4. Thomas Zimmermann and Andreas Zeller. Visualizing memory graphs. In Stephan Diehl, editor, *Proc. of the International Dagstuhl Seminar on Software Visualization*, volume 2269 of *Lecture Notes in Computer Science*, pages 191–204, Dagstuhl, Germany, May 2002. Springer-Verlag.

Source-Level Debugging for Multiple Languages with Modest Programming Effort

Sukyoung Ryu and Norman Ramsey

Division of Engineering and Applied Sciences, Harvard University
{syryu, nr}@eecs.harvard.edu

Abstract. We present techniques that enable source-level debugging for multiple languages at the cost of only modest programming effort. The key idea is to avoid letting debugging requirements constrain the internal structure of the compiler. Constraints are minimized primarily by hiding the source-language type system and target-machine representations from the debugger. This approach enables us to support a new language and compiler while reusing existing elements: a multi-language, multi-platform debugger; the compiler's implementation of source-language types and expressions; information already present in the compiler's private data structures; and our *compile-time support library*, which helps the compiler meet its obligations to the debugger without exposing language-dependent details. We evaluate our approach using two case studies: the production compiler `lcc` and an instructional compiler for MiniJava.

1 Introduction

Wouldn't it be nice if every high-level programming language came with a source-level debugger? Unfortunately, debugging requires a wealth of information that depends on both source language and target machine: what the source-level type system is, how source-level values are represented on the target machine, how such values should be displayed to the user, and so on. A typical debugger receives this information through an interface like `dbx` "stabs" or DWARF (Linton 1990; Unix Int'l 1993). It is bad enough that these interfaces are complex and difficult to use, but what is worse, they overconstrain the compiler: the compiler writer must shoehorn the source language into the debugger's type model, and the compiler writer's choices of representations are limited by the debugger's assumptions.[1]

We address these problems by changing the contract between the compiler and debugger. Our new contract enables us to reduce programming effort by reusing code, by reusing information already present in the compiler's private data structures, and by avoiding constraints on the compiler's representation choices and phase ordering.

- We have implemented a debugger which, except for its stack walker, can be reused even with a language or compiler that it did not previously support.

[1] For example, many debuggers won't let a compiler put a record value in a register, even if the representation of the record fits in a machine word.

R. Bodik (Ed.): CC 2005, LNCS 3443, pp. 10–26, 2005.

- Rather than implement an interpreter for source-language expressions, our debugger reuses the compiler's code to parse expressions, type-check them, and translate them to intermediate form.
- Our debugger receives information from a compiler through a reusable *compile-time support library*. The library helps the compiler meet its obligations to the debugger while hiding language-dependent details. Our library does not force the compiler's private data structures to fit the debugger's model, does not require changing the timing or ordering of the compiler's phases, and does not artificially prolong the lifetimes of the compiler's internal data structures.
  To be used with a particular compiler, the library must provide an interface in the implementation language of that compiler. We have therefore designed the interface in two layers: an abstract layer that is independent of implementation language (Ryu and Ramsey 2004), and a concrete layer that contains instances for four implementation languages (C, Java, Standard ML, and Objective Caml). Each concrete instance is backed up by an implementation.

Our primary goal is to reduce programming effort, which is notoriously difficult to evaluate. As usual, we cannot afford a quantitative, comparative study of different implementation techniques. Instead, we rely on simple metrics and one basic principle.

- Once we have added debugging support to a compiler, we measure the code:
  - How many modules were changed? How many new modules were added?
  - How big are the new modules? In changed modules, how many lines of code were added or changed?
  - How much code is duplicated (in both compiler and debugger)?

  There are other software metrics, but these suffice to show that our technique requires significantly less programming effort than standard techniques.
- Our basic principle is that the less the compiler writer is constrained, the smaller the programming effort will be. Relevant constraints include requiring that the compiler writer present certain information to the debugger; requiring that the information be presented in a certain order; requiring that the information be kept live for a certain time during compilation; and requiring that the compiler use only certain source-language types and representations. Minimizing these constraints has been the major idea behind the design of our support library.

Our work builds on earlier work with `ldb`, which used information hiding to make it easier to retarget a debugger (Ramsey and Hanson 1992; Ramsey 1993). That work applied only to a single language and compiler, and the contract between compiler and debugger was too complex and put too many constraints on the compiler writer. Our novel research contribution is a new contract, which reduces programming effort in two ways: it minimizes constraints on the compiler, and it removes the intellectual burden of organizing the compiler's information in the way the debugger wants it. Instead of falling on the compiler writer, this burden is carried by the support library.

Our new contract supports not only multiple machines, but also multiple source languages. This does not mean *every* language—we assume that a language can be executed by threads with stacks, has mutable state that can be examined, has a meaningful notion of breakpoint, and so on. While these assumptions apply to most languages, they

```
ldb Fib (stopped) > t
  0 <_print:2> (Mips/mjr.c:25,2)  void _print(char *s = (0x1000008c) " ")
* 1 <fib:51+0x24> (Fib.java:23,32)
        void fib(Fib this = {int buffer = 10,
                             int[] a = {1, 1, 2, 3, 5, 8, 13, 21, 34, 55,
                                        0, 0, 0, 0, 0, 0, 0, 0, 0, 0}
                            }, int n = 10)
  2 <main:3+0x18> (Fib.java:5,23)  void main(String[] argv = {})
  3 <mAiN:end+0x1c> (mininub.c:7,9)
        int mAiN(int argc = 2, char **argv = 0x7fff7b24,
                char **envp = 0x7fff7b34)
```

Fig. 1. Example stack trace showing support for multiple languages. Frame 0 contains a C procedure that is part of the MiniJava run-time system; frames 1 and 2 contain MiniJava methods; and frame 3 contains startup code written in C

may not apply to a lazy functional language, a logic language, or a constraint language, for example. Even so, `ldb` can easily be applied to an interesting class of multi-language programs. For example, Fig. 1 shows a debugger stack trace in which some frames are implemented in C and others in the instructional language MiniJava.

2 Overview

Under a debugging contract, a compiler provides information about each program it compiles, and the debugger uses this information to give users a source-level view at run time. Information about a program is highly structured and may describe such elements as source-language types, variables, statements, functions, methods, and so on. We assume that in any given compiler, such elements have natural, native representations, which we call *language-level objects*. But a debugger that works with multiple languages and compilers must use a representation that is independent of any compiler; this representation is composed of elements we call *debug-level objects*. Under our contract, a compiler uses its language-level objects to create debug-level objects, which encapsulate the compiler's knowledge about the source program and its representation on the target machine. Both kinds of objects are described in Section 3.

A key property of debug-level objects is that language-dependent and machine-dependent information is hidden from the debugger. This information hiding leaves the compiler writer free to reflect the structure of the compiler's language-level objects directly in the structure of debug-level objects, reducing the effort required to create the debug-level objects. For example, if the compiler's natural representation of a record type contains a list of pointers to representations of the types of the record's fields, the compiler writer is free to create a debug-level representation of the record type that contains a similar list. But if the compiler's representation of a record type instead keeps the field information in an auxiliary symbol-table entry (Fraser and Hanson 1995, p 54), the compiler writer is free to reflect that representation instead.

To help the compiler create debug-level objects from language-level objects, we provide a compile-time support library. Each library function places a constraint on the

```
void fib(int n) throws
        java.io.IOException {
    int[] a = new int[20];
    if (n > 20) n = 20;
    a[0] = 1;
    a[1] = 1;
    { int i = 1;
      while (i<=n) {
          i = i+1;
          a[i] = a[i-1] + a[i-2];
      }
    }
    { int j = 0;
      while (j<n) {
          this.printint(a[j]);
          System.out.print(" ");
          j = j+1;
      }
    System.out.println();
    }
}
```

Fig. 2. `Fib.java`: MiniJava code

```
          ⋮
    .text
    .globl  $L.Fib.fib
    .ent    $L.Fib.fib
$L.Fib.fib:
$L.Fib.fib_framesize=52
          ⋮
    addu $22, $0, $5
.set noreorder
$L.X6:
.set reorder
    addu $fp, $0, $21
    beq $fp, 0, _BADPTR1
$L1:
    add $8, $fp, 4
    addu $fp, $0, $8
.set noreorder
$L.X7:
.set reorder
    ori $8, $0, 20
          ⋮
```

Fig. 3. `Fib.s`: assembly code

lifetimes of language-level objects: all the language-level objects needed to create a debug-level object must be live at the same time. Section 4 describes these constraints and explains how we minimize them.

Section 5 presents two case studies and makes comparisons with gdb, and Section 6 discusses related work.

3 What a Compiler Must Represent

Creating debug-level objects from language-level objects accounts for most of the programming effort of using `ldb`. To explain the effort, we discuss the language-level objects the compiler needs, the debug-level objects the compiler must create, and the associated programming effort. We also discuss expression evaluation, which not only requires its own effort but also affects the effort of creating debug-level objects.

To make examples concrete, we use procedure `fib`, shown in Fig. 2, which is written in MiniJava. Procedure `fib` computes and prints Fibonacci numbers. It is translated into the assembly file `Fib.s`, an excerpt of which is shown in Fig. 3.

3.1 Language-Level Objects

To create the debug-level objects that `ldb` requires, a compiler needs the following language-level objects.

- *Source-code locations*. The compiler must associate a source-code location with each instance of an interesting language construct, such as the declaration of a variable or the start of a statement. For example, in Fig. 2, the source-code location of variable `i` is line 7, column 11 of file `Fib.java`.
- *Variable placements*. The compiler must know where each live variable is placed at run time. Typically, a variable is placed either in a stack slot or in a machine register. For example, the compiler might place variable `i` in a stack slot addressed at offset −4 from register `$r2`. Placement may vary as the program counter changes.
- *Labels*. On request from the support library, the compiler must insert a label into assembly-language output. For example, the library may ask the compiler to insert a label to mark the start of a statement. In Fig. 3, label `$L.X6` is such a label.
- *Types*. The compiler must know the source-language type of a variable or expression. (If the source language is dynamically typed, it suffices that every variable and expression have the same type, "value.") For example, `i`'s type is `int`.
- *Symbols*. If a named entity is to be visible at debug time, the compiler must describe it with a symbol. For example, if a user can ask the debugger for `i`'s value, the compiler must describe `i` with a symbol.
- *Stopping points*. The compiler must identify *stopping points*: source-code locations where execution of a program might stop at debug time. For example, MiniJava uses very fine-grained stopping points: not only before and between statements, but also before each expression, even nested expressions.
- *Environments*. The compiler must build an environment (symbol table) mapping names to symbols. In a language that allows local declarations, a single name can mean different things at different points in a program, so the compiler must be able to reconstruct a suitable environment at each stopping point. For example, in Fig. 2, variable `i` is visible in line 8's environment but not in line 14's environment.

Because such language-level objects already exist in a typical compiler, even a student compiler (Aho, Sethi, and Ullman 1986; Appel 1998), providing them usually takes little programming effort. The two exceptions are stopping points and source-code locations. Here we have room to discuss only stopping points; source-code locations are discussed in an expanded version of this paper (Ryu and Ramsey 2005).

Stopping points require two kinds of effort. First is the intellectual effort of determining what sorts of program points should be considered stopping points. This determination is language-specific but should not be difficult; common choices include statements, control-flow points, and declarations of named variables. (We recommend against another common choice: source lines.) Second is the programming effort, which we discuss in more detail in Section 3.2.

3.2 Debug-Level Objects to be Created by the Compiler

The language-level objects listed above are used to create debug-level objects. The structure of the language-level objects, especially types and symbols, necessarily reflects the structure of the language being compiled. But different languages have different structures. How, then, can we define one set of debug-level objects that supports multiple languages? The answer is that `ldb`'s debug-level objects make it *possible* to reflect linguistic structure at debug level, but they do not *require* any particular linguistic structure at debug level.

The interface to our support library is based on a hierarchy of types. The base type of a debug-level object is *info*. Some debug-level objects can be extended with key-value pairs (property lists) that hold information private to the compiler; such objects are *tables*. Private key-value pairs (properties) are added to a table using `ldbTable_put`. In the C version of our interface, its declaration is

```
void ldbTable_put(LdbTable *t, const char *key, LdbInfo *val);
```

Particular instances of tables include *symbols* and *types*.

Simple objects: Source-code locations, labels, and variable placements To `ldb`, a source-code location is a triple containing a file name, line number, and column number; a label is a string; and a placement is a term in an algebra with labels, registers, and address arithmetic. Such objects are created using constructor functions like these:

```
LdbSrcLoc *ldbSrcLoc_make         (const char *file, int line, int col);
LdbLabel  *ldbLabel_makeInCodeSpace(const char *asmname);
LdbLabel  *ldbLabel_makeInDataSpace(const char *asmname);
LdbPlcmt  *ldbPlcmt_makeAtLabel    (LdbLabel   *label);
LdbPlcmt  *ldbPlcmt_makeAbsolute   (char space,                int offset);
LdbPlcmt  *ldbPlcmt_makeShifted    (             LdbPlcmt *loc, int offset);
LdbPlcmt  *ldbPlcmt_makeIndirect   (char space, LdbPlcmt *loc, int offset);
```

Creating these objects typically requires modifying only a couple of existing modules. For example, `lcc` required 19 lines to create label names and 13 lines to translate its register names into `ldb`'s placement algebra.

Types. `ldb` imposes no structure on types; it uses a debug-level type only to determine how a value is printed. To support printing, each debug-level type must include a procedure or method that prints values of that type. Writing these procedures requires significant effort. For each type constructor in the source language, the compiler writer must write a procedure that `ldb` can use to print a value whose type is formed using that type constructor. To write such a procedure, one must know how values are represented and how they should be printed. For printing, `ldb` provides a flexible prettyprinter, but for manipulating representations, `ldb` provides only basic machine-level primitives like load, store, and arithmetic. But because expressing source-level manipulations using machine-level primitives is what a compiler does, a compiler writer is well equipped to write printing procedures.

In what language are these printing procedures to be written? They can't be written in the source language of the target program, because `ldb` must work with multiple source languages. They could be written in machine language, but this is a bad idea; not only can machine code be tricky to load dynamically, but because `ldb` can debug over a network, machine code compiled for `ldb`'s target might not run on `ldb`'s machine. Ideally, printing procedures would be written in a simple, high-level scripting language. Today, popular languages like Perl, Python, and Scheme can be embedded in applications; there are even languages designed expressly to be embedded, like Lua and Tcl. Any of these languages could work in `ldb`. But when the `ldb` project was started, these options did not exist.

Instead, Ramsey and Hanson (1992, §5) chose to extend `ldb` with a new implementation of an existing language: PostScript. PostScript does have some advantages, but if we were to rebuild `ldb` from scratch, we would choose a language that is better known and more friendly to programmers.

The choice of language affects the effort required to write printing procedures. This effort, while modest, is not trivial; some examples may help you judge. A PostScript printing procedure receives three arguments on the stack: an "abstract memory," which represents the state of the target program; the location of the value to be printed; and a debug-level object containing the printing procedure. This last argument means that printing procedures are effectively equivalent to methods in an object-oriented setting.

The basic technique can be illustrated by a very simple example; more examples can be found in the expanded version of this paper. The `lcc` compiler supports two different machine-level representations of floating-point numbers. In the debug-level object representing a floating-point type, `lcc` identifies the representation by using a private property `mtype`. This property, which is bound into the debug-level object using the support-library function `ldbTable_put`, is then used in the printing procedure:

```
/PF { /mtype get Memory.Fetch Put } def
```

The PostScript code "`/mtype get`" fetches the value of the `mtype` property, after which the PostScript stack holds exactly the arguments needed by `Memory.Fetch`, which leaves the floating-point number on the stack. As a primitive machine-level value, the floating-point number can then be printed using `ldb`'s primitive `Put`. Crucially, the very existence of the `mtype` field is hidden from the debugger.

The printing procedures that `lcc` uses for unsigned integers and for characters are similar. The printing procedure for signed integers is `PI`:

```
/PI { dup 4 1 roll /mtype get Memory.Fetch
      exch /bitsize get SignExtend Put } def
```

"`dup 4 1 roll`" saves a copy of the debug-level type before extracting `mtype` and fetching the value. In the debug-level type, the private key `bitsize` is associated with the number of bits in the integer, and it is used to sign-extend the integer before printing.

MiniJava supports only one basic type integer type, whose printing procedure is

```
/INT { pop Memory.Type.I32 Memory.Fetch 32 SignExtend Put } def
```

Because every MiniJava value fits in one word, this procedure is simpler than `lcc`'s printing procedure for integers.

The examples above may be slightly intimidating, but once one masters some rudimentary PostScript, writing printing procedures is straightforward. Moreover, our case studies showed that printing procedures for `lcc` and MiniJava are very similar. We expect, therefore, that one could use existing printing procedures as guides to implement new ones. And our case-study compilers do not require many printing procedures. For example, the `lcc` front end recognizes 14 language-level type constructors, which it prints using 13 printing procedures. (Some type constructors share a printing procedure, and some types, notably `char *`, require specialized printing procedures.)

Symbols. Debug-level symbols come in four flavors: bare, with type, with type and value, and procedure. Each flavor is also a *table* and so can be extended with private properties. A bare symbol has a name and a source-code location but no other information; such a symbol is not directly useful to `ldb`, but it may help a compiler writer embed the compiler's private data structures into debug-level objects. A symbol with only a type can have its type printed; such a symbol might represent a language-level type. A symbol with a type and value can have both its type and its value printed; such a symbol might represent a language-level variable or constant. A procedure symbol can support many debug-time operations, including enumerating formal parameters and local variables, searching stopping points, and walking a call stack. To support these operations, a procedure symbol must provide the name of its return type, an environment that includes its arguments, its stack-frame size, information about callee-saved registers, its assembly-output label, and a list of stopping points.

Because the linguistic structure of symbols is not part of the contract between `ldb` and the compiler, this contract supports multiple languages and compilers. The compiler writer must embed the compiler's symbols into `ldb`'s symbols, but because each flavor can be extended with private properties, this does not require too much programming effort. For example, `lcc` maintains five kinds of symbols: types, constants, variables, procedures, and `typesyms`. (The `typesym` is part of `lcc`'s private representation of a C-language type.) Each kind is easily embedded in a debug-level symbol.

Stopping Points. At debug time, stopping points are used not only to plant breakpoints by source-code location but also to identify the source-code location nearest the point of a program fault. These operations require the debugger to map between object-code locations and source-code locations. The map is defined by the set of all stopping points in the program, so `ldb` requires the compiler to associate each stopping point with both a source-code location and an object-code location. (The object-code location is represented by an assembly-language label like `$L.X6` in Fig. 3.) At a stopping point, the debugger must be able to look up symbols, so `ldb` requires the compiler to associate each stopping point with an environment.

As described in Section 3.1, the primary effort required to support stopping points is to create an explicit, language-level representation in the compiler. Given a suitable language-level representation, creating the corresponding debug-level object is straightforward. Section 5.2 discusses how we modified the `lcc` and MiniJava compilers to create stopping points.

Environments. At debug time, looking up symbols by name requires an environment. Because a compiler already maintains its own language-level environments, creating debug-level environments should not require much programming effort. Some extra effort may be required to propagate environments through the intermediate representation so they can be associated with stopping points.

Compilation Unit. The `ldb` support library maintains an abstraction that represents the compiler's knowledge about the entire compilation unit. This debug-level compilation unit is created incrementally: every time the compiler processes a top-level symbol, it should announce the symbol to the compilation unit. Because a symbol can be announced from wherever it is created, little programming effort is required.

3.3 Expression Evaluation

Unlike other debuggers, which require that the source language be reimplemented inside the debugger, `ldb` evaluates expressions by reusing a key component of the compiler: the translation from source language to low-level intermediate code. After being wrapped in a thin layer that communicates with the debugger, this translation component acts as an *expression-evaluation server*. The server communicates with `ldb` over a TCP connection: `ldb` sends ASCII to the server, and the server replies with PostScript code that `ldb` interprets. To evaluate an expression, `ldb` sends the text of the expression to the server, which parses the expression, type-checks it, and replies with a PostScript procedure followed by code that, when interpreted, has the effect of evaluating the expression (Ramsey and Hanson 1992).

Building an expression-evaluation server may require significant intellectual effort as well as programming effort: one must define what it means to evaluate an expression at a stopping point. For an explicitly typed language such as Java or C, this task is easy; one can simply reconstruct the original environment in which the stopping point occurs. But for an implicitly typed language such as Haskell or ML, an expression that is evaluated at debug time cannot participate in type inference in the same way as an expression that is part of the original program. For example, Hindley-Milner type variables cannot be unified with known types but must be treated as abstract types. For such languages, the semantics of debug-time evaluation remains a topic for future work.

Even given a semantics, implementing expression evaluation requires significant programming effort. The process is described in detail by Ramsey (1993, Chapter 5), but we summarize here.

- The expression server must reconstruct the language-level objects that represent the context at a stopping point. The private contents of these objects can be stored in property lists on `ldb`'s debug-level objects. An additional property, "serialize," should be PostScript code that, when interpreted, sends the private properties to the expression server. To get its private data, the server asks `ldb` to execute "serialize."
- Once the context has been reconstructed and an expression translated to intermediate code, the server must turn this code into PostScript. As a stack-based language, PostScript is an ideal target for such translation, so there is not much intellectual effort involved. But the programming effort is proportional to the number of different kinds of nodes in the compiler's intermediate code, which can be considerable.
- If the expressions to be evaluated include procedure calls, the target-language run-time system may have to be modified to be able to execute a procedure call on behalf of `ldb`. Depending on the complexity of the calling convention, this feature can be quite difficult to implement.
- If the compiler supports multiple target machines, the expression server must be specialized to the requirements of the target being debugged. For example, the expression server must know the sizes and alignments of basic data types. The compiler writer may create a specialized expression server for each target, or better, create a single expression server that is specialized at startup time.

It is worth noting that this effort is not absolutely required—because a debugger is useful even without an expression-evaluation server, we can trade programming effort for debugging functionality. In particular, if no expression-evaluation server is provided, `ldb` uses a "default" evaluator that can print the values of variables only.

4 When Representations Must be Available

Section 3 explains what language-level objects a compiler must provide in order to create debug-level objects for `ldb`. But when must these objects be provided? One strategy is to accumulate *all* the objects, and once compilation is over, emit them (Ramsey 1993, Chapter 4). Although this strategy has the merit of simplicity, it prolongs the lifetimes of the compiler's language-level objects, and it can complicate memory management and slow the compiler. A better strategy is as follows:

- *Create* debug-level objects as soon as is convenient, possibly leaving out some parts. For example, a procedure's object might be created without stopping points.
- Incrementally *mutate* debug-level objects to accumulate missing parts.
- When all information has been accumulated, *externalize* the object by writing it to assembly-language output.

The create-mutate-externalize strategy is built into the design of our support library. The library provides the create and mutate operations for each type of debug-level object. For example, a debug-level procedure is created without stopping points; when a stopping point becomes available, the compiler mutates the procedure by calling `ldbProc_addLocus`. In the library interface, an externalize operation is exported only for a compilation unit; other objects are externalized by the library's implementation.

The primary benefit of our approach is that the compiler writer need not worry about how long objects should live or when objects should be written to disk; these tasks are handled by the support library. A secondary benefit is that the support library becomes free to change and experiment with the external representation of debug-level objects, perhaps to improve performance. For example, it is possible to externalize individual objects incrementally, by writing create and mutate operations to a log. Experimentation with these possibilities is a topic for future work.

5 Results

To assess the programming effort required by our approach, we undertook case studies with the `lcc` (Fraser and Hanson 1995) and MiniJava (Appel and Palsberg 2002; Hosking 2003) compilers. We explain how programming effort is decomposed, present internal metrics for the modifications done to each compiler, discuss the effort of creating the compile-time support library, and compare with gdb.

5.1 Decomposition of Programming Effort

We distinguish two kinds of programming effort: modifying the compiler's existing *phase modules* and adding new *utility modules*. A phase module implements a phase

		lcc			MiniJava		
		core	driver & back ends	total	core	driver & back ends	total
original compiler	total modules	36	9	45	132	6	138
	total source lines	13,730	4,839	18,569	5,673	1,472	7,145
	Driver source		268			121	
	Alpha source		1,192				
	MIPS source		1,129			1,351	
	SPARC source		1,163				
	x86-linux source		1,087				
effort to add source locations & stopping points	utility modules added	(none)			(none)		
	phase modules changed				8	0	8
	• lines added				131	0	131
	• lines changed				53	0	53
effort to support MIPS hardware	utility modules added	(none)			0	1	1
	• lines therein				0	49	49
	phase modules changed				4	3	7
	• lines added				45	429	474
	• lines changed				9	1	10
effort to add debugging support	utility modules added	6	0	6	2	0	2
	• lines therein	990	0	990	343	0	343
	phase modules changed	4	4	8	29	2	31
	• lines added	18	43	61	340	46	386
	• lines changed	0	4	4	57	9	66
effort to add an expression-evaluation server	utility modules added	0	8	8	(none)		
	• lines therein	0	1,172	1,172			
	phase modules changed	24	0	24			
	• lines added	730	0	730			
	• lines changed	105	0	105			
total source lines added or changed		**1,843**	**1,219**	**3,062**	**978**	**534**	**1,512**

Fig. 4. Case studies: `lcc` and MiniJava

	C/C++	Java	Fortran	Pascal	Modula-2
lang-`exp.y`	1,715	1,462	1,175	1,485	1,094
lang-`lang.c`	522	1,097	957	465	468
lang-`lang.h`	84	66	98	75	31
lang-`typeprint.c`	1,154	343	435	858	41
lang-`valprint.c`	573	527	739	1,115	39
total source lines	**4,048**	**3,495**	**3,404**	**3,998**	**1,673**

Fig. 5. Lines of code for `gdb`'s language support

of the compiler; a utility module is used by phase modules or by the support library. Utility modules have well-defined interfaces and do not depend on other parts of the code, so it is easy to add them. To modify an existing phase module requires more effort: the compiler writer must understand how to do the modification safely. We therefore reduce programming effort by putting most new code, especially most of the intellectual work of creating debug-level objects, into utility modules. This organization requires less programming effort than would be required to do the same work in phase modules.

5.2 Internal Metrics

Measurements of our two case-study compilers are summarized in Fig. 4. The block at the top of Fig. 4 shows the sizes of the original compilers; back-end code is split by target machine. The next four blocks summarize four kinds of modifications:

- We modified MiniJava to propagate source-code locations into intermediate code and to define stopping points.
- We modified MiniJava to generate code that could run on MIPS hardware, not only on the SPIM simulator (Larus 2003).
- We modified both compilers to add debugging support.
- We implemented an expression-evaluation server for `lcc`.

We describe three of these modifications below.

The original MiniJava compiler provided no source-code locations for symbols and no stopping points. We modified MiniJava's parser to capture each symbol's source-code location and to propagate the locations into MiniJava's intermediate representation. We also modified MiniJava to include a stopping point before each expression, including nested expressions, as well as before each statement and at the end of each block. Adding source-code locations changed only 17 lines; adding stopping points added 131 lines and changed 36 lines.

The bulk of our effort was invested in true debugging support, which we did for both MiniJava and `lcc`. Because `lcc` has a well-defined internal interface for emitting debugging information, most of our effort was in writing a new implementation of that interface. We added 6 modules to `lcc`: 1 big module emits debugging information, and the other 5 implement utility functions. For MiniJava, we added 2 modules to the core of MiniJava: 1 for variable placements and 1 for printing procedures. We had to change 31 modules, but because MiniJava uses visitor patterns, this number is deceptively large: of the 31 changed modules, 22 collaborate to define MiniJava's intermediate form, defining one type of node per module. Leaving aside these modules, we changed roughly the same fraction of modules as in `lcc`: about 10%.

We implemented an expression-evaluation server only for `lcc`. To implement communication between `ldb` and the server, we modified 105 lines and added 1,172 lines. Of the 8 modules added, 1 module of 239 lines is a driver, and 1 module of 617 lines implements a new back end that generates PostScript. The remaining 6 modules, totalling 316 lines, enable the expression server to be specialized at startup time; there is one specialization module for each of 6 different architectures.

We also consider duplication of effort. Only name resolution is implemented both by `ldb` and by our case-study compilers. The code is 316 lines for `lcc` and 77 lines for

MiniJava. Because the compiler and debugger both need name resolution, and because they can be implemented in different languages, we see no way to avoid this duplication.

5.3 The Compile-Time Support Library

Our case studies do not include the effort required to create `ldb`'s support library. We have invested significant effort in developing four implementations of this library: one in each of C, Java, Standard ML, and Objective Caml. If a compiler is written in one of these languages, the appropriate library can be reused with no additional programming effort. But if a compiler is written in another language, the library interface must be instantiated for the new language, and the new interface must be implemented.

To instantiate the interface requires choosing suitable idioms in the new language. But our four existing instances already embody idioms from a range of paradigms: Java is object-oriented, Standard ML is functional, Objective Caml is both, and C is neither. We expect, therefore, that one of the existing instances would be a good guide to creating a new one. Furthermore, the library itself is not large; for example, the C interface is 1,154 lines, of which only 366 are non-blank, non-comment lines. The corresponding implementation is 1,001 lines. Given a new programming language, we could probably instantiate the library interface and implementation in less than a week.

5.4 Comparisons with `gdb`

Our case studies look at programming effort for individual compilers. Here, we compare our method with `gdb`. According to our basic principle—the less the compiler writer is constrained, the smaller the programming effort will be—we compare how our method and `gdb` constrain the compiler writer.

The compiler writer must present certain information to the debugger. In Section 3, we describe what language-level objects the compiler must provide. We didn't need to add any language-level objects to `lcc`; to MiniJava, we added 131 lines and modified 53 lines for source-code locations of symbols and for stopping points. These changes affected only small, isolated parts of the compiler.

`gdb` does not describe its requirements clearly. Gilmore (2000, Chapter 7) tells a compiler writer to add a new source language to `gdb` by providing 5 files. Fig. 5 shows the sizes of the files for the source languages supported by `gdb-5.1.1`: C/C++, Java, Fortran, Pascal, and Modula-2. Language support is three or four thousand lines of C code, except for Modula-2. The support for Modula-2 is much smaller because it reuses the modules for printing C types and values. Comments in the source code indicate that this reuse is a stopgap measure, and `gdb`'s implementors intend eventually to implement correct printing support for Modula-2. By contrast, `ldb`'s language support is three thousand lines of C code for `lcc`, including its expression-evaluation server, and half that for MiniJava, which lacks an expression server. According to Gilmore, a compiler writer who wants to add a new language to `gdb` must understand at least 3 header files and 5 source files, which are 11,521 lines altogether, of which 7,727 lines are non-blank, non-comment lines. Our support library is far smaller and simpler.

The information must be presented in a certain order and be kept live for a certain time during compilation. For each symbol, gdb represents the symbol information as a "stabstring" which is the symbol's name appended by the encoding of type information. While the stabstring requires a compiler to generate a symbol's information all at once, our support library can accumulate information incrementally, which gives the compiler the freedom to generate different parts of the information in any order. Moreover, because `ldb` uses a native-language interface, not strings, our support library can guarantee the well-formedness of the generated information.

The less the source language is constrained, the smaller the programming effort. To work with gdb, a compiler must use only types that gdb understands, and it must use gdb's representation. By contrast, our techniques hide the source-language type system and data representations, so the compiler writer never has to change them in order to suit the debugger—this is a whole category of programming effort we guarantee to eliminate. For example, we kept `lcc`'s and MiniJava's data representations unchanged.

The more the compiler's code is reused, the smaller the programming effort. gdb's code for expression evaluation duplicates substantial functionality that is already present in the compiler, including parsing, type checking, and generation of intermediate code. Because the code in gdb must respect gdb's naming conventions and other internal constraints, it is not possible simply to reuse the corresponding code in the compiler, even if the compiler happens to be implemented in C. By contrast, as described in Section 3.3, our method reuses the compiler's code.

The less the debugger's code is revealed, the smaller the programming effort. The compiler writer interacts with `ldb` only through the compiler-support interface, which hides the details of the debugger. By contrast, gdb requires the compiler writer read and understand large chunks of C code.

6 Related Work

There are two fundamental approaches to source-level debugging of compiled code. To support the *reverse engineering* approach, a compiler generates code much as it normally would, and it emits additional information that enables the debugger to analyze the object code and report information at the source level. To support the *instrumentation* approach, a compiler or other tool modifies the program before code generation; for example, a compiler might insert a conditional branch at every stopping point. Debuggers that use reverse engineering include `ldb`, gdb, and `dbx`; debuggers that use instrumentation include `smld` (Tolmach and Appel 1990; Tolmach 1992) and `cdb` (Hanson and Raghavachari 1996).

Instrumentation can support debugging with modest programming effort. Instrumentation can also support advanced debugging features such as time travel, which is more difficult to support using reverse engineering (Feldman and Brown 1988). Unfortunately, the convenience comes at a substantial cost in performance: code instrumented for debugging typically runs 3–4 times as long as uninstrumented code.

The standard approach to reverse engineering, which is exemplified by `dbx`, `gdb`, and DWARF, is for the debugger to provide a *union model* of all languages it supports. Because the union model provides the interface by which the compiler tells the debugger about the types of variables, it must include every type constructor used in any language the debugger might support.

There are two difficulties with a union model:

- The compiler and debugger must agree on a representation for each type. Because the representation may be machine-dependent, a different agreement may be needed for each target machine. Typically, the compiler writer cannot choose representations for high-level values such as records and strings; the compiler must use the representations that are assumed by the debugger.
- A union model might not include the types needed by a new language. Forcing a new language to fit an old union model may require substantial effort, and success is not guaranteed.

A union model exposes the details of source-language types and target-machine representations. By hiding these details, we leave the compiler writer free to change them, so no programming effort is expended forcing the compiler to be compatible with an unsuitable union model.

Like `ldb`, the Acid debugger avoids a union model and instead prints values by using functions written in an internal programming language (Winterbottom 1994). As with `ldb`, these functions must be emitted by the compiler. It is difficult to evaluate the programming effort required for a compiler to work with Acid, but it looks similar to the effort required to work with early versions of `ldb`: it appears to be up to the compiler writer, without assistance, to emit information in the form that the debugger expects.

A great deal of related work has been invested in debugging optimized code. To debug optimized code, the debugger needs to know the relation between optimized code and source code. In particular, when execution is suspended, the debugger must find a way to explain the actual state of the machine, even if that state is not consistent with a sequential execution of the source program. This may happen if, for example, the optimizer has changed the order of execution, eliminated dead assignments, eliminated induction variables from loops, and so on. Even for a fairly simple optimization, building a debugger that is capable of finding such explanations requires substantial intellectual and programming effort. This problem has engendered a large body of literature, which falls into two broad camps. Hennessy (1982) exemplifies the camp that tries to "undo" optimizations so that the debugger can present an explanation that makes it appear as if the program had never been optimized. Brooks, Hansen, and Simmons (1992), Tice and Graham (1998), and Jaramillo, Gupta, and Soffa (1999, 2000) exemplify the camp that tries to explain how the optimized code is executed as it is. In either camp, building a debugger requires lots of compiler support and also a deep understanding of optimization. We believe that debugging optimized code is orthogonal to the problem of building a debugger that supports multiple languages, compilers, and machines.

7 Conclusion

We have presented a new kind of contract between a compiler and debugger. The key ideas are to distinguish language-level objects from debug-level objects; to build debug-level objects incrementally; to hide the memory management and external representation of debug-level objects in a reusable support library; and to hide language-dependent, machine-dependent information behind the methods of the debug-level objects. The contract supports multiple programming languages and target machines, and it helps a compiler writer add debugging support while expending only modest programming effort.

Acknowledgements

Anonymous referees provided helpful comments on an earlier version of this paper.

This work has been funded by an Alfred P. Sloan Research Fellowship and by National Science Foundation grant EIA-0096091.

Bibliography

Alfred V. Aho, Ravi Sethi, and Jeffrey D. Ullman. 1986. *Compilers, Principles, Techniques, and Tools*. Addison-Wesley.

Andrew W. Appel. 1998. *Modern Compiler Implementation.* Cambridge University Press. Available in three editions: C, Java, and ML.

Andrew W. Appel and Jens Palsberg. 2002. *Modern Compiler Implementation in Java*. Cambridge University Press, second edition.

Gary Brooks, Gilbert J. Hansen, and Steve Simmons. 1992 (July). A new approach to debugging optimized code. *Proceedings of the ACM SIGPLAN '92 Conference on Programming Language Design and Implementation,* in *SIGPLAN Notices*, 27(7):1–11.

Stuart I. Feldman and Channing B. Brown. 1988 (May). IGOR: A system for program debugging via reversible execution. *Proceedings of the ACM SIGPLAN/SIGOPS Workshop on Parallel and Distributed Debugging,* in *SIGPLAN Notices*, 24(1):112–123.

Christopher W. Fraser and David R. Hanson. 1995. *A Retargetable C Compiler: Design and Implementation.* Addison-Wesley.

John Gilmore. 2000. GDB internals—a guide to the internals of the GNU debugger. Found in the `doc` directory of `gdb` distribution version 5.1.1.

David R. Hanson and Mukund Raghavachari. 1996. A machine-independent debugger. *Software–Practice and Experience*, 26(11):1277–1299.

John Hennessy. 1982. Symbolic debugging of optimized code. *ACM Transactions on Programming Languages and Systems*, 4(3):323–344.

Antony Hosking. 2003. The MiniJava compiler. Provided by the author, whose email address is `hosking@acm.org`.

Clara Jaramillo, Rajiv Gupta, and Mary Lou Soffa. 1999 (March). Comparison checking: an approach to avoid debugging of optimized code. In *Proceedings of the 7th European Software Engineering Conference (ESEC) held jointly with the 7th ACM SIGSOFT International Symposium on Foundations of Software Engineering (FSE)*, volume 1687 of *Lecture Notes in Computer Science*, pages 268–284. Springer-Verlag.

Clara Jaramillo, Rajiv Gupta, and Mary Lou Soffa. 2000 (July). FULLDOC: A full reporting debugger for optimized code. In *Proceedings of the 7th International Symposium on Static Analysis*, volume 1824 of *Lecture Notes in Computer Science*, pages 240–259. Springer-Verlag.

James Larus. 2003. SPIM: A MIPS R2000/R3000 simulator. http://www.cs.wisc.edu/ larus/spim.html.

Mark A. Linton. 1990 (June). The evolution of Dbx. In *Proceedings of the Summer USENIX Conference*, pages 211–220.

Norman Ramsey. 1993 (January). *A Retargetable Debugger*. PhD thesis, Princeton University. Also technical report CS-TR-403-92.

Norman Ramsey and David R. Hanson. 1992 (July). A retargetable debugger. *ACM SIGPLAN '92 Conference on Programming Language Design and Implementation,* in *SIGPLAN Notices*, 27(7):22–31.

Sukyoung Ryu and Norman Ramsey. 2004. The `ldb` interface. Technical Report TR-23-04, Division of Engineering and Applied Sciences, Harvard University.

Sukyoung Ryu and Norman Ramsey. 2005 (January). Source-level debugging for multiple languages with modest programming effort (expanded version). Technical Report TR-01-05, Division of Engineering and Applied Sciences, Harvard University.

Caroline Tice and Susan L. Graham. 1998 (July). OPTVIEW: A new approach for examining optimized code. *Proceedings of the 1998 ACM SIGPLAN/SIGSOFT Workshop on Program Analysis for Software Tools and Engineering,* in *SIGPLAN Notices*, 33(7):19–26.

Andrew P. Tolmach. 1992 (October). *Debugging Standard ML.* PhD thesis, Princeton University. Also technical report CS-TR-378-92.

Andrew P. Tolmach and Andrew W. Appel. 1990 (June). Debugging Standard ML without reverse engineering. In *Proceedings of the 1990 ACM Conference on LISP and Functional Programming*, pages 1–12.

Unix Int'l. 1993 (July). *DWARF Debugging Information Format.* Unix International, Parsippany, NJ.

Philip Winterbottom. 1994. Acid: A debugger based on a language. In *Proceedings of the Winter 1994 USENIX Conference*, pages 211–222.

Compilation of Generic Regular Path Expressions Using C++ Class Templates

Luca Padovani*

University of Bologna, Department of Computer Science,
Mura Anteo Zamboni 7, 40127 Bologna, Italy
lpadovan@cs.unibo.it

Abstract. Various techniques for the navigation and matching of data structures using path expressions have been the subject of extensive investigations. No matter whether such techniques are based on type information, indexing, automata, it is desirable to synthesize implementations automatically, starting from a high-level description of the path expressions to be traversed.

In this paper we present a library of C++ templates for the representation of regular path expressions and their compilation into efficient backtracking algorithms. The resulting code can be used to implement visitors, pattern matchers, node collectors on regular paths over possibly heterogeneous, linked data structures.

The point of the paper is on the path compilation technique, which was inspired by a continuation-passing, functional semantics of the path expressions. We rely on some peculiar aspects of C++ templates to create a compilation framework that closely follows the given semantics.

1 Introduction

The traversal of linked data structures along paths with a certain pattern is an operation that underlies many kinds of more complex queries: the recognition of a context in the proximity of a node in the data structure, the selection, the iteration, the visit of a set of nodes that are related by a pattern.

Regular path expressions extend the concept of plain regular expressions to the traversal of linked data structures. The recent diffusion of XML technologies has made path expressions the subject of a renewed interest. Among proposed standards we cite XPath [11, 17] and XQuery [19], but a whole plethora of languages and techniques have been studied and developed. Optimized implementations are possibly based on type information, indexing, finite state automata [20], tree automata [12, 15].

There are contexts, however, where optimizations are not applicable or give little advantage if compared to backtracking algorithms for path traversal. These contexts are often characterized by the following aspects:

* This work has been supported by the European Project IST-2001-33562 MoWGLI.

R. Bodik (Ed.): CC 2005, LNCS 3443, pp. 27–42, 2005.

- the data structure evolves under the effect of frequent editing operations;
- operations may change the structure arbitrarily, making it infeasible to keep track of the state of the structure if not by considering the whole structure as "the state";
- the patterns to be matched are sparse or linear, that is we are interested in checking only a limited number of objects around a focused node (which is sometimes called *cursor*), rather than performing an exhaustive query on whole documents.

The problem of backtracking algorithms is that their complexity grows unmanageably as the path expressions become more complicated, the strive to make them efficient contributes significantly to their complexity, they are seldom generic, reusable, and they cannot be easily composed together. It is generally desirable to be able to specify the path expressions to be traversed in a high-level language which would be compiled into efficient traversal code.

In this paper we describe a framework for the compilation of generic regular path expressions into backtracking algorithms. The framework is based on C++ class templates that represent path expressions. The same class templates are able to synthesize the traversal code following the functional semantics of the path expressions being compiled. The bottom line is that there is no need for any tool other than the C++ compiler itself, and the generated algorithm integrates seamlessly with the rest of the code.

The structure of the paper is as follows: in Section 2 we overview the basic constructs of generic regular path expressions and define their set-based semantics in a way similar to what was done for XPath in [10]. In Section 3 we define a continuation-passing, functional semantics for path expressions that is equivalent to the set-based semantics. Section 4 gives the stateless implementation of a simple but limited compilation framework that closely follows the functional semantics. Section 5 elaborates the stateless implementation into a stateful one and shows how the library can be adapted so as to accomplish specific tasks. Section 6 gives a brief account of related work. We conclude in Section 7 with some performance comparisons. The source code of the PET library is publicly available at `http://www.cs.unibo.it/~lpadovan/PET/index.html`.

Some knowledge of C++ templates and of the λ-calculus notation is assumed.

2 Syntax and Set-Based Semantics

We consider a linked data structure where links are represented as labelled arcs. For the sake of simplicity, in this paper we assume that the data structure is uniform and that its elements have all the same type *Object*. This assumption is relaxed in the implementation of the library. We consider generic regular path expressions generated by the grammar of Table 1. The expressions are generic in the sense that the finite set of *atomic expressions*, denoted by the nonterminal $\langle atom \rangle$, is left unspecified. Conceptually atoms can be classified as *selectors* and *filters*. Selectors follow labelled arcs in the data structure: for each $x, y \in Object$, we say that $s \in \langle atom \rangle$ selects y from x if there is an arc $x \xrightarrow{s} y$ in the data structure. For example, in a tree data structure we may have the "first child of" or "parent of" selectors (links), with their usual meaning. Filters can be thought of as *predicates* on objects in the *Object* domain. In data structures with labeled objects a typical filter is "has label l" (examples of "labels" are names, types, identifiers).

Table 1. Abstract syntax of generic regular path expressions

$$
\begin{array}{lllr}
\langle atom \rangle ::= & \mathbf{0} & & \\
\mid & \mathbf{1} & & \\
\mid & \ldots & & \\
\langle expr \rangle ::= & a & & a \in \langle atom \rangle \\
\mid & e_1 \mid e_2 & & \\
\mid & e_1\, e_2 & & \\
\mid & e^* & & \\
\mid & e? & \mathbf{1} \mid e & \\
\mid & e^+ & ee^* & \\
\mid & e^n & \underbrace{ee\cdots e}_{n} & 0 \leq n \\
\mid & e^{n,m} & e^n \mid e^{n+1} \mid \cdots \mid e^m & 0 \leq n \leq m
\end{array}
$$

Table 2. Set-based semantics of regular path expressions

$$
\begin{aligned}
\mathcal{S}[\![]\!] &: \mathit{Expr} \to \mathit{Object} \to \mathit{Set}(\mathit{Object}) \\
\mathcal{S}[\![\mathbf{0}]\!]x &= \emptyset \\
\mathcal{S}[\![\mathbf{1}]\!]x &= \{x\} \\
\mathcal{S}[\![a]\!]x &= a(x) \\
\mathcal{S}[\![e_1 \mid e_2]\!]x &= \mathcal{S}[\![e_1]\!]x \cup \mathcal{S}[\![e_2]\!]x \\
\mathcal{S}[\![e_1\, e_2]\!]x &= \mathcal{S}[\![e_2]\!]\mathcal{S}[\![e_1]\!]x = \textstyle\bigcup_{y \in \mathcal{S}[\![e_1]\!]x} \mathcal{S}[\![e_2]\!]y \\
\mathcal{S}[\![e^*]\!]x &= \textstyle\bigcup_{i=0}^{\infty} \mathcal{S}[\![e^i]\!]x
\end{aligned}
$$

Only two atoms are pre-defined, they are the identity selector **1** and the null selector **0** (equivalently the filters for the always-true and always-false predicates respectively).

A *core* path expression can be a single atom a, the alternative $e_1 \mid e_2$ between two path expressions e_1 and e_2, the composition $e_1\, e_2$ of two path expressions e_1 and e_2, or the closure e^* of a path expression e. The remaining regular path expressions can be expressed in terms of these core expressions as shown in Table 1, hence they will not be considered any further; the implementation, however, supports them. Note that given two filters p_1 and p_2, the composition $p_1\, p_2$ represents the conjunction $p_1 \wedge p_2$ and $p_1 \mid p_2$ represents the disjunction $p_1 \vee p_2$.

We define the set-based semantics of a path expression e focused on an object x as the finite set of objects selected (or reached) by e starting from x (Table 2). Borrowing the notation from [10], we write $\mathit{Set}(\mathit{Object})$ for the type of a set where each element is of type Object and $\mathit{Set}_1(\mathit{Object})$ for the subtype of sets with at most one element. Each atom is modelled as a function $a : \mathit{Object} \to \mathit{Set}_1(\mathit{Object})$. A selector s is modelled as a function s such that, given an object x, $s(x) = \{y\}$ if $x \xrightarrow{s} y$, and $s(x) = \emptyset$ if there is no arc from x labelled s. A filter p is modelled as a function p such that, given an object x, $p(x) = \{x\}$ if x satisfies p, and $p(x) = \emptyset$ otherwise.

Example 1 (Plain Regular Expressions). Regular expressions over sequences of symbols in a finite vocabulary V can be seen as a special case of regular path expressions where there is only one selector "next character" and there is one filter for each symbol $a \in V$ with the meaning "the current character is a". As there is only one selector, the syntax of plain regular expression does not normally have any notation for it, juxtaposition of symbols has the meaning of concatenation.

Example 2 (XPath Expressions). The subset of XPath (version 1.0 [11]) expressions without qualifiers can be encoded as regular path expressions. Assuming that the *parent*, *first_child*, *next_sibling* selectors are defined, we encode XPath axes as follows:

`self`	$\Rightarrow \mathbf{1}$
`child`	$\Rightarrow$ *first_child next_sibling**
`descendant`	$\Rightarrow$ (*first_child next_sibling**)$^+$
`ancestor`	$\Rightarrow$ *parent*$^+$
`following_sibling`	$\Rightarrow$ *next_sibling*$^+$
`following`	$\Rightarrow$ *parent** *next_sibling*$^+$(*first_child next_sibling**)*

The remaining XPath axes are symmetric to the shown ones.

3 Functional Semantics

The set-based semantics is very concise and clear in giving the meaning of path expressions, and its naive implementation is naturally based on object sets and union operations. If we were to compile an expression e to a function that way, the type of such functions would be $\mathcal{F}_O[\![e]\!] : \mathit{Object} \rightarrow \mathit{Set}(\mathit{Object})$ and, for instance, the compilation rule for a compound expression $e_1\, e_2$ would look something like

$$\mathcal{F}_O[\![e_1\, e_2]\!] = \lambda x.\, \cup_{y \in (\mathcal{F}_O[\![e_1]\!]\; x)} (\mathcal{F}_O[\![e_2]\!]\; y)\,.$$

This implementation, which is typical for several XPath engines, is unsatisfactory when

1. we are not interested to knowing which nodes have been selected, but only if at least one node was selected, or
2. we are interested to bind only a limited subset of the selected objects, or
3. we want to bind different objects to different names (perhaps because objects have different types), or
4. we want to visit the selected objects as they are discovered.

The heart of the problem is the composition $e_1\, e_2$, in particular when the path e_1 selects more than one object. We cannot avoid the set-union operation as long as e_1 and e_2 are completely evaluated in isolation. What we need is a way to tell $\mathcal{F}[\![e_1]\!]$ that, whenever it selects a node, it should proceed along the path e_2 from this node and, if this path fails, search for the next object selected by e_1. We do this by adding to $\mathcal{F}[\![e_1]\!]$ one more parameter, called the *continuation*.

Table 3 shows the continuation-passing, functional semantics of regular path expressions. We adopt the λ-calculus notation with the following extensions. We use $\{x\}$ to

Table 3. Functional semantics of regular path expressions

$$
\begin{aligned}
\mathsf{null} &\equiv \lambda x.\emptyset \\
\mathsf{id} &\equiv \lambda x.\{x\} \\
\mathsf{fork} &\equiv \lambda k_1.\lambda k_2.\lambda k_3.\lambda x.\mathbf{match}\ (k_1\ x)\ \mathbf{with} \\
&\qquad\qquad\qquad\qquad \{y\} \to (k_2\ y) \\
&\qquad\qquad\qquad\qquad \emptyset \to (k_3\ x)
\end{aligned}
$$

$$
\begin{aligned}
\mathcal{A}[\![\mathbf{0}]\!] &= \mathsf{null} \\
\mathcal{A}[\![\mathbf{1}]\!] &= \mathsf{id} \\
\mathcal{A}[\![a]\!] &= \lambda x.a(x)
\end{aligned}
$$

$$
\mathcal{F}[\![]\!] \ :\ \mathit{Expr} \to (\mathit{Object} \to \mathit{Set}_1(\mathit{Object})) \to \mathit{Object} \to \mathit{Set}_1(\mathit{Object})
$$

$$
\begin{aligned}
\mathcal{F}[\![a]\!] &= \lambda k.(\mathsf{fork}\ \mathcal{A}[\![a]\!]\ k\ \mathsf{null}) \\
\mathcal{F}[\![e_1 \mid e_2]\!] &= \lambda k.(\mathsf{fork}\ (\mathcal{F}[\![e_1]\!]\ k)\ \mathsf{id}\ (\mathcal{F}[\![e_2]\!]\ k)) \\
\mathcal{F}[\![e_1\, e_2]\!] &= \lambda k.(\mathcal{F}[\![e_1]\!]\ (\mathcal{F}[\![e_2]\!]\ k)) \\
\mathcal{F}[\![e^*]\!] &= \lambda k.(\mathsf{fix}\ \lambda f.(\mathsf{fork}\ k\ \mathsf{id}\ (\mathcal{F}[\![e]\!]\ f)))
\end{aligned}
$$

denote "some object x" and $\emptyset$ to denote "no object". These correspond to the `Some` x and `None` values in languages like ML or OCaml. We destruct optional values using a simplified form of pattern matching which is only capable of discriminating a singleton and the empty set and optionally binding a name to the value of the singleton.

The terms null, id, fork, and fix are called *basic terms*. The first two terms correspond to the compiled versions of the **0** and **1** paths respectively. The fork term is the basic term for backtracking: (fork e_1 e_2 e_3 x) tries to follow the path e_1 with focus x. If it succeeds (thus reaching an object y), it continues along e_2 with focus y. If it fails, it continues along e_3 with focus x. The composition of two paths $e_1\, e_2$ is translated as the function corresponding to e_1 to which the function corresponding to e_2 is passed as continuation. The compilation of e^* makes use of the fix-point basic term, fix, which is left unspecified in the semantics as it will be implemented using a peculiar feature of C++ class templates. As usual, we require that (fix F) $=$ (F (fix F)) for all functions F.

Note that the function we obtain from a path expression e expects a continuation k that "receives" the selected objects. We will see in Section 5.3 that, by varying k, one can use the path expression to accomplish different tasks.

Let us conclude this section with a proposition stating that the set-based semantics and the functional semantics are in a way equivalent:

Proposition 1. *Let*

$$
\mathsf{eq} = \lambda x.\lambda y.\begin{cases} \{x\}, & \text{if } x = y \\ \emptyset, & \text{otherwise} \end{cases}
$$

be the filter that tests whether two objects are the same object, then we have

$$
\forall x, y \in \mathit{Object}, x \in \mathcal{S}[\![e]\!]y \iff (\mathcal{F}[\![e]\!]\ (\mathsf{eq}\ x)\ y) = \{x\}\,.
$$

The proof follows by a structural induction on the path expression e.

4 Implementation

If we were to generate code for a functional language, the rules of the functional semantics in Table 3 could be used directly. As a matter of fact, when we first attacked the problem it seemed that the only way of producing a code close to the functional semantics was to use a functional language as target (a concrete attempt was done with Objective Caml [21]). In C++ functions are not first-class entities (let alone continuations) and moreover they can only be declared at the top-level or inside a class, hence the compilation process would not be compositional. In particular, it would not be possible to compile a local path expression within another C++ function, for instance as a test expression of an `if` statement. We can circumvent these limitations using C++ class templates.

C++ class templates allow the programmer to abstract the definition of a class with respect to one or more *template parameters*. This way it is possible to design generic classes that can be used with arbitrary data types. For example, the type

```
template <typename A, typename B>
struct Pair {
  A first;
  B second;
};
```

defines a generic `Pair` structure with two template parameters `A` and `B` for representing pairs of values of arbitrary types. In order to be used, parameterized classes must be *instantiated* with the appropriate types. The instantiation acts by substituting the abstracted types with the provided ones. For example `Pair<int, float>` represents the type of `Pairs` where the `first` component has type `int` and the `second` component has type `float`. Roughly speaking, class templates can be thought of as functions operating on and returning types.

In addition to member fields, class templates can contain member methods, member types, and member templates as well, all of which may depend on template parameters. Member methods of class templates are instantiated (that is, their actual object code is output by the compiler) on demand when they are invoked. Upon instantiation of a method of a class template, the compiler may decide to do code inlining for the method's body, or to output a standalone instance of the method to be called one or more times.

Going back to our problem, we can let the C++ compiler output functions on demand using templates, thus: for each basic term we define a template that has as many template parameters as the continuation parameters of the term (none for null and id, three for fork) and has a static member function `walk` accepting one parameter (the cursor) and implementing the term semantics. This approach is possible as long as all the continuation parameters are known at compile-time, because template instantiation must be resolved by the C++ compiler. This condition holds: given a compiled path expression $\mathcal{F}[\![e]\!]$ and a statically-known receiving term t, no redex in $(\mathcal{F}[\![e]\!]\ t)$ involving continuations does depend on runtime information.

The use of templates also allows us to relax the constraint of working on homogeneous data structures. As anticipated in the introduction, we will focus on the compilation framework rather than on these details of the implementation. From now on we assume that the objects of the data structure being traversed are accessed by a pointer `Object*`: the `walk` method will accept and return a `Object*` value.

4.1 Basic Terms

The user has to provide a class (template) for each atom occurring in the path expressions. Typically, selectors corresponds to accessors in the `Object` class and filters are predicates over `Object` objects. The class for an atom a must provide a static `walk` method accepting the current object in the path (the x variable in the specification, the `x` parameter in the C++ code below) and returning a possibly null object.

Following these guidelines, the id and null atoms are implemented as follows:

```
struct IdTerm
{ static Object* walk(Object* x) const { return x; } };
struct NullTerm
{ static Object* walk(Object*) const { return 0; } };
```

According to Table 3 the term fork has four parameters. However, the first three parameters (k_1, k_2, and k_3) are continuations so they are represented by template parameters:

```
template <typename K1, typename K2, typename K3>
struct ForkTerm {
  static Object* walk(Object* x) const {
    if (Object* y = K1::walk(x)) return K2::walk(y);
    else return K3::walk(x);
  }
};
```

Finally, we need to implement the fix-point operator and we do so by exploiting a special case of parameterized inheritance. The function for which we have to compute the fixed point is represented by the template template parameter `F`:

```
template <template <typename> class F>
struct FixTerm : public F<FixTerm<F> > { };
```

A variant of this construct, in which the class itself is a parameter of the class it derives from, is known under the name of Curiously Recurring Template Pattern [7, 5]. Although there are other slightly more compact ways of implementing recursive types, this one closely resembles the functional semantics and, anyway, it introduces no overhead if compared to the equivalent variants (however see note 1 in Section 4.2).

Example 3. The path expression $parent\ (parent \mid \mathbf{1})$, which selects both the parent and the grandparent of the cursor, is represented by the type

```
ForkTerm<ParentTerm,
         ForkTerm<ForkTerm<ParentTerm, k, NullTerm>,
                  IdTerm, ForkTerm<IdTerm, k, NullTerm> >,
         NullTerm>
```

where `Parent` implements the *parent* atom and k is the atom that is supposed to receive the selected objects.

4.2 A Template-Based Compiler

It is clear from Example 3 that types representing path expressions are not readable and handy to work with: it would be better to use some syntax that is more closely related to the structure of the path expressions those types derive from. Although the concrete syntax of path expressions is affected by the application domain (as the two examples at the end of Section 2 have shown), we can lift from the level of basic terms to the level of the path structure. The idea, the same used in expression templates [5, 18], is to encode the structure of a path expression using types so that, for instance, the type

```
SeqPath<AtomPath<ParentTerm>,
        OrPath<AtomPath<ParentTerm>, AtomPath<IdTerm> > >
```

would represent the path expression $parent\ (parent \mid \mathbf{1})$.

C++ classes (and class templates) may contain other class template declarations. We exploit this feature for implementing the compilation rules shown in Table 3. To this aim, each template representing the structure of a path expression defines a member class template `Compile` with a template parameter `K` for the continuation. The inner `Compile` class must define a member type `RES` representing the basic term resulting from the compilation. A look at the actual code for the `AtomPath`, `OrPath`, and `SeqPath` templates should clarify the basic idea:

```
template <typename A> struct AtomPath {
  template <typename K> struct Compile
  { typedef ForkTerm<A, K, NullTerm> RES; };
};

template <typename P1, typename P2> struct OrPath {
  template <typename K> struct Compile {
    typedef typename P1::template Compile<K>::RES T1;
    typedef typename P2::template Compile<K>::RES T2;
    typedef ForkTerm<T1, IdTerm, T2> RES;
  };
};

template <typename P1, typename P2> struct SeqPath {
  template <typename K> struct Compile {
    typedef typename P2::template Compile<K>::RES T1;
    typedef typename P1::template Compile<T1>::RES RES;
  };
};
```

For the compilation of the `StarPath` construct we first define an auxiliary template `F` representing $\lambda f.(\mathsf{fork}\ \ k\ \ \mathsf{id}\ \ (\mathcal{F}[\![e]\!]\ f))$ and then we apply the fix-point operator `FixTerm` to `F`:[1]

```
template <typename P> struct StarPath {
  template <typename K> struct Compile {
    template <typename f>
    struct F : public ForkTerm<K, IdTerm,
                 typename P::template Compile<f>::RES> { };
    typedef FixTerm<F> RES;
  };
};
```

4.3 Code Improvement

The uniform treatment of selectors and filters simplifies the framework but can result into inefficient code. When the first template argument of `ForkTerm` is a filter, `ForkTerm`'s `walk` method is exceedingly complex because a filter never returns an object different from the cursor. Depending on the type of the `walk`'s parameter (which need not necessarily be an actual pointer), a compiler may be unable to optimize the code by itself. Fortunately we can help the compiler improving the generated code in such cases by using partial template specialization. Below we show an example of such optimization:

```
template <typename Object, typename K2, typename K3>
struct ForkTerm<IdTerm, K2, K3> {
  static Object* walk(Object* x) { return K2::walk(x); }
};
```

Any time a `ForkTerm` is instantiated with `IdTerm` as its first template argument, this specialization, which defines a shorter and more efficient implementation of the `walk` method, will be "preferred" by the C++ compiler to the more general one.

5 Stateful Implementation

The library developed so far is relatively simple and clean and the compilation scheme closely follows the functional semantics of path expressions. However, the use of static walking methods prevents methods from accessing any data that is not constant or at the global scope. For example, if we were to design a *sink* atom collecting any object that it is passed to, we would have to declare a global container and access that container from the `walk` method of the `Sink` class. More generally, terms can only be parameterized by

[1] At the time of this writing not every C++ compiler is capable of handling correctly the `StarPath` template. An alternative formulation for the `RES` member type which can be successfully compiled with GCC version 3.3.3 is `struct RES : public ForkTerm<K, IdTerm, typename P::template Compile<RES>::RES> { };` Note that this type too is defined using a variant of the CRTP even if the `FixTerm` template is not needed anymore.

values that are constants with internal static linkage, because this is the only category of values that can be passed as template parameters. Not even constant strings nor floating point numbers, for example, can be used as template parameters.

It is possible to extend the implementation seen so far to a stateful one, that is an implementation where term classes are allowed to have non-static member fields that can affect (or can be affected by) the evaluation of the `walk` method. Since most of the changes needed to the classes already seen are either trivial or technical, in the section that follows we only give a few examples and a brief account for them. The interested reader can have a look at the source code for the details.

5.1 Stateful Basic Terms

The changes required to implement stateful terms are the following:

- terms containing subterms (like fork) must have a constructor that accepts objects representing the compiled subterms and stores them as member fields;
- the `walk` method must no longer be static;
- calls to the continuations must no longer be static but rather are proper method invocations on the continuation member fields.

In `IdTerm` and `NullTerm` only the `walk` method changes, which is no longer static. The stateful variant of `ForkTerm` is as follows, with the relevant changes underlined:

```
template <typename K1, typename K2, typename K3>
struct ForkTerm {
  ForkTerm(const K1& _k1, const K2& _k2, const K3& _k3)
    : k1(_k1), k2(_k2), k3(_k3) { }
  Object* walk(Object* x) const {
    if (Object* y = k1.walk(x)) return k2.walk(y);
    else return k3.walk(x);
  }
  const K1 k1;
  const K2 k2;
  const K3 k3;
};
```

The instances corresponding to the three continuations are passed to the constructor and embedded in the instance of `ForkTerm`. Embedding the subterms (as opposed to referencing them via pointers) is necessary because most of the time terms will be instantiated by the C++ compiler into temporaries, and storing references to such temporaries would likely result into dangling pointers.

Not surprisingly, the most delicate class to change is `FixTerm`. The problem arises because not only the type of the stateful `FixTerm` must be circular (which, as we have seen in Section 4.1, can be achieved in a relatively easy way), but also its instance as well. The circularity of the instance must be broken somehow using a reference for otherwise we end up with the paradoxical situation of an instance object containing a proper copy of itself. Also, such a circular term must be constructed in "one shot" by the default C++

constructor mechanism for we do not want the user to have to manually patch circular terms after their compilation!

The initialization of a recursive term is possible because during the instantiation of a class, and precisely when the constructor of a derived class is initializing the base class, it is already possible to refer to `this`, since the memory for the object is allocated *before* initialization takes place. In particular, in the initialization of the base class it is possible to pass `*this` as a constant reference to the object being instantiated. If the base class, or any other class this reference is passed to, stores it somewhere we have the desired circularity. To make sure that no attempt is done to copy `*this`, we introduce a new term, which we call `WeakRefTerm`, that stores its child term as a reference rather than as an embedded object. The `WeakRefTerm`'s `walk` method just forwards the invocation to the child term hence it is semantically transparent:

```
template <typename K> struct WeakRefTerm {
  WeakRefTerm(const K& _k) : k(_k) { }
  Object* walk(Object* x) const { return k.walk(x); }
  const K& k;
};
```

It is sufficient to pass `WeakRefTerm(*this)` to the base class to have the desired effect of creating a finite circularity. This solution is still problematic, though, because if a circular object gets copied (this eventually happens as continuations may be duplicated) the default field-by-field copy constructor will break the circularity. Nor it is possible to define a specific copy constructor that restores the circular references in the new copy.

The only possibility is to forbid the copy of circular objects, and to actually share them when continuations are duplicated. This implies that circular objects must be allocated in the heap, that they must provide a reference-counter for keeping track of their sharing, and that they must be managed by a special `RefTerm` class which stores a pointer to such a heap allocated object forwarding any call to it. The `RefTerm` is similar to `WeakRefTerm` as far as the expression semantics is concerned. In addition, it acts as a smart pointer that increases and decreases the reference counter appropriately and eventually releases the circular object when it is no longer used.

5.2 Expression Templates

The stateful implementation also allows us to define a set of overloaded operators that can be used to construct complex path expression types (and corresponding instances) in a transparent way. In our implementation we have overloaded the infix operators >> and | to be used for composition and alternatives, respectively, and the prefix operators * and + to be used for "zero or more" and "one or more" closure operators, respectively. We have also overloaded the bracketing operator `[]` to implement qualifiers (these are special filters that verify a structural predicate, similar to XPath qualifiers) and the function application operator `()` that, given a path expression e and a node x, starts up the compilation process and evaluates e starting from x.

Example 4. The following C++ expression implements the `following` axes as defined in the example 2, assuming that the `Parent`, `NextSibling`, and `FirstChild` terms have been defined with their intuitive meaning, and evaluates the expression from the node x:

```
(*atom(Parent()) >> +atom(NextSibling())
 >> *atom(FirstChild()) >> *atom(NextSibling()))(x)
```

5.3 Usage Patterns

Once the basic framework has been designed and implemented, it is possible to add atoms to perform more specific operations.

Example 5 (Pattern Matching). To test whether the data structure matches a pattern (specified as a regular path expression) p from a node x, we just write the statement

```
if (p(x)) { /* there is a match */ }
```

Example 6 (Collecting). In order to collect all the nodes selected by a regular path expression from a node x, we introduce a filter atom `Sink` that stores each node that has been encountered. The filter does not propagate nodes encountered in an earlier traversal:

```
struct Sink {
  Object* walk(Object* x) const {
    if (sink.find(x) == sink.end()) {
      sink.add(x);
      return x;
    } else return 0;
  }
  std::set<Object*> sink;
};
```

After the visit is completed, the `Sink` term can be queried to retrive the set of collected nodes:

```
Sink sink;
(p >> atom(sink) >> empty())(x);
/* do something with sink */
```

where the expression `empty()` is the library's implementation of the **0** atom.

Example 7 (visitor). To perform a user-provided operation on each node selected by a regular path expression from a node x (without necessarily collecting the visited nodes), a visitor class is implemented as an atom that always fails, thus forcing the backtracking algorithm to search for any possible alternative path:

```
template <typename Object> struct Visitor {
  bool walk(Object* x) const {
    /* visit x */
    return false;
  }
};
```

Example 8 (Unique Visitor). If the data structure contains cycles, and more generally if one wants to be sure that the each selected node is not visited more than once, a sink term can be composed just before the `Visitor` atom:

```
Visitor visitor;
(p >> atom(Sink()) >> atom(visitor))(x);
```

6 Related Work

The compilation framework that we have presented builds on top of a standard C++ compiler and heavily relies on template metaprogramming, with no need for external tools. Although this work does not introduce new concepts, the used techniques have been applied in original ways.

Continuations are well-known and date back to the construction of compilers based on Continuation Passing Style (CPS, see [3]) and also to the field of denotational semantics [1, 2]. In the latter case, continuations become critical in specifying the semantics of the sequential composition of commands in imperative programming languages with `gotos`. In [1], the semantics of a construct $S_1; S_2$ in an environment ρ and with continuation θ is defined to be $\mathcal{C}[\![S_1; S_2]\!]\ \rho\ \theta = \mathcal{C}[\![S_1]\!]\ \rho\ (\mathcal{C}[\![S_2]\!]\ \rho\ \theta)$ which basically is the same rule for path composition of Table 3, except that in our context the environment ρ plays no role.

The use of C++ templates for metaprogramming is also well-known [4, 18], and the synthesis of types from other types using template classes is related to C++ *traits* [6]. In our development it is crucial the capability of class templates to be instantiated everywhere in the source program. The compiler keeps track of which templates have been instantiated, hence it can decide whether to do instantiation or to retrieve a previous instantiation. Compared to higher-order functions in a functional programming language, templates have the advantage that they can be expanded by inlining. The Curiously Recurring Template Pattern (CRTP [7]), which occurs in the bibliography mainly as a twisted mix of genericity and inheritance, is also crucial since it represents the only way to generate implicitly recursive functions (where the recursive nature is not apparent from the source code). Other approaches that relate templates and functional programming (like the FC++ library [14, 16] or the BOOST Lambda library[2]) do not address recursion but rather rely on explicitly recursive functions.

Our use of class templates is just an application of offline partial evaluation [8, 9]: C++ may be regarded as a two-level language where template parameters represent statically known values, and method parameters represent dynamically known values. A path expression compiled using the rules in Table 3 results into a function where all the continuation parameters are statically known. The C++ compiler partially evaluates the functions obtained from the compilation process by unfolding the continuations and recursively evaluating the resulting code.

---

[2] `http://www.boost.org/libs/lambda/doc/`

7 Final Remarks

There are several contexts where it is desirable to use backtracking algorithms for the evaluation of regular path expressions. The code generated by the PET library is efficient and modern C++ compilers (such as the latest versions of GCC[3] or LLVM[4]) are capable of tail-optimizing function calls and simple (but not trivial) path expressions are compiled as loops instead of recursive function calls. The library is generic in that it makes no assumptions on the data structures being traversed. The user is free to add atoms to fit her own needs, while the library of basic terms can be written once and for all without loosing genericity.

Table 4. Comparing PET against other query engines. The times are in milliseconds and refer to 20 evaluations of the indicated paths, excluding parsing time. The factor f is the ratio $matching\ time/(parsing\ time + matching\ time)$

XPath expression	Nodes	PET		Xalan		`libxml2`		`Fxgrep`	
	n	ms	f	ms	f	ms	f	ms	f
`//node()`	33806	238	.079	100	.008	18368	.869	4102	.054
`//mrow[@xref]`	750	158	.054	120	.010	3807	.579	4007	.052
`//mrow[@xref]/text()`	3162	161	.054	190	.015	5435	.661	3942	.053
`//text()[../mrow[@xref]]`	3162	202	.068	930	.068	8298	.750	-	-
`//*[@xref][text()]`	2486	147	.050	510	.042	5634	.671	3603	.054
`//text()/../*[@xref]`	2486	175	.059	1220	.092	14729	.824	-	-

We have made some (non-exhaustive) comparative tests of the PET library against the implementations of XPath provided by Xalan[5] and `libxml2`[6] and against the `Fxgrep` XML querying tool [20]. It should be kept in mind that the compared libraries have very different architectures. While PET produces native code, `Fxgrep` translates paths into finite state automata, and `libxml2` and Xalan provide interpreters for XPath expressions. Table 4 shows the absolute times spent for the matching phase, as well as the ratio given by the matching time over the total time (parsing and matching). This way, we have tried to give a performance score that roughly measures the matching algorithm regardless of the implementation language and architecture.

By looking at the absolute times PET outperforms the other tools in most cases. We have to remark that while PET, Xalan, and `libxml2` are C/C++ libraries, `Fxgrep` is written in SML/NJ (Standard ML of New Jersey) and, as the author of `Fxgrep` has recognized, this might be the main cause of its modest absolute performance. By looking at the f ratio, PET performances are rather good. The important thing to notice in this case is how much the ratio f varies, that is how much the absolute time depends on the particular query. On one side we have `Fxgrep`, which is almost unaffected by the kind

[3] `http://gcc.gnu.org/`

[4] `http://llvm.cs.uiuc.edu/`

[5] C++ version, see `http://xml.apache.org/xalan-c/`

[6] `http://xmlsoft.org/`

of query, and this is consequence of the fact that `Fxgrep` uses an optimized automaton that scans the whole document. On the opposite side, Xalan and particularly `libxml2` show a significant variance. In these tools the time spent on union operations on node-set becomes predominant in certain queries. In some cases `libxml2` spends more than 90% of the total time merging node sets. The cost of computing a node set is also relative to whether we are actually interested to know *which* nodes have been selected, or just if *some* node has been selected (this is relevant in XPath when a path occurs within a qualifier). The PET library roughly sits in between these two situations, and proves to be an effective and cheap tool for the programmer.

It is also important to remark that while the other tools are targeted to XML processing, PET is completely generic and provides an easily extensible compilation framework that can be adapted to specific tasks.

References

1. Stoy, J. E. "*Denotational Semantics: The Scott-Strachey Approach to Programming Language Semantics*", MIT Press, Cambridge, Massachusetts, 1977.
2. Schmidt, D. A. "*Denotational Semantics: A Methodology for Language Development*", Wm. C. Brown Publishers, 1988.
3. Appel, A. "*Compiling with Continuations*", Cambridge University Press, 1992.
4. Veldhuizen, T. "*Using C++ Template Metaprograms*", C++ Report Vol. 7 No. 4, pp. 36–43, May 1995.
5. Veldhuizen, T. "*Expression Templates*", C++ Report, Vol. 7 No. 5, pp. 26–31, June 1995.
6. Myers, N. "*A new and useful template technique: Traits*", C++ Report, Vol. 7 No. 5, pp. 33–35, June 1995.
7. Coplien, J. O. "*Curiously Recurring Template Patterns*", in Stanley B. Lippman, editor, C++ Gems, 135–144. Cambridge University Press, New York, 1996.
8. Jones, N. D. "*An introduction to partial evaluation*", ACM Computing Surveys 28, 3, pp. 480–503, September 1996.
9. Veldhuizen, T. "*C++ templates as partial evaluation*", in ACM SIGPLAN Workshop on Partial Evaluation and Semantics-Based Program Manipula-tion (PEPM 1998), pp. 13–18, San Antonio, TX, USA, January, 1999.
10. Wadler, P. "*A formal semantics of patterns in XSLT*", in B. Tommie Usdin, D. A. Lapeyre, and C. M. Sperberg-McQueen, editors, Proceedings of Markup Technologies, Philadelphia, 1999.
11. Clark, J., and DeRose, S. "*XML Path Language (XPath)*", W3C Recommendation, 1999, `http://www.w3.org/TR/xpath`
12. Comon, H., Dauchet, M., Gilleron, R., Jacquemard, F., Lugiez, D., Tison, S., and Tommasi, M. "*Tree Automata Techniques and Applications*", 1999, `http://www.grappa.univ-lille3.fr/tata`
13. Eisenecker, U. W., Czarnecki, K. "*Generative Programming: Methods, Tools, and Applications*", Addison-Wesley, 2000.
14. Mcnamara, B., Smaragdakis, Y. "*Functional Programming in C++ using the FC++ Library*", ACM SIGPLAN Notices, 36(4), pp. 25–30, April 2001.
15. Hosoya, H., Pierce, B. "*Regular expression pattern matching for XML*", in Proceedings of the 28th ACM SIGPLAN-SIGACT symposium on Principles of programming languages, pp. 67–80, 2001.

16. Mcnamara, B., Smaragdakis, Y., "*Functional Programming with the FC++ Library*", under consideration for publication in Journal of Functional Programming, July 2002.
17. Clark, J., and DeRose, S. "*XML Path Language (XPath) 2.0*", W3C Working Draft, 2002, `http://www.w3.org/TR/xpath20`
18. Vandevoorde, D., Josuttis, N. M. "*C++ Templates: The Complete Guide*", Addison-Wesley, 2002.
19. Boag S. et al., "*XQuery 1.0: An XML Query Language*", W3C Working Draft, November 2003, `http://www.w3.org/TR/xquery/`
20. Neumann, A., Berlea, A., and Seidl, H. "*fxgrep, The Functional XML Querying Tool*", `http://www.informatik.uni-trier.de/~aberlea/Fxgrep/`
21. Leroy X. et al., "*Objective Caml*", `http://caml.inria.fr/ocaml/`

XML Goes Native: Run-Time Representations for XTATIC

Vladimir Gapeyev, Michael Y. Levin, Benjamin C. Pierce, and Alan Schmitt

University of Pennsylvania

Abstract. XTATIC is a lightweight extension of C♯ offering native support for statically typed XML processing. XML trees are built-in values in XTATIC, and static analysis of the trees manipulated by programs is part of the ordinary job of the typechecker. "Tree grep" pattern matching is used to investigate and transform XML trees. XTATIC's surface syntax and type system are tightly integrated with those of C♯. Beneath the hood, however, an implementation of XTATIC must address a number of issues common to any language supporting a declarative style of XML processing (e.g., XQUERY, XSLT, XDUCE, CDUCE, XACT, XEN, etc.). In particular, it must provide representations for XML tags, trees, and textual data that use memory efficiently, support efficient pattern matching, allow maximal sharing of common substructures, and permit separate compilation. We analyze these representation choices in detail and describe the solutions used by the XTATIC compiler.

1 Introduction

XTATIC inherits its key features from XDUCE [1, 2], a domain-specific language for statically typed XML processing. These features include XML trees as built-in values, a type system based on *regular types* (closely related to popular schema languages such as DTD and XML-Schema) for static typechecking of computations involving XML, and a powerful form of pattern matching called *regular patterns*. The goals of the XTATIC project are to bring these technologies to a wide audience by integrating them with a mainstream object-oriented language and to demonstrate an implementation with good performance. We use C♯ as the host language, but our results should also be applicable in a Java setting.

At the source level, the integration of XML trees with the object-oriented data model of C♯ is accomplished by two steps. First, the subtype hierarchy of tree types from XDUCE is grafted into the C♯ class hierarchy by making all regular types be subtypes of a special class `Seq`. This allows XML trees to be passed to generic library facilities such as collection classes, stored in fields of objects, etc. Conversely, the roles of tree labels and their types from XDUCE are played by objects and classes in XTATIC; XML trees are represented using objects from a special `Tag` class as labels.

Subtyping in XTATIC subsumes both the object-oriented subclass relation and the richer subtype relation of regular types. XDUCE's simple "semantic"

R. Bodik (Ed.): CC 2005, LNCS 3443, pp. 43–58, 2005.

definition of subtyping (sans inference rules) extends naturally to XTATIC's object-labeled trees and classes. The combined data model and type system, dubbed *regular object types*, have been formalized in [3]. Algorithms for checking subtyping and inferring types for variables bound in patterns can be adapted straightforwardly from those of XDUCE ([2] and [4]).

XTATIC's tree construction and pattern matching primitives eschew all forms of destructive update—instead, the language promotes a declarative style of tree processing, in which values and subtrees are extracted from existing trees and used to construct entirely new trees. This style is attractive from many points of view: it is easy to reason about (no need to worry about aliasing), it integrates smoothly with other language features such as threads, and it allows rich forms of subtyping that would be unsound in the presence of update. Many other high-level XML processing languages, including XSLT [5], XQUERY [6], CDUCE [7], and XACT [8], have made the same choice, for similar reasons. However, the declarative style makes some significant demands on the implementation, since it involves a great deal of replicated substructure that must be shared to achieve acceptable efficiency.

Our implementation is based on a source to source compiler from XTATIC to C$^\sharp$. One major function of this compiler is to translate the high-level pattern matching statements of XTATIC into low-level C$^\sharp$ code that is efficient and compact. A previous paper [9] addressed this issue by introducing a formalism of *matching automata* and using it to define both backtracking and non-backtracking compilation algorithms for regular patterns.

The present paper addresses the lower-level issue of how to compile XML values and value-constructing primitives into appropriate run-time representations. We explore several alternative representation choices and analyze them with respect to their support for efficient pattern matching, common XTATIC programming idioms, and safe integration with foreign XML representations such as the standard Document Object Model (DOM). Our contributions may be summarized as follows: (1) a data structure for sequences of XML trees that supports efficient repeated concatenation on both ends of a sequence, equipped with a fast algorithm for calculating the subsequences bound to pattern variables; (2) a compact and efficient hybrid representation of textual data (PCDATA) that supports regular pattern matching over character sequences (i.e., a statically typed form of string grep); (3) a type-tagging scheme allowing fast dynamic revalidation of XML values whose static types have been lost, e.g., by upcasting to `object` for storage in a generic collection; and (4) a proxy scheme allowing foreign XML representations such as DOM to be manipulated by XTATIC programs without first translating them to our representation. (Because of space constraints, we present only the first here; details of the others can be found in an extended version of the paper [10].) We have implemented these designs and measured their performance both against some natural variants and against implementations of other XML processing languages. The results show that a declarative statically typed embedding of XML transformation operations into a stock object-oriented language can be competitive with existing mainstream XML processing frameworks.

The next section briefly reviews the XTATIC language design. The heart of the paper is Section 3, which describes and evaluates our representations for trees. Section 4 summarizes results of benchmarking programs compiled by XTATIC against other XML processing tools. Section 5 discusses related work.

2 Language Overview

This section sketches just the aspects of the XTATIC design that directly impact runtime representation issues. More details can be found in [11, 3].

Consider the following document fragment—a sequence of two entries from an address book—given here side-by side in XML and XTATIC concrete syntax.

```
<person>                                [[ <person>
  <name>Haruo Hosoya</name>                  <name>'Haruo Hosoya'</name>
  <email>hahasoya</email>                    <email>'hahasoya'</email>
</person>                                  </person>
<person>                                   <person>
  <name>Jerome Vouillon</name>               <name>'Jerome Vouillon'</name>
  <tel>123</tel>                             <tel>'123'</tel>
</person>                                  </person> ]]
```

XTATIC's syntax for this document is very close to XML, the only differences being the outer double brackets, which segregate the world of XML values and types from the regular syntax of C♯, and backquotes, which distinguish PCDATA (XML textual data) from arbitrary XTATIC expressions yielding XML elements.

One possible type for the above value is a list of persons, each containing a name, an optional phone number, and a list of emails:

```
<person> <name>pcdata</> <tel>pcdata</>? <email>pcdata</>* </person>*
```

The type constructor "?" marks optional components, and "*" marks repeated sub-sequences. XTATIC also includes the type constructor "|" for non-disjoint unions of types. The shorthand `</>` is a closing bracket matching an arbitrarily named opening bracket. Every regular type in XTATIC denotes a set of sequences. Concatenation of sequences (and sequence types) is written either as simple juxtaposition or (for readability) with a comma. The constructors "*" and "?" bind stronger than ",", which is stronger than "|". The type "`pcdata`" describes sequences of characters.

Types can be given names that may be mentioned in other types. E.g., our address book could be given the type `APers*` in the presence of definitions

```
regtype Name  [[ <name>pcdata</> ]]
regtype Tel   [[ <tel>pcdata</>  ]]
regtype Email [[ <email>pcdata</> ]]
regtype TPers [[ <person> Name Tel </> ]]
regtype APers [[ <person> Name Tel? Email* </> ]]
```

A *regular pattern* is just a regular type decorated with variable binders. A value v can be matched against a pattern p, binding variables occurring in p to the corresponding parts of v, if v belongs to the language denoted by the regular type obtained from p by stripping variable binders. For matching against multiple patterns, XTATIC provides a match construct that is similar to the switch statement of C♯ and the match expression of functional languages such as ML. For example, the following program extracts a sequence of type TPers from a sequence of type APers, removing persons that do not have a phone number and eliding emails.

```
static [[ TPers* ]] addrbook ([[ APers* ]] ps) {
 [[ TPers* ]] res = [[ ]];     bool cont = true;
 while (cont) {
   match (ps) {
    case [[<person> <name>any</> n, <tel>any</> t, any </>, any rest]]:
      res = [[ res, <person> n, t </> ]];    ps = rest;
    case [[ <person> any </person>, any rest ]]:      ps = rest;
    case [[ ]]:    cont = false;  } }
 return res; }
```

The integration of XML sequences with C♯ objects is accomplished in two steps. First, XTATIC introduces a special class named Seq that is a supertype of every XML type—i.e., every XML value may be regarded as an object this class. The regular type [[any]] is equivalent to the class type Seq. Second, XTATIC allows any object—not just an XML tag—to be the label of an element. For instance, we can write <(1)/> for the singleton sequence labeled with the integer 1 (the parentheses distinguish an XTATIC expression from an XML tag); similarly, we can recursively define the type any as any = [[<(object)>any</>*]].

We close this overview by describing how XTATIC views textual data. Formally, the type pcdata is defined by associating each character with a singleton class that is a subclass of the C♯ char classand taking pcdata to be an abbreviation for <(char)/>*. In the concrete syntax, we write 'foo' for the sequence type <(char$_f$)/><(char$_o$)/><(char$_o$)/> and for the corresponding sequence value. This treatment of character data has two advantages. First, there is no need to introduce a special concatenation operator for pcdata, as the sequence 'ab','cd' is identical to 'abcd'. This can also be seen at the type level:

```
pcdata,pcdata = <(char)/>*,<(char)/>* = <(char)/>* = pcdata
```

Equating pcdata with string would not allow such a seamless integration of the string concatenation operator with the sequence operator. Second, singleton character classes can be used in pattern matching to obtain functionality very similar to string regular expressions [12]. For instance, the XTATIC type 'a',pcdata,'b' corresponds to the regular expression a.*b.

3 Representing Trees

We now turn to the design of efficient representations for XML trees. First, we design a tree representation that supports XTATIC's view of trees as shared and immutable structures (Section 3.1). The main constraint on the design is that the programming style favored by XTATIC involves a great deal of appending (and consing) of sequences. To avoid too much re-copying of sub-sequences, we enhance the naive design to do this appending lazily (Section 3.2). Finally, XTATIC needs to inter-operate with other XML representations available in .NET, in particular DOM. In the full version of this paper [10], we show how DOM structures can masquerade as instances of our XTATIC trees in a type-safe manner.

3.1 Simple Sequences

Every XTATIC value with a regular type is a *sequence* of trees. XTATIC's pattern-matching algorithms, based on tree automata, require access to the label of the first tree in the sequence, its children, and its following sibling. This access style is naturally supported by a simple singly linked structure.

Figure 1 summarizes the classes implementing sequences. `Seq` is an abstract superclass representing all sequences regardless of their form. As the exact class of a `Seq` object is often needed by XTATIC-generated code, it is stored as an enumeration value in the field `kind` of every `Seq` object. Maintaining this field allows us to use a `switch` statement instead of a chain of `if-then-else` statements relying on the "`is`" operator to test class membership.

The subclass `SeqObject` includes two fields, `next` and `contents`, that point to the rest of the sequence—the right sibling—and the first child of the node. The field `label` holds a C♯ object. Empty sequences are represented using a single, statically allocated object of class `SeqEmpty`. (Using `null` would require an extra test before `switch`ing on the kind of the sequence—in effect, optimizing the empty-sequence case instead of the more common non-empty case.)

In principle, the classes `SeqEmpty` and `SeqObject` can encode all XTATIC trees. But to avoid downcasting when dealing with labels containing primitive values (most critically, characters), we also include specialized classes `SeqBool`, `SeqInt`, `SeqChar`, etc. for storing values of base types.

XML data is encoded using `SeqObjects` that contain, in their `label` field, instances of the special class `Tag` that represent XML tags. A tag object has a

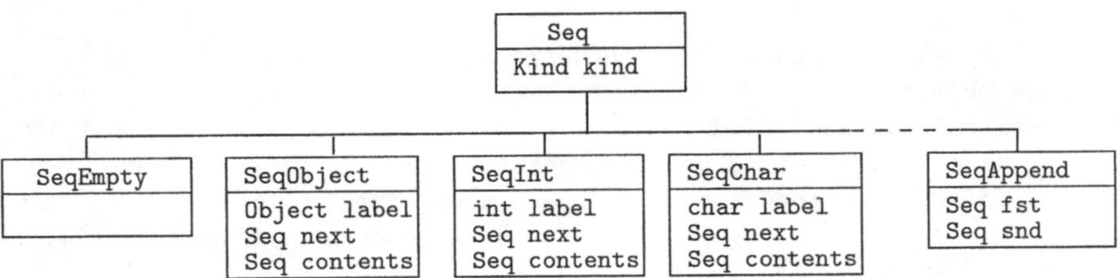

Fig. 1. Classes used for representing sequences

string field for the tag's local name and a field for its namespace URI. We use memoisation (interning) to ensure that there is a single run-time object for each known tag, making tag matching a simple matter of physical object comparison.

Pattern matching of labels is implemented as follows. The object (or value) in a label matches a label pattern when: the pattern is a class `C` and the object belongs to a subclass of `C`, the pattern is a tag and the object is physically equal to the tag, the pattern is a base value `v` and the label holds a value equal to `v`.

3.2 Lazy Sequences

In the programming style encouraged by XTATIC, sequence concatenation is a pervasive operation. Unfortunately, the run-time representation outlined so far renders concatenation linear in the size of the first sequence, leading to unacceptable performance when elements are repeatedly appended at the end of a sequence, as in the assignment of `res` in the `addrbook` example in Section 2.

This observation naturally suggests a lazy approach to concatenation: we introduce a new kind of sequence node, `SeqAppend`, that contains two fields, `fst` and `snd`. The concatenation of (non-empty) sequences `Seq1` and `Seq2` is now compiled into the constant time creation of a `SeqAppend` node, with `fst` pointing to `Seq1`, and `snd` to `Seq2`. We preserve the invariant that neither field of a `SeqAppend` node points to the empty sequence.

To support pattern matching, we need a *normalization* operation that exposes at least the first element of a sequence. The simplest approach, *eager* normalization, just transforms the whole sequence so that it does not contain any top-level `SeqAppend` nodes (children of the nodes in the sequence are not normalized). However, there are cases when it is not necessary to normalize the whole sequence, e.g. when a program inspects only the first few elements of a long list. To this end we introduce a *lazy* normalization algorithm, given in pseudocode form in Figure 2.

The algorithm fetches the first concrete element—that is, the leftmost non-`SeqAppend` node of the tree—copies it (so that the contexts that possibly share

```
Seq lazy_norm(Seq node) {
  switch (node.kind) {
    case Append: return norm_rec(node.fst, node.snd);
    default:     return node;   } }

Seq norm_rec(Seq node, Seq acc) {
  switch (node.kind) {
    case Append: return norm_rec(node.fst, new SeqAppend(node.snd, acc));
    case Object:
      switch node.next.kind {
        case Empty: return new SeqObject(node.label, node.contents, acc);
        default:    return new SeqObject(node.label, node.contents,
                                         new SeqAppend(node.next, acc)); }
    /* similar cases for SeqInt, SeqBool, ... */   } }
```

Fig. 2. Lazy Normalization Algorithm

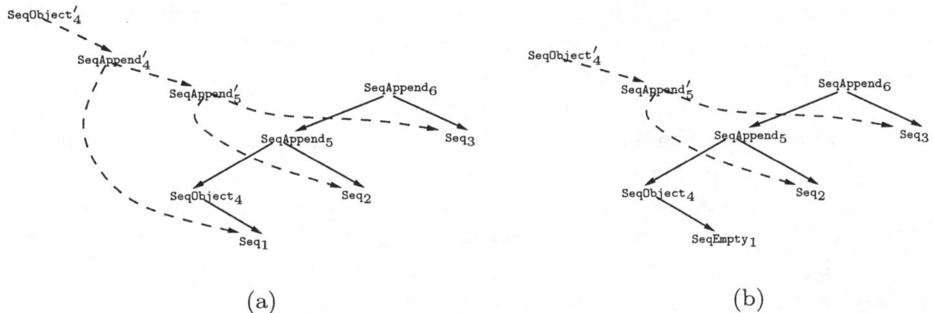

(a) (b)

Fig. 3. Lazy normalization of lazy sequences. In (a), the leftmost concrete element has a right sibling; in (b) it does not. Dotted pointers are created during normalization

it are not affected), and makes it the first element of a new sequence consisting of (copies of) the traversed `SeqAppend` nodes arranged into an equivalent, but right-skewed tree. Figure 3 illustrates this algorithm, normalizing the sequence starting at node $\texttt{SeqAppend}_6$ to the equivalent sequence starting at node $\texttt{SeqObject}'_4$.

Since parts of sequence values are often shared, it is not uncommon to process (and normalize) the same sequence several times. As described so far, the normalization algorithm returns a new sequence, e.g. $\texttt{SeqObject}'_4$, but leaves the original lazy sequence unchanged. To avoid redoing the same work during subsequent normalizations of the same sequence, we also modify *in-place* the root `SeqAppend` node, setting the `snd` field to `null` (indicating that this `SeqAppend` has been normalized), and the `fst` field to the result of normalization:

```
Seq lazy_norm_in_place(Seq node) {
  switch (node.kind) {
    case Append:
      if (node.snd == null) return node.fst;
      node.fst = norm_rec(node.fst, node.snd); node.snd = null;
      return node.fst;
    default: return node;   }   }
```

Interestingly, this in-place modification is required for the *correctness* of binding of non-tail variables in patterns. The pattern matching algorithm [4] naturally supports only those pattern variables that bind to tails of sequence values; variables binding to non-tail sequences are handled by a trick. Namely, binding a non-tail variable `x` is accomplished in two stages. The first stage performs pattern matching and—as it traverses the input sequence—sets auxiliary variables $\texttt{x}_b$ and $\texttt{x}_e$ to the beginning and end of the subsequence. The second stage computes `x` from $\texttt{x}_b$ and $\texttt{x}_e$ by traversing the sequence beginning at $\texttt{x}_b$ and copying nodes until it reaches $\texttt{x}_e$. In both stages, the program traverses the same sequence, performing normalization along the way. In-place modification guarantees that during both traversals we will encounter *physically* the same concrete nodes, and so, in the second stage, we are justified in detecting the end of the subsequence by checking physical equality between the current node and $\texttt{x}_e$.

Because of creation of fresh SeqAppend nodes, the lazy normalization algorithm can allocate more memory than its eager counterpart. However, we can show that this results in no more than a constant factor overhead. A node is said to be a *left node* if it is pointed by the fst pointer of a SeqAppend. There are two cases when the algorithm creates a new SeqAppend node: when it traverses a left SeqAppend node, and when it reaches the leftmost concrete element. In both cases, the newly created nodes are *not* left nodes and so will not lead to further creation of SeqAppend nodes during subsequent normalizations. Hence, lazy normalization allocates at most twice as much memory as eager normalization.

We now present some measurements quantifying the consequences of this overhead on running time. The table below shows running times for two variants of the phone book application from Section 2, executed on an address book of 250,000 entries. (Our experimental setup is described below in Section 4.) The first variant constructs the result as in Section 2, appending to the end. The second variant constructs the result by by appending to the front:

```
res = [[ <person> n, t </>, res ]];
```

This variant favors the non-lazy tree representation from the previous subsection, which serves as a baseline for our lazy optimizations. Since our implementation recognizes prepending singleton sequences as a special case, no lazy structures are created when the second program is executed, and, consequently all concatenation approaches behave the same. For the back-appending program, the system runs out of memory using eager concatenation, while both lazy concatenation approaches perform reasonably well. Indeed, the performance of the lazy representations for the back-appending program is within 10% of the performance of the non-lazy representation for the front-appending program, which favors such a representation.

	eager concatenations	eager normalization	lazy normalization
back appending	∞	1,050 ms	1,050 ms
front appending	950 ms	950 ms	950 ms

This comparison does not show any difference between the lazy and eager normalization approaches. We have also compared performance of eager vs. lazy normalization on the benchmarks discussed below in Section 4. Their performance is always close, with slight advantage for one or the other depending on workload. On the other hand, for programs that explore only part of a sequence, lazy normalization can be *arbitrarily* faster, making it a clear winner overall.

Our experience suggests that, in common usage patterns, our representation exhibits constant amortized time for all operations. It is possible, however, to come up with scenarios where repeatedly accessing the first element of a sequence may take linear time for each access. Consider the following program fragment:

```
[[any]] res1 = [[]];    [[any]] res2 = [[]];
while (true) {
  res1 = [[res1, <a/>]];   res2 = [[res1, <b/>]];
  match (res2) {
    case [[<(Tag x)/>, any]]: ...use x...    } }
```

Since the pattern matching expression extracts only the first element of `res2`, only the top-level `SeqAppend` object of the sequence stored in `res2` is modified in-place during normalization. The `SeqAppend` object of the sequence stored in `res1` is not modified in-place, and, consequently, is completely renormalized during each iteration of the loop.

Kaplan, Tarjan and Okasaki [13] describe *catenable steques*, which provide all the functionality required by XTATIC pattern-matching algorithms with operations that run in constant amortized time in the presence of sharing. We have implemented their algorithms in C♯ and compared their performance with that of our representation using the lazy normalization algorithm. The steque implementation is slightly more compact—on average it requires between 1.5 and 2 times less memory than our representation. For the above tricky example, catenable steques are also fast, while XTATIC's representation fails on sufficiently large sequences. For more common patterns of operations, our representation is more efficient. The following table shows running times of a program that builds a sequence by back-appending one element at a time and fully traverses the constructed sequence. We ran the experiment for sequences of four different sizes. The implementation using catenable steques is significantly slower than our much simpler representation because of the overhead arising from the complexity of the steque data structures.

	Steques	XTATIC
n = 10,000	70 ms	6 ms
n = 20,000	140 ms	12 ms
n = 30,000	230 ms	19 ms
n = 40,000	325 ms	31 ms

4 Measurements

This section describes performance measurements comparing XTATIC with some other XML processing systems. Our goal in gathering these numbers has been to verify that our current implementation gives reasonable performance on a range of tasks and datasets, rather than to draw detailed conclusions about relative speeds of the different systems. (Differences in implementation platforms and languages, XML processing styles, etc. make the latter task well nigh impossible!)

Our tests were executed on a 2GHz Pentium 4 with 512MB of RAM running Windows XP. The XTATIC and DOM experiments were executed on Microsoft .NET version 1.1. The CDUCE interpreter (CVS version of November 25th, 2003) was compiled natively using ocamlopt 3.07+2. QIZX/OPEN and Xalan XSLTC were executed on SUN JAVA version 1.4.2. Since this paper is concerned with run-time data structures, our measurements do not include static costs of typechecking and compilation. Also, since the current implementation of XTATIC's

XML parser is inefficient and does not reveal much information about the performance of our data model, we factor out parsing and loading of input XML documents from our analysis. Each measurement was obtained by running a program with given parameters ten times and averaging the results. We selected sufficiently large input documents to ensure low variance of time measurements and to make the overhead of just-in-time compilation negligible. The XTATIC programs were compiled using the lazy append with lazy normalization policy described in Section 3.

We start by comparing XTATIC with the QIZX/OPEN [14] implementation of XQUERY. Our test is a small query named `shake` that counts the number of distinct words in the complete Shakespeare plays, represented by a collection of XML documents with combined size of 8Mb. The core of the `shake` implementation in XQUERY is a call to a function `tokenize` that splits a chunk of character data into a collection of white-space-separated words. In XTATIC, this is implemented by a generic pattern matching statement that extracts the leading word or white space, processes it, and proceeds to handle the remainder of the `pcdata`. Each time, this remainder is boxed into a `SeqSubstring` object, only to be immediately unboxed during the next iteration of the loop. We believe this superfluous manipulation is the main reason why XTATIC is more than twice slower than QIZX/OPEN in this example.

	shake
XTATIC	7,500 ms
QIZX/OPEN	3,200 ms

We also implemented several XQUERY examples from the XMark suite [15], and ran them on an 11MB data file generated by XMark (at "factor 0.1"). XTATIC substantially outperforms QIZX/OPEN on all of these benchmarks—by 500 times on `q01`, by 700 times on `q02`, by six times on `q02`, and by over a thousand times on `q08`. This huge discrepancy appears to be a consequence of two factors. Firstly, QIZX/OPEN, unlike its commercial counterpart, does not use indexing, which for examples such as `q01` and `q02` can make a dramatic performance improvement. Secondly, we are translating high-level XQUERY programs into low-level XTATIC programs—in effect, performing manual query optimization. This makes a comparison between the two systems problematic, since the result does not provide much insight about the underlying representations.

Next, we compare XTATIC with two XSLT implementations: .NET XSLT and Xalan XSLTC. The former is part of the standard C♯ library; the latter is an XSLT compiler that generates a JAVA class file from a given XSLT template.

We implemented several transformations from the XSLTMark benchmark suite [16]. The `backwards` program traverses the input document and reverses every element sequence; `identity` copies the input document; `dbonerow` searches a database of person records for a particular entry, and `reverser` reads a `PCDATA` fragment, splits it into words, and outputs a new `PCDATA` fragment in which the words are reversed. The first three programs are run on a 2MB XML document containing 10,000 top-level elements; the last program is executed on a small text fragment.

	backwards	identity	dbonerow	reverser
XTATIC	450 ms	450 ms	13 ms	2.5 ms
.NET XSLT	2,500 ms	750 ms	300 ms	9 ms
Xalan XSLTC	2,200 ms	250 ms	90 ms	0.5 ms

XTATIC exhibits equivalent speed for `backwards` and `identity` since the cost of reversing is approximately equal to the cost of copying a sequence in the presence of lazy concatenation. The corresponding XSLT programs behave differently since `backwards` is implemented by copying *and* sorting every sequence according to the position of the elements. The XSLT implementations are relatively efficient on `identity`. This may be partially due to the fact that they use a much more compact read-only representation of XML documents. XTATIC is substantially slower than Xalan XSLTC on the `pcdata`-intensive `reverser` example. We believe the reason for this is, as in the case of `shake` in the comparison with QIZX/OPEN, the overhead of our `pcdata` implementation for performing text traversal. Conversely, XTATIC is much faster on `dbonerow`. As with QIZX/OPEN, this can be explained by the difference in the level of programming detail—a single XPATH line in the XSLTC program corresponds to a low-level XTATIC program that specifies how to search the input document efficiently.

In the next pair of experiments, we compare XTATIC with CDUCE [7] on two programs: `addrbook` and `split`. The first of these was introduced in Section 2 (the CDUCE version was coded to mimick the XTATIC version, i.e. we did not use CDUCE's higher-level `transform` primitive); it is run on a 25MB data file containing 250,000 `APers` elements. The second program traverses a 5MB XML document containing information about people and sorts the children of each person according to gender. Although it is difficult to compare programs executed in different run-time frameworks and written in different source languages, we can say that, to a rough first approximation, XTATIC and CDUCE exhibit comparable performance. An important advantage of CDUCE is a very memory-efficient representation of sequences. This is compensated by the fact that XTATIC programs are (just-in-time) compiled while CDUCE programs are interpreted.

	split	addrbook
XTATIC	950 ms	1,050 ms
CDUCE	650 ms	1,300 ms

The next experiment compares XTATIC with XACT [17]. We use two programs that are part of the XACT distribution—`recipe` processes a database of recipes and outputs its HTML presentation; `sortedaddrbook` is a version of the address book program introduced in Section 2 that sorts the output entries. We ran `recipe` on a file containing 525 recipes and `sortedaddrbook` on a 10,000 entry address book.(Because of problems installing XACT under Windows, unlike the other experiments, comparisons with XACT were executed on a 1GHz Pentium III with 256MB of RAM running Linux.) For both programs XTATIC is substantially faster. As with XQUERY, this comparison is not precise because of a mismatch between

	recipe	sortedaddrbook
XTATIC	250 ms	1,600 ms
XACT	60,000 ms	10,000 ms

XML processing mechanisms of XTATIC and XACT. In particular, the large discrepancy in the case of `recipe` can be partly attributed to the fact that its style of processing in which the whole document is traversed and completely rebuilt in a different form is foreign to the relatively high level XML manipulation primitives of XACT but is quite natural to the relatively low level constructs of XTATIC.

The last experiment compares XTATIC with a C♯ program using DOM and the .NET XPATH library, again using the `addrbook` example on the 25MB input file. The C♯ program employs XPATH to extract all the `APers` elements with `tel` children, destructively removes their `email` children, and returns the obtained result. This experiment confirms that DOM is not very well-suited for the kind of functional manipulation of sequences prevalent in XTATIC. The DOM data model is geared for destructive modification and random access traversal of elements and, as a result, is much more heavyweight.

	addrbook
XTATIC	1,050 ms
DOM/Xpath	5,100 ms

5 Related Work

We have concentrated here on the runtime representation issues that we addressed while building an implementation of XTATIC that is both efficient and tightly integrated with C♯. Other aspects of the XTATIC design and implementation are described in several companion papers—one surveying the most significant issues faced during the design of the language [11], another presenting the core language design, integrating the object and tree data models and establishing basic soundness results [3], and the third proposing a technique for compiling regular patterns based on *matching automata* [9].

There is considerable current research and development activity aimed at providing convenient support for XML processing in both general-purpose and domain-specific languages. In the latter category, XQUERY [6] and XSLT [5] are special-purpose XML processing languages specified by W3C that have strong industrial support, including a variety of implementations and wide user base. In the former, the CDUCE language of Benzaken, Castagna, and Frisch [7] generalizes XDUCE's type system with intersection and function types. The XEN language of Meijer, Schulte, and Bierman [18] is a proposal to significantly modify the core design of C♯ in order to integrate support for objects, relations, and XML (in particular, XML itself simply becomes a syntax for serialized object instances). XACT [17, 8] extends JAVA with XML processing, proposing an elegant programming idiom: the creation of XML values is done using XML templates, which are immutable first-class structures representing XML with named gaps that may be filled to obtain ordinary XML trees. XJ [19] is another extension of JAVA for native XML processing that uses W3C Schema as a type system and XPATH as a navigation language for XML. XOBE [20] is a source to source compiler for an extension of JAVA that, from language design point of view, is very similar to XTATIC. SCALA is a developing general-purpose web services language that compiles into JAVA bytecode; it is currently being extended with XML support [21].

So far, most of the above projects have concentrated on developing basic language designs; there is little published work on serious implementations. (Even for XQUERY and XSLT, we have been unable to find detailed descriptions of their run-time representations.) We summarize here the available information.

Considerable effort, briefly sketched in [7], has been put into making the CDUCE's OCAML-based interpreter efficient. They address similar issues of text and tree representations and use similar solutions. CDUCE's user-visible datatype for strings is also the character list, and they also implement its optimized alternatives—the one described in the paper resembles our `SeqSubstring`. CDUCE uses lazy list concatenation, but apparently only with eager normalization. Another difference is the object-oriented flavor of our representations.

XACT's implementation, developed independently and in parallel with XTATIC but driven by similar needs (supporting efficient sharing, etc.) and targeting a similar (object-oriented) runtime environment, has strong similarities to ours; in particular, lazy data structures are used to support efficient gap plugging. Our preliminary performance measurements may be viewed as validating the representation choices of both implementations. XTATIC's special treatment of `pcdata` does not appear to be used in XACT. The current implementations of XOBE and XJ are based on DOM, although the designs are amenable to alternative back-ends.

Kay [22] describes the implementation of Version 6.1 of his XSLT processor Saxon. The processor is implemented in JAVA and, like in our approach, does not rely on a pre-existing JAVA DOM library for XML data representation, since DOM is again too heavyweight for the task at hand: e.g. it carries information unnecessary for XPATH and XSLT (like entity nodes) and supports updates. Saxon comes with two variants of run time structures. One is object-oriented and is similar in spirit to ours. Another represents tree information as arrays of integers, creating node objects only on demand and destroying them after use. This model is reportedly more memory efficient and quicker to build, at the cost of slightly slower tree navigation. Overall, it appears to perform better and is provided as the default in Saxon.

In the broader context of functional language implementations, efficient support for list (and string) concatenation has long been recognized as an important issue. An early paper by Morris, Schmidt and Wadler [23] describes a technique similar to our eager normalization in their string processing language Poplar. Sleep and Holmström [24] propose a modification to a lazy evaluator that corresponds to our lazy normalization. Keller [25] suggests using a lazy representation without normalization at all, which behaves similarly to database B-trees, but without balancing. We are not aware of prior studies comparing the lazy and eager alternatives, as we have done here.

More recently, the algorithmic problem of efficient representation for lists with concatenation has been studied in detail by Kaplan, Tarjan and Okasaki [13].

They describe *catenable steques* which support constant amortized time sequence operations. We opted for the simpler representations described here out of concern for excessive constant factors in running time arising from the complexity of their data structures (see Section 3.2.)

Another line of work, started by Hughes [26] and continued by Wadler [27] and more recently Voigtlander [28] considers how certain uses of list concatenation (and similar operations) in an applicative program can be eliminated by a systematic program transformation, sometimes resulting in improved asymptotic running times. In particular, these techniques capture the well-known transformation from the quadratic to the linear version of the reverse function. It is not clear, however, whether the techniques are applicable outside the pure functional language setting: e.g., they transform a recursive function f that uses append to a function f' that uses only list construction, while in our setting problematic uses of append often occur inside imperative loops.

Prolog's difference lists [29] is a logic programming solution to constant time list concatenation. Using this technique requires transforming programs operating on regular lists into programs operating on difference lists. This is not always possible. Marriott and Søndergaard [30] introduce a dataflow analysis that determines whether such transformation is achievable and define the automatic transformation algorithm. We leave a more detailed comparison of our lazy concatenation approach and the difference list approach for future work.

Acknowledgements

Parts of the XTATIC compiler were implemented by Eijiro Sumii and Stephen Tse. Conversations with Eijiro contributed many ideas to XTATIC and this paper. We also thank Haruo Hosoya, Alain Frisch, Christian Kirkegaard, and Xavier Franc for discussing various aspects of this work. Our work on XTATIC has been supported by the National Science Foundation under Career grant CCR-9701826 and ITR CCR-0219945, and by gifts from Microsoft.

References

1. Hosoya, H., Pierce, B.C.: XDuce: A statically typed XML processing language. ACM Transactions on Internet Technology **3** (2003) 117–148
2. Hosoya, H., Vouillon, J., Pierce, B.C.: Regular expression types for XML. In: Proceedings of the International Conference on Functional Programming (ICFP). (2000)
3. Gapeyev, V., Pierce, B.C.: Regular object types. In: European Conference on Object-Oriented Programming (ECOOP), Darmstadt, Germany. (2003) A preliminary version was presented at FOOL '03.
4. Hosoya, H., Pierce, B.C.: Regular expression pattern matching. In: ACM SIGPLAN–SIGACT Symposium on Principles of Programming Languages (POPL), London, England. (2001) Full version in *Journal of Functional Programming*, 13(6), Nov. 2003, pp. 961–1004.

5. W3C: XSL Transformations (XSLT) (1999) `http://www.w3.org/TR/xslt`.
6. XQuery 1.0: An XML Query Language, W3C Working Draft (2004) `http://www.w3.org/TR/xquery/`.
7. Benzaken, V., Castagna, G., Frisch, A.: CDuce: An XML-centric general-purpose language. In: ACM SIGPLAN International Conference on Functional Programming (ICFP), Uppsala, Sweden. (2003) 51–63
8. Christensen, A.S., Kirkegaard, C., Møller, A.: A runtime system for XML transformations in Java. In Bellahsène, Z., Milo, T., Michael Rys, e.a., eds.: Database and XML Technologies: International XML Database Symposium (XSym). Volume 3186 of Lecture Notes in Computer Science., Springer (2004) 143–157
9. Levin, M.Y.: Compiling regular patterns. In: ACM SIGPLAN International Conference on Functional Programming (ICFP), Uppsala, Sweden. (2003)
10. Gapeyev, V., Levin, M.Y., Pierce, B.C., Schmitt, A.: XML goes native: Run-time representations for Xtatic. Technical Report MS-CIS-04-23, University of Pennsylvania (2004)
11. Gapeyev, V., Levin, M.Y., Pierce, B.C., Schmitt, A.: The Xtatic experience. Technical Report MS-CIS-04-24, University of Pennsylvania (2004)
12. Tabuchi, N., Sumii, E., Yonezawa, A.: Regular expression types for strings in a text processing language. In den Bussche, J.V., Vianu, V., eds.: Proceedings of Workshop on Types in Programming (TIP). (2002) 1–18
13. Kaplan, H., Okasaki, C., Tarjan, R.E.: Simple confluently persistent catenable lists. SIAM Journal on Computing **30** (2000) 965–977
14. Franc, X.: Qizx. `http://www.xfra.net/qizxopen` (2003)
15. Schmidt, A.R., Waas, F., Kersten, M.L., Carey, M.J., Manolescu, I., Busse, R.: XMark: A benchmark for XML data management. In: Proceedings of the International Conference on Very Large Data Bases (VLDB), Hong Kong, China (2002) 974–985 See also `http://www.xml-benchmark.org/`.
16. DataPower Technology, Inc.: XSLTMark. `http://www.datapower.com/xml_community/xsltmark.html` (2001)
17. Kirkegaard, C., Møller, A., Schwartzbach, M.I.: Static analysis of XML transformations in Java. IEEE Transactions on Software Engineering **30** (2004) 181–192
18. Meijer, E., Schulte, W., Bierman, G.: Programming with circles, triangles and rectangles. In: XML Conference and Exposition. (2003)
19. Harren, M., Raghavachari, B.M., Shmueli, O., Burke, M., Sarkar, V., Bordawekar, R.: XJ: Integration of XML processing into Java. Technical Report rc23007, IBM Research (2003)
20. Kempa, M., Linnemann, V.: On XML objects. In: Workshop on Programming Language Technologies for XML (PLAN-X). (2003)
21. Emir, B.: Extending pattern matching with regular tree expressions for XML processing in Scala. Diploma thesis, EPFL, Lausanne; `http://lamp.epfl.ch/~buraq` (2003)
22. Kay, M.H.: Saxon: Anatomy of an xslt processor (2001) `http://www-106.ibm.com/developerworks/library/x-xslt2/`.
23. Morris, J.H., Schmidt, E., Wadler, P.: Experience with an applicative string processing language. In: ACM Symposium on Principles of Programming Languages (POPL), Las Vegas, Nevada. (1980) 32–46
24. Sleep, M.R., Holmström, S.: A short note concerning lazy reduction rules for append. Software Practice and Experience **12** (1982) 1082–4
25. Keller, R.M.: Divide and CONCer: Data structuring in applicative multiprocessing systems. In: Proceedings of the 1980 ACM conference on LISP and functional programming. (1980) 196–202

26. Hughes, J.: A novel representation of lists and its application to the function "reverse". Information Processing Letters **22** (1986) 141–144
27. Wadler, P.: The concatenate vanishes. Note, University of Glasgow (1987) (revised 1989).
28. Voigtländer, J.: Concatenate, reverse and map vanish for free. In: ACM SIGPLAN International Conference on Functional Programming (ICFP), Pittsburgh, Pennsylvania. (2002) 14–25
29. Sterling, L., Shapiro, E.: The Art of Prolog. MIT Press (1986)
30. Marriott, K., Søndergaard, H.: Difference-list transformation for prolog. New Generation Computing **11** (1993) 125–157

Boosting the Performance of Multimedia Applications Using SIMD Instructions*

Weihua Jiang[1,2], Chao Mei[1], Bo Huang[2], Jianhui Li[2], Jiahua Zhu[1], Binyu Zang[1], and Chuanqi Zhu[1]

[1] Parallel Processing Institute, Fudan University,
220 Handan Rd, Shanghai, China, 200433
{021021073, 0022704, jhzhu, byzang, cqzhu}@fudan.edu.cn
[2] Intel China Software Center, Intel China Ltd,
22nd Floor, No. 2299 Yan'an Road (West), Shanghai, China, 200336
{weihua.jiang, bo.huang, jian.hui.li}@intel.com

Abstract. Modern processors' multimedia extensions (MME) provide SIMD ISAs to boost the performance of typical operations in multimedia applications. However, automatic vectorization support for them is not very mature. The key difficulty is how to vectorize those SIMD-ISA-supported idioms in source code in an efficient and general way. In this paper, we introduce a powerful and extendable recognition engine to solve this problem, which only needs a small amount of rules to recognize many such idioms and generate efficient SIMD instructions. We integrated this engine into the classic vectorization framework and obtained very good performance speedup for some real-life applications.

1 Introduction

Multimedia extensions (MME), e.g. Intel MMX/SSE/SSE2 [13][14], Motorola AltiVec [21] etc, have become an integral part of modern processors. They enable the exploitation of SIMD parallelism in multimedia applications. These SIMD ISA include not only simple SIMD arithmetic instructions (addition, subtraction etc) but also many domain-specific SIMD instructions to accelerate multimedia typical operations, e.g. saturated arithmetic, which are widely used in multimedia applications.

However, these MMEs have been underutilized so far due to the immaturity of compiler automatic vectorization support. Programmers are largely restricted to time-consuming methods such as inline assembly or intrinsic functions [16].

Many researches have been conducted in automatic vectorization for MMEs. Most of them have regarded this utilization as a similar problem with the vectorization for

* This research supported by: NSF of China (60273046), Science and Technology Committee of Shanghai, China (02JC14013) and Intel-University Cooperation Project (Optimizing Compiler for Intel NetBurst Microarchitecture).

R. Bodik (Ed.): CC 2005, LNCS 3443, pp. 59 – 75, 2005.

vector machines [7][11][15][16]. However, these two problems have different key points [3]. Traditional vectorization [1][2] focuses on how to transform source code into vector form correctly, while the utilization of MMEs shall concentrate on how to automatically recognize and then vectorize MME supported idioms in multimedia applications [3]. There are so many idioms needed to be recognized that an efficient and general way is of critical importance. Some researchers exerted efforts in this direction, the typical work is Bik *et al* [12]'s use of tree-rewriting technique to recognize two kinds of operations, saturation and MAX/MIN. Simple rigid pattern match methods [6] and specific languages (e.g. SWARC [17]) have also been used.

In this paper, we solve the key problem by introducing a powerful and extendable recognition engine and integrating it into the classic vectorization algorithm [1] as an extra stage. In this stage, we first normalize the program representation. Then we use an extended Bottom-Up Rewriting System (BURS) [9] to decide possible vectorization plans (VP) for each statement. Based on these single-statement VPs, we find out multi-statement vectorizable idioms and their VPs. Finally, we determine the best VP set for the loop. Experimental results show that we can vectorize many operations in real-life multimedia applications and the performances are quite satisfactory. We achieved a 10.86% average speedup for Accelerating Suite of Berkeley Multimedia Workload [4][5]. Compared with the vectorization ability of Intel C Compiler (ICC) version 8 [10], our compiler outperforms it by about 8% on average.

In short, this paper offers: (1) a uniform and flexible engine to recognize many vectorizable idioms, (2) a mechanism to generate efficient code for vectorized idioms and (3) very good performance for several real-life multimedia applications.

The rest of paper is organized as follows: In section 2, we show the key points in utilizing MMEs. After briefly introducing related techniques in section 3, we present our algorithm and discuss it in detail in section 4. In section 5, experiment results are presented. Then comparisons between our research and previous works are made in section 6. Finally, we end this paper by drawing conclusions in section 7.

2 Key Points in Fully Utilizing MMEs

MMEs include more domain-specific instructions than vector processors [3]. Table 1 lists those in Intel MMX/SSE/SSE2. The corresponding operations are heavily used in real-life multimedia applications. And after manual vectorization, they contribute to almost all speedups [4][5]. This fact shows that the recognition of these ISA-supported multimedia typical operations should be the focus of compiler support for MMEs.

As a result of more domain-specific instructions on MMEs, more idioms need to be recognized than traditional vectorization. Furthermore, because of lacking direct support in high-level languages, programmers often have to use multiple statements to express a multimedia typical operation. In such case, statements composing it are often connected by complex control structure. Sometimes, the statements may even not be adjacent. This fact greatly increases the number of idioms needed to be recognized. For example, Fig. 1 gives three typical idioms to express the signed short saturated operation in C language. Therefore, it is impractical to use the traditional 1:1 special treat

Table 1. Multimedia typical arithmetic instructions provided by MMX/SSE/SSE2

Function	Instruction
Saturated add	PADDSB/PADDSW/PADDUSB/PADDUSW
Saturated subtract	PSUBSB/PSUBSW/PSUBUSB/PSUBUSW
Saturated pack	PACKSSWB/PACKSSDW/PACKUSWB
Sum of absolute difference	PSADBW
Min/max	PMINUB/.../PMINSW/PMAXUB/.../PMAXSW
Average	PAVGB/PAVGW
Multiply and add	PMADDWD
Logical	PAND/PANDN/PXOR/POR
Compare	PCMPEQB/PCMPGTW/.../PCMPGTB

```
/* short a, b; int ltmp; */
#define GSM_SUB(a, b) \
   ((ltmp=(int)a-(int)b)\
   > MAX_WORD ? MAX_WORD:\
   ltmp < MIN_WORD ? \
   MIN_WORD: ltmp

t = GSM_SUB(a, b)
     (a)
```

```
/*short *a,*b,*c;
 int t;*/
t = a[i] - b[i];
if(t>32767||t<-32768){
   if(t>32767)
      c[i] = 32767;
   else
      c[i] = -32768;
} else  c[i] = t;
     (b)
```

```
/*float sum; int clip;
short *sample; */
if(sum>32767.0) {
   *samples = 32767;
   clip++;
}elseif(sum<-32768.0)
{ *samples = -32768;
   clip++;
}else   *samples = sum;
     (c)
```

Fig. 1. Three variations of signed short saturated operation

ment to recognize each idiom as the number of idioms is now largely increased. It follows that a uniform and flexible way to recognize them is much preferred.

3 Background

3.1 Classic Vectorization Algorithm

The classic algorithm for automatic vectorization [1] is illustrated in Fig. 2. Its main idea is to reorder and vectorize statements in the loop according to data dependence.

```
for each loop in source code {
  construct its data dependence graph.
  condense each maximal strongly connected component in the graph.
  topological sort the condensed graph and number the nodes
  (1..m).
  for i = 1 to m {             // code generation
     distribute node_i into a loop.
     if node_i is not strongly-connected    //not in a dep cycle
       or can be recognized as vectorizable idiom then
          vectorize node_i.
  }
}
```

Fig. 2. Classic vectorization algorithm

Because its objects mostly are simple arithmetic operations, it pays little attention to code pattern and ISA support. For other few important idioms in numerical applications, e.g. MAX/MIN, it uses special treatment to recognize them.

3.2 Bottom-Up Rewriting System (BURS)

Bottom-Up Rewriting System (BURS) [9] is a code generator's generator, which is widely used in compiler to help generate code from IR tree. For a certain IR tree and a set of tree patterns, there may be more than one match (covering) of the tree. BURS uses dynamic programming to choose the lowest cost one. It accepts rules in the form of **non-terminal→pattern (cost) [action]** and produces tree matchers that make two passes over each subject tree. The first bottom-up pass finds a set of patterns that cover the tree with minimum cost. The second top-down pass executes the actions associated with minimum-cost patterns at the nodes they matched, which is driven by the goal non-terminal at tree root (similar with the *start* symbol in LR parsing).

According to the grammar in Fig. 3(a), tree *FETCH(PLUS(REG,INT))* has two coverings, namely, rule tree 1(4(6(5(2,3)))) and 1(4(8(2))) with costs 5 and 2, respectively.

In the first traversal of the BURS tree matcher, the tree is labeled as Fig. 3(b), in which each node is associated with minimum cost matching rule set for this subtree and corresponding costs. The best covering 1(4(8(2))) is indicated by the goal non-terminal *goal* at tree root.

```
#   NT→Pattern (Cost)
#1  goal→reg          (0)
#2  reg→REG           (0)
#3  reg→INT           (1)
#4  reg→FETCH(addr)      (2)
#5  reg→PLUS(reg, reg)   (2)
#6  addr→reg          (0)
#7  addr→INT          (0)
#8  addr→PLUS(reg, INT)  (0)
```
(a)

```
                                        FETCH   #4 reg->FETCH(addr)  (2)
                                                #6 addr->reg         (2)
#5 reg->PLUS(reg, reg)  (3)                     #1 goal->reg         (2)
#8 addr->PLUS(reg,INT)  (0)              PLUS
#1 goal->reg            (3)
      #2 reg->REG    (0)                                #7 addr->INT   (0)
      #6 addr->reg   (0)      REG        INT            #3 reg->INT    (1)
      #1 goal->reg   (0)                                #1 goal->reg   (1)
```
(b)

Fig. 3. Example BURS Matches. Action of each rule is omitted

4 Compiler Support for MMEs

To solve the idiom recognition problem in compiler support for MMEs, we design a powerful recognition engine and add it as an extra stage at the beginning of the classic algorithm in Fig. 2. The enhanced algorithm, as a whole, works as follows: our engine deals with the recognition of vectorizable language constructs (simple statements and idioms) in each loop and the dependence relations within each construct. Besides, the engine decides vectorization plan (VP) for each construct, i.e. the way to generate its SIMD code. Then it comes to the classic algorithm part that handles other issues, e.g. dependence relations between these constructs and other statements. During dependence graph construction, the statement(s) in each construct share one node in the graph. After graph condensing, we discard those recognized constructs that are strongly connected. For those survived, SIMD code is generated according to their VPs.

4.1 Basic Ideas in Vectorizable Construct Recognition

A vectorizable construct is a code block in source code to express one or several related vectorizable operations as a whole. It can be transformed into efficient SIMD code. Recognizing such constructs and finding how to vectorize them i.e. their VPs are the two tasks the recognition engine needs to accomplish. These two tasks are closely related. To recognize such construct, we have to know whether it is supported by MME's ISA and whether its vectorized form is profitable. Only during deciding its VPs can such information be obtained. To find how to vectorize a construct, i.e. its VP, we have to use a series of patterns (rules) to match the construct. Thus, a VP actually is a rule set covering the construct and VP finding is a process of recognition. Therefore, we prefer to perform these two tasks together.

During the recognition of single-statement vectorizable construct, VP selection is needed since a construct may have more than one VP. E.g. on Intel SSE/SSE2, construct *c[i]=(a[i]+b[i]+1)>>1;* have two VPs: one is *add/add/shift/store* instruction sequence and the other is instructions *average/store*. If we express each statement as a tree, then BURS is a tool available to find the best one of all the coverings (VPs).

As to the recognition of multi-statement construct, the first key problem is to uniform variations of multimedia operations. As mentioned in section 2, such variations result from the complex control structure. If relations between statements were simplified, the number of variations and the difficulty of recognition would be lowered. Therefore, we first normalize the program representation. IF-conversion [18] is the technique we used to convert control dependence to data dependence. After conversion, statements are flattened and only related by data dependence. Besides, each statement is composed of a statement body and several guard conditions. In this way, it does not matter what statements look like in original source code since they are now all related by data dependence.

Then, we have to find which statements constitute such a construct. Each statement's semantic information and their relations are thus needed. The latter can be obtained from variables' DU chains. The former can be obtained from VPs of statements since certain VP is only linked with certain statement structure. Thus, we reuse the result of single-statement construct recognition (represented by goal non-terminals of VP) here to avoid redundant computation. E.g., we can know that the first statement in Fig. 1(b) can be part of a vectorizable saturated sub construct since its VP shows that it is a signed short subtract operation.

However, not every single statement in a vectorizable multi-statement construct can be vectorized. E.g. though statements in Fig. 1(b) as a whole are vectorizable on MMEs, the second statement itself is not vectorizable. To solve this problem, we regard each statement in a vectorizable multi-statement operation as partially vectorizable and design a goal non-terminal and a VP rule to represent it. After multi-statement construct recognition, these partial VPs will be discarded.

After multi-statement construct recognition, selection is also needed since constructs may have conflicts, i.e. a statement may belong to more than one construct.

To ease the introduction of our recognition algorithm, we define several concepts.

Definition 1. A vectorization plan (VP) for tree t defines a possible way to vectorize the tree. It consists of a series of 6-tuples *<r, vl, vc, sc, def, use>* associated with tree nodes, which means using rule *r* to vectorize the subtree rooted at the node, *vl* is the vector length, *vc* is the amortized vectorized execution cost, *sc* is the sequential execution cost, *def* and *use* mean the definition and use operands respectively.

In our system, VP rules are expressed similarly with BURS rules. In each tuple, field *sc* is used to compare with field *vc* to show whether the VP is profitable. When recognizing a multi-statement construct, we need to know its operands from VPs of its statements. Thus, we add field *def* and *use* here.

As mentioned above, the result of VP can be represented by its goal non-terminal. Thus, for simplicity, we denote the vectorization plan as *VP(t, n)*, in which *t* is the tree and *n* is the goal non-terminal.

To be easy, we encode the VP rule information into its left-side non-terminal. It is named as *[<op>_]<category>[suffix]*$_{[datatype]}$. E.g. *ssub_expr*$_{s16}$ denotes the result of using signed short saturated subtract rule to vectorize an expression.

Op	category	Datatype
sub(normal subtract)	*expr*(vectorizable expression)	*s16* (signed short)
ssub(saturated subtract), etc.	*stmt*(vectorizable statement)	*u32*(unsigned int), etc

In our system, we express statements as trees. For each statement, its body and every condition in its guard are expressed as a tree, respectively. For a tree *t*, *t* is vectorizable if

$$\begin{cases} \exists VP(t,n) \wedge n \in stmt \text{ category} & t \text{ is statememt body} \\ \exists VP(t,n) \wedge n \in expr \text{ category} & t \text{ is guard condition} \end{cases}.$$

Definition 2. Best vectorization plan BVP(t, n) is the minimal vectorized cost VP of all VP(t, n).

Definition 3. Candidate vectorization plan set CVP_Set(t) contains all the BVPs for tree t.

If we ignore fields *vl, sc, def* and *use* of each tuple in VP, we can find that CVP_Set is just the result set of using BURS and rules to match a tree.

Definition 4. Multi-statement vectorization plan $MVP(s_1,s_2,\ldots,s_n)$ is a vectorization plan for multi-statement construct which is composed of statements $s_1, s_2,\ldots,s_n$. It is a tree of 6-tuples *<MVP rule, vl, vc, sc, def, use>* (one for each multi-statement operation). Each field has similar meaning as its counterpart in VP tuple.

Our recognition algorithm is shown in Fig. 4. Each main step is discussed below.

```
Normalize program respresention;
for each statement s in loop {
  compute CVP_Set(s.body);
  for each condition expression c in s.guard
    compute CVP_Set(c);
}
find all MVPs in the loop;
select best VPs for loop;
```

Fig. 4. Recognition Algorithm

4.2 Normalize the Program Representation

To normalize the program representation, first, we perform a series of normalization techniques: e.g. scalar expansion, variable range analysis [20], loop rerolling [3] etc.

As mentioned above, we perform IF-conversion [18] in the loop body to reduce variations of multi-statement operations and eliminate complex control flow. It removes branches by replacing the statements in the loop body with an equivalent set of guarded statements. Besides normal statement body, every guarded statement includes a guard (relative to the loop) which is composed of several condition expressions combined by *and* operation. As to nested loops, the inner loop as a whole is regarded as a statement when outer loop is processed. The below code illustrates the conversion for the outer loop.

```
if(guard1)                            if(guard1)
   for(…){                              for(…){
     if(guard2){              S1:          (guard2, guard3)    stmt1;
      if(guard3)         ⇒    S2:          (guard2)     for(…) stmt2;
          stmt1;                        }
      for(…)
          stmt2;
}}
```

Thus, variation (a) and (b) in Fig. 1 have the same code sequence as in Fig. 5(a) after scalar expansion and IF-conversion. And variation (c) has the form as in Fig. 5(b).

```
S1:   ( )         t[i]=a[i]-b[i];
S2:  (t[i]>32767)   c[i]=32767;
S3:  (t[i]<-32768)   c[i]=-32768;
S4:   (t[i]≥-32768,  t[i]≤32767)
                    c[i]=t[i];
                (a)
```

```
S1:(sum[i]>32767.0)    samples[i]=32767;
S2:(sum[i]>32767.0)    clip++;
S3:(sum[i]<-32768.0)  samples[i]=-32768;
S4:(sum[i]<-32768.0)   clip++;
(sum[i]≥-32768, sum[i]≤32767)
                       samples[i]=sum;
                         (b)
```

Fig. 5. Saturated Operations after IF-conversion

Generally, IF-conversion can be used to utilize bit-masking instructions on MMEs [3]. Here, we extend its usage. We regard program representation after IF-conversion as a new IR on which our further recognition is based. After recognition, we roll back those converted statements (including their guard) if they are not vectorizable.

4.3 Compute CVP_Sets

As mentioned above, we use BURS [9] to generate CVP_Sets for every statement's body and guard conditions. The first bottom-up pass of BURS matcher is performed here while the second top-down pass is performed at code generation stage.

To use BURS to compute CVP_Set, we define VP rule as extended BURS rule. The extension is the addition of 5 fields: *vl*, *sc*, *def*, *use* and *constraint*. Field *constraint* is added to represent constraints, e.g. dependence issues, data type etc., that are required before applying this rule. Original *cost* field in BURS rule is used as *vc*.

We define costs of VP rule as $\begin{cases} \mathrm{vc} \cong (\textit{latency of SIMD instrcutions})/(\textit{vector length}) \\ \mathrm{sc} \cong \textit{latency of sequential instrcutions} \end{cases}$.

In its bottom-up traversal, BURS matcher matches a tree and labels each tree node its CVP_Set. In each tuple <*r, vl, vc, sc, def, use*>, cost *vc* and *sc* are set as the sum of VP rule *r*'s *vc, sc* and each subtree's *vc*, *sc*, respectively. Field *def* and *use* are simply set as VP rule *r*'s *def* and *use*.

As to vector length *vl*, its computation is a little bit subtle because vector length of VP rule and that of each subtree may not be equal. E.g. Assuming we have an expression *a[i]+b[i]*, the element type of *a*, *b* is *short* and *int*, respectively. According to the rules in Fig. 6, Rule tree *11(10(2),4)* can successfully match it. Vector length of each rule is 4, 4, 8 and 4, respectively. If vector length of the tree is 4, then part of load result *a[i+4:i+7]* will be discarded. To avoid such waste, we set *vl* as the least common multiply (LCM) of vector length of VP rule and that of each subtree. This means the tree will be executed LCM times in one vectorized loop iteration. Thus, SIMD code generated by VP rule's and subtrees' semantic actions will be duplicated LCM/vl_i times respectively. As to the above example, we will generate code:

```
load a[i:i+7];                                                  #rule 2
load b[i:i+3]; load b[i+4:i+7];                                 #rule 4
convert a[i:i+7] to int vectors a'[i:i+3] and a'[i+4:i+7]; #rule 10
a'[i:i+3]+b[i:i+3]; a'[i+4:i+7]+b[i+4:i+7];                     #rule 11
```

Take the process of computing CVP_Set for statements in Fig. 5(a) as an example. Parts of the related VP rules are shown in Fig. 6. Fig. 7 shows BURS matching result.

#	Rule	vl	vc	sc	def	use	constraint
1	lval_expr$_{s16}$ → arr[index]	8	0.75	1.5	root		vec_arr(arr,index, s16)
2	expr$_{s16}$ → arr[index]	8	0.75	1.5		{root}	vec_arr(arr,index, s16)
3	lval_expr$_{s32}$ → arr[index]	4	1.5	1.5	root		vec_arr(arr,index, s32)
4	expr$_{s32}$ → arr[index]	4	1.5	1.5		{root}	vec_arr(arr,index, s32)
5	ssub_stmt1$_{s16}$ → lval_expr$_{s32}$ =expr$_{s16}$–expr$_{s16}$	4	0.5	0.5	lval_expr$_{s32}$	{expr$_{s16}$[1], expr$_{s16}$[2]}	no_dep(def, use[1]) no_dep(def,use[2])
6	sub_stmt$_{s32}$ → ssub_stmt1$_{s16}$	4	0	0	ssub_stmt1$_{s16}$.def	ssub_stmt1$_{s16}$.use	
7	upplimit_expr$_{s32}$ → expr$_{s32}$>32767	4	0.5	0.5		{expr$_{s32}$}	
8	lowlimit_expr$_{s32}$ → expr$_{s32}$<-32768	4	0.5	0.5		{expr$_{s32}$}	
9	ssub_stmt2$_{s16}$ → lval_expr$_{s16}$=32767	8	0.5	0.5	lval_expr$_{s16}$		
10	expr$_{s32}$ → expr$_{s16}$	4	0.5	0.5		{expr$_{s16}$}	
11	expr$_{s32}$ → expr$_{s32}$ + expr$_{s32}$	4	0.5	0.5		{expr$_{s32}$[1],expr$_{s32}$[2]}	

Fig. 6. Some VP Rules. Function *vec_arr(arr, index, type)* checks if *arr[index]* is a vectorizable continuous array visit expression with element type as *type*. Function *no_dep(a, b)* checks if there is no dependence between *a* and *b*

The final work before MVP finding is to compute sequential cost *sc* of each statement (including its body and guard). It is set as the sum of each part's lowest *sc* and the fixed instruction latency for *if* statement dispatch.

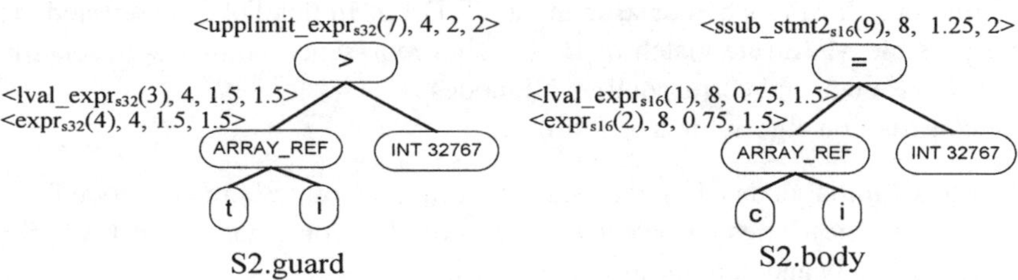

Fig. 7. CVP_Set Computation Result for S2 in Fig. 5(a). The VP rules for S1, S3 and S4 and their match processes are similar, hence omitted. Their results are:
CVP_Set(S1.guard) = ∅, CVP_Set(S1.body) = {<ssub_stmt1$_{s16}$,...>, <sub_stmt$_{s32}$,...>},
CVP_Set(S3.guard) = {<lowlimit_expr$_{s32}$,...>}, CVP_Set(S3.body)={<ssub_stmt3$_{s16}$,...>},
CVP_Set(S4.guard.condition1)={<!upplimit_expr$_{s32}$,...>}, CVP_Set(S4.guard.condition2) = {<!lowlimit_expr$_{s32}$,...>}. , CVP_Set(S4.body) = {< ssub_stmt4$_{s16}$,...>}

4.4 Find All MVPs

Based on CVP_Sets, we now begin to find all MVPs in the loop according to predefined MVP rules. We define each MVP rule as *<non-terminal→Stmt_Set, vl, vc, def, use, constraint, action>*. Set *Stmt_Set* contains statements (represented by goal non-terminals to indicate their roles). Other fields have the same meaning with their counterparts in VP rules. As an example, Fig. 8 shows some MVP rules.

NT	Stmt_Set	vl	vc	def	use	constraint
ssub_stmt s16	{s1: () ssub_stmt1$_{s16}$, s2: (upplimit_expr$_{s32}$) ssub_stmt2$_{s16}$, s3: (lowlimit_expr$_{s32}$) ssub_stmt3$_{s16}$, s4: (!upplimit_expr$_{s32}$, !lowlimit_expr$_{s32}$) ssub_stmt4$_{s16}$}	8	0.5	s4.body.def	s1.body.use	DU_Chain(def(s1.body)) ≡{s2.guard, s3.guard, s4.guard, s4.body.right} def(s2.body)≡def(s3.body) def(s2.body)≡def(s4.body)
stmt$_{s16}$	{s1: () ssub_stmt$_{s16}$}	8	0	s1.def	s1.use[1].parent	
bitmask- ing_stmt s16	{s1: (expr$_{s16}$) stmt$_{s16}$ s2: (expr$_{s16}$) stmt$_{s16}$}	8	0.75	s1.body.def	{s1.guard.use, s1.body.use, s2.body.use}	def(s1.body)≡def(s2.body) s1.guard≡!s2.guard

Fig. 8. MVP Rules Expamples. Action part of each rule is straightforward, thus omitted. E.g. action of the last rule will generate code (in form of ICC intrinsic function): "xmm1 = _mm_and_si128(use[1], use[2]); xmm2 = _mm_andnot_si128(use[1] , use[3]); xmm3 = _mm_or_si128(xmm1, xmm2); _mm_store_si128(def, xmm3)"

Since a MVP rule represents a vectorizable operation, statements in it as a whole constitute a simpler semantic expression than their respective original expressions. As a result, we use the action of MVP rule and those of operands in *use* and *def* to generate code, instead of using the actions in each statement's CVP_Set. Semantic actions of operands will be executed before that of MVP rule.

We find out all MVPs by constructing a VP DAG. In this DAG, every node represents a possible MVP rule match or BVP. Edge represents the inclusion relationship between MVP node and corresponding VP nodes.

The construction algorithm is as follows:

1) Construct initial nodes. For each statement in the loop, we create a node for every element in the Cartesian product (every possible combination) of CVP_Sets of statement body and conditions in the guard.
2) Find a MVP rule match. It means to find a node set that meets the MVP rule, i.e. node set is an instance of the *Stmt_Set* (possible with additional guards) and constraints are satisfied. For each found MVP rule match, we construct a new node for it and make the node set as its children.
3) Repeat step 2 until no new MVP rule match can be found.

When a MVP rule successfully matched, a MVP node is created and annotated as *<MVP rule, vl, vc, sc, def, use>*. Field *def* and *use* are set according to the *def* and *use* field of MVP rule. E.g. the MVP rule match node for Fig. 5(a) has {a[i], b[i]} as *use* and c[i] as *def*. Field *vl* is set as the least common multiply of MVP rule's *vl* and *vl* of each operand (*def* and *use*). Field *vc* is set as the sum of MVP rule's *vc* and *vc* of each operand. Field *sc* is set as the sum of *sc* of each original statement it included.

For example, for statements in Fig. 5(a), we first construct node 1 to 5 in Fig. 9 according to their CVP_Set. Then, after matching saturated subtract MVP rule, we

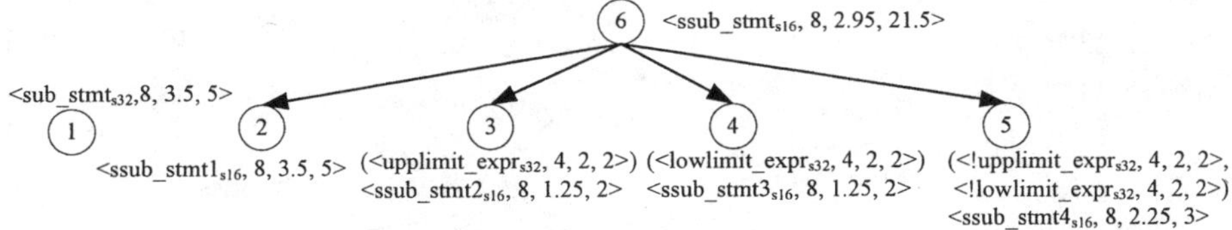

Fig. 9. MVP DAG for Fig. 5(a). The *def* and *use* field in each node is ignored for simpilicity

construct node 6. Thus, all the MVP matches have been found and shown in this DAG. For statements in Fig. 5(b), similar DAG can be created.

When matching MVP rules, it may be found that the statements constituting the MVP match node have additional guard conditions besides the ones needed by the MVP rule. If different statement has different additional conditions, this MVP rule cannot be matched because these statements actually are embraced by different *if* statements. However, if there is only one additional condition, we decompose each node representing the related statement that hasn't such condition into two node and continue the match. E.g. assuming there are two nodes: *(guard)S1* and *S2*. *S1* and *S2* constitute a MVP match *M* if *guard* does not exist. In such case, we decompose *S2* into two new nodes: *(guard)S2* and *(!guard)S2*. Then *(guard)S1* and *(guard)S2* are matched as a MVP node *(guard)M*. Such decomposition is performed on DAG. Only when the related MVP is finally chosen will the decomposition really be performed on statements. Such decomposition may increase the number of possible MVPs. However, our goal of this step is to find all the possibilities. Next step will choose from them the best ones. Thus, such treatment is harmless.

Fig. 10(a) introduces an example to show the MVP recognition process. It is slightly modified from a code segment (Fig. 10(b)) in ADPCM Decoder to make it vectorizable. The original version is similar to a saturated operation, but not vectorizable because *valpred* is a reduction variable and has different type from *vpdiff*. This test case is hard to recognize because saturated subtract operation is mingled with the saturated add in that they share the clip statement (the second *if* statement). We have not found any previous research work that could deal with it. However, our approach can vectorize

```
if(sign[i])
  t[i]=valpred[i]
       -vpdiff[i];
else
  t[i]=valpred[i]
       +vpdiff[i];
if(t[i]>32767)
  valpred[i]=32767;
else if (t[i]<-32768)
  valpred[i]=-32768;
else valpred[i]=t[i]
```
(a)

```
if(sign)
   valpred-=vpdiff;
else
   valpred+=vpdiff;
if(valpred>32767)
   valpred=32767;
else
if(valpred<-32768)
   valpred=-32768;
```
(b)

```
S1:(sign[i])
     t[i]=valpred[i]-vpdiff[i];
S2:(!sign[i])
     t[i]=valpred[i]+vpdiff[i];
S3:(t[i]>32767)
     valpred[i]=32767;
S4:(t[i]<-32768)
     valpred[i]=-32768;
S5:(t[i]≤32767,t[i]≥-32768)
      valpred[i]=t[i]
```
(c)

Fig. 10. Code Segment in ADPCM Decoder

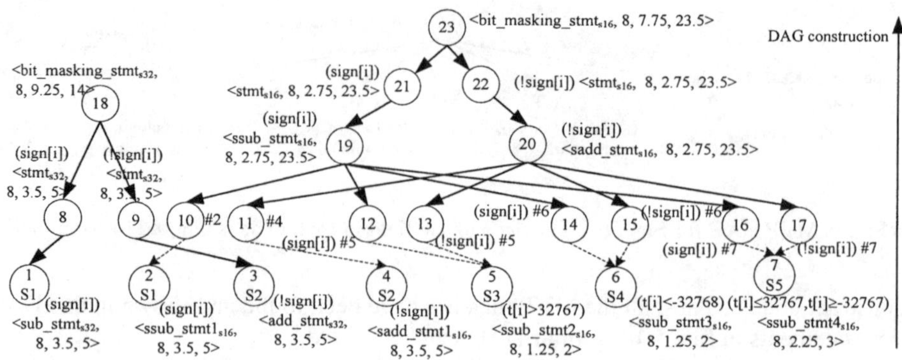

Fig. 11. Match Result for Fig. 10(c). Guards are shown as real conditions instead of VPs for easy understanding. The *def* and *use* field in each node is ignored. Dotted line is used to show the node decomposition process. For example, node 12 and 13 are decomposed from node 5(S3 of Fig. 10(c)). So, node 13 is *(!sign[i], t[i]>32767) <ssub_stmt2*$_{s16}$*, 8, 1.25, 2>* ,which represents statement: *(!sign[i], t[i]>32767) valpred[i] = 32767;*. Solid line shows the inclusion relationship. E.g. MVP *sadd_stmt*$_{s16}$ (node 20) needs 4 statements (node 11, 13, 15, 17) to constitute. Therefore, they are connected by directed lines

this example very well. Its normalized code is shown in Fig. 10(c). According to the MVP rules in Fig. 8 and some other similar MVP rules, we can get the MVP matching DAG in Fig. 11. It clearly shows our system's power.

4.5 Select VPs for the Loop

After constructing the DAG, the problem now becomes how to select for each statement its best VP because each statement can only be vectorized using one VP.

First, we decompose the DAG into a series of connected components (trees) (ignoring dotted lines). For example, DAG in Fig. 11 is decomposed as following trees: {1, 3, 8, 9, 18}, {2}, {4}, {5}, {6}, {7}, {10–17, 19–23}. Each tree as a whole shows how to vectorize a construct.

Then, we delete those trees whose root satisfies any of the following conditions: 1) root.VP is only meaningful as part of MVP; 2) root.guard $\neq \varnothing$. It means vectorized code shall be embraced by a vectorized *if* statement (not bit-masking operation) which is impossible; 3) root.sc $\leq$ root.vc. Such MVP is not profitable. After it, DAG in Fig. 11 has trees {1, 3, 8, 9, 18} and {10–17, 19–23} left. The former will vectorize statements S1-S2 while the latter will vectorize S1-S5. However, S1-S2 can only be vectorized by one VP tree. Thus, these two trees are incompatible.

We try to find the compatible tree subset with maximum weight. We define each tree's weight (time save of vectorization) as its root.sc–root.vc. This problem can be formulated as a NP-complete set-covering problem (by using similar technique in [19]). In practice, because conflicts are rare and easy to solve, we use the greedy algorithm: choose the tree that has the most number of statements and lowest cost first. Thus, VP tree {10–17, 19–23} is selected for Fig. 11.

At dependence-graph-construction stage, we make all the statements in each chosen tree share one node in the graph. The dependence relations between these statements are ignored since they are already checked by the constraints of VP/MVP rules.

4.6 Code Generation

In code generation stage, vectorizable nodes in the dependence graph, i.e. those that are associated with a VP tree and not strongly connected, are vectorized on IR in the classic way: first distribute it into a loop; then generate vectorized code according to actions of its VP tree; loop step is set as the *vl* field of the VP tree root; rest loop is generated for un-vectorizable iterations.

Since we regard each VP tree as a high-level operation, it shall contain assignment(s) only to one variable. Thus, the "store" action in each non-root VP node is not performed. E.g. the store operations to variable *valpred* in nodes 19-22 of Fig. 11 are prohibited.

After vectorization on IR, two optimizations: alignment analysis and redundant load/store are performed. Because MMEs prefer aligned data load/store, we need to lay out the arrays and determine the alignment information for each memory access. At present, we only scan alignment requirements for array references and try to meet them as many as possible. For pointer references, we conservatively regard them as unaligned. This strategy seems to work well for our benchmarks.

To reduce the redundant load/store for arrays in vectorized constructs, we perform common sub-expression elimination for loads and dead code elimination for stores.

5 Experimental Results

In this section, we demonstrate the effectiveness of the presented algorithm with experimental results. All experiments were conducted on a 2.8G Pentium 4E Processor and 1G memory system with Redhat 9.0. The benchmark we use is Accelerating Suite of Berkeley Multimedia Workload (ASBMW) [4][5]. We also compare the results of our method with ICC[10], the Intel compiler that has the state of the art vectorization techniques. We use two versions of ICC, *v7* and the latest *v8*, to vectorize the applications. We implement our vectorization algorithm in our C-to-C compiler Agassiz [8] which is a research compiler developed by University of Minnesota and us. Agassiz transforms vectorizable parts of multimedia source code into Intel SSE/SSE2 instruction set (in form of ICC intrinsic functions). The rules we added to our system are the ones we found profitable and general enough in our real-life application study. The output of Agassiz is compiled by ICC 7 and ICC 8 with vectorization off, respectively. Fig.12 lists the results. All results are obtained as the average of 5 runs.

As illustrated by Fig.12, Agassiz achieved an average more than 10% speedup. In contrast, ICC 7 and ICC 8 only achieved 1.94% and 2.37% speedup, respectively. This is because Agassiz can vectorize almost all the constructs ICC can, which mainly are memory copies, arithmetic operations, MAX/MIN operations, etc. Moreover, Agassiz

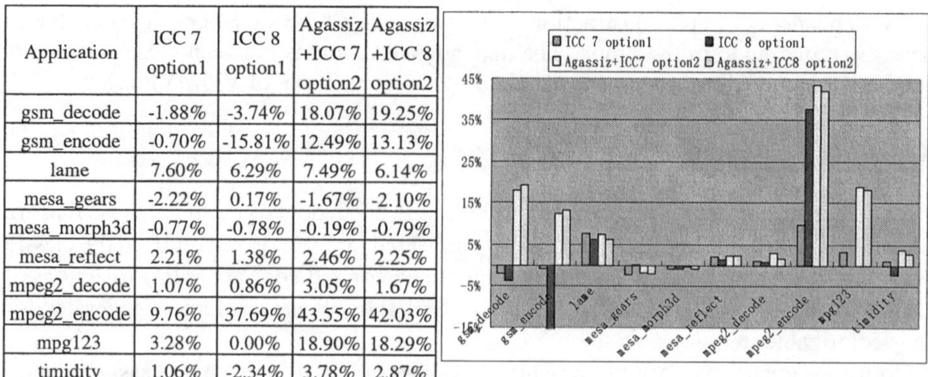

Application	ICC 7 option1	ICC 8 option1	Agassiz +ICC 7 option2	Agassiz +ICC 8 option2
gsm_decode	-1.88%	-3.74%	18.07%	19.25%
gsm_encode	-0.70%	-15.81%	12.49%	13.13%
lame	7.60%	6.29%	7.49%	6.14%
mesa_gears	-2.22%	0.17%	-1.67%	-2.10%
mesa_morph3d	-0.77%	-0.78%	-0.19%	-0.79%
mesa_reflect	2.21%	1.38%	2.46%	2.25%
mpeg2_decode	1.07%	0.86%	3.05%	1.67%
mpeg2_encode	9.76%	37.69%	43.55%	42.03%
mpg123	3.28%	0.00%	18.90%	18.29%
timidity	1.06%	-2.34%	3.78%	2.87%

Fig. 12. Speedup of vectorization. ICC compiling option1: *-O2 -xW* (with vectorization turned on); ICC compiling option2: *-O2 -xW -vec-* (with vectorization turned off). The baseline is compiled with option2

can vectorize constructs that ICC cannot. This fact leads to the results that Agassiz outperforms ICC on six applications while the rest have similar performance.

We can also find that ICC 8 generated better scalar code than ICC 7 since Agassiz+ICC 8 had slightly smaller speedup than Agassiz+ICC 7 on most applications. As to the vectorization capability, ICC 8 greatly outperformed ICC 7 on *mpeg2_encode* since it vectorized the Sum of Absolute Difference (SAD) operation. A very strange thing is that, though they vectorized the same parts of *gsm_encode*, ICC 8 greatly slowed down it.

Though Agassiz have vectorized lots of constructs, the most important ones (contributing most to speedup) are just variations of several important operations. As to *gsm_decode* and *gsm_encode*, the most important one is saturated operation. Concerning *lame*, the most important one is MAX operation. As to *mpeg2_encode*, the key operations are SAD operation and float arithmetic operation. As to *mpeg2_decode*, it is saturated pack. To *mpg123*, it is also saturated arithmetic. Regarding *timidity*, it is floating-point operation.

Fig. 13 lists the comparison of two performance monitors after Agassiz+ICC 8 vectorization and its scalar counterparts.

We can see that execution time (clockticks, column 2) is somewhat proportional to the number of dynamic instructions retired (column 3). In the listed applications, the great reduction of dynamic instructions is attributed to the vectorization of multimedia typical operations (mainly multi-statement operations) in hot loops. Thus, these operations contribute to most of the speedups. The rest speedups mainly come from float operation and integer operation of small data type. Other performance monitors such as mis-predicted branches and L2 cache miss etc. have not changed much due to vectorization. Thus, they are not listed here.

	Clockticks	Instructions
gsm_decode	86.47%	62.18%
gsm_encode	88.73%	83.98%
lame	92.77%	85.22%
mesa_gears	98.03%	100.91%
mesa_morph3d	97.18%	100.69%
mesa_reflect	96.96%	89.48%
mpeg2_decode	98.41%	96.46%
mpeg2_encode	68.72%	42.99%
mpg123	84.42%	75.94%
timidity	96.39%	99.68%

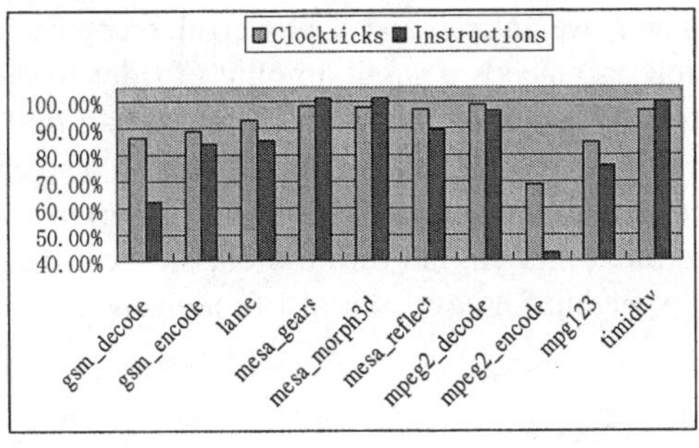

Fig. 13. Performance monitors after vectorization vs. its scalar counterparts

6 Related Work

The application of traditional automatic vectorization techniques on MMEs [11][15][16] and new methods such as SLP [7] neither recognize nor vectorize those important multi-statement idioms in real-life multimedia programs.

Realizing the importance of recognizing multimedia typical idioms, researchers have proposed other methods. Simple pattern match based algorithm [6] requires compiler to have one pattern for each variation of multimedia operations, thus too rigid to be acceptable. Domain-specific language, SWARC [17], is developed to provide a portable way to program for MMEs. But it is not popular enough.

In [12], a preprocessing before classic vectorization algorithm to detect two multimedia typical operations (saturation and max/min) is presented. It uses tree rewriting system to rewrite the tree step by step to recognize them. Speedup was reported for several small kernels and 164.gzip in SPEC2000. In comparison, our algorithm shows more applicability and power. First, our algorithm can recognize almost all kinds of SIMD idioms in a uniform and flexible way. Second, as to the two kind operations this method focuses on, our method puts much less constraints on the recognizable operations. For example, ours does not require the exact order of statements in a multi-statement construct, e.g. statements *s2, s3, s4* in Fig. 5(a) can appear in any order and any other irrelevant statements could be inserted between these three statements. We also allow the multi-statement operations appearing in forms that are more complex. Thus, our method is able to recognize those variations such as Fig. 1(b), Fig. 1(c) and Fig. 10(a) which cannot be handled by [12].

7 Conclusion

In this paper, we first showed that the key difficulty in utilizing MMEs to boost the performance of real-life multimedia applications is how to recognize many different profitable and vectorizable operations, especially how to recognize the variations of the same multimedia typical operation in an efficient and general way.

Then, we introduced a powerful recognition engine to overcome such difficulty, which only needs a small amount of rules to recognize and vectorize many operations in real-life source code. In addition, it can find the best VP set for each loop. Thus, it can fully exploit benefits from MMEs. It also enjoys great extendibility in that we only need to add new operation patterns (rules) into it if new SIMD instructions appear. We integrated this engine into the classic vectorization framework and obtained satisfactory speedup for several real-life multimedia applications.

References

[1] Allen R, Kennedy K. Automatic Translation of Fortran Programs to Vector Form. *ACM Trans. on Programming Languages and Systems*, 1987, 9(4): 491-542.

[2] Padua D, Wolfe M. Advanced Compiler Optimizations for Supercomputers. *Comm. of the ACM*. 1986, 29(12): 1184-1201.

[3] Ren G, Wu P, Padua D. A Preliminary Study On the Vectorization of Multimedia Applications for Multimedia Extensions. *Proc. of the 16th Int'l Workshop on Languages and Compilers for Parallel Computing,* 2003.

[4] Slingerland N, Smith A J. Design and Characterization of the Berkeley Multimedia Workload. *Multimedia Systems,* 2002, 8(4): 315-327.

[5] Slingerland N, Smith A J. Measuring the Performance of Multimedia Instruction Sets. *IEEE Trans. Computers*, 2002, 51(11): 1317-1332.

[6] Boekhold M, Karkowski I, Corporaal H. Transforming and Parallelizing ANSI C Programs Using Pattern Recognition. *Lecture Notes in Computer Science*, 1999, 1593: 673.

[7] Larsen S, Amarasinghe S. Exploiting Superword Level Parallelism with Multimedia Instruction Sets. *ACM SIGPLAN Notices*, 2000, 35(5): 145-156.

[8] Zheng B, Tsai J Y, Zhang BY, Chen T, Huang B, Li J H, Ding Y H, Liang J, Zhen Y, Yew P C, Zhu C Q. Designing the Agassiz Compiler for Concurrent Multithreaded Architectures. *Proc. of the 12th Int'l Workshop on Languages and Compilers for Parallel Computing*, 1999: 380-398.

[9] Fraser C W, Hanson DR, Proebsting T A. Engineering Efficient Code Generators Using Tree Matching and Dynamic Programming. TR-386-92, Princeton University.

[10] Intel Corporation. Intel C++ Compiler User's Guide. 2003: http://developer.intel.com/.

[11] Sreraman N, Govindarajan R. A Vectorizing Compiler for Multimedia Extensions. *Int'l Journal on Parallel Processing*, 2000.

[12] Bik A J C, Girkar M, Grey P M, Tian X. Automatic Detection of Saturation and Clipping Idioms. *Proc. of the 15th Int'l Workshop on Languages and Compilers for Parallel Computers,* July 2002.

[13] Intel Corporation. Intel Architecture Software Developer's Manual, Volume 1: Basic Architecture. 2001: http://developer.intel.com/.

[14] Intel Corporation. Intel Architecture Optimization Reference Manual. 2001: http://developer.intel.com/.

[15] Cheong G, Lam M S. An Optimizer for Multimedia Instruction Sets. *Second SUIF Compiler Workshop*, Stanford, August 1997.

[16] Krall A, Lelait S. Compilation Techniques for Multimedia Processors. *Int'l Journal of Parallel Programming*, 2000, 28(4): 347-361.

[17] Fisher R J, Dietz H G. Compiling for SIMD within a Register. *Workshop on Languages and Compilers for Parallel Computing*, University of North Carolina, August 1998.

[18] Allen J R, Kennedy K, Porterfield C, Warren J. Conversion of Control Dependence to Data Dependence. *Proc. of the 10th ACM SIGACT-SIGPLAN symp. on Principles of Programming Languages,* Austin, Texas, 1983: 177-189.

[19] Liao S, Devadas S, Keutzer K. A Text-Compression-Based Method for Code Size Minimization in Embedded Systems. *ACM Trans. on Design Automation of Electronic Systems, 1999, 4(1): 12-38*

[20] Stephenson M, Babb J, Amarasinghe S. Bitwidth Analysis with Application to Silicon Compilation. *ACM SIGPLAN Conf. on Programming Language Design and Implementation,* June 2000

[21] Fuller S. Motorola's AltiVec Technology. White Paper, May 6, 1998

Task Partitioning for Multi-core Network Processors

Robert Ennals[1], Richard Sharp[1], and Alan Mycroft[2]

[1] Intel Research Cambridge,
15 JJ Thomson Avenue, Cambridge, CB3 0FD, UK
[2] Computer Laboratory, Cambridge University,
15 JJ Thomson Avenue, Cambridge, CB3 0FD, UK
{robert.ennals, richard.sharp}@intel.com
am@cl.cam.ac.uk

Abstract. Network processors (NPs) typically contain multiple concurrent processing cores. State-of-the-art programming techniques for NPs are invariably low-level, requiring programmers to partition code into concurrent tasks early in the design process. This results in programs that are hard to maintain and hard to port to alternative architectures. This paper presents a new approach in which a high-level program is separated from its partitioning into concurrent tasks. Designers write their programs in a high-level, domain-specific, architecturally-neutral language, but also provide a separate Architecture Mapping Script (AMS). An AMS specifies semantics-preserving transformations that are applied to the program to re-arrange it into a set of tasks appropriate for execution on a particular target architecture. We (i) describe three such transformations: pipeline introduction, pipeline elimination and queue multiplexing; and (ii) specify when each can be safely applied.

As a case study we describe an IP packet-forwarder and present an AMS script that partitions it into a form capable of running at 3Gb/s on an Intel IXP2400 Network Processor.

1 Introduction

This paper addresses *an instance* of a perennial general problem in the compilation of concurrent systems to parallel hardware architectures:

> *Given a program which expresses problem-oriented concurrency, and hardware which has multiple processing elements, how can we efficiently map one to the other?*

The instance we attack concerns the domain of packet processing applications such as Internet routers, firewalls and similar network devices. The parallel hardware architectures we target are Network Processors (NPs) [1, 6, 10, 23]: specialised programmable chips designed for high-speed packet processing.

NPs typically contain multiple processor cores, allowing multiple network packets to be processed concurrently. To make a program run fast on such an

R. Bodik (Ed.): CC 2005, LNCS 3443, pp. 76–90, 2005.

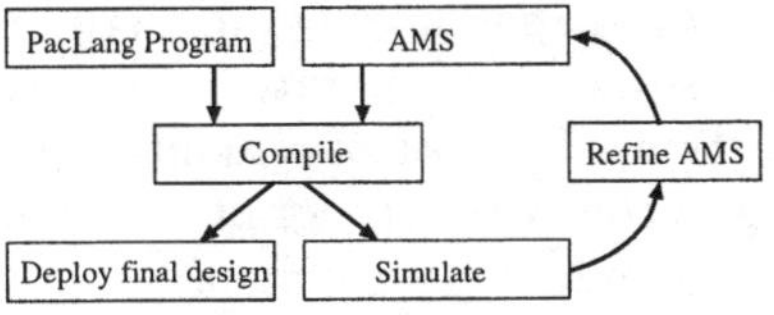

Fig. 1. Design flow using our compiler

architecture it is necessary to partition it into a number of separate concurrent tasks, such that the number of tasks matches the number of cores on the target architecture. Furthermore, tasks arranged in a pipeline configuration should be balanced, with similar latencies.

State-of-the-art programming techniques for NPs are invariably low level, requiring the programmer to explicitly code a separate process for each core and explicitly pass state between processes. In this way, the programmer is forced to combine high-level application functionality with low-level architectural details in a way that makes them difficult to separate. This results in programs that are hard to maintain and strongly tied to a particular revision of a particular architecture.

This paper describes a new approach, in which the high-level application functionality is completely separated from the architectural details of any specific NP. Our compiler takes two files as input: a high-level packet processing program and an *Architecture Mapping Script* (AMS). The AMS specifies (*i*) how the high-level program should be transformed into a new set of concurrent tasks suitable for execution on a particular NP architecture; and (*ii*) how these tasks should be mapped to the NP's processing cores[1]. The compiler checks that the transformations specified in the AMS are semantics-preserving.

We use the domain-specific language PacLang [4] to express the high-level behaviour of packet processing applications in an *architecturally-neutral* way (i.e. without encoding assumptions about any particular target architecture). A PacLang program consists of multiple concurrent tasks that communicate via shared queues. Such parallelism, and the controlled non-determinism it introduces, is essential if one is to conveniently express packet processing algorithms. For example, in an IP forwarder, non-critical, computationally expensive packets can be processed on different tasks to critical packets, allowing critical packets to overtake the non-critical ones.

Figure 1 illustrates the design flow that we intend programmers to follow when using our compiler. After writing a PacLang specification and an initial AMS for a particular architecture, the compiler is invoked and the resulting code simulated using architecture-specific tools. Based on the profiling results derived from simulation, the AMS is iteratively refined to explore different partitionings and timing behaviours.

[1] Although there is scope for generating an Architecture Mapping Script automatically for particular architectures, that is not the topic of this paper.

The contributions of this paper are: (*i*) a methodology for programming multi-core Network Processors that separates architectural-details from high-level application specification; (*ii*) a set of semantics-preserving program transformations that re-arrange a concurrent program into a different set of concurrent units (i.e. tasks and queues); and (*iii*) a whole-program analysis that determines when it is safe to pipeline a specified task in the wider context of a whole concurrent program.

We have implemented a PacLang compiler targeting Intel IXP2400 Network Processors [10]. To demonstrate that the techniques described in this paper are applicable to realistic networking applications, we present a case-study showing how an architecturally-neutral PacLang IP packet-forwarder can be transformed into a form suitable for implementation on an Intel IXP2400 chip. We present performance figures, showing that executing the compiled code on a 3-port Gigabit Ethernet IXP2400-based system [20] achieves a forwarding rate of 3 Gb/s (full line-rate).

For expository purposes, this paper initially presents our partitioning transformations (Section 3) and safety analysis (Section 4) in the domain of *Core PacLang*—a simplified version of PacLang. Later, the transformations and safety analysis are then extended from Core PacLang to the full PacLang language (Section 5). We finish by presenting a case-study (Section 6), related work (Section 7), and our conclusions (Section 8).

2 Core PacLang Language

We start by considering Core PacLang: a simplified version of the PacLang language. Unlike PacLang proper, Core PacLang is untyped, supports only value types (no references or pointers) and has no user-defined functions.

$e \leftarrow c \mid x \mid op\ (e_1, \ldots, e_k)$	constant, local variable, primitive op
$s \leftarrow$ `if` (e) s_1 `else` s_2	conditional
$\mid$ `while` (e) s	while loop
$\mid$ s; s	sequence
$\mid$ `skip`	do nothing
$\mid$ x = e	imperative assignment
$\mid$ q.`enq` $(e_1, \ldots, e_k)$	enqueue
$\mid$ $(x_1, \ldots, x_k)$ = q.`deq()`	dequeue
$d \leftarrow$ `task` t $\{s\}$	task t with body s
$\mid$ `queue` q;	global queue q
$p \leftarrow d_1 \ldots d_n$	Core PacLang program

Fig. 2. Abstract Syntax of CORE PACLANG

The abstract syntax of Core PacLang is presented in Figure 2. A program consists of a set of declarations, each of which is either a *task*, t, or a *queue*, q. Tasks are the unit of concurrent execution: during program execution, all task bodies run concurrently. Tasks are statically declared; there is no dynamic thread creation in PacLang. (Note that tasks' names have no significance other than providing a convenient way of referencing them in AMSes.)

Each task has a body, s, which it executes repeatedly. One can imagine that task bodies are surrounded by an invisible "`while (true)`" loop. When a task body restarts all its local variables are uninitialised. This ensures that there are no loop-carried-dependencies between subsequent iterations of a task body.

Queues provide inter-thread communication. In Core PacLang we assume that queue-read operations block when the queue is empty and queue-write operations never block (i.e. queues are unbounded). We write `q.enq(`$v_1, \ldots, v_n$`)` to atomically enqueue values $v_1, \ldots, v_n$ in the queue declared with name `q`. Similarly, `q.deq()` returns (multiple) values dequeued from `q`. Built-in queues, `receive` and `transmit` represent the external network interface. `receive.deq()` reads a value from the network[2]; `transmit.enq(`v`)` schedules value v for transmission.

In untyped Core PacLang, variables do not have to be declared explicitly and are scoped by their enclosing task.[3] To simplify the presentation of subsequent transformations we assume that all declared names (i.e. local variable names, queue names and task names) are globally distinct.

3 Semantics-Preserving Transformations for Partitioning

In this section we present three semantics-preserving transformations that allow programs to be repartitioned into different numbers of concurrent tasks. The first transformation, *PipeIntro* (Section 3.1), divides a single task into two separate, concurrent tasks connected in a pipeline configuration. The second transformation, *PipeElim* (Section 3.2), allows two pipeline stages connected via a queue to be fused into a single task. The third transformation, *QueueMux* (Section 3.3), allows multiple queues to be multiplexed onto a single queue. We first present the transformations in the domain of Core PacLang; Section 5 shows that they naturally extend to deal with the full PacLang language.

Although we do not prove our transformations formally in this paper, it is necessary nonetheless to define precisely what we mean by semantics-preserving. In previous work we presented a small-step transition semantics for PacLang [4]. The semantics is non-deterministic, making no guarantees about the interleaving of concurrent tasks' operations and making no guarantees about progress or fairness. With reference to this semantics, we say that a transformation is semantics-preserving iff the set of *possible behaviours* of the transformed program is a *subset* of the possible behaviours of the source program, where the

[2] Full PacLang supports a structured *packet* datatype to represent such packets.

[3] In contrast, full PacLang supports C-like variable declaration and lexical scoping.

possible behaviours of a PacLang program are the set of possible traces of values on external queues (`receive` and `transmit`). In other words, transformations can increase determinism, narrowing the set of possible behaviours, but any behaviour exhibited by the transformed program must have also been a possible behaviour of the source program.

3.1 PipeIntro Transformation

The PipeIntro transformation facilitates pipelining, allowing a task t to be transformed into two separate, concurrent tasks, t_1 and t_2—see Figure 3. Here, and throughout the rest of this paper, we let $\mathcal{A}$ and $\mathcal{B}$ range over statements. Queue Q is used to transfer the variables required by $\mathcal{B}$ (i.e. the live variables in task t at the program point between $\mathcal{A}$ and $\mathcal{B}$) from t_1 to t_2. Recall that statements may themselves include sequences of other statements. This, and the fact that we make the ";" operator associative, allows the PipeIntro transformation presented in Figure 3 to split task t between any two statements that are not nested within a `while` loop or a conditional.

In order to preserve the semantics of a Core PacLang program, the PipeIntro transformation can only be applied under certain conditions. In Section 4 we present the technical details of a static analysis that determines when it is safe to apply PipeIntro. We spend the remainder of this section highlighting the need for a safety analysis, by giving examples of *unsafe* applications of PipeIntro. First consider:

```
queue q1;
task t { x=q1.deq(); y=q1.deq(); transmit.enq(x,y); }
```

Task `t` continually reads pairs of values from `q1` and writes them to `transmit` in the order they were read. If we were allowed to apply the PipeIntro transformation arbitrarily we might choose to split between the two queue read operations, yielding:

```
queue q1; queue Q;
task t1 { x=q1.deq(); Q.enq(x); }
task t2 { x=Q.deq(); y=q1.deq(); transmit.enq(x,y); }
```

`task` t $\{\mathcal{A};\mathcal{B}\}$	$\longrightarrow$	`queue` Q; `task` t_1 $\{\mathcal{A};\ Q$`.enq(`$x_1,\ldots,x_k$`)`$\}$ `task` t_2 $\{$`(`$x_1,\ldots,x_k$`) =` Q`.deq();` $\mathcal{B}\}$

where Q, t_1 and t_2 are fresh names and $x_1,\ldots,x_k$ are the live variables of task t at the program point between statements $\mathcal{A}$ and $\mathcal{B}$. (Recall the x's in t_1 are different from the x's in t_2 because they are locally scoped.)

Fig. 3. The PipeIntro Transformation

In the transformed program, the values on `transmit` might not appear in the same order that they were read from `q1`. For example, task `t1` may consume the first 5 elements from the `q1` before task `t2` has had a chance to read `q1` at all.

The unsafe application of PipeIntro given above may lead the reader to think that a suitable safety condition may be that, in the source program, the queues accessed (read or written) by the statements before the split point should be disjoint from the queues accessed by the statements after the split point. However, this condition is not sufficient in general. Consider the following program:

```
queue q;
task t { q.enq(1); transmit.enq(2); }
task connect_q_to_transmit { transmit.enq(q.deq()); }
```

Task `t` task writes a "1" to `q`, then writes a "2" to the `transmit` queue and then loops. Task `connect_q_to_transmit` reads elements from `q` and writes them to the `transmit` queue. If we now apply PipeIntro to `t`, splitting between the two queue write operations, we get:

```
queue q; queue Q;
task t1 { q.enq(1); Q.enq(); }
task t2 { ignore = Q.deq(); transmit.enq(2); }
task connect_q_to_transmit { transmit.enq(q.deq()); }
```

These two programs are not semantically equivalent (even though, in the source program, the statements on either side of the split point access disjoint queues)—e.g. in the transformed program the trace $\langle 1, 1, 1\rangle$ may appear on the `transmit` queue; this is not a valid trace of the source program[4].

Informally the problem is that `t1` affects `connect_q_to_transmit` which shares a queue with `t2`. In Section 4 we present a static analysis that determines when PipeIntro can be safely applied.

3.2 PipeElim Transformation

The PipeElim transformation allows two tasks t_1 and t_2 connected by a single-reader, single-writer queue q to be fused into a single task t. In essence the code for t_2 is inlined into t_1 in place of its write to q—see Figure 4. Since the queue write operation can occur anywhere within a t_1 (e.g. nested inside conditionals or while loops) we express PipeElim in terms of a *context* [22], $\mathcal{C}$, defined below:

$$\mathcal{C} \leftarrow [\cdot] \mid s;\mathcal{C} \mid \mathcal{C};s \mid \texttt{while } (e)\ \mathcal{C} \\ \mid \texttt{if } (e) \texttt{ then } \mathcal{C} \texttt{ else } s \mid \texttt{if } (e) \texttt{ then } s \texttt{ else } \mathcal{C}$$

In joining concurrent tasks, the PipeElim transformation essentially picks a static interleaving of operations from t_1 and t_2, encoding this schedule explicitly in the order of statements in t. For the sake of simplicity, the transformation shown in

---

[4] The source program ensures that: (the number of 1's on the transmit queue) $\leq$ (the number of 2's on the transmit queue) + 1.

`queue` q		`task` t $\{$
`task` t_1 $\{\mathcal{C}[q$`.enq(`$e_1,\ldots,e_i$`)`$]\}$	$\longrightarrow$	$\mathcal{C}[\mathcal{A}$`;` x_1`=`e_1`;`$\ldots$`;` x_i`=`e_i`;` $\mathcal{B}]$
`task` t_2 $\{\mathcal{A}$`; (`$x_1,\ldots,x_i$`) =` q`.deq();` $\mathcal{B}\}$		$\}$

where there are no other references to q in the rest of the program; we assume that task-local variables in t_1 and t_2 have been renamed so as to be disjoint.

Fig. 4. The PipeElim Transformation

Figure 4 just inlines the body of t_2 into t_1. Note, however, that PipeElim is merely an instance of a more general *transformation schema* which may interleave the statements from $\mathcal{A}$ and $\mathcal{B}$ with the statements of t_1's body in a variety of ways, exploring different static schedules.

Depending on the static schedule implicitly specified by an application of PipeElim, deadlock may be introduced. For example $\mathcal{B}$ might block waiting for a queue that t_1 would have written to immediately after writing to q. Although such deadlocks are consistent with our subset interpretation of semantics-preserving, they are clearly undesirable. In this paper we do not consider deadlock detection further; however, we are currently implementing a "deadlock and timing analyser"[5] that checks whether (transformed) PacLang programs meet user-specified timing constraints.

3.3 QueueMux Transformation

The QueueMux transformation is used in conjunction with PipeElim to fuse concurrent tasks that are *not* connected in a pipeline configuration (i.e. concurrent tasks that cannot be fused using PipeElim alone).

The effect of a QueueMux transformation on program structure is shown in Figure 5. We start with n queues $(q_1,\ldots,q_n)$ each read by a single reader task. After transformation, a task body that previously wrote a value, v, to q_i $(1 \le i \le n)$ now writes a *pair* of values (i, v) to a *Combined Queue*, Q. A *Demux* task dequeues these (i, v) pairs, testing the value of i to determine which of the original queues v should be forwarded to.

Once a QueueMux has been applied, PipeElim can be applied as many times as required to combine each of the reader tasks with the Demux task (see Figure 5). The case study in Section 6 demonstrates this technique in practice.

3.4 Architecture Mapping Scripts

For a particular NP architecture, A, and an architecturally-neutral PacLang program, $\mathcal{P}$, an Architecture Mapping Script (AMS) specifies both:

---

[5] After all, for real-time reactive systems, deadlocks are just a special case of failing to meet timing requirements!

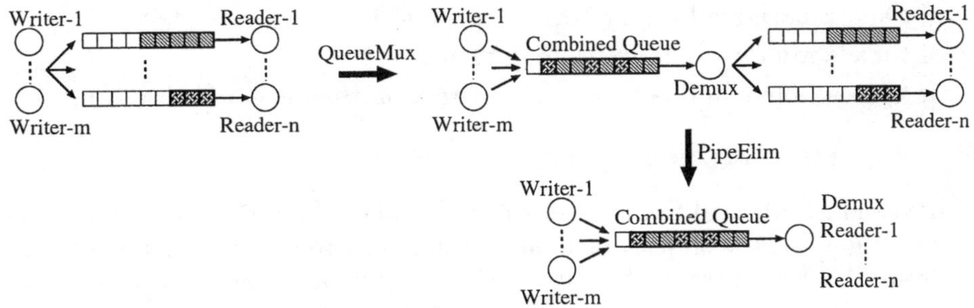

Fig. 5. Applying the QueueMux Transformation, followed by PipeElim

- how the PipeElim, PipeIntro and QueueMux transformations should be applied to $\mathcal{P}$ in order to refine it into a form suitable for execution on A; and
- how the tasks and queues after transformation are to be mapped onto the low-level resources of A.

The precise syntax of Architecture Mapping Scripts is straightforward. Although the technical details are omitted from this paper due to space constraints, the interested reader may download real examples of AMSes from the web [11].

4 Safety Analysis for PipeIntro Transformation

Here we present a static analysis which enables the PipeIntro transformation by conservatively determining whether the transformation is safe.

The PipeIntro transformation (as presented in Figure 3) allows a subsequent iteration of $\mathcal{A}$ to start before a previous iteration of $\mathcal{B}$ has finished. Therefore, the transformation is safe if an *observer* (who reads from transmit queues) is unable to infer that an execution step in an iteration of $\mathcal{A}$ *occurs before* an execution step in an iteration of $\mathcal{B}$. We model this observer by adding a task to the program that reads from all transmit queues. The analysis then determines whether this observer task might be able to infer that an execution step in an iteration of $\mathcal{A}$ occurs before an execution step in an iteration of $\mathcal{B}$.

We start by considering what information a task, t, might infer about the ordering of execution steps in other tasks. We note that a task can only infer ordering information about other tasks' execution steps by reading from a shared queue. (One cannot infer anything by performing a queue write, as writes return no information.)

We let u, v, w (in addition to t) range over tasks. We write $u \overset{t}{\rightsquigarrow} v$ to mean that task t may infer that an execution step of task u occurred before an execution step of task v by reading a queue. The relation '$\overset{t}{\rightsquigarrow}$' is defined as follows:

1. if t and u both read from q, then $t \overset{t}{\rightsquigarrow} u$ and $u \overset{t}{\rightsquigarrow} t$;
2. if t reads from q and u writes to q, then $u \overset{t}{\rightsquigarrow} t$;
3. if t reads from q and both u and v write to q, then $u \overset{t}{\rightsquigarrow} v$ and $v \overset{t}{\rightsquigarrow} u$.

We justify these three cases as follows:

1. If u and t both read from q then t may be able to infer the order of its reads w.r.t. u's reads—e.g. let q be a queue containing sequential integers starting from "1". If t's first read returns "2" then it knows that u must have read first.
2. If u writes to q and t reads from q then t may be able to determine that its read occurred after u's write—e.g. if t read the value written by u. However, it is not possible for t to infer that its read occurred *before* u's write. Nor is it possible for t to infer that any other task's read from q has occurred before any further task's write to q.
3. If u and v both write to q then t may be able to infer the order in which the writes occurred—e.g. t may perform two read operations and compare the values returned with those expected.

But we cannot just apply these rules and ask "can the observer infer that an execution step of $\mathcal{A}$ occurs before an execution step of $\mathcal{B}$". Firstly, consider the case where task u passes information (via a shared queue) to task v. The data transferred may reveal, to task v, the event orderings observed by task u. To simplify the analysis we conservatively assume that every task may get to know all orderings observed by all other tasks. Therefore, we define:

$$u \rightsquigarrow v \overset{\text{def}}{\iff} \exists t.u \overset{t}{\rightsquigarrow} v$$

i.e. $u \rightsquigarrow v$ holds iff *any task* may observe that an execution step in u occurs before an execution step in v. Secondly, we note that, if $u \rightsquigarrow v$ and $v \rightsquigarrow w$ then one *may* use this information to deduce that an execution step of u occurs before an execution step of w. It is thus necessary to consider $\rightsquigarrow^*$, the transitive closure of $\rightsquigarrow$.

The PipeIntro transform as presented in Figure 3 is safe if in the transformed program with queue Q removed, it is not the case that $t_1 \rightsquigarrow^* t_2$.

4.1 Algorithm for PipeIntro Safety Analysis

Taking the safety analysis presented above, and making the conservative assumption that all queues have readers, leads to the following simple algorithm for determining whether a PipeIntro transformation (as presented in Figure 3) can be applied:

1. Construct a graph, G, where nodes are tasks in the transformed program.
2. In the transformed program with queue Q removed (see Figure 3) consider each pair of tasks, u and v, that share a queue, q. Place a directed edge from u to v if:

   (a) u and v both read from q; or
   (b) u writes to q and v reads from q; or
   (c) u and v both write to q.
3. If, there is no path in G from t_1 to t_2 then the PipeIntro transformation can be applied.

5 Dealing with the Full PacLang Language

The full PacLang language supports a number of constructs omitted from the core language of Section 2 including user-defined functions, references, arrays (of values or of queues) and global variables. Here we discuss how these additional features impact the transformations presented in Section 3.

User-defined functions can be dealt with straightforwardly: for the purposes of this paper we simply restrict functions to being non-recursive and then assume all user-defined function calls are inlined (although, in practice one need only inline a function call if the AMS requests that it be split across several tasks).

The introduction of generalised global variables is also largely straightforward[6]. The PipeElim and QueueMux transformations are unaffected by the introduction of global variables. However, the PipeIntro safety analysis needs to be extended accordingly (see Section 5.2).

The impact of introducing references needs to be considered more carefully. If we permitted the *unrestricted* use of references then the PipeElim and QueueMux transformations would remain sound, but PipeIntro would not. In the following subsection we explain informally why PacLang's linear type system [4] is sufficient to ensure that PipeIntro (as already presented) remains sound in the PacLang domain, even when references are used.

5.1 References, Linearity and the PipeIntro Transform

The full PacLang language provides a *packet* datatype. Packets are dynamically allocated blocks of structured data that can be passed-by-reference. PacLang's linear type system restricts the ways in which these references can be manipulated, with the aim of enabling a number of optimisations, including PipeIntro.

Before considering PacLang's linear type system, let us first consider what would happen to the PipeIntro transformation if we permitted the *unrestricted* use of packet references. Figure 6 gives an example of how unrestricted references can lead to an unsound application of PipeIntro. For the sake of simplicity let us consider the case where `q` contains a single packet reference. In this case task `t` uses `q` to simulate a global packet variable: the first line of `t` reads a packet reference from `q` and then immediately writes it back again. Executing the program results in the packet's first word being repeatedly incremented and written to `q1`. As a result, a series of consecutive integers appears on `q1`.

[6] Recall that Core PacLang already supports global queues.

```
queue<packet*> q;
queue<int> q1;

task t {
   packet* p = q.deq();
   q.enq(p);
   p[0]++;
   q1.enq(p[0]);
}
```

$\longrightarrow$

```
queue<packet*> q, Q;
queue<int> q1;
task t1 {
   packet* p = q.deq();
   q.enq(p);
   p[0]++;
   Q.enq(p);
}
task t2 {
   packet* p = Q.deq();
   q1.enq(p[0]);
}
```

Fig. 6. This code, written in a PacLang-like language without a linear type system, shows that the unrestricted use of references can break the PipeIntro transformation

In the transformed program, task `t1` can loop round many times before `t2` has read anything from `Q` (the queue introduced by the PipeIntro transformation). As a result, by the time `t2` gets round to dereferencing its local copy of the packet pointer, the packet's first word may have been incremented several times. This allows traces to appear on `q1` that were not possible in the source program (e.g. $\langle 0, 5, 10 \rangle$). The problem is that `t1` and `t2` access shared state via their packet references. The PipeIntro safety analysis, in the form presented in Section 4, is not able to detect this sharing since it does not model aliasing. One solution would be to perform full alias analysis as a precursor to the PipeIntro safety analysis, using this approximate aliasing information to detect potential accesses to shared state. Fortunately this is unnecessary as PacLang's linear type system [4] prevents aliasing and so would disallow the source program in Figure 6. Thus, the PipeIntro safety analysis does not need to be modified at all.

PacLang's linear type system does not exist merely to make PipeIntro easier. It has a number of notable features that simplify the compilation of high-level programs for Network Processors, while naturally capturing the style in which many packet processing programs are already written [4].

5.2 Extending PipeIntro Safety Analysis to Full PacLang

Global Variables: The algorithm for determining safety of PipeIntro (Section 4.1) can be extended to deal with global variables by extending the graph, G, as follows. For each pair of tasks, u and v, that share a global variable, g, place directed edges from both u to v and v to u if: (i) both u and v write to g; or (ii) one of u and v writes to g and the other reads from g.

We note that global variables could be translated into operations on shared queues. However, if we do this then the safety analysis as presented in Section 4 would deduce that the order of two reads from the same global variable may be observed. Dealing with global variables directly leads to a more accurate analysis.

Bounded Queues: Consider adding language primitive *HowFull*(q) that returns the number of elements currently on queue q. We can extend the algorithm for determining safety of PipeIntro (Section 4.1) by extending the graph, G, as follows. For every task, u, that does *HowFull*(q) add edges (u, v) and (v, u) for any task, v, that reads or writes q.

The intuition is that if a task tests the fullness of a queue, q, then it may be able to determine the order of its *HowFull* operation w.r.t. reads and writes to q.

6 Case Study

We have written a simple IPv4 unicast packet forwarding engine that employs a longest-prefix-match route-lookup algorithm in 500 lines of architecturally neutral PacLang. In this section we illustrate how our tools allow the program to be transformed into a form capable of achieving 3Gb/s (line rate) on an Intel IXP2400 Network Processor.

The details of IP packet forwarding are not described here (for more technical information the interested reader is referred directly to the IETF standards [18] and our PacLang code [11]). The purpose of this case study is to show that our transformations can be applied to realistic, non-trivial programs.

Figure 7(i) shows the initial structure of the PacLang IP forwarder. The program has five tasks, represented by white circles: Classify (`C`), IP options (`O`), ARP (`A`), IP Route Lookup (`I`) and ICMP Error (`E`). Queues are represented by filled circles. The receive (`r`) and transmit (`t`) queues are sources and sinks of network packets respectively.

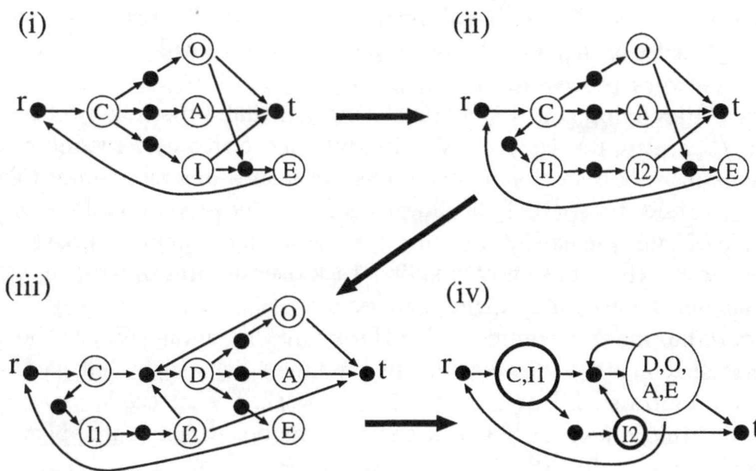

Fig. 7. Transforming the IPv4 unicast packet forwarder for IXP implementation. White circles represent tasks, filled circles represent queues

Our AMS for Intel IXP-series NPs applies the transformations shown graphically in Figure 7. First, PipeIntro splits `I` into `I1` and `I2`. Next, QueueMux is applied to the input queues of `O`, `A`, and `E`, creating a new Demux (`D`) task. Finally, PipeElim merges `D`, `O`, `A`, and `E` together, and merges `C` and `I1` together.

Our safety analysis deems that the PipeIntro transformation is applicable since, in the graph, G, constructed by the algorithm of Section 4.1, there is no edge from `I1` to any other task. Thus, there is no path from `I1` to `I2`—the two tasks created by the PipeIntro transformation.

The final structure of the transformed program (Figure 7(iv)) is well suited for IXP implementation. The tasks on the packet forwarder's critical path (the path taken by the vast majority of incoming packets) are highlighted with thick-lined circles. Timing analysis and simulation shows that, for our IXP2400, a 2-stage pipelined version of the critical path is sufficient to achieve 3Gb/s packet throughput (full line-rate on our 3-port Gigabit Ethernet board), for worst-case, min-size packets. If greater throughput was required (e.g. if we wanted line-rate for more than 3 ports) then we could apply PipeIntro again to increase the pipeline depth. Our AMS maps the two tasks on the critical path to separate micro-engines (small RISC processor cores on the IXP chip), the remaining task to the IXP's XScale processor core, and the queues to hardware scratch queues.

Both the source code, and the AMS that transforms it are available for download [11].

7 Related Work

Transformation-based approaches to program development have been around for a long time [3, 5] and applied to a variety of problems including circuit design [17] and hardware/software co-design [2]. The contribution of our research is to show that program-transformation is an appealing technique for bridging the gap between a high-level packet processing program and its low-level realisation on a multi-core network processor.

Software Pipelining [13, 8] is a transformation that superficially sounds similar to our *PipeIntro*, but is actually quite different. Software Pipelining reorders instructions in a loop so that instructions for future iterations may take place during the current iteration. This allows loads to be hoisted and allows better use to be made of multiple execution units on VLIW and superscalar architectures. Unlike our work, the aim is not to split a task over several processing elements, but to make better use of a single processor.

Our work has more in common with Hardware Pipelining [16, 19]: the division of a circuit specification into concurrent pipeline stages such that each stage is of roughly uniform size. However, unlike our work, the successive stages run in lock-step with no queueing between them—a model which is inappropriate for packet processing systems.

Previous work on automatic pipelining typically focuses on transforming a complete sequential program into a single pipeline. In contrast, our PipeIntro transformation and associated safety analysis extends this work, addressing the more general problem of determining when it is safe to pipeline a *particular* concurrent task within the wider context of a whole concurrent program.

Task Assignment [15, 9] addresses the problem of assigning tasks to processors, taking into account the sizes of the tasks and the communication between them. While this work is similar to ours in that it explores the way in which a program can be mapped to several processors, there is no attempt to pipeline one task between several processors.

A number of other languages for multi-core processors have been developed [7, 12, 21, 14], but these are all significantly lower level and do not allow the task structure of a program to be changed.

8 Conclusions and Future Work

We have (*i*) presented a transformation-based methodology for programming Network Processors that allows architectural details to be separated from high-level program specification; and (*ii*) validated this methodology by showing how it can be applied to a realistic packet processing application.

We have also presented a whole-program analysis that determines when it is safe to pipeline a PacLang task. This extends previous work on automatic pipelining by addressing the more general problem of determining when it is safe to pipeline a *particular* concurrent task within the wider context of a whole concurrent program.

We hope that the ideas presented in this paper can be applied to the automatic partitioning of high-level code across multi-core architectures more generally (i.e. not just Network Processors). Since industrial trends suggest that such architectures will become more prevalent (as silicon densities continue to increase) we believe that this is an important topic for future research.

Acknowledgements

This research was supported by (UK) EPSRC grant GR/S68941: "High-Level Languages for Network Processors".

References

1. Allen, J. R., Bass, B. M., Basso, C., Boivie, R. H., Calvignac, J. L., Davis, G. T., Frelechoux, L., Heddes, M., Herkesdorf, A., Kind, A., Logan, J. F., Peyravian, M., Sabhikhi, M. A. R. R. K., Siegel, M. S., and Waldvogel, M. PowerNP network processor: Hardware, software and applications. *IBM Journal of research and development 47*, 2–3 (3003), 177–194.
2. Barros, E., and Sampaio, A. Towards provably correct hardware/software partitioning using occam. In *Proceedings of the 3rd international workshop on Hardware/software co-design* (1994), IEEE Computer Society Press, pp. 210–217.
3. Burstall, R., and Darlington, J. A transformation system for developing recursive programs. In *JACM 24(1)* (1977).

4. Ennals, R., Sharp, R., and Mycroft, A. Linear types for packet processing. In *Proceedings of the European Symposium on Programming (ESOP) 2004* (2004).
5. Feather, M. A system for assisting program transformation. *ACM Transactions on Programming Languages and Systems 4*, 1 (January 1982), 1–20.
6. Freescale. *C-5 Network Processor Architecture Guide*, 2001.
7. George, L., and Blume, M. Taming the IXP network processor. In *Proceedings of the ACM SIGPLAN 2003 conference on Programming Language Design and Implementation* (2003), pp. 26–37.
8. Hwang, C.-T., Hsu, Y.-C., and Lin, Y.-L. Scheduling for functional pipelining and loop winding. In *Proceedings of the 28th conference on ACM/IEEE design automation* (1991), ACM Press, pp. 764–769.
9. Ikinci, M. Multilevel heuristics for task assignment in distributed systems. Master's thesis, Bilkent University, Turkey, 1998.
10. Intel Corporation. Intel IXP2400 Network Processor: Flexible, high-performance solution for access and edge applications. Available from: `http://www.intel.com/design/network/papers/ixp2400.htm`.
11. Intel Corporation. PacLang. `http://sourceforge.net/projects/paclang/`.
12. Intel Corporation. *Microengine C Language Support Reference Manual*, 2003.
13. Lam, M. Software pipelining: An effective scheduling technique for VLIW machines. In *Proceedings of the ACM SIGPLAN conference on Programming Language Design and Implementation* (1988), pp. 318–328.
14. Lam, M. Compiler optimizations for asynchronous systolic array programs. In *Proceedings of the ACM SIGPLAN-SIGACT symposium on Principles of Programming Languages* (1998).
15. Lo, V. Heuristic algorithms for task assignment in distributed systems. *IEEE Transactions on Computers* (1988), 1384–1397.
16. Marinescu, M.-C. V., and Rinard, M. High-level automatic pipelining for sequential circuits. In *Proceedings of the 14th international symposium on Systems Synthesis* (2001), ACM Press, pp. 215–220.
17. Mycroft, A., and Sharp, R. A statically allocated parallel functional language. In *Proceedings of the International Conference on Automata, Languages and Programming* (2000), vol. 1853 of *LNCS*, Springer-Verlag.
18. Network Working Group. RFC1812: Requirements for IP version 4 routers.
19. Papaefthymiou, M. C. On retiming synchronous circuitry and mixed integer optimization. Master's thesis, Massachusetts Institute of Technology, 1990.
20. Radisys. ENP-2611 network processor board. `http://www.radisys.com`.
21. Teja. Teja NP: The first software platform for multiprocessor system-on-chip architectures. `http://www.teja.com`.
22. Winskel, G. *The formal semantics of programming languages: an introduction.* Foundations of computing. MIT Press, 1993.
23. Yavatkar, R., and H. Vin (eds.). *IEEE Network Magazine. Special issue on Network Processors: Architecture, Tools, and Applications 17*, 4 (July 2003).

Experiences with Enumeration of Integer Projections of Parametric Polytopes

Sven Verdoolaege[1], Kristof Beyls[2], Maurice Bruynooghe[1], and Francky Catthoor[3]

[1] Katholieke Universiteit Leuven, Department of Computer Science, Celestijnenlaan 200A, B-3001 Leuven, Belgium
[2] Department of Electronics and Information Systems, Ghent University – UGent, Sint-Pietersnieuwstraat 41, B-9000 Ghent, Belgium
[3] IMEC, Kapeldreef 75, B-3001 Leuven, Belgium; also at Katholieke Universiteit Leuven, Department of Electrical Engineering

Abstract. Many compiler optimization techniques depend on the ability to calculate the number of integer values that satisfy a given set of linear constraints. This count (the enumerator of a parametric polytope) is a function of the symbolic parameters that may appear in the constraints. In an extended problem (the "integer projection" of a parametric polytope), some of the variables that appear in the constraints may be existentially quantified and then the enumerated set corresponds to the projection of the integer points in a parametric polytope.
This paper shows how to reduce the enumeration of the integer projection of parametric polytopes to the enumeration of parametric polytopes. Two approaches are described and experimentally compared. Both can solve problems that were considered very difficult to solve analytically.

1 Introduction

Many compiler optimization techniques require the enumeration of objects of a certain class. Examples include counting the number of calculations, accessed memory locations or statement executions in a loop nest or parts thereof [6, 21, 23, 28, 29, 38]; calculating the number of cache misses in a loop [12, 16, 24]; computing the number of dynamically allocated bytes [11]; enumerating the number of live array elements at a given iteration (i, j) [27, 42]; counting how many parallel processing elements can be used when executing a loop on an FPGA [5, 22, 25] and computing the amount of communication for a given schedule of parallel tasks on a distributed computing system [9, 26, 37].

These counts are used to drive optimizations such as increasing parallelism [38], minimizing memory size [1, 2, 27, 38, 42], estimating worst case execution time [28], increasing cache effectiveness [6, 16], high-level transformations for DSP applications [23], converting software loops into parallel hardware implementations [5, 18, 22, 25, 38] and minimizing communication overhead in distributed applications [9, 26, 37]. In many of these optimizations, the objects or

R. Bodik (Ed.): CC 2005, LNCS 3443, pp. 91–105, 2005.

events to be counted are modeled as the integer solutions to systems of linear inequalities, i.e., as the elements of a set $S = \{\mathbf{x} \in \mathbb{Z}^d \mid A\mathbf{x} + \mathbf{c} \geq \mathbf{0}\}$, with $A \in \mathbb{Z}^{n \times d}$ and $\mathbf{c} \in \mathbb{Z}^n$. Furthermore, they often need the count in terms of a vector of parameters $\mathbf{p}$ (e.g., in the presence of symbolic loop bounds):

$$S_{\mathbf{p}} = \{\mathbf{x} \in \mathbb{Z}^d \mid A\mathbf{x} + B\mathbf{p} + \mathbf{c} \geq \mathbf{0}\}. \tag{1}$$

A recent efficient algorithm that computes the function from specific values of $\mathbf{p}$ to the number of elements in $S_{\mathbf{p}}$ is presented in [40]. This paper considers the more general counting problem, where some of the variables can be existentially quantified. We propose a general solution for counting the number of elements (in terms of parameters $\mathbf{p}$) for sets that can be expressed in the form

$$\left\{\mathbf{x} \in \mathbb{Z}^d \mid \exists \mathbf{y} \in \mathbb{Z}^{d'} : A\mathbf{x} + D\mathbf{y} + B\mathbf{p} + \mathbf{c} \geq \mathbf{0}\right\}. \tag{2}$$

Computing the number of elements in such a set is, amongst others, needed in the program analyses described in [1, 2, 5, 6, 9, 12, 16, 25, 26, 37, 42]. Practical examples are discussed in an extended version of this paper, see [39].

Example 1. Consider an example adapted from [14] (Figure 1(a)). Assume we want to know the total number of array elements accessed by the statement in the inner loop as a function of the symbolic parameter p. This problem is equivalent to counting the number of elements in the set

$$S_p = \{\, l \in \mathbb{Z} \mid \exists i, j \in \mathbb{Z} : l = 6i + 9j - 7 \wedge 1 \leq j \leq p \wedge 1 \leq i \leq 8\,\}, \tag{3}$$

which can be written in the same form as (2):

$$\left\{ l \in \mathbb{Z} \mid \exists \begin{pmatrix} i \\ j \end{pmatrix} \in \mathbb{Z}^2 : \begin{pmatrix} 1 \\ -1 \\ 0 \\ 0 \\ 0 \\ 0 \end{pmatrix} l + \begin{pmatrix} -6 & -9 \\ 6 & 9 \\ 0 & 1 \\ 0 & -1 \\ 1 & 0 \\ -1 & 0 \end{pmatrix} \begin{pmatrix} i \\ j \end{pmatrix} + \begin{pmatrix} 0 \\ 0 \\ 0 \\ 1 \\ 0 \\ 0 \end{pmatrix} p + \begin{pmatrix} 7 \\ -7 \\ -1 \\ 0 \\ -1 \\ 8 \end{pmatrix} \geq \begin{pmatrix} 0 \\ 0 \\ 0 \\ 0 \\ 0 \\ 0 \end{pmatrix} \right\}.$$

Figure 1(b) shows the array elements that are accessed for $p = 3$. These elements do not correspond to the integer points in a polytope. Even after scaling by 3 it still contains two "holes" (marked by $\times$ on the figure). These holes complicate the enumeration. For $p = 3$, the set S_p contains 19 points, see Figure 1(b). In general, the number of points in S_p can be described by the function. Different polynomials represent the count in different regions of the parameter space. Following [36], we call these regions *chambers*. In general, the count in each chamber is described by a *step-polynomial*, as defined in Section 2.

The solution to a counting problem is called the enumerator of the set of constraints. Without parametric variables in the counting problem, the enumerator is an integer; otherwise the enumerator is a function that maps the values of the parametric variables to an integer. Different applications for different types of

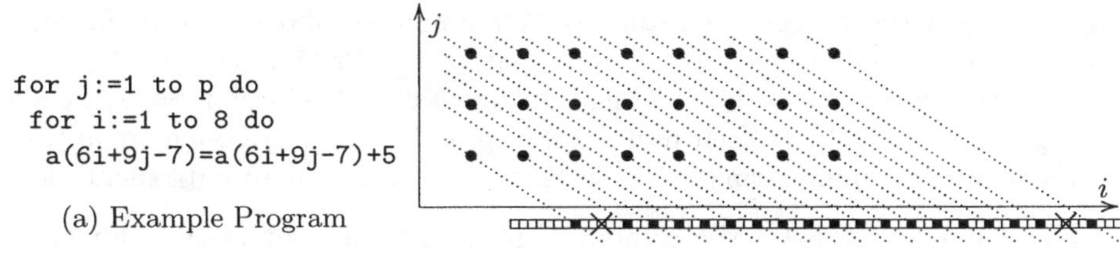

for j:=1 to p do
for i:=1 to 8 do
a(6i+9j-7)=a(6i+9j-7)+5
j
i

(a) Example Program

(b) Array elements accessed for $p = 3$

Fig. 1. Example adapted from [14]

constraints has led to different proposals. Below, when we refer to the complexity of algorithms, we always mean for a fixed number of variables. Note that the enumeration of even parametric polytopes is NP-hard.

Linear Inequalities. Barvinok [3] was first to propose an algorithm for enumerating sets defined by linear inequalities that is polynomial-time.

Parametric Linear Inequalities. Ehrhart [19] showed that the general form of the enumerator for a certain form of parametric linear inequalities with a single parameter is a quasi-polynomial. Clauss et al. [15] extended this theory to handle the more general form shown in Equation (1), albeit in exponential time complexity. De Loera et al. [17] implemented Barvinok's [3] polynomial-time algorithm for enumerating sets defined by linear inequalities and its extension to compute the Ehrhart series corresponding to the dilation nP of a polytope P. Finally, Verdoolaege et al. [40] implemented a polynomial time algorithm for the counting problem of Equation (1).

Linear Inequalities with Existential Variables. Barvinok and Woods [4] propose a polynomial time algorithm. No implementation has been reported, and the extension to parameters is not obvious.

Parametric Linear Inequalities with Existential Variables. Boulet [9] proposes to compute the enumerator of a set of parametric linear inequalities with existential variables in two steps. First, parametric integer programming (PIP) [20] is used to eliminate the existential variables, after which Clauss's [15] method is used to enumerate the resulting set of linear inequalities. However, no extensive evaluation has been reported and the appendix in [10] indicates that the method cannot compute the enumerator fully automatically. Meister [30] proposes a similar technique using his more general periodic polyhedra instead of PIP. No implementation has been reported. Clauss [13] proposed a method (recently implemented [35]) based on "thick facets" that works for a single existential variable.

Non-parametric Presburger Formula. Presburger formulas consist of linear inequalities of integer variables, combined by existential and universal quantifiers, disjunction, conjunction and negation. ($\exists, \forall, \vee, \wedge, \neg$). Two recent methods [8, 31] represent the formula as a finite automaton to count the number of its integer solutions in exponential time.

Parametric Presburger Formula. In [33], a number of rewrite rules are proposed to compute the enumerator of a parametric Presburger formula. However, the rules seem ad-hoc and no implementation has been reported, making it hard to evaluate their usefulness in practice. In [41], a polynomial-time algorithm for enumerating sets as in (2) is proposed without implementation.

This paper investigates the combination of PIP with our method for parametric polytopes [40]. This combination can handle the parametric counting problems with existential variables reported in [2, 6, 9, 12] that were previously considered difficult or even unsolvable. Since PIP is worst-case exponential, we also investigate an alternative method that uses a number of simple polynomial rewriting rules to eliminate existential quantifiers. While all existential quantifiers are eliminated in our experiments on a wide range of practical applications, some could remain. In that case, PIP can be used as a back-up to solve the reduced problem. Theoretically, parametric Presburger formulas can be transformed into a disjoint union of sets of the form (2). For the majority of the parametric Presburger formulas we considered, this transformation could be performed efficiently and automatically by the Omega library.

Section 2 introduces background on parametric polytopes and enumerators and Section 3 two extensions for handling existential variables. An experimental evaluation is performed in Section 4, and concluding remarks follow in Section 5.

2 Parametric Polytopes

Before tackling integer projections of parametric polytopes, we review the results on enumeration of parametric polytopes. We refer to [40] for the details.

Definition 1. *A* rational polyhedron $P \in \mathbb{Q}^d$ *is a set of rational d-dimensional vectors* $\mathbf{x}$ *defined by linear inequalities*

$$P = \left\{ \mathbf{x} \in \mathbb{Q}^d \mid A\mathbf{x} + \mathbf{c} \geq \mathbf{0} \right\}, \text{ with } A \in \mathbb{Z}^{m\times d} \text{ and } \mathbf{c} \in \mathbb{Z}^m. \tag{4}$$

A rational polytope *is a bounded rational polyhedron.*

Definition 2. *A* rational parametric polytope $P_\mathbf{p}$ *with n parameters* $\mathbf{p}$ *is a set of rational d-dimensional vectors* $\mathbf{x}$ *defined by linear inequalities on* $\mathbf{x}$ *and* $\mathbf{p}$

$$P_\mathbf{p} = \left\{ \mathbf{x} \in \mathbb{Q}^d \mid A\mathbf{x} + B\mathbf{p} + \mathbf{c} \geq \mathbf{0} \right\} \tag{5}$$

with $A \in \mathbb{Z}^{m\times d}$, $B \in \mathbb{Z}^{m\times n}$ *and* $\mathbf{c} \in \mathbb{Z}^m$, *and such that for each fixed value* $\mathbf{p}_0$ *of* $\mathbf{p}$, $P_{\mathbf{p}_0}$ *defines a (possibly empty) rational polytope in* $\mathbb{Q}^d$.

All the polyhedra in this paper are rational. If the parametrization of a polytope is clear from the context, subscript $\mathbf{p}$ is omitted. Note that the same equations that define a parametric polytope also define a potentially unbounded $(d+n)$-dimensional polyhedron in the combined data and parameter space.

$$P' = \left\{ (\mathbf{x}, \mathbf{p}) \in \mathbb{Q}^{d+n} \mid A\mathbf{x} + B\mathbf{p} + \mathbf{c} \geq \mathbf{0} \right\}$$

Definition 3. *The* enumerator $c_P(\mathbf{p})$ *of a parametric polytope* $P_\mathbf{p}$ *is a function from the set of n-dimensional integer vectors* $\mathbb{Z}^n$ *to the set of natural numbers* $\mathbb{N}$.[4] *The function value at* $\mathbf{p}_0$*, denoted* $c_P(\mathbf{p}_0)$*, is the number of integer points in the polytope* $P_{\mathbf{p}_0}$*.*

$$\begin{aligned} c_P : \mathbb{Z}^n &\to \mathbb{N} \\ \mathbf{p}_0 &\mapsto c_P(\mathbf{p}_0) = \# \left(\mathbb{Z}^d \cap \{\, \mathbf{x} \in \mathbb{Q}^d \mid A\mathbf{x} + B\mathbf{p}_0 + \mathbf{c} \geq \mathbf{0} \,\} \right) \end{aligned}$$

Definition 4. *A* step-polynomial $g : \mathbb{Z}^n \to \mathbb{Q}$ *of degree d is a function written in the form*

$$g(\mathbf{p}) = \sum_{j=1}^{m} \alpha_j \prod_{k=1}^{d_j} \lfloor \langle \mathbf{a}_{jk}, \mathbf{p} \rangle + b_{jk} \rfloor ,$$

with $\alpha_j \in \mathbb{Q}$*,* $\mathbf{a}_{jk} \in \mathbb{Q}^n$*,* $b_{jk} \in \mathbb{Q}$*,* $\langle \cdot, \cdot \rangle$ *the inproduct, and* $\lfloor \cdot \rfloor$ *is the floor (greatest integer) function. A* piecewise step-polynomial $f : \mathbb{Z}^n \to \mathbb{Q}$ *consists of a subdivision of* $\mathbb{Z}^n$*, called the* chambers,[5] *each with an associated step-polynomial.*

Proposition 1 ([40]). *For fixed dimensions d and n, the enumerator of a parametric polytope can be computed as a piecewise step-polynomial in a time polynomial in the input size (the number of bits needed to represent the input [34]).*

Example 2. Consider the parametric polytope P_p

$$\{\, (x, y) \in \mathbb{Q}^2 \mid x + 3y \leq 8 \wedge x + 2y + 1 \leq 0 \wedge x + 2y + p \geq 0 \wedge x + 3p + 11 \leq 0 \,\}.$$

Figure 2 shows P_p for different values of p. The number of integer points is given by

$$c_P(p) = \begin{cases} 5 & \text{if } p \geq 3 \\ -\frac{3}{4}p^2 + \frac{15}{4}p + \frac{1}{2}\lfloor \frac{1}{2}p \rfloor & \text{if } 1 \leq p \leq 2 \end{cases}.$$

This enumerator has two chambers: $\{\, p \mid p \geq 3 \,\}$ and $\{\, p \mid 1 \leq p \leq 2 \,\}$. The step-polynomial associated with the first chamber is a constant. For the second chamber, we obtain a polynomial in the floors of p and $\frac{1}{2}p$. Note that this is only one of the possible representations of $c_P(p)$. For this particular example, a much simpler representation exists with chambers $\{\, p \mid p \geq 2 \,\}$ and $\{\, 1 \,\}$, and the constants 5 and 3 for the corresponding functions.

3 Existential Variables

This section considers the extension with existential variables. The general form of these counting problems, given in Equation 2, is equivalent to

$$\#\pi_d \left(\mathbb{Z}^{(d+d')} \cap \left\{ (\mathbf{x}, \mathbf{y}) \in \mathbb{Q}^{(d+d')} \mid A\mathbf{x} + D\mathbf{y} + B\mathbf{p} + \mathbf{c} \geq \mathbf{0} \right\} \right)$$

[4] In [40], the symbol $\mathcal{E}$ is used instead of c.

[5] Chambers are also called validity domains in some publications.

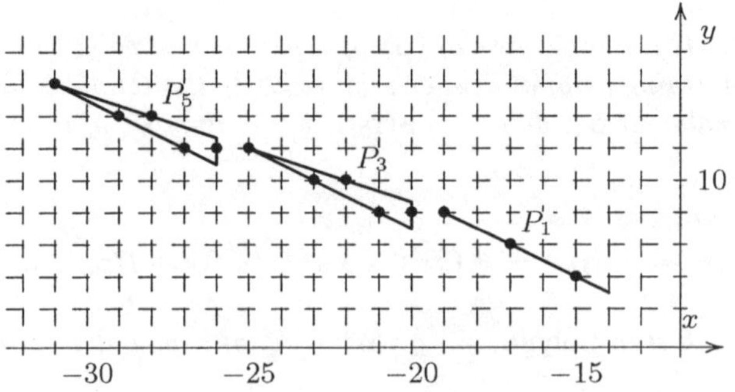

Fig. 2. Different instantiations of the parametric polytope from Example 2

where π_d is the projection onto the first d dimensions. This parametric count corresponds to the number of points in the projection of the integer points in a parametric polytope, or integer projection of a parametric polytope for short.

Note that we cannot simply ignore the existential quantifier and count the number of points as if the set were a parametric polytope, since for any particular value of $\mathbf{x}$ there may be several values of $\mathbf{y}$ that satisfy the constraints. We also cannot simply project out the existential variables since there may exist values of $\mathbf{x}$ in this projection for which there is no *integer* value of $\mathbf{y}$ satisfying the constraints. E.g., if we project P_5 in Figure 2 onto the x-axis, then this projection will contain the value −30, while there is no integer y such that $(-30, y) \in P_5$.

We consider three techniques for eliminating existential variables; they are polynomial in the input size (for fixed dimensions) but not always applicable. In the latter case, one can fall back upon parametric integer programming to count the set. However, this is worst-case exponential, even for fixed dimensions.

3.1 Elimination

Unique Existential Variables. The existential quantifiers introduced by tools that automatically extract counting problems from source code can sometimes be redundant. This occurs when for each $\mathbf{x}$ in the set, there is at most one integer value for y_i that satisfies the constraints. In such a case, the existential quantifier for y_i can be omitted without affecting the cardinality of the set.

Many cases can be detected when there is a constraint that involves y_i but none of the other existential variables $\overline{\mathbf{y}}$. Without loss of generality, we assume the constraint establishes a lower bound on the variable y_i, i.e., it is of the form

$$n_l y_i + \langle \mathbf{a}_l, \mathbf{x} \rangle + \langle \mathbf{b}_l, \mathbf{p} \rangle + c_l \geq 0 \tag{6}$$

with $n_l \in \mathbb{N}$. Combining this constraint with an upper bound

$$-n_u y_i + \langle \mathbf{a}_u, \mathbf{x} \rangle + \langle \overline{\mathbf{d}}_u, \overline{\mathbf{y}} \rangle + \langle \mathbf{b}_u, \mathbf{p} \rangle + c_u \geq 0 \tag{7}$$

we obtain

$$-n_u(\langle \mathbf{a}_l, \mathbf{x} \rangle + \langle \mathbf{b}_l, \mathbf{p} \rangle + c_l) \leq n_u n_l y_i \leq n_l(\langle \mathbf{a}_u, \mathbf{x} \rangle + \langle \overline{\mathbf{d}}_u, \overline{\mathbf{y}} \rangle + \langle \mathbf{b}_u, \mathbf{p} \rangle + c_u). \tag{8}$$

The number of distinct integer values for $n_u n_l y_i$ is given by the upper bound minus the lower bound plus one. If this number is smaller than $n_u n_l$, then the two constraints admit at most one integer value for y_i. That is, if

$$n_l(\langle \mathbf{a}_u, \mathbf{x}\rangle + \langle \overline{\mathbf{d}}_u, \overline{\mathbf{y}}\rangle + \langle \mathbf{b}_u, \mathbf{p}\rangle + c_u) + n_u(\langle \mathbf{a}_l, \mathbf{x}\rangle + \langle \mathbf{b}_l, \mathbf{p}\rangle + c_l) + 1 \le n_l n_u \quad (9)$$

for all integer values that satisfy the constraints, then y_i is uniquely determined by $\mathbf{x}$ and $\mathbf{p}$ and can therefore be treated as a regular variable, without existential quantification. It is independent of the other existential variables because of our assumption that one of the constraints does not involve these other variables. Condition (9) can easily be checked by adding the negation to the existing set of constraints and testing for satisfiability. Note that it is sufficient to find one such pair to be able to drop the existential quantification of the variable.

Example 3. Consider the set S

$$\{ x \in \mathbb{Z} \mid \exists y \in \mathbb{Z} : x+3y \le 8 \wedge x+2y+1 \le 0 \wedge x+2y+p \ge 0 \wedge x+3p+11 \le 0 \}.$$

This is the same set that appeared in Example 2, except that y is now an existential variable. Since there is only a single existential variable, all constraints are independent of the "other existential variables". Using $x + 2y + p \ge 0$ and $-x - 3y + 8 \ge 0$ as constraints, condition (9) yields

$$x + 3p + 17 \le 6. \quad (10)$$

All elements of the set satisfy this constraint so we can remove the existential quantification and the set S is then $P_p \cap \mathbb{Z}$, with P_p the set from Example 2.

Even if there is no single existential variable that is unique, some linear combination of existential variables may still be unique. To avoid enumerating all possible combinations, we only consider this case if we have two constraints that are "parallel in the existential space", i.e., such that $\mathbf{d}_l = n_l \mathbf{d}$ and $\mathbf{d}_u = -n_u \mathbf{d}$ for some positive integers n_l and n_u and an integer vector $\mathbf{d}$ with greatest common divisor (gcd) 1. We compute condition (9) from (6) and (7) with y_i replaced by $\langle \mathbf{d}, \mathbf{y}\rangle$ ($\overline{\mathbf{d}}_u$ is $\mathbf{0}$ in this case). If this condition holds, we perform a change of basis such that $y'_1 = \langle \mathbf{d}, \mathbf{y}\rangle$, which we now know to be unique. Such a change of basis can be obtained through transformation by the unimodular extension of $\mathbf{d}$ [7].

Example 4. Consider the set S (3) from Section 1. This set satisfies the equality $l = 6i + 9j - 7$, which means that $2i + 3j$ is unique. Transforming this set using the unimodular extension of $\mathbf{d} = (2, 3)$

$$\begin{pmatrix} x \\ y \end{pmatrix} = \begin{pmatrix} 2 & 3 \\ -1 & -1 \end{pmatrix} \begin{pmatrix} i \\ j \end{pmatrix}$$

we obtain

$$S = \{ l \in \mathbb{Z} \mid \exists x, y \in \mathbb{Z} : l = 3x-7 \wedge -x-p \le 2y \le -x-1 \wedge -x+1 \le 3y \le -x+8 \}.$$

Equation $l = 3x - 7$ provides an upper and a lower bound on x, hence Equation (9) is trivially satisfied, $\exists x$ can be removed and also l as it is now redundant.

$$S' = \{ x \in \mathbb{Z} \mid \exists y \in \mathbb{Z} : -x - p \leq 2y \leq -x - 1 \wedge -x + 1 \leq 3y \leq -x + 8 \}. \quad (11)$$

Redundant Existential Variables. Consider again a lower bound on the existential variable y_i: $n_l y_i + \langle \mathbf{c}_l, \mathbf{w} \rangle \geq 0$, where we used $\mathbf{c}_l := (\mathbf{a}_l, \overline{\mathbf{d}}_l, \mathbf{b}_l, c_l)$ and $\mathbf{w} := (\mathbf{x}, \overline{\mathbf{y}}, \mathbf{p}, 1)$ for brevity. Since we are only interested in integer values of y_i, this is equivalent to $n_u(n_l y_i + \langle \mathbf{c}_l, \mathbf{w} \rangle) + n_u - 1 \geq 0$, for any positive integer n_u. Similarly, for an upper bound we obtain $n_l(-n_u y_i + \langle \mathbf{c}_u, \mathbf{w} \rangle) + n_l - 1 \geq 0$. The range in (8) can therefore be expanded to

$$-n_u \langle \mathbf{c}_l, \mathbf{w} \rangle - n_u + 1 \leq n_u n_l y_i \leq n_l \langle \mathbf{c}_u, \mathbf{w} \rangle + n_l - 1.$$

If this range is larger than $n_u n_l$, i.e., if

$$n_l \langle \mathbf{c}_u, \mathbf{w} \rangle + n_u \langle \mathbf{c}_l, \mathbf{w} \rangle + n_l - 1 + n_u - 1 + 1 \geq n_l n_u, \quad (12)$$

then there is *at least* one integer value for each given value of the other variables. If this holds for all pairs of constraints, then variable y_i does not restrict the solutions in any way and can be eliminated (known as the Omega test [32]). Note that the constraints need not be independent of the other variables.

Example 5. Consider the set

$$S = \{ x \in \mathbb{Z} \mid \exists y \in \mathbb{Z} : -x - p \leq 2y \leq -x - 1 \wedge x \leq -11 \wedge \\ -x + 1 \leq 3y \leq -x + 8 \wedge x + 3p + 10 \leq 0 \wedge p \geq 3 \}.$$

This set is shown (■) in Figure 3. Pairwise combining the two upper and two lower bounds to form condition (12), we obtain $2p + 1 \geq 4$, $26 \geq 9$, $-x - 1 \geq 6$ and $x + 20 + 3p \geq 6$. All of these are true in S. (In practice we would use the least common multiple of n_l and n_u instead of their product.) Variable y can therefore be eliminated and we obtain $S = \{ x \in \mathbb{Z} \mid x \leq -11 \wedge p \geq 3 \wedge x + 3p + 10 \geq 0 \}$.

Independent Splits. If neither of the two heuristics above apply, we can split the set into two or more parts by cutting the polyhedron in the combined space along a hyperplane. By considering hyperplanes that are independent of the existential variables, we ensure that the enumerator of the original set is the sum of the enumerators of the parts; otherwise we would obtain sets that may intersect, requiring the computation of a disjoint union.

In particular, we consider all pairs of a lower and an upper bound on an existential variable that do not depend on other existential variables, i.e., they are of the form (6). If neither condition (9) nor condition (12) is satisfied over the whole set, then we cut off that part of the set where condition (9) does hold. In the remaining part, condition (12) holds for this particular pair of constraints.

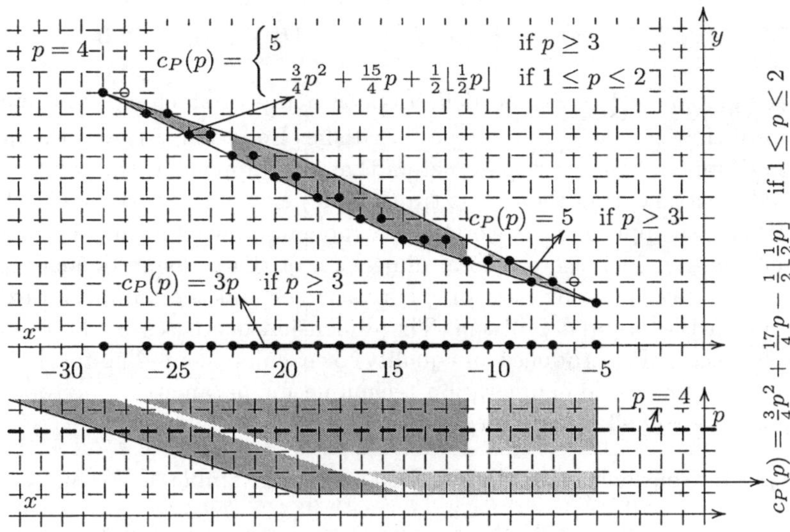

Fig. 3. Decomposition of the set from Example 6

Since the number of pairs of constraints is polynomial in the input size, the number of sets we split off is also polynomial and so the whole technique, if it applies, is polynomial in the input size (for fixed dimension). As a special case, this technique always applies if there is only a single existential variable.

Example 6. Consider once more the set S' (11) from Example 4. The bottom of Figure 3 shows the projection of the corresponding polyhedron in the combined data-parameter space onto the xp-plane and the top shows the xy-slice at $p = 4$. The two constraints we considered in Example 3 also appear in this set. Condition (10) does not hold for the whole set, but instead is used to cut off the part that we considered in Example 3. This is the leftmost part (■) in Figure 3. Using the other constraints, we further split off $p \leq 2$ and $x \geq -10$. The remaining part is the set discussed in Example 5.

3.2 Parametric Integer Programming

Parametric integer programming (PIP) [20] is a technique for computing the lexicographical minimum of a parametric polytope as a function of the parameters. The solution is defined by rational linear expressions in both the original parameters and possibly some extra parameters, defined as the floors of rational linear expressions of other parameters. Different solutions may exist in different parts of the parameter space, each defined by linear inequalities in the parameters (both original and extra).

PIP can help in the enumeration of integer projections of parametric polytopes. Consider a set S (2) with d regular variables, d' existential variables and n parameters. Compute the lexicographical minimum of the d' existential variables with the regular variables and the original parameters as parameters, i.e.,

$$\mathbf{y}^{\mathrm{m}}_{(\mathbf{x},\mathbf{p})} = \operatorname{lexmin}\left\{ \mathbf{y} \in \mathbb{Z}^{d'} \mid A\mathbf{x} + D\mathbf{y} + B\mathbf{p} + \mathbf{c} \geq \mathbf{0} \right\}.$$

Replacing $\mathbf{y}$ by $\mathbf{y}^{\mathrm{m}}_{(\mathbf{x},\mathbf{p})}$ in the definition of S does not change the number of solutions. However, $\mathbf{y}^{\mathrm{m}}_{(\mathbf{x},\mathbf{p})}$ is unique (it satisfies Equation (9)) and the quantifier can be dropped. The extra parameters that may appear in the solution can be handled by considering them as extra (unique) existential variables in the set S.

PIP always applies but is worst-case exponential, even for fixed dimension. It may decrease or increase the total dimension of the problem depending on the difference between the number of extra variables and the number of existential variables in the original problem. The dimension decreases by 1 for each such variable since PIP introduces an equality for each of them. The total dimension is important since the enumeration technique for parametric polytopes is only polynomial for fixed dimension.

Example 7. Consider again the set S' (11) from Example 4. We have:

$$\begin{aligned} y^{\mathrm{m}}_{(x,p)} &= \operatorname{lexmin}\left\{ y \in \mathbb{Z} \mid -x-p \leq 2y \leq -x-1 \wedge -x+1 \leq 3y \leq -x+8 \right\} \\ &= \begin{cases} 1-x-\left\lfloor \frac{2-2x}{3} \right\rfloor & \text{if } x+3p+2 \geq 0 \\ -x-\left\lfloor \frac{p-x}{2} \right\rfloor & \text{otherwise} \end{cases}. \end{aligned}$$

Hence S' is the (disjoint) union of two sets $S_1 \sqcup S_2$. E.g., S_1 is defined as

$$\begin{aligned} S_1 = \{\, x \in \mathbb{Z} \mid \exists y, q \in \mathbb{Z} : y = 1-x-q \wedge 2-2x \leq 3q \leq 4-2x \wedge \\ x+3p+2 \geq 0 \wedge -x-p \leq 2y \leq -x-1 \wedge -x+1 \leq 3y \leq -x+8 \,\}, \end{aligned}$$

where q is the new "parameter" $q = \lfloor (2-2x)/3 \rfloor$. Each new set has exactly one extra (unique) existential variable, hence the total dimension remains constant.

4 Experiments

We count the number of integer points in formulas resulting from reuse distance equations [6], cache miss analysis [12], memory size estimation [2] and communication volume computation [9]. An overview of these problems and details on the specific versions of the `PolyLib` and `Barvinok` libraries we used are in [39].

4.1 Reuse Distances

We performed extensive experiments calculating reuse distances of a set of relatively small but representative test programs including matrix-matrix multiplication and Cholesky factorization. The second column of Table 1(a) shows the number of times a particular rule from Section 3.1 was used. The remaining columns are explained in Section 4.2. The row "Fixed" refers to the special case of a unique existential variable determined by an equality; "Change" refers to a change of basis. In most of the tests we assume a cache line size of four words. Frequently, the matrix size is a multiple of the cache line size. The resulting

Table 1. Tables with experimental results

type	RD	Chatterjee	Balasa	Boulet
Sets	19177	8+13	4	1
Fixed	3470	0+2	14	5
Change+Fixed	0	0+0	0	2
Unique	4890	8+9	0	0
Change+Unique	18	0+0	0	0
Redundant	684	0+0	2	1
Split	286	0+0	0	0
PIP	0	0+0	0	0

(a) Rule application distribution for polytopes originating from reuse distance equations (RD), cache miss analysis (Chatterjee), memory size estimation (Balasa) and communication volume computation (Boulet)

#EV	Dimension Decrease						
	?	-1	0	1	2	3	4
1			6186	527	25		
2		6	779	102	41	10	
3	2	2	122	66	11	6	
4			6	38	5		7
5			3	1	5		1
6	2					3	

(b) Dimension decrease induced by PIP in terms of the number of existential variables (#*EV*)

enumerators for such cases were experimentally verified through a cache simulation. PIP was never needed in these experiments. Simply ignoring the existential quantifiers would have produced the wrong result, however, since we had to split some sets. Curiously, some sets contained redundant existential variables, even though they were created by Omega which should have removed them.

We also investigated the impact of the input size. For reuse distance calculation for matrix–matrix multiplication varying the sizes of the matrices, ranging from 20×20 to 640×640, produced no measurable increase in computation time. However, on tests where matrix sizes are not multiples of the cache line size, Omega fails to simplify the resulting Presburger formulas, and produces inexact formulas containing `Unknowns`. We were forced to devise a way that avoids Omega as much as possible. This modification increases the number of sets to enumerate. For matrices of size 19×19 and 41×41, some of the resulting sets proved too difficult to handle. For both sizes, we found at least one set where we had to abort `PolyLib` after one hour while it was calculating step-polynomials. Directly applying PIP also did not produce a result; moreover, PIP failed also on two other sets that were handled by our reduction rules.

Next, we compared the relative performance of PIP and our rules when combined with our polytope enumeration technique. A priori, we would expect that the method with PIP would perform worse since PIP itself is worst-case exponential and the use of PIP may significantly increase the dimension of the problem. Table 1(b) shows that this increase did not occur for our set of examples. Ignoring the 4 sets that failed to produce an answer (column "?") as well as the 11355 sets without existential variables (not shown in the table), of the 7952 resulting polytopes, almost 90% have the same dimension as the original set. Furthermore, except for 8 polytopes which experience an increase in dimension, all others have a dimension that is smaller than that of the original set. There are even 35 polytopes with a decrease in dimension that is *larger* than the number

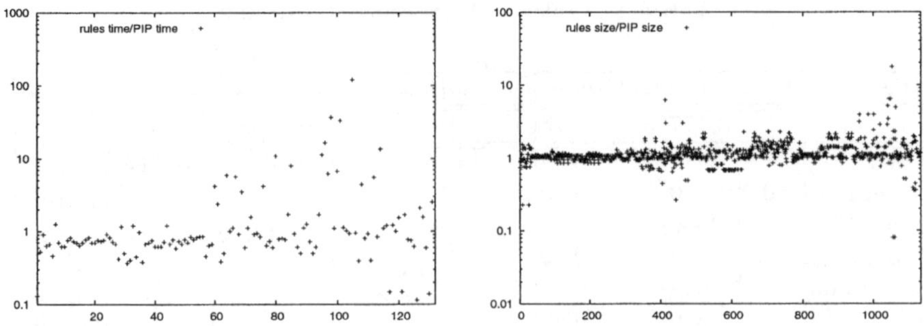

Fig. 4. Comparison between PIP and our rules

of existential variables. The explanation for this phenomenon is that some of the sets allow a range of rational values in one of the dimension, but only a single integer value, e.g., $4 \leq 5i \leq 7$. Again, this is surprising since Omega should have discovered the corresponding equality. For the sets that PIP was able to handle, Figure 4 shows the relative execution time on the left, for sets with an execution time larger than 0.1s, and the relative size of the resulting enumerator on the right, for sets where this relative size is not exactly one. We conclude that for our set of examples, neither method has a clear performance gain over the other.

We previously reported [40] that our method for enumerating parametric polytopes is faster, sometimes significantly, than Clauss's method. Figure 5 provides further evidence of this improvement. The inputs are the parametric polytopes generated by PIP on the reuse distance sets. From a total of 18951 polytopes, 907 had a computation time of more than 0.1s. The implementation of Clauss's method failed to produce a complete result for 190 of these polytopes, due to "degenerate domains". The ratio of the execution times for the remaining polytopes is shown for the "raw" polytopes on the left and for the polytopes with redundant equalities removed on the right. For 17 polytopes on the left and 8 polytopes on the right, the computation with Clauss's method exceeds 10 minutes. The "ratio" for these polytopes is fixed to 100000 on the figures.

4.2 Other Applications

In this section, we mainly compare the combination of PIP with either Clauss's method or our method [40]. Applying Clauss's method on a problem for an 8×8 processor array presented in [10] leads to a computation time of 713s. The same problem for a 64×64 array, requires 6855s. Apparently, Clauss's method does not exploit equalities; first removing them reduces times to 0.04s and 1.43s. Using our own method, which removes equalities automatically, we obtain both results in 0.01s. The applied rules are shown in column 5 of Table 1(a).

An example in [2] counts the number of array elements accessed by 4 references in a motion estimation loop kernel, for a number of different values of the symbolic loop bounds. We handled the symbolic loop bounds parametrically,

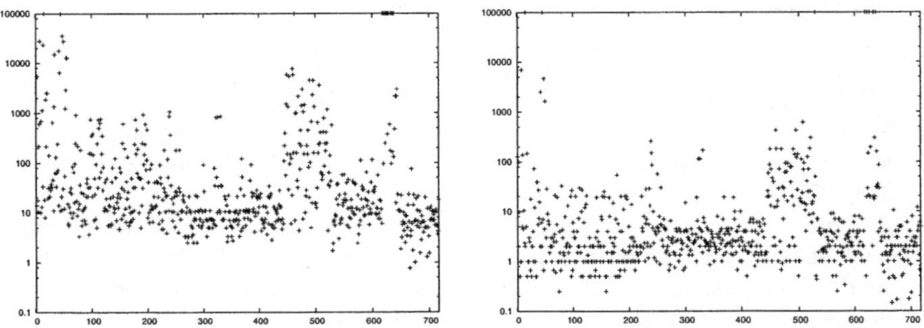

Fig. 5. Execution time ratio for Clauss's method compared to ours for the original polytopes on the left and preprocessed polytopes on the right

thereby obtaining a single solution for all possible values of the symbolic loop bounds. Using Clauss's method (after removing equalities), counting takes respectively 1.38s, 0.01s, 1.41s and 1.41s. With our method, times are 0.06s, 0.01s, 0.07s and 0.04s. The applied rules are shown in column 4 of Table 1(a).

Finally, we considered a large formula from [12]. Computation times for the 8 disjuncts range from a couple of seconds to 1.5 minutes while Clauss's method for one of the parametric polytopes did not finish in 15 hours. To enumerate the whole formula, a disjoint union consisting of 13 sets was computed in less than a second using Omega. Their enumeration times are in the same range as those of the original disjuncts. The applied rules are shown in column 3 of Table 1(a), with the original disjuncts on the left and the disjoint sets on the right.

5 Conclusions

Many compiler analyses and optimizations require the enumeration of the integer projection of a parametric polytope. As shown, this problem can be reduced to a problem of enumerating parametric polytopes, either by using PIP or by applying a number of rewriting rules. This reduction, together with our polynomial method for enumerating parametric polytopes [40], yields a method that works well in practice and can solve many problems that were previously considered very difficult or even unsolvable. Although both approaches usually have comparable performance, there are some examples where PIP runs out of time. Since the applicability of the rules is easy to check, it seems appropriate to apply the rules first and to use PIP only when no complete reduction is achieved.

Acknowledgements. Sven Verdoolaege was supported by FWO-Vlaanderen. Kristof Beyls was supported by research project GOA-12051002.

References

[1] S. Anantharaman and S. Pande. Compiler optimizations for real time execution of loops on limited memory embedded systems. In *RTSS*, 1998.

[2] F. Balasa, F. Catthoor, and H. De Man. Background memory area estimation for multidimensional signal processing systems. *IEEE Transactions on VLSI*, 3(2):157–172, 1995.

[3] A. Barvinok and J. Pommersheim. An algorithmic theory of lattice points in polyhedra. *New Perspectives in Algebraic Combinatorics*, 38:91–147, 1999.

[4] A. Barvinok and K. Woods. Short rational generating functions for lattice point problems. *J. Amer. Math. Soc.*, 16:957–979, Apr. 2003.

[5] M. Bednara, F. Hannig, and J. Teich. Generation of distributed loop control. In *SAMOS*, volume 2268 of *LNCS*, pages 154–170, 2002.

[6] K. Beyls. *Software Methods to Improve Data Locality and Cache Behavior.* PhD thesis, Ghent University, 2004.

[7] A. J. C. Bik. *Compiler Support for Sparse Matrix Computations.* PhD thesis, University of Leiden, The Netherlands, 1996.

[8] B. Boigelot and L. Latour. Counting the solutions of Presburger equations without enumerating them. *Theoretical Computer Science*, 313(1):17–29, Feb. 2004.

[9] P. Boulet and X. Redon. Communication pre-evaluation in HPF. In *EUROPAR'98*, volume 1470 of *LNCS*, pages 263–272. Springer Verlag, 1998.

[10] P. Boulet and X. Redon. Communication pre-evaluation in HPF. Technical report, Université des Sciences et Technologies de Lille, 1998. AS-182.

[11] V. Braberman, D. Garbervetsky, and S. Yovine. On synthesizing parametric specifications of dynamic memory utilization. Technical Report TR-2004-03, VERIMAG, Oct. 2003.

[12] S. Chatterjee, E. Parker, P. J. Hanlon, and A. R. Lebeck. Exact analysis of the cache behavior of nested loops. In *PLDI*, pages 286–297, 2001.

[13] P. Clauss. Counting solutions to linear and nonlinear constraints through Ehrhart polynomials: Applications to analyze and transform scientific programs. In *International Conference on Supercomputing*, pages 278–285, 1996.

[14] P. Clauss. Handling memory cache policy with integer points counting. In *European Conference on Parallel Processing*, pages 285–293, 1997.

[15] P. Clauss and V. Loechner. Parametric analysis of polyhedral iteration spaces. *Journal of VLSI Signal Processing*, 19(2):179–194, July 1998.

[16] P. D'Alberto, A. Veidembaum, A. Nicolau, and R. Gupta. Static analysis of parameterized loop nests for energy efficient use of data caches. In *COLP*, 2001.

[17] J. A. De Loera, R. Hemmecke, J. Tauzer, and R. Yoshida. Effective lattice point counting in rational convex polytopes. *The Journal of Symbolic Computation*, 38(4):1273–1302, 2004.

[18] S. Derrien, A. Turjan, C. Zissulescu, B. Kienhuis, and E. Deprettere. Deriving efficient control in Kahn process network. In *SAMOS*, 2003.

[19] E. Ehrhart. Polynômes arithmétiques et méthode des polyèdres en combinatoire. *International Series of Numerical Mathematics*, 35, 1977.

[20] P. Feautrier. Parametric integer programming. *Operationnelle/Operations Research*, 22(3):243–268, 1988.

[21] J. Ferrante, V. Sarkar, and W. Thrash. On estimating and enhancing cache effectiveness. In *LCPC*, volume 589 of *LNCS*, pages 328–343, 1991.

[22] D. Fimmel and R. Merker. Design of processor arrays for real-time applications. In *Euro-Par '98*, LNCS, pages 1018–1028, 1998.

[23] B. Franke and M. O'Boyle. Array recovery and high-level transformations for DSP applications. *ACM TECS*, 2(2):132–162, May 2003.

[24] S. Ghosh, M. Martonosi, and S. Malik. Cache miss equations: a compiler framework for analyzing and tuning memory behavior. *ACM Transactions on Programming Languages and Systems*, 21(4):703–746, 1999.

[25] F. Hannig and J. Teich. Design space exploration for massively parallel processor arrays. In *PaCT*, volume 2127 of *LNCS*, pages 51–65, 2001.

[26] F. Heine and A. Slowik. Volume driven data distribution for NUMA-machines. In *Euro-Par*, LNCS, pages 415–424, 2000.

[27] P. G. Kjeldsberg, F. Catthoor, and E. J. Aas. Data dependency size estimation for use in memory optimization. *IEEE Transactions on Computer-Aided Design of Integrated Circuits and Systems*, 22(7), July 2003.

[28] B. Lisper. Fully automatic, parametric worst-case execution time analysis. In *Workshop on Worst-Case Execution Time (WCET) Analysis*, pages 77–80, 2003.

[29] V. Loechner, B. Meister, and P. Clauss. Precise data locality optimization of nested loops. *J. Supercomput.*, 21(1):37–76, 2002.

[30] B. Meister. Projecting periodic polyhedra for loop nest analysis. In *CPC*, pages 13–24, 2004.

[31] E. Parker and S. Chatterjee. An automata-theoretic algorithm for counting solutions to Presburger formulas. In *Compiler Construction*, volume 2985 of *LNCS*, pages 104–119, 2004.

[32] W. Pugh. The Omega test: a fast and practical integer programming algorithm for dependence analysis. In *Conference on Supercomputing*, pages 4–13, 1991.

[33] W. Pugh. Counting solutions to Presburger formulas: How and why. In *PLDI*, pages 121–134, 1994.

[34] A. Schrijver. *Theory of Linear and Integer Programming.* John Wiley & Sons, 1986.

[35] R. Seghir. Dénombrement des point entiers de l'union et de l'image des polyédres paramétrés. Master's thesis, ICPS, Strasbourg, France, June 2002.

[36] B. Sturmfels. On vector partition functions. *J. Comb. Theory Ser. A*, 72(2):302–309, 1995.

[37] E. Su and A. L. et al. Advanced compilation techniques in the PARADIGM compiler for distributed-memory multicomputers. In *ICS*, pages 424–433, 1995.

[38] A. Turjan, B. Kienhuis, and E. Deprettere. A compile time based approach for solving out-of-order communication in Kahn process networks. In *ASAP*, 2002.

[39] S. Verdoolaege, K. Beyls, M. Bruynooghe, and F. Catthoor. Experiences with enumeration of integer projections of parametric polytopes. Report CW 395, Department of Computer Science, K.U. Leuven, Leuven, Belgium, Oct. 2004.

[40] S. Verdoolaege, R. Seghir, K. Beyls, V. Loechner, and M. Bruynooghe. Analytical computation of Ehrhart polynomials: Enabling more compiler analyses and optimizations. In *CASES*, pages 248–258, 2004.

[41] S. Verdoolaege, K. M. Woods, M. Bruynooghe, and R. Cools. Computation and manipulation of enumerators of integer projections of +parametric polytopes. Report CW 392, Dept. of Computer Science, K.U. Leuven, Leuven, Belgium, 2005.

[42] Y. Zhao and S. Malik. Exact memory size estimation for array computations. *IEEE Transactions on VLSI Systems*, 8(5):517–521, October 2000.

Generalized Index-Set Splitting

Christopher Barton[1], Arie Tal[2], Bob Blainey[2], and José Nelson Amaral[1]

[1] Department of Computing Science,
University of Alberta, Edmonton, Canada
{cbarton, amaral}@cs.ualberta.ca
[2] IBM Toronto Software Laboratory, Toronto, Canada
{arietal, blainey}@ca.ibm.com

Abstract. This paper introduces *Index-Set Splitting* (ISS), a technique that splits a loop containing several conditional statements into several loops with less complex control flow. Contrary to the classic *loop unswitching* technique, ISS splits loops when the conditional is loop variant. ISS uses an *Index Sub-range Tree* (IST) to identify the structure of the conditionals in the loop and to select which conditionals should be eliminated. This decision is based on an estimation of the code growth for each splitting: a greedy algorithm spends a pre-determined code growth budget. ISTs separate the decision about which splits to perform from the actual code generation for the split loops. The use of ISS to improve a loop fusion framework is then discussed. ISS opportunity identification in the SPEC2000 benchmark suite and three other suites demonstrate that ISS is a general technique that may benefit other compilers.

1 Introduction

This paper describes *Index-Set Splitting* (ISS), a code transformation motivated by the implementation of loop fusion in the commercially distributed IBM XL Compilers. ISS is an enabling technique that increases the code scope where other optimizations, such as software pipelining, loop unroll-and-jam, unimodular transformations, loop-based common expression elimination, can be applied.

A loop that does not contain branch statements is a Single Basic Block Loop (SBBL). A loop that contains branches is a Multi-Basic Block Loop (MBBL). SBBLs are easier to optimize than MBBLs. For instance, MBBLs with complex control flow are not candidates for conventional software pipelining. Loop unswitching is a transformation that can convert a MBBL into two non-control flow equivalent SBBLs by moving a branch statement out of the original loop [1]. Loop unswitching is applicable only to loop invariant branches.

ISS recursively splits a loop with several branches into loops with smaller index ranges and fewer branches. Contrary to loop unswitching, ISS splits loops based on loop variant branches. In order to minimize its impact on compilation time and code growth, ISS performs a profitability analysis to control the number of loops that are generated. ISS is effective in removing branches that are found

R. Bodik (Ed.): CC 2005, LNCS 3443, pp. 106–120, 2005.

in the original code as well as branches that are inserted into the code by the compiler.

Loop fusion is a code transformation that may insert branches into a loop. Barton *et al.* list three fusion-preventing conditions that, if present, must be dealt with before two control flow equivalent loops can be fused: (1) intervening code; (2) non-identical loop bounds; and (3) negative distance dependencies between loop bodies [2]. The classical solution to deal with the second and third conditions requires the generation of compensatory code outside of the loops. This compensatory code will contain one or more iterations of the loop. If this code is generated during the loop fusion process, it becomes intervening code between other fusion candidates. This new intervening code has, in turn, to be moved elsewhere. Thus a cumbersome loop fusion code transformation is created.

The proliferation of intervening code during the loop fusion process can be avoided by inserting guard branches within the loops. Guards are conditional statements that prevent a portion of the loop code from being executed on certain iterations. Once the loop fusion process has completed, ISS can be run to remove the guard branches from inside the fused loops, thereby turning a single MBBL into many SBBLs.

The main contributions of this paper are:

- A description of the new index-set splitting technique that selectively eliminates loop variant branches from a loop.
- An example of the use of guards followed by index-set splitting to improve the loop fusion framework.
- An example of the use of index-set splitting to enable other optimizations.
- Measurements indicating the changes caused by ISS in the compilation time of applications in the development version of the IBM XL compiler.
- Run-time measurements indicating the impact of ISS on the performance of the code generated.

The paper is organized as follows. Section 2 presents an example to motivate ISS. Section 3 introduces the Index Sub-range Tree that is used to handle loops with multiple split points. Section 4 describes how code growth is controlled by the ISS algorithm. Section 5 describes how ISS is used to produce a cleaner framework for loop fusion. Section 6 shows the use of guards for run-time bounds checks in loop fusion. These guards are then split points for the ISS algorithm. A discussion of how ISS can be used to enable other optimizations is provided in Section 7. An experimental evaluation of ISS is presented in Section 8.

2 A Motivating Example

The code in Figure 1(a) executes a branch in every iteration of the loop. Although in most modern architectures this branch is likely to be predicted correctly, the execution of the branch requires an additional instruction in each loop iteration and has the potential of disrupting the operation of the execution pipeline. Removing a branch from inside a loop by splitting the loop into two separate,

```
for(i=0; i<100; i++) {
  if(i < m)
    A[i] = A[i] * 2;
  else
    A[i] = A[i] * 5;
  B[i] = A[i]*A[i];
}
```

(a) Original loops

```
for(i=0; i<m; i++) {
  A[i] = A[i] * 2;
  B[i] = A[i]*A[i];
}
for(i=m; i<100; i++) {
  A[i] = A[i] * 5;
  B[i] = A[i]*A[i];
}
```

(b) Incorrect ISS

```
for(i=0; i<min(m,100); i++) {
  A[i] = A[i] * 2;
  B[i] = A[i]*A[i];
}
for(i=max(m,0); i<100; i++) {
  A[i] = A[i] * 5;
  B[i] = A[i]*A[i];
}
```

(c) Correct ISS

```
for(i=lb; i<min(m,ub); i++) {
  A[i] = A[i] * 2;
  B[i] = A[i]*A[i];
}
for(i=max(m,lb); i<ub; i++) {
  A[i] = A[i] * 5;
  B[i] = A[i]*A[i];
}
```

(d) General code generated by ISS

Fig. 1. Example of application of ISS

control flow equivalent, loops is desirable because it results in a reduction of the number of instructions executed. This splitting also produces loops with simpler control flow that are easier to optimize.

However, the code in Figure 1(b) may produce incorrect results. Consider the case in which `m > 100`. The first loop in Figure 1(b) would execute more iterations than the original loop. A similar problem occurs with the second loop if `m < 0`. Thus the correct transformation must replace these loop bounds by `min(m, 100)` and `max(m, 0)`, respectively, as shown in Figure 1(c). In general, for a loop with lower bound `lb`, upper bound `ub`, and split point `m`, the code shown in Figure 1(d) should be produced. This code transformation is called *Index-Set Splitting* (ISS).

ISS is always safe, *i.e.,* no other condition besides the structure of the loop has to be analyzed. ISS can be applied even when the bounds and the split points are not known at compile time. However, if relations between these values can be discovered at compile time, loops may be eliminated or their bodies may be simplified.

3 Index Sub-range Tree

When a loop contains two split points, ISS could be applied iteratively. For example, ISS could be applied on the original loop creating two new loops, both containing a single split point. ISS would then be applied to each of the new

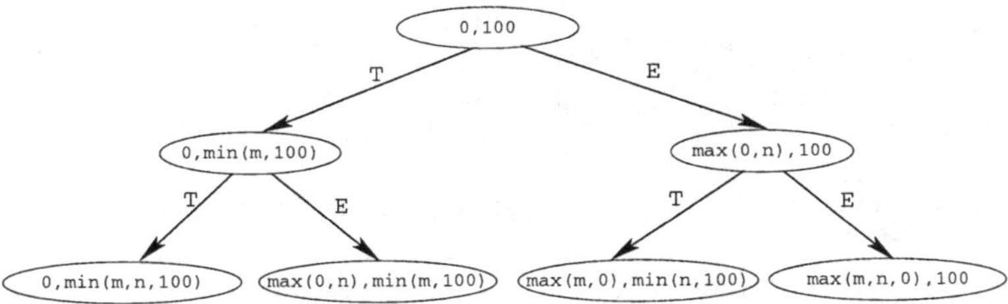

Fig. 2. Index sub-range tree (IST)

loops, creating two new SBBLs. However, iterative ISS would make estimating the potential gain of ISS and controlling the amount of code growth difficult. An alternative solution is to build an *Index Sub-range Tree* (IST). For instance, the following loop contains two split points, `m` and `n`:

```
for(i=0; i < 100; i++) {
    if(i < m)
      A[i] = A[i] * 2;
    else
      A[i] = A[i] * 5;
    B[i] = A[i]*A[i];
  }
```

The IST for the loop above is shown in Figure 2. The root of the IST corresponds to the index range for the original loop. The second level of the tree corresponds to the two loops that are created to eliminate the first test, `(i < m)`, from the loop. If ISS stops at this level of the tree, two loops, each with one branch, are created as shown in Figure 3(a). The nodes in the leaf level in the IST correspond to the four loops that have to be created in order to eliminate all split points, as shown in Figure 3(b).

Edges in the IST labeled with `T` represent the true or "`then`" branch of a test, and edges labeled with `E` represent the "`else`" branch of a test. This labeling is a convenience for the generation of code for the loop representing each node in the tree. The code generation algorithm for a node v_i starts with the original loop code, and traverses the tree from the root to v_i. At each level, if the `then` path is taken, the corresponding branch is eliminated and its `then` code is preserved. If the `else` path is taken, the `else` code is preserved. This process is referred to as the elimination of "dead" inductive branches.

Figure 4 shows the elimination of dead inductive branches to generate the loop body for the leaf node `max(0,n), min(m,100)` in the IST of Figure 2 (the second loop in Figure 3(b)). Starting at the root, to reach this leaf node, the algorithm first follows the `then` path, thus the text `if (i < m)` is eliminated but its `then` code is preserved. At the next level the `else` path is taken. Because the `else` code of the test `if(i < n)` is empty, the entire `if` statement is eliminated.

The IST correctly models nested branches. In the case of a nested branch, the inner level branch only splits the range of the nodes for which they apply. The IST for the loop with nested branch of Figure 5 is shown in Figure 6.

```
for(i=0; i < min(m,100); i++) {
    A[i] = A[i] * 2;
    if(i < n)
      A[i] = A[i] * 5;
    B[i] = A[i]*A[i];
  }
for(i=max(m, 0); i < 100; i++) {
    if(i < n)
      A[i] = A[i] * 5;
    B[i] = A[i]*A[i];
  }
```

(a) Elimination of first split point

```
for(i=0; i < min(m,n,100); i++) {
    A[i] = A[i] * 2;
    A[i] = A[i] * 5;
    B[i] = A[i]*A[i];
  }
for(i=max(0,n); i < min(m,100); i++) {
    A[i] = A[i] * 2;
    B[i] = A[i]*A[i];
  }
for(i=max(m, 0); i < min(n,100); i++) {
    A[i] = A[i] * 5;
    B[i] = A[i]*A[i];
  }
for(i=max(m,n,0); i < 100; i++) {
    B[i] = A[i]*A[i];
  }
```

(b) Elimination of second split point

Fig. 3. Handling loops with multiple split points

```
for(i=max(0,n); i < min(m,100); i++) {
    if(i < m)
      A[i] = A[i] * 2;
    if(i < n)
      A[i] = A[i] * 5;
    B[i] = A[i]*A[i];
  }
```

Fig. 4. Elimination of dead inductive branches

```
for(i=0; i < 100; i++) {
    if(i < m)
      A[i] = A[i] * 2;
    else
      if(i < n)
        A[i] = A[i]*5;
    B[i] = A[i]*A[i];
  }
```

Fig. 5. A loop with nested branches

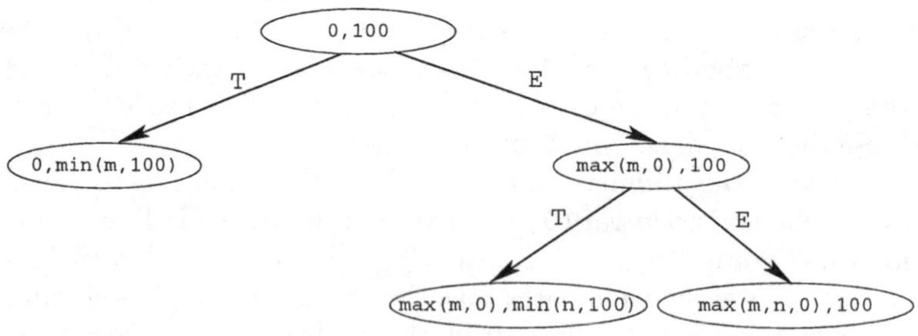

Fig. 6. Index sub-range tree for nested branches

4 Controlling Code Growth

Each index splitting requires the duplication of the loop that it splits. Therefore, there is a potential for significant code growth. If this code growth is left unchecked it may (1) prohibitively slow down the compiler by consuming compilation time that would be put to better use elsewhere and (2) generate negative instruction cache effects at run time.

To control code growth the ISS algorithm marks the root of the sub-range tree with the code size estimate for the original loop. The code size estimate is based on the number of machine instructions that would have been generated for the loop being analyzed. Each node of the subtree is annotated with an estimate of the code size that would be produced by ISS. This estimate is based on doubling the size of the loop at the current level and subtracting the code that is removed from each loop because of the splitting.

In the resulting IST each node is annotated with a code size estimate for its children. The ISS is a greedy algorithm that executes a top-down breadth first traversal of this annotated tree until either all the leaves are processed or a specified code growth budget is consumed. If the budget is exhausted, the lowest nodes that were visited in each branch of the tree represent the loops that are generated by ISS.

5 Applying ISS to Loop Fusion

A loop is normalized if it has a lower bound of 0, and an increment of 1. Thus all normalized loops have the same lower bound, increment, and direction (both loops increase their indexes). If L_i and L_j are normalized and their upper bounds are not the same, the loops are *non-conforming*. Non-conforming loops can be fused if iterations are peeled from the longer loop. However peeling iterations from a loop is not desirable in a loop fusion framework because the peeled iterations may become intervening code that, in turn, has to be moved to allow future loop fusions. For instance, to fuse loops `L1` and `L2` of Figure 7(a), two iterations of `L2` have to be peeled as shown in Figure 7(b). Once `L1` and `L2` are fused (forming `L4`) the code for the peeled iterations becomes intervening code

```
L1: for(i=0; i<n-2; i++)
        A[i] = A[i] * 2;
L2: for(j=0; j<n; j++)
        A[j] = A[j] + 3;
L3: for(k=0; k<n-2; k++)
        A[k] = A[k] - 5;
```

(a) Original loops

```
L1: for(i=0; i<n-2; i++)
        A[i] = A[i] * 2;
L2: for(j=0; j<n-2; j++)
        A[j] = A[j] + 3;
    A[n-2] = A[n-2] + 3;
    A[n-1] = A[n-1] + 3;
L3: for(k=0; k<n-2; k++)
        A[k] = A[k] - 5;
```

(b) After peeling second loop

Fig. 7. Loop peeling example

```
L4: for(i=0; i<n-2; i++) {
        A[i] = A[i] * 2;
        A[i] = A[i] + 3;
    }
    A[n-2] = A[n-2] + 3;
    A[n-1] = A[n-1] + 3;
L3: for(k=0; k<n-2; i++)
        A[k] = A[k] - 5;
```

(a) First fusion

```
L5: for(i=0; i<n-2; i++) {
        A[i] = A[i] * 2;
        A[i] = A[i] + 3;
        A[i] = A[i] - 5;
    }
    A[n-2] = A[n-2] + 3;
    A[n-1] = A[n-1] + 3;
```

(b) Last fusion

Fig. 8. Loop fusion and movement of intervening code example

```
L1: for(i=0; i<n-2; i++)
        A[i]=A[i]*2;
L2: for(j=0; j<n; j++)
        A[j]=A[j]+3;
L3: for(k=0; k<n-2; k++)
        A[k]=A[k]-5;
```

(a) Original loops

```
L4: for(i=0; i<n; i++)
      if (i < n-2)
        A[i]=A[i]*2;
        A[j]=A[j]+3;
      else
        A[j]=A[j]+3;
L3: for(k=0; k<n-2; k++)
      A[k]=A[k]-5;
```

(b) First fusion

```
L5: for(i=0; i<n; i++)
      if (i < n-2)
        if (i < n-2)
          A[i]=A[i]*2;
          A[i]=A[i]+3;
        else
          A[i]=A[i]+3;
        A[k]=A[k]-5;
      else
        if (i<n-2)
          A[i]=A[i]*2;
          A[j]=A[j]+3;
        else
          A[j]=A[j]+3;
```

(c) Second fusion

Fig. 9. Loop fusion using guards

between L4 and L3, as shown in Figure 8(a). This new intervening code has to be moved before the next fusion, as shown in Figure 8(b).

An alternative to iteration peeling is to introduce *guards* in the fused loop, as shown in Figure 9. The introduction of guards prevents the generation of additional intervening code. However, it creates fused loops with complex control flow. These complex control structures: (1) cause the dynamic execution of more branch operations, (2) may prevent future optimizations such as software pipelining, and (3) make instruction scheduling and register allocation more difficult. Thus once all fusions are performed, ISS separates loops fused with guards into individual simpler loops.

6 Runtime Bounds Check

When the relationship between the upper bounds of the two loops cannot be determined at compile time, a run-time bounds check must be performed. The

```
for(i=0; i<n; i++)
   A[i] = A[i] * 2;


for(j=0; j<m; j++)
   A[j] = A[j] * 3;
```

(a) Original loops

```
S = max(n,m);
T = min(n,m);
for(i=0; i<S; i++) {
  if (i<T) {
   A[i] = A[i] * 2;
   A[i] = A[i] * 3;
  }
  else {
   if(i<n)
     A[i] = A[i] * 2;
   else
     A[i] = A[i] * 3;
  }
}
```

(b) After Fusion

```
S=max(n,m);
T=min(n,m);
for (i=0; i < T; i++) {
   A[i] = A[i] * 2 ;
   A[i] = A[i] * 3 ;
}
for (i=max(T,0); i < n; i++)
   A[i] = A[i] * 2 ;
for (i=max(n,0); i < S; i++)
   A[i] = A[i] * 3 ;
```

(c) After ISS

Fig. 10. Run time bounds check example

fused loop combines the bodies of the two original loops for the minimum iteration count. Residuals of the two loops can then be executed depending on the iteration counts of the original loops.

For instance, assume that `n` and `m` in Figure 10(a) are not known at compile time. During loop fusion we want to generate the code shown in Figure 10(b). The upper bound of the fused loop is the maximum of the two original upper bounds. The execution of the composition of the bodies of the two loops is guarded by a test comparing with the minimum of the original bounds. Finally, the remainder iterations of the longer loop are executed. Applying ISS results in the code shown in Figure 10(c). The `max(T,0)` and `max(n,0)` in the resulting loops are necessary to preserve program semantics.

7 ISS as an Enabling Technique

The previous sections showed that ISS can be used to simplify code generated by optimizations such as loop fusion. ISS also enables optimizations that could not be performed in the presence of dynamic branches. For example, consider the loop in Figure 11(a).

This loop initializes the first 25 columns of each row in the two dimensional array `A` to zero and doubles all other entries in the array. However, `A` is traversed in column-major order while multidimensional arrays are stored in row-major order in the C programming language. Thus the data reference in this loop is extremely inefficient as it will result in a cache miss for every iteration of the inner loop (provided that the dimensions of `A` are larger than a cache line). Loop interchange, is an optimization that detects this type of memory access and interchanges the outer and inner loops to improve cache performance [3]. Unfortunately, these

```
for (int j=0; j < 10000; j++) {
  if (j < 25) {
    for (int i=0; i < 10000; i++) {
      A[i][j] = 0;
    }
  }
  else {
    for (int i=0; i < 10000; i++) {
      A[i][j] += A[i][j];
    }
  }
}
```

(a) Original Loop

```
for (int j=0; j < 25; j++) {
  for (int i=0; i < 10000; i++) {
    A[i][j] = 0;
  }
}
for (int j=25; j < 10000; j++) {
  for (int i=0; i < 10000; i++) {
    A[i][j] += A[i][j];
  }
}
```

(b) After ISS-enabled interchange

Fig. 11. Loop interchange enabled by ISS

loops cannot be interchanged because of the dynamic branch guarding the innermost loop. After ISS has removed the dynamic branch, the code shown in Figure 11(b) is generated. Loop interchange will then be able to interchange the outer loop with the inner loop, resulting in a more efficient traversal of `A`.

Using a small test program containing the above code example, the runtime went from 12.88 seconds without Index-Set Splitting to 0.40 seconds using Index-Set Splitting.[1] This performance improvement is a result of the two loops being interchanged, resulting in increased cache performance. However, this transformation would not be possible if ISS did not eliminate the dynamic branch guarding the inner loops, thereby creating perfect loop nests. This demonstrates the ability of ISS to enable other optimizations, resulting in improved performance.

8 Experimental Evaluation

This section presents an experimental evaluation of a robust implementation of ISS in the development version of the IBM XL compiler suite. When introduced by itself in a compiler suite, ISS has the potential to degrade both compilation time and execution time. The appeal of ISS is its integration with other loop optimizations, as discussed in Section 7. Compile time degradation can be attributed to the processing of additional loops by later optimizations. Runtime degradation will occur if ISS creates many loops with small iteration counts or loops that are not executed at all. When control flow reaches a loop that is not executed, it still has to execute a test for the loop terminating condition. Also, if the compiler is not able to eliminate *min* and *max* computations introduced by ISS in hot paths, performance may also degrade. A careful implementation of ISS should have only minor impact on compilation and execution time, and

[1] This test program was run on the same machine used to collect results in Section 8.

thus enable subsequent optimizations to profit from a simpler loop structure in the code. The results of this experimental study can be summarized as follows:

- A total of 107 opportunities for ISS are found in several benchmark suites before loop fusion is applied. With the application of loop fusion, the number of ISS opportunities increased to 133.
- ISS does not increase compilation time. For the SPEC 2000 suite the compilation time is reduced by 17 seconds (0.3%). For a combination of benchmarks from Perfect, Quetzal and NAS, this reduction is of 34 seconds (1.6 %).
- Execution time variations due to ISS alone are very small for the SPEC 2000 benchmark suite (less than 3%). For benchmarks in the Perfect suite this variation can be larger (from 8% slower to 8% faster), but these benchmarks have very short runtimes (less than 5 seconds).

We prototyped ISS in the development version of the IBM XL compiler suite. Benchmarks were compiled using this development compiler and run on an IBM p630 machine, equipped with two POWER4™processors, 2048 MB of memory and running AIX®5.1.

8.1 Opportunities for ISS

Table 1 shows the number of opportunities to apply ISS in standard benchmark suites. These opportunities were counted using compile-time instrumentation. The benchmark suites listed on Table 1 were tested in their entirety. The benchmarks not shown had no opportunities for ISS. An opportunity to apply ISS is a loop that contains a loop variant branch that splits the range of the loop index. The table shows that in some benchmarks there is a significant number of loops to which ISS applies even when loop fusion is not performed. This empirical result is evidence that ISS is a general technique that may benefit the implementation of optimizations in a compiler beyond the loop restructuring framework. The results also show that loop fusion creates additional ISS opportunities that can be detected and handled by our implementation.

8.2 Variations in Compilation and Execution Time

The variations in compilation time and execution time are presented in Figure 12. The bar graphs show the percentage *increase* in compilation time and the percentage *reduction* in execution time. Thus, a negative number in Figures 12(a) and 12(c) means the compilation process is taking less time when ISS is applied (*i.e.,* a larger-magnitude negative number is better). Similarly, a positive number in Figures 12(b) and 12(d) means the program execution time is lower when ISS is applied (*i.e.,* a higher positive number is better). The baseline for the comparison is an optimized compilation (at level *-O3 -qhot*) without ISS. In both the baseline and the ISS versions of the compiler all standard, and most advanced, optimizations found in a commercial compiler are performed. ISS has complex interactions with other optimizations.

Table 1. Number of times that an opportunity to apply ISS was identified

Suite	Bench-mark	No Loop Fusion ISS Opportunities	Loop Fusion Loops Fused	Loop Fusion ISS Opportunities
SPEC2000	bzip2	1	4	2
	crafty	2	7	4
	eon	1	0	1
	gap	7	4	9
	gzip	0	4	3
	perlbmk	2	0	2
	twolf	4	0	4
	vpr	1	0	1
	applu	2	4	3
	apsi	8	4	8
	equake	1	0	1
	fma3d	1	36	3
	galgel	6	21	6
	lucas	1	2	1
	sixtrack	16	26	24
Perfect	W.CS	2	1	2
	W.LG	0	2	1
	W.MT	1	1	2
	W.SR	2	4	3
	W.OC	2	0	2
	W.TF	1	4	2
	W.AP	8	4	8
	W.SD	3	4	3
	W.NA	2	4	4
	W.TI	3	4	4
Quetzal	lu	17	15	17
	rnflow	6	8	6
NAS PBN-S	BT	1	8	1
	LU	1	11	1
	SP	1	9	1
NAS PBN-H	BT	1	9	1
	FT	1	0	1
	LU	1	7	1
	SP	1	12	1
	Total	**107**		**133**

The normalization to the baseline times in the presentation of percentage variations may be misleading. Thus, for convenience, the benchmarks in Figure 12 are sorted from left to right based on their baseline compilation time. In Figure 12(a) benchmarks located to the left of `apsi` have a compilation time of less than one minute. `apsi` and `twolf` have a compilation time of less than two minutes. Similarly, in Figure 12(c) all benchmarks to the left of `W.TF` have a compilation time of less than one minute and all benchmarks to the left of

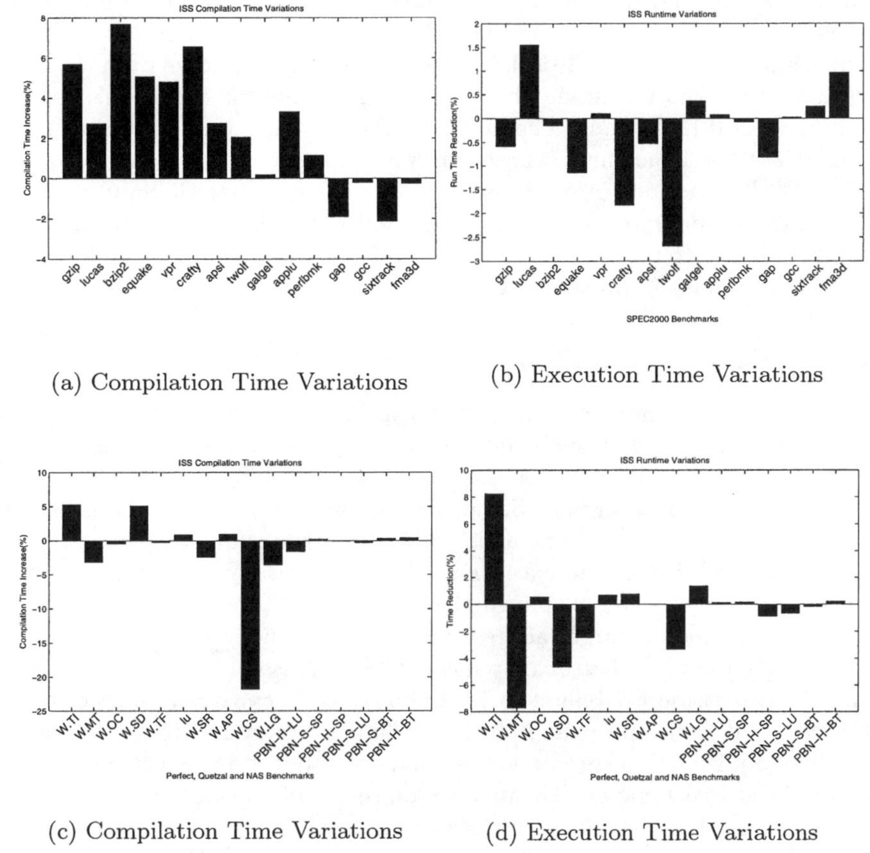

(a) Compilation Time Variations

(b) Execution Time Variations

(c) Compilation Time Variations

(d) Execution Time Variations

Fig. 12. Variation in the compilation time and run time using ISS on SPEC2000 (a and b) and on the Perfect, Quetzal and NAS (c and d) benchmark suite[2]

`W.LG` have a compilation time of less than two minutes. The compilation time of most benchmarks is not significantly impacted by ISS. `applu`'s compile time increases from 207 seconds to 214 seconds. Furthermore, compilation is faster for the benchmarks with the longest compilation times: `gap`, `gcc`, `sixtrack` and `fma3d`. The total aggregated compilation time for the SPEC2000 suite does not change significantly: it is reduced by 17 seconds (or 0.3%) when ISS is applied. Thus the simplified loop structure provided to later optimizations compensates for the time spent on ISS. Similarly, the aggregated compilation time for benchmarks listed in Figure 12(c) is reduced by 34 seconds (1.6 %) with ISS.

The variations on execution time because of ISS are very small. As shown in Figure 12(b) execution time variations are under 3% (reductions of 3.3 seconds in

[2] Measurements did not use the official SPEC tools.

lucas and fma3d and additional 3.5 seconds in crafty and 12.5 seconds in twolf are the largest time variations). While the percentage variation in run times for the benchmarks in Figure 12(d) are larger, the W.* benchmarks from the Perfect suite have very short running time. The largest runtime variation in the W.* benchmarks is 0.11 seconds. The largest variation in runtime in Figure 12(d) is for the PBN-H-SP benchmark whose runtime increases by 1.7 seconds.

The small variations in execution time is evidence that the implementation of ISS in this industry-strong compiler is robust. Further improvements to loop optimizations, currently underway, that were enabled by ISS should produce overall performance improvements.

8.3 Micro-Architecture Study

ISS does not have a significant impact on the runtime performance of the benchmarks tested. However, a large number of loops contained ISS opportunities. Thus, the question still arises as to the effects that ISS code changes have on the execution of the program. Since ISS removes loop variant branches from loops, one metric that should be affected by ISS is the number of branch mispredictions incurred during the execution of a program. By monitoring hardware performance counters, we examined the execution of several benchmarks to determine the number of target address branch mispredictions.

The study revealed that crafty has a 30% increase in the number of branch mispredictions (from 5.7 billion to 7.4 billion), while twolf's branch mispredictions increased from approximately 122 million without ISS to 1.1 billion with ISS. These additional mispredictions should contribute to the increased running time of these benchmarks. An analysis of the code generated for twolf and crafty reveals that the values of the *min* and *max* statements inserted by ISS could not be computed at compile time. The runtime execution of these *min* and *max* statements should be the cause of the performance degradation.

Significant reductions in branch mispredictions occur in apsi (82%, from 630 million to 111 million) and fma3d (31%, from 15 billion to 10 billion). However, these reductions did not translate into improved running times. A possible explanation is that the hardware was able to recover effectively from these branch mispredictions in the code generate by the baseline compiler.

9 Related Work

Loop unswitching is a similar technique to index-set splitting in the sense that a loop with a condition is converted into two non-control flow equivalent simpler loops [1]. However, as defined by Frances Allen and John Cocke, unswitching only does the conversion when the test's conditional is loop-independent [4]. In contrast index-set splitting performs multiple unswitches of tests on the value of the index variable of the loop. Another distinction between loop unswitching and ISS is that the separate loops created by unswitching are not control flow equivalent, while ISS creates control flow equivalent loops.

Loop fusion has been implemented in compilers for over twenty years [5]. Optimizations to loop fusion have been proposed by Gao [6], Ding [7, 8], McKinley [9, 10], Allen, and Kennedy [11] among others. Most research papers on loop transformations prescribe selective fusion of loops, *i.e.,* a decision about the profitability of fusing two or more loops is made during the loop fusion phase. Placing the decision about loop groupings in the fusion leads to several graph-based optimization algorithms. The IBM XL compilers take a different approach to loop restructuring: maximal loop fusion is applied first and then selective loop distribution, using several heuristics, takes place.

Allen, Callahan, and Kennedy described loop alignment as a solution to eliminate synchronization in the execution of parallel loops [5]. Alignment is used to describe the Global Alignment Network (GAN) by Padua *et al.* GAN distributes data in a multiprocessor system. For instance GAN could partition a vector and distribute its elements to several processors in the system to eliminate cross-iteration dependencies when creating fully parallel loops [12].

Yang *et al.* propose a technique to improve the order of branches based on run-time profile [13]. However, their technique does not reverse the order of loops and conditionals.

10 Conclusions

This paper introduced a new code transformation that enables the unswitching of loops that contain conditionals that are loop-dependent. Index-set splitting was implemented in the development version of the commercial IBM XL compilers and tested with four benchmark suites, including the industry standard SPEC2000 suite. The use of ISS as a convenient tool to implement a cleaner loop fusion transformation was also discussed.

ISS removes loop variant branches from inside a loop body, splitting the original loop into several loops with varying ranges. The compiler can then remove ranges that it can prove will never execute. ISS significantly impacts the generated code: the resulting loop bodies are smaller, making it easier to perform resource allocation and instruction scheduling (including modulo scheduling). ISS enables loop interchange, resulting in improved cache performance. ISS can also benefit other loop optimizations, such as loop parallelization, by removing loop-carried dependencies. On architectures where predicated instructions are available, the removal of the loop variant branch will remove the necessity of predicating the instructions that are control dependent on the branch. This will prevent aborted predicated instructions from polluting execution streams.

The static evaluation of ISS discovered opportunities for application of ISS even when loop fusion is not performed, thus indicating that ISS is a general technique that may benefit other compilers. The dynamic measurements of performance indicate that there is no significant variation in compile time and run time due to ISS alone. Thus downstream optimizations enabled by ISS shall produce overall performance improvements.

Acknowledgments

This research was supported by the IBM Center for Advanced Studies (CAS), and by a grant from the Collaborative Research Development (CRD) Grants program of the National Sciences and Engineering Council of Canada (NSERC) of Canada. Some of the infrastructure used for the experimental evaluation was acquired through a grant from the Canadian Foundation for Innovation (CFI).

Trademarks

The following terms are trademarks or registered trademarks of International Business Machines Corporation in the United States, other countries, or both: IBM, POWER4, AIX and pSeries. Other company, product, and service names may be trademarks or service marks of others.

References

1. Cooper, K.D., Torczon, L., *Engineering a Compiler.* Morgan Kaufmann (2004)
2. Blainey, B., Barton, C., Amaral, J.N., Removing impediments to loop fusion through code transformations. *Workshop on Languages and Compilers for Parallel Computing*, College Park, MD (2002)
3. Wolfe, M., *High Performance Compilers for Parallel Computing.* Addison Wesley, Longman (1994)
4. Allen, F.E., Cocke, J., A catalogue of optimizing transformations. In Rustin, R., ed., *Design and Optimization of Compilers.* Prentice-Hall (1972) 1–30
5. Allen, R., Callahan, D., Kennedy, K., Automatic decomposition of scientific programs for parallel execution. *Symposium on Principles of Programming Languages*, Munich, Germany (1987) 63–76
6. Gao, G.R., Olsen, R., Sarkar, V., Thekkath, R., Collective loop fusion for array contraction. *Workshop on Languages and Compilers for Parallel Computing*, New Haven, Conn., Berlin: Springer Verlag (1992) 281–295
7. Ding, C., Kennedy, K., The memory bandwidth bottleneck and its amelioration by a compiler. *International Parallel and Distributed Processing Symposium*, Cancun, Mexico (2000) 181–189
8. Ding, C., Kennedy, K., Improving effective bandwidth through compiler enhancement of global cache reuse. *International Parallel and Distribute Processing Symposium*, San Francisco, CA (2001)
9. Kennedy, K., McKinley, K.S., Maximizing loop parallelism and improving data locality via loop fusion and distribution. *Workshop on Languages and Compilers for Parallel Computing*, Portland, Ore., (1993) 301–320
10. Singhai, S., McKinley, K., A parameterized loop fusion algorithm for improving parallelism and cache locality. *The Computer Journal*, **40** (1997) 340–355
11. Allen, R., Kennedy, K., *Optimizing Compilers for Modern Architectures*, Morgan Kaufmann Publishers (2002)
12. Padua, D.A., Kuck, D.J., Lawrie, D.H., High-speed multiprocessors and compilation techniques, *IEEE Transactions on Computers*, **29** (1980) 763–776
13. Yang, M., Uh, G.R., Whalley, D.B., Improving performance by branch reordering. *Programming Language Design and Implementation* (PLDI), Montreal, Canada, (1998) 130–141

Age-Oriented Concurrent Garbage Collection

Harel Paz[1], Erez Petrank[1,*], and Stephen M. Blackburn[2]

[1]Dept. of Computer Science, Technion, Haifa 32000, Israel
{pharel, erez}@cs.technion.ac.il
[2]Dept. of Computer Science, ANU, Canberra ACT 0200, Australia
Steve.Blackburn@anu.edu.au

Abstract. Generational collectors are well known as a tool for shortening pause times incurred by garbage collection and for improving garbage collection efficiency. In this paper, we investigate how to best use generations with on-the-fly collectors. On-the-fly collectors run concurrently with the program threads and induce very short program pauses. Thus, the motivation for incorporating generations is focused at improving the throughput; pauses do not matter, since they are already very short. We propose a new collection approach, denoted *age-oriented* collection, for exploiting the generational hypothesis to obtain better efficiency. This approach is particularly useful when reference counting is used to collect the old generation, yielding a highly efficient and non-obtrusive on-the-fly collector. Finally, an implementation is provided demonstrating how the age-oriented collector outperforms both the non-generational and the generational collectors' efficiency.

1 Introduction

Dynamic memory management and garbage collection is arguably a key factor in supporting fast and reliable large software products. However, naive garbage collection algorithms may have undesirable effects on program behavior, most notably long pauses and reduced throughput[3]. Generational garbage collection [20, 27] ameliorates both problems by reducing the average pause times and increasing efficiency. The basic assumption underlying generational collectors design is the weak generational hypothesis: "most objects have short lifetimes". Given this hypothesis, it makes sense to concentrate the effort on young objects which are most likely to be unreachable. Generational collectors segregate objects according to their age into two or more groups called generations, and run frequent collections of the young generation. Keeping the young generation small yields frequent short collections that make room for further allocations. The older generation (or the entire heap) is collected infrequently when space is exhausted. Full heap collections require long pauses, but are infrequent.

* Research supported by the Bar-Nir Bergreen Software Technology Center of Excellence and by the IBM Faculty Partnership Award.

[3] *Throughput* is the amount of work completed in a fixed time period.

R. Bodik (Ed.): CC 2005, LNCS 3443, pp. 121–136, 2005.

If the generational hypothesis is indeed correct, we get several advantages. First, reducing pauses is achieved for most collections. Second, collections are more efficient since they concentrate on the young part of the heap where a high percentage of garbage is found. Finally, the working set size is smaller both for the program (because it repeatedly reuses the young area) and for the collector (because most of the collections trace over a smaller portion of the heap).

On-the-Fly Garbage Collection for Multiprocessors
Many garbage collectors work while program threads are stopped. On multiprocessor platforms, it is not desirable to stop the program and perform the collection in a single thread on one processor, as this leads both to long pause times and poor processor utilization. A concurrent collector runs concurrently with the program threads. The program threads may be stopped for a short time to initiate and/or finish the collection. An *on-the-fly* collector is a concurrent collector that does not need to stop the program threads simultaneously, not even for the initialization or the completion of the collection cycle. Such collectors are targeted at multiprocessors, usually employed as server machines.

1.1 This Work

In this work, we propose a new way, denoted *age-oriented* collection, to better exploit the generational hypothesis with concurrent and on-the-fly garbage collectors. Concurrent collectors already achieve short pause times and therefore the main interest in using the generational hypothesis is to try and improve the application throughput. An age-oriented collector is defined as follows.

Definition 1: *An* age-oriented *collector is a collector that*
- *always collects the entire heap (unlike generational collectors),*
- *during a collection it treats each generation differently (like generational collectors).*

Age-oriented collectors differ from generational collectors because the entire heap is always collected (infrequently). Like the generational framework, an age-oriented collector may be instantiated in various ways, depending on the choice of collector for the young generation and the choice of collector for the old generation. Reasonable instantiations should handle the young generation with a collector that is efficient with a high death rate, and handle the old generation with a collector that is efficient with lower death rates. In particular, our flagship instantiation of the generic age-oriented collector employs reference counting for the old generation and mark and sweep for the young generation. The complexity of reference counting is proportional to the number of pointer updates and the amount of unreachable space. Therefore, it can handle huge live spaces efficiently. Mark and sweep benefits from a high death rate since its complexity bottleneck is the scanning of the live objects[4].

[4] Avoiding the sweep by using copying collectors may be even better for the young generation, but concurrent versions of copying collectors are not easy to obtain.

One other instantiation that we have tried (and is now delivered) with the Jikes RVM is a parallel age-oriented collector denoted *copyMS*, employing mark and sweep for the old generation, and copying for the young generation. In this paper, we focus on the use of *concurrent* age-oriented collectors, which was most successful in practice.

We build on three previous on-the-fly collectors.

1. The on-the-fly reference counting collector of Levanoni and Petrank [19].
2. The on-the-fly mark and sweep collector of Azatchi et al. [3].
3. The *generational* on-the-fly collector of Azatchi and Petrank [4] that uses collector (2) for the young generation and collector (1) for full heap collections.

The third (generational) collector that builds on the first two collectors outperformed the original collectors. In this paper, we also use the first and second collector, but we combine them in an age-oriented manner. We show that the obtained age-oriented collector outperforms even the more efficient third (generational) collector of [4].

Organization. In Section 2, we introduce the age-oriented framework and our proposed instantiation. In Section 3, an overview of the original reference counting collector [19] is presented. An overview of the age-oriented collector algorithm is introduced in Section 4. Performance results are described in Section 5. Related work is discussed in Section 6. We conclude in Section 7.

2 Age-Oriented Collection: Motivation and Overview

Although generational collectors reduce pauses and improve efficiency, they also impose some overhead. One major overhead is the manipulation of inter-generational pointers. These are pointers that point from the old generation to the young generation. If the young generation is collected while the old generation is not, these pointers must be accounted for: they may be the only evidence that a young object is reachable. Keeping record of all inter-generational pointers and using them as roots for the young generation collection poses an overhead. Many papers investigate reducing this overhead via efficient recording methods (e.g., card marking). A second overhead of generational collection is the frequent initiation of young generation collections, which repeatedly involves synchronization with the program threads, marking of all roots, etc. Using a large young generation implies less frequent collections and better throughput, but also longer pauses (for young generation collections).

Previous on-the-fly generational collectors [14, 4] have used a fixed sized young generation. Using a small fixed sized young generation is useful for the stop-the-world framework as they shorten most pause times. However, the size of the young generation does not determine the pause times with on-the-fly collectors[5]. Hence, we can use a larger young generation in order to achieve better throughput. It has been noted in [2, 7] that the larger the young generation is, the more efficient the generational collector gets.

Age-oriented collectors, i.e., collectors which follow definition 1, have the following advantages over generational collectors. Such collectors use the largest possible young generation as they collect the old generation each time to make more young generation space. Age-oriented collectors may usually avoid recording inter-generational pointers because the entire heap is collected and inter-generational pointers may be determined during the collection. Finally, age-oriented collectors perform fewer collections than a generational collector. All these properties potentially make an age-oriented collector more efficient than a generational collector, when instantiated appropriately. Let us now motivate reference counting for use with age-oriented collection by making a couple of observations.

First, there is a difference between using tracing and using reference counting to collect the old generation. A tracing collection work is proportional to the number of reachable objects, hence there is a (relatively) fixed cost for each full collection. Delaying a tracing collection of an old generation as far as possible is desirable as it decreases the accumulated garbage collection work. On the other hand, the work of reference-counting is proportional to the mutators' work and to the number of dead objects. This work is accumulative. Thus, delaying a reference-counting collection does not decrease the overall garbage collection work (it only delays and accumulates it).

A second point to note is that on-the-fly collections are triggered way before the heap gets exhausted in order to let the collection terminate concurrently *before* the free space in the heap is exhausted. If the heap does get exhausted, concurrency is lost as the program threads must wait for the collector to finish before they can next allocate. Mutators' halting yields poor processor utilization: only one processor actually works (while the rest are idle).

Putting the above two observations together we get a good match for using reference counting with the old generation in an age-oriented collector. First, when running a collection on-the-fly we may need to trigger it more frequently to let it terminate on time. Furthermore, whereas a generational collector collects the young generation repeatedly in order to defer as much as possible the collection of the old generation, an age-oriented collector does not make such a deferring attempt. When reference counting is used, running a bit more frequent old collections because of the concurrent setting or due to the age-oriented framework, does not hurt the throughput.

To summarize this motivational discussion with an overview, we instantiate the age-oriented generic collector by choosing reference counting for the old

[5] We normally measure pauses induced by on-the-fly collectors when the number of program threads is smaller than the number of CPU's. If the number of threads exceeds the number of processors, than large pause are induced by threads losing the CPU to one another. The lengths of such pauses depend on the operating system scheduler and is not attributed to the garbage collector.

generation and mark and sweep for the young generation. We build on a previous generational collector of [4]. The underlying techniques come from [19], which is reviewed in the next section.

3 Reviewing the Original Reference-Counting Collector

Section 4 describes our age-oriented collector. For completeness, we start with a review of the sliding-views reference-counting collector [19]. The age-oriented collector is constructed by adding some simple modifications to this collector.

The sliding-views collector [19] is an on-the-fly collector. It is a reference-counting collector that eliminates many of the reference count updates by the following coalescing strategy. Consider a pointer slot p that is assigned the values $o_0, o_1, o_2, \ldots, o_n$ between two garbage collections. All previous reference counting collectors execute $2n$ reference count updates for these assignments: RC(o_0)−−, RC(o_1)++, RC(o_1)−−, RC(o_2)++, ..., RC(o_n)++. However, only two updates are required: RC(o_0)−− and RC(o_n)++.

Suppose the reference counts we have represent the heap view at the previous collection time and we would like to update them for the current collection time. In light of the observation above, it suffices to do the following. For each pointer p that was modified between the two collections:

1. find p's referent in the previous collection time (corresponding to o_0 above) and decrement its reference count, and
2. find p's referent in the current collection time (corresponding to o_n above) and increment its reference count.

It remains to devise a mechanism that records all pointers that were modified after the previous collection. Furthermore, this mechanism should provide, for each such pointer, its referent at the previous collection time and its referent at the current collection time. To achieve this, a program thread maintains a local buffer, denoted *Updates* buffer, in which all updated pointers are logged. For efficiency, all pointers of an updated object are logged rather than each single updated pointer. To make sure that each object is logged only once, a *dirty* bit per object is employed to signify whether the object is logged. During a collection, all objects are marked not dirty. Then, at the first time a thread modifies an object, it marks the object dirty and it logs all its pointers' previous referents in the *Updates* buffer. Further modification to the (dirty) object will not be recorded. When a new collection begins, the *Updates* buffer provides all the information required to update the reference counts: it lists all modified pointers, and keeps a record of their values before the first modification (these are the referents of these pointers in the previous collection time). In the current collection, the collector finds the current referent of the pointer on the heap.

A special case of modified objects are newly created objects. Such objects do not have referents at the previous collection time since they did not exist then. Newly created objects are created dirty (to prevent logging in the *Updates* buffer) and are logged (upon creation) in a special buffer, denoted the *YoungObjects* buffer. The collector increments the reference counts of their referents at the current collection time, but does not need to do any related decrements.

An example appears in Figure 1. It depicts the heap and the buffers in two subsequent collections, where the view of the former collection appears on the left side. The *YoungObjects* buffer contains the six objects that were created after the last collection. Between the two collections a pointer in A was modified to reference C. Hence, A was logged in the *Updates* buffer, together with its previous referent B (which appears next to A in a smaller font). The collector uses this information in the following way. It iterates over the objects logged in the *Updates* buffer and finds A. It decrements the reference count of B, which is A's descendant in the previous collection, and it increments the reference count of C, A's descendant at the current collection time. It then iterates over the six

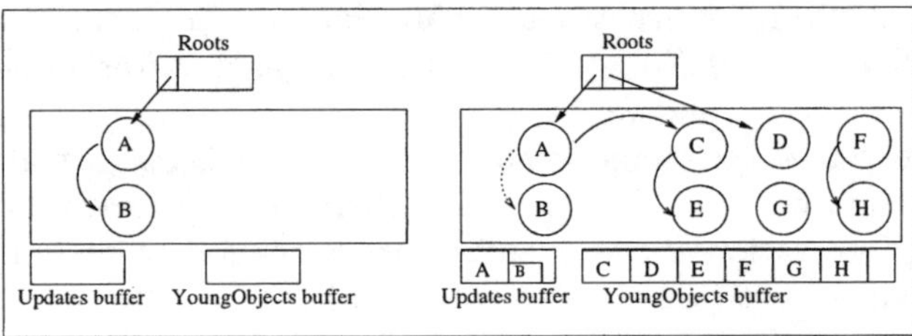

Fig. 1. An example: heap and buffers view in 2 subsequent collections

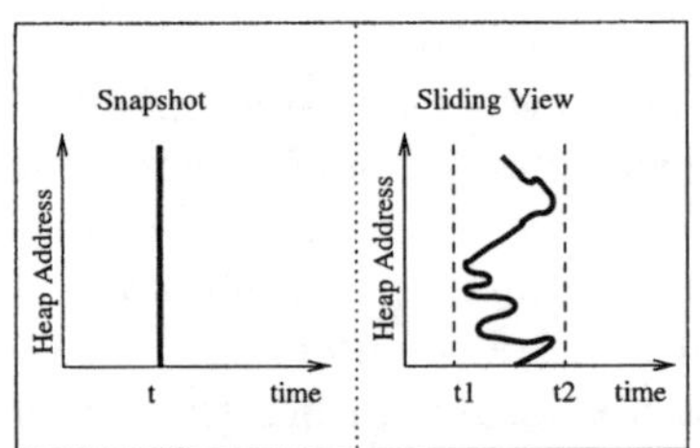

Fig. 2. A snapshot view at time t vs. a sliding view at interval $[t1,t2]$

X Y Z
Y is recorded into sliding view.
(a)
Y is modified to reference Z.
(b)
X is set to null.
(c)
X is recorded into sliding view.
(d)

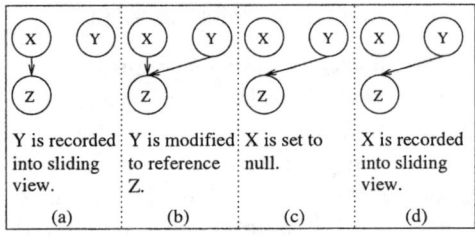

Fig. 3. An example in which the reachability of Object Z is missed by a sliding view

```
Roots := programRoots ∪ SnoopedObjects
for each object logged in Updates do
        - decrement rc of its previous sliding-view descendants
        - increment rc of its current sliding-view descendants
for each object logged in YoungObjects do
        increment rc of its current sliding-view descendants
reclaim objects with zero rc which do not belong to Roots recursively
```

Fig. 4. Reference-Counting: Collection Cycle

objects in the *YoungObjects* buffer. It increments the reference counts of their descendants at the current collection time. For example, for the object F the reference count of H is incremented.

Virtually, the above algorithm uses a snapshot of the heap. A snapshot at time t is a copy of the content of each object in the heap at time t. To get an on-the-fly collector, the program threads are not stopped simultaneously and thus a snapshot cannot be used. Instead, a collection works with a *sliding view* of the heap. A sliding view of the heap is associated with a time interval [$t1$,$t2$] (rather than a single point in time). It provides the content of each object in the heap at an arbitrary time t, satisfying $t_1 \leq t \leq t_2$. In contrast to a snapshot, objects are not all viewed at the same time. Figure 2 depicts the difference between a sliding view and a snapshot. Using a sliding view for collection introduces a correctness danger: objects reachability may not be reflected correctly in the view. Figure 3 shows such example, where the reachability of Z is missed in the sliding view, although it is reachable. A solution to this problem is a *snooping* mechanism. The *snooping* mechanism (via the write-barrier) records any object to which a new reference is created in the heap during the time interval [$t1$,$t2$]. Snooped objects are considered roots, and are not reclaimed in the current collection cycle.

The main phases of the sliding views algorithm (a simplified version) are presented in Figure 4. Further details are irrelevant for this paper and can be found in the original paper [19].

4 The Age-Oriented Collector

This section presents our age-oriented collector. Full details (including pseudo-code) are omitted for lack of space, and appear in our technical report [22]. Our age-oriented collector extends the reference counting collector of [19] by using it for the old generation and adding a tracing collection for the young generation. The tracing collection is in the spirit of the tracing collector in [3].

The original reference counting collector of [19] iterates over all the young objects recorded in the *YoungObjects* buffer, incrementing the reference counts of their descendants, only to find out later that most of them are dead (assuming the weak generational hypothesis). Thus, it then decrements the reference counts of all their descendants (before deleting them). The source of this inefficiency is that the collector does not know in advance which of the young objects are dead, and which are reachable. The age-oriented collector avoids this problem by wisely detecting the roots of the young generation and tracing only the small number of reachable young objects, updating the reference counts of reachable young objects and their descendants during the trace.

The main phases of the age-oriented collector (ignoring irrelevant on-the-fly issues) are presented in Figure 5. As with generational collectors, one needs to identify all young objects directly referenced by the program roots and by old objects. We denote these objects *youngGenerationRoots*. The age-oriented collector obtains these roots for free from the data structure of the original collector. An old object that references a young object must have been modified after the pre-

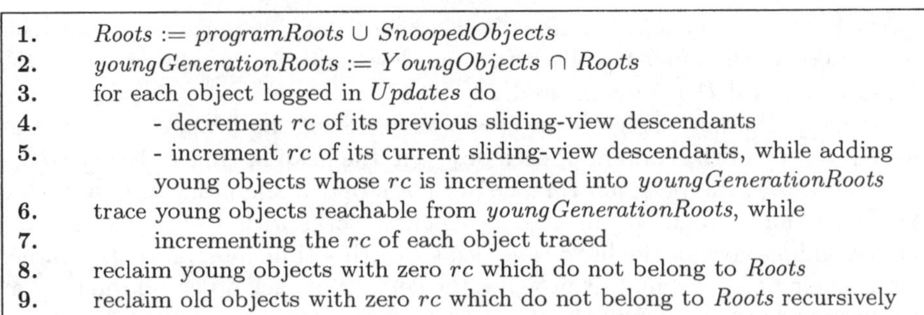

```
1.  Roots := programRoots ∪ SnoopedObjects
2.  youngGenerationRoots := YoungObjects ∩ Roots
3.  for each object logged in Updates do
4.      - decrement rc of its previous sliding-view descendants
5.      - increment rc of its current sliding-view descendants, while adding
        young objects whose rc is incremented into youngGenerationRoots
6.  trace young objects reachable from youngGenerationRoots, while
7.      incrementing the rc of each object traced
8.  reclaim young objects with zero rc which do not belong to Roots
9.  reclaim old objects with zero rc which do not belong to Roots recursively
```

Fig. 5. Age-Oriented: Collection Cycle

vious collection, as the young object did not exist earlier. All modified objects are logged in the *Updates* buffer. After locating the roots, the tracing of the young generation uses the current sliding views as explained in Section 3. Dead young objects are freed via sweep on the *YoungObjects* buffer and dead old objects are freed as usual by recursive freeing of the reference counting algorithm.

Example. We use Figure 1 to present the principles of the age-oriented collector. The previous sliding view is depicted on the left side, and the current sliding view is depicted on the right. The roots are depicted above the heap and the old generation (containing A and B) is visibly separated on the left side of the heap from the young generation, which is depicted on the right side of the heap. When the age-oriented collector scans the objects logged in the *Updates* buffer (line 3 in the pseudo-code of Figure 5), it finds A. It decrements the reference count of B, its descendant in the previous sliding view (line 4 in the pseudo-code), and increments the reference count of C, its current sliding-view values (line 5). The incremented values that belong to the young generation (C) are considered roots for the young generation tracing (line 5). An additional young generation root is D which is directly referenced by the program roots (line 2). Hence, the age-oriented collector traces the young generation from C and D (line 6). In comparison, the original reference counting collector would have iterated over the six young objects incrementing the reference counts of their current sliding view, only to find out later that the work spent on F, G, and H was redundant.

As with any reference counting collector, this age-oriented algorithm cannot reclaim cyclic data structures in the old generation (cyclic structures in the young generation are collected immediately). To reclaim such structures, the tracing sliding view algorithm of [3] is run infrequently on the full heap.

Since the on-the-fly collector we build on [19] does not move objects, the partitioning to young and old generations is logical (as in [10, 14, 4]). A bit per object indicates whether the object is young or old. If a young object survives a collection, it is considered old in the next collection.

The new collector retains the characteristics of the original collector. In particular, it is adequate for a multithreaded environment and a multiprocessor platform, it retains the short pauses of the original collectors, and it has the potential to be efficient (which indeed is shown in the measurements below).

5 Platforms, Benchmarks, and Measurements

An Implementation for Java. The age-oriented collector was implemented in the Jikes RVM [1] (using the baseline compiler of version 2.0.3), a research Java virtual machine. The collector is suitable for any other JVM as well.

Platform and Benchmarks. We run measurements on a 4-way IBM Netfinity 8500R server with a 550MHz Intel Pentium III Xeon processor and 2GB of physical memory. The benchmarks used were the SPECjvm98 benchmark suite and the SPECjbb2000 benchmark (described in [24]). The multithreaded SPECjbb2000 benchmark is more important, as the SPECjvm98 are mostly single-threaded and our algorithm, being on-the-fly, is targeted at multithreaded programs running on multi-processors. SPECjbb2000 runs in a single JVM in which threads represent terminals in a warehouse. It is run with one terminal per warehouse, thus, the number of warehouses signifies the number of threads.

Testing Procedure. We used the benchmark suite using the test harness, performing standard automated runs of all the benchmarks in the suite. Each benchmark was run five times for each of the JVM's involved (each implementing a different collector). The average of this 5 runs is reported. Finally, each JVM was run on varying heap sizes. For the SPECjvm98 suite, we started with a 24MB heap size and extended the sizes by 8MB increments until a final large size of 96MB. For SPECjbb2000 we started from 256MB heap size and extended by 64MB increments until a final large size of 704MB. It should be noted that Jikes requires larger sizes than other JVMs because the same heap is used both for the application and for the data structures of the JVM itself.

The Compared Collectors. The age-oriented collector was tested against 3 collectors. First, against the original reference counting collector [19], denoted *the original collector*. Second, against the generational collector of [4], denoted *the generational collector*. And finally, against the Jikes parallel stop-the-world mark and sweep collector. Recall that the second (generational) collector of [4] is a collector that builds on exactly the same two collectors of [19, 3], but it combines them in the standard generational manner, whereas we combined them according to the age-oriented framework.

5.1 Comparison with Related On-the-Fly Collectors

SPECjbb2000. In Figure 6 we report the throughput results for the generational collector and the age-oriented collector against the original collector with the SPECjbb2000 benchmark. With 1-3 warehouses, the collectors do not differ

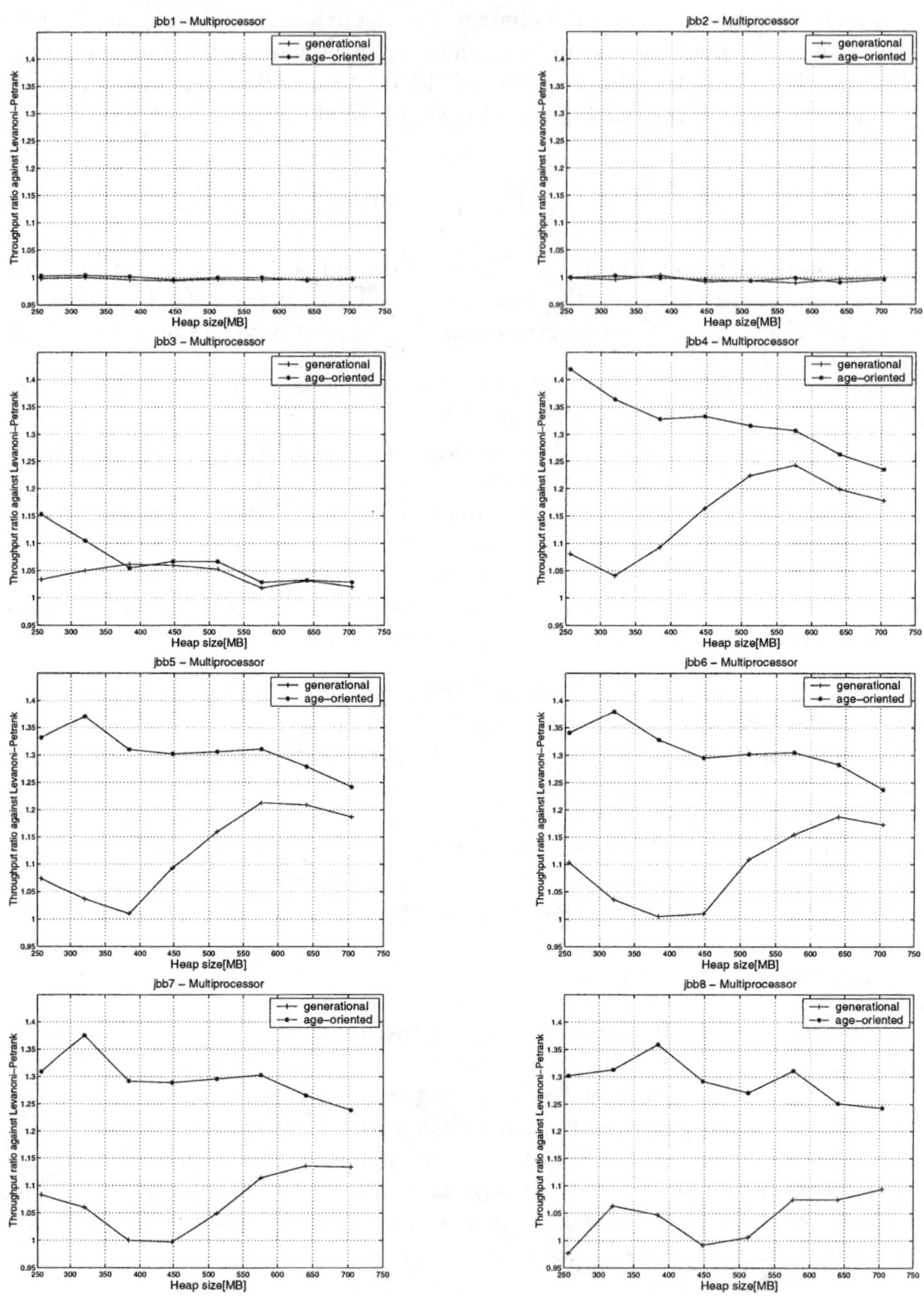

Fig. 6. SPECjbb2000 on a multiprocessor: throughput ratio of the generational and the age-oriented collector for 1-8 warehouses. The higher the ratio, the better the measured collector performs compared to the original reference counting collector. jbb*i* stands for running with *i* terminals, i.e., *i* program threads

much, as they run concurrently on a spare processor (on our 4-way machine), and usually manage to handle all their work while mutators are running. With 4-8 warehouses, the collector shares a processor with the program threads (yet, given a higher priority). Thus, the efficiency of the collector influences the throughput of the whole system. The results show that the age-oriented collector substantially outperforms the generational collector, which already performs better than the original collector. The superiority of the age-oriented collector is usually higher with (relatively) small heaps where more garbage collections are required. The generational collector is less efficient on tight heaps, since full collections cannot be postponed much. The improvements of the age-oriented are less visible with larger heaps simply because there are fewer collections, and less time spent on collections.

SPECjvm98. Figure 7 presents comparison of the age-oriented collector with the original collector and with the generational collector over all the suite's benchmarks[6]. When running the SPECjvm98 benchmarks on a multiprocessor, the collector thread can run on a designated processor and hardly influence the throughput[7]. The results show that the age-oriented collector performs slightly better than both the original collector and the generational collector. Large variations in performance are especially noticeable with _213_javac. The reason for these fluctuations is that _213_javac creates many garbage cycles in the old generation. All three collectors (the age-oriented, the generational and the original) rely on a backup tracing collector to collect these cycles. Collection of these cycles is triggered at irregular times resulting in the observed fluctuations.

5.2 Comparison to a Stop-the-World Collector

Using an on-the-fly collector leads to extremely short pause times, but has a throughput cost. To measure this cost, we have compared the performance of the age-oriented collector against the Jikes parallel stop-the-world mark and sweep collector. In this comparison, the multithreaded SPECjbb2000 was run on a 4-way platform, and SPECjvm98 benchmarks were run on a uniprocessor. The results, appearing in figure 8, show that unless the heap is tight (and then the mutators exhaust the heap before the concurrent collector is done) the overhead incurred by running the collector concurrently is up to 10%. Obtaining short pauses normally require a pay in the throughput. A 10% throughput reduction is considered a small pay for a two orders of magnitude reduction in the pause times (see pause time measurements in Section 5.3 below). The tight conditions highlight the advantage of parallel collectors in this setting. Parallel collectors always exploit all CPUs, while our on-the-fly collector uses only one processor while all program threads wait for free space to allocate. An exception is seen

[6] Measurements of _222_mpegaudio and _201_compress are not presented. _222_mpegaudio does not perform meaningful allocation activity. _201_compress heavily depends on a tracing collector as it creates substantial garbage cycles, so its measurements are not relevant for a comparison to a reference counting collector.

[7] Further uniprocessor results are given in our technical report [22].

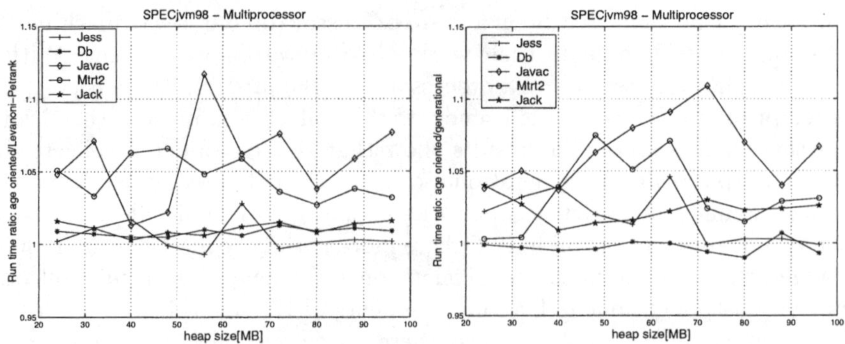

Fig. 7. SPECjvm98 on a multiprocessor: run-time ratio of the age-oriented collector compared to the original collector (left) and compared to the generational collector (right). The higher the ratio, the better the age-oriented collector performs compared to the other collector

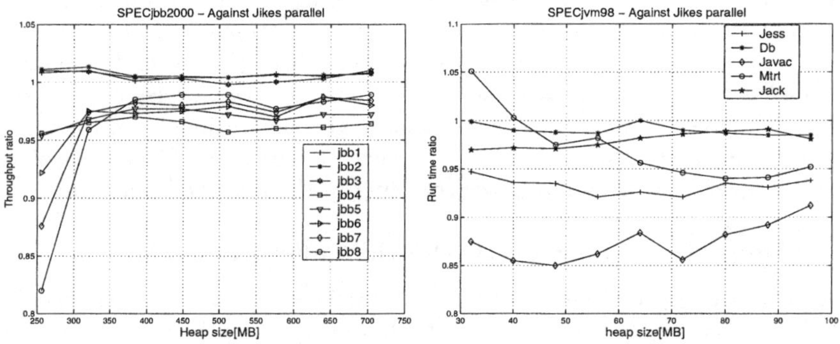

Fig. 8. SPECjbb2000 on a multiprocessor (left) and SPECjvm98 on a uniprocessor (right): comparison against Jikes parallel mark and sweep collector. The higher the ratio, the better the age-oriented collector performs compared to Jikes collector

with the _213_javac benchmark. This benchmark creates cycles that are promoted to the old generation and die there. Since the age-oriented collector employs reference-counting with the old-generation, it does not collect these garbage cycles, causing frequent garbage collection invocations.

5.3 Pause Times

Table 1 presents the maximum pause times of the age-oriented collector and Jikes parallel collector. Pauses were measured with a 64MB heap for SPECjvm98 benchmarks, and a 256MB heap for SPECjbb2000 with 1, 2, and 3 warehouses. For this number of threads, no thread gets swapped out, and so pauses are due to the garbage collection only. If we run more program threads, large pause

Table 1. Maximum pause time in milliseconds

Maximum pause time(ms)	compress	jess	db	javac	mtrt	jack	jbb-1	jbb-2	jbb-3
Age-oriented	1.0	1.7	1.1	2.1	1.4	1.2	1.1	1.4	1.9
Jikes Parallel	195	261	188	643	225	376	322	417	511

times (whose lengths depend on the operating system scheduler) appear because threads lose the CPU to other threads.

The maximum pause time of 2.1ms, measured for the age-oriented collector, is two orders of magnitude shorter than that of Jikes parallel collector. The length of the age-oriented pause time is dominated by the time it takes to scan the roots of a single thread (occurring in one of the handshakes). This operation also dominates the pause time of the previous on-the-fly collectors [19, 4], and thus their pause times are similar (see [19, 4] for specific measurements of pause times for these collectors). Hence, the age-oriented collector achieves a significant throughput improvement over the original reference counting collector and over the generational collectors, while retaining the short pause times.

It is important to note that the pauses induced by the collector do not happen frequently. If pauses of 2ms occurred once every 3ms, then pause times would loose their meaning and we should look at mutator's minimum utilization (MMU). However, in our case, the pauses form a negligible part of the collection cycle, and are split far apart from each other.

6 Related Work

Generational garbage collection was introduced by Lieberman and Hewitt [20], and the first published implementation was by Ungar [27]. Both algorithms aimed to reduce the running time of most collections by focusing on the young objects.

Appel [2] presented a generational collector with variable young generation size: all its free space is devoted to the young generation. When the young generation becomes full, it collects the young generation, copying surviving objects to the older generation, and reducing the young generation size by this space. Major collections are executed only when the old generation occupies the entire heap. We push this idea further by proposing to always collect the old generation together with the young generation to make room for a large young generation.

Demers, et al. [10] presented a generational collector which does not move objects, hence appropriate for conservative garbage collection. They partition the heap logically (instead of physically separating between generations) by keeping a bit per object indicating whether it is young or old. We adopt this idea. However, their collector is not concurrent.

The study of on-the-fly garbage collectors was initiated by Steele and Dijkstra, et al. [25, 26, 11] and continued in a series of papers culminating in [14, 5, 17, 19, 3]. The advantage of an on-the-fly collector over a parallel collector and other types of concurrent collectors [6, 23, 9, 15, 16, 18], is that it avoids the operation of stopping all the program threads and incurs very short pauses.

Incorporations of generational collectors into on-the-fly collectors were done by Domani et al. [14], and by Azatchi and Petrank [4][8]. Both works employed fixed-sized young generation and both showed that combining generations with on-the-fly collectors may be useful. Domani et al. used the Doligez-Leroy-Gonthier mark and sweep collector [13, 12] both for the collection of the young generation and the collection of the full heap. The generational collector of [4] used the same basic collectors that we use here for the age-oriented collector. Results show that using these collectors for an age-oriented collection is more efficient than using them for a generational collection.

Blackburn and McKinley [8] implemented a uniprocessor stop-the-world generational collector with reference counting for the old generation and copying for the young. Their goal was to shorten the pauses a stop-the-world reference counting incurs, while obtaining good throughput. They run part of the old generation collection together with the young collection in order to avoid the need for a full collection that requires a long pause. The (controlled) pause times they obtain are an order of magnitude larger than those obtained by on-the-fly collectors.

7 Conclusion

We have proposed a framework of garbage collectors called age-oriented collectors. These collectors exploit the generational hypothesis in a different manner than standard generational collectors. Instead of running frequent young generation collections, the entire heap is collected infrequently, but young objects are treated differently from old objects. An age-oriented collector does not need to record inter-generational pointers, and avoids the overhead of initiating frequent young generation collections. The most fitting use of age-oriented collectors is with on-the-fly collectors and particularly when the old generation is collected via reference counting.

We have designed and implemented an instantiation of an age-oriented collector, based on the reference counting collector of [19] and the tracing collector of [3], in which reference counting collects the old objects and mark and sweep collects the young objects. This age-oriented collector was implemented on the Jikes RVM. Our measurements show that this collector maintains the short pauses of the original collectors and significantly outperforms both the original reference counting collector as well as the generational variant.

Acknowledgements. We thank Elliot (Hillel) Kolodner for helpful discussions, and Michael Philippsen for the numerous helpful remarks on improving the readability of this manuscript.

[8] A partial incorporation of generations with an on-the-fly collector was used by Doligez, Leroy, and Gonthier [13, 12]. The whole scheme depends on the fact that many objects in ML are immutable. This is not true for Java and other imperative languages. Furthermore, the collection of the young generation is not concurrent.

References

1. Bowen Alpern, C. R. Attanasio, Anthony Cocchi, Derek Lieber, Stephen Smith, Ton Ngo, John J. Barton, Susan Flynn Hummel, Janice C. Sheperd, and Mark Mergen. Implementing Jalapeño in Java. In *ACM Conference on Object-Oriented Systems, Languages and Applications*, 34(10), pages 314–324, 1999.
2. Andrew W. Appel. Simple generational garbage collection and fast allocation. *Software Practice and Experience*, 19(2):171–183, 1989.
3. Hezi Azatchi, Yossi Levanoni, Harel Paz, and Erez Petrank. An on-the-fly mark and sweep garbage collector based on sliding view. In OOPSLA [21].
4. Hezi Azatchi and Erez Petrank. Integrating generations with advanced reference counting garbage collectors. In *Proceedings of the 12th International Conference on Compiler Construction, CC 2003*, volume 2622 of *LNCS*, pages 185–199, 2003.
5. David F. Bacon, Clement R. Attanasio, Han B. Lee, V. T. Rajan, and Stephen Smith. Java without the coffee breaks: A nonintrusive multiprocessor garbage collector. In *Proceedings of Conference on Prog. Lang. Design and Impl.*, 2001.
6. Henry G. Baker. List processing in real-time on a serial computer. *Communications of the ACM*, 21(4):280–94, 1978.
7. Stephen M. Blackburn, Richard Jones, Kathryn S. McKinley, and J. Eliot B. Moss. Beltway: Getting around garbage collection gridlock. In *Proceedings of SIGPLAN 2002 Conference on Prog. Lang. Design and Impl.*, pages 153–164, 2002.
8. Stephen M. Blackburn and Kathryn S. McKinley. Ulterior reference counting: Fast garbage collection without a long wait. In OOPSLA [21].
9. Hans-Juergen Boehm, Alan J. Demers, and Scott Shenker. Mostly parallel garbage collection. *ACM SIGPLAN Notices*, 26(6):157–164, 1991.
10. Alan Demers, Mark Weiser, Barry Hayes, Daniel G. Bobrow, and Scott Shenker. Combining generational and conservative garbage collection: Framework and implementations. In *17 ACM Symp. on Prin. of Prog. Lang.*, pages 261–269, 1990.
11. Edsgar W. Dijkstra, Leslie Lamport, A. J. Martin, C. S. Scholten, and E. F. M. Steffens. On-the-fly garbage collection: An exercise in cooperation. *Communications of the ACM*, 21(11):965–975, November 1978.
12. Damien Doligez and Georges Gonthier. Portable, unobtrusive garbage collection for multiprocessor systems. In *21 ACM Symp. on Principles of Prog. Lang.*, 1994.
13. Damien Doligez and Xavier Leroy. A concurrent generational garbage collector for a multi-threaded implementation of ML. In *the Twentieth ACM Symp. on Principles of Prog. Lang.*, pages 113–123. January 1993.
14. Tamar Domani, Elliot Kolodner, and Erez Petrank. A generational on-the-fly garbage collector for Java. In *Proceedings of SIGPLAN 2000 Conference on Programming Languages Design and Implementation.*
15. Toshio Endo, Kenjiro Taura, and Akinori Yonezawa. A scalable mark-sweep garbage collector on large-scale shared-memory machines. In *Proceedings of High Performance Computing and Networking (SC'97)*, 1997.
16. Christine Flood, Dave Detlefs, Nir Shavit, and Catherine Zhang. Parallel garbage collection for shared memory multiprocessors. In *Usenix Java Virtual Machine Research and Technology Symposium (JVM '01)*, April 2001.
17. Richard L. Hudson and J. Eliot B. Moss. Sapphire: Copying GC without stopping the world. In *Joint ACM Java Grande — ISCOPE 2001 Conference.*
18. Elliot K. Kolodner and Erez Petrank. Parallel copying garbage collection using delayed allocation. In *Parallel Processing Letters*, volume 14, June 2004.
19. Yossi Levanoni and Erez Petrank. An on-the-fly reference counting garbage collector for Java. In *ACM Conf. on Object-Oriented Systems, Lang. & Appl.*, 2001.

20. Henry Lieberman and Carl E. Hewitt. A real-time garbage collector based on the lifetimes of objects. *Communications of the ACM*, 26(6):419–429, 1983.
21. *OOPSLA'03 ACM Conf. on Object-Oriented Systems, Lang. & Applications*, 2003.
22. Harel Paz and Erez Petrank. Age-oriented garbage collection. Technical Report CS-2003-08, Technion, Israel, October 2003. http://www.cs.technion.ac.il/users/wwwb/cgi-bin/tr-info.cgi?2003/CS/CS-2003-08.
23. Tony Printezis and David Detlefs. A generational mostly-concurrent garbage collector. In Tony Hosking, editor, *Proceedings of the Second International Symp. on Memory Management*, volume 36(1) of *ACM SIGPLAN Notices*, October 2000.
24. SPEC Benchmarks. Standard Performance Evaluation Corporation. http://www.spec.org/, 1998,2000.
25. Guy L. Steele. Multiprocessing compactifying garbage collection. *Communications of the ACM*, 18(9):495–508, September 1975.
26. Guy L. Steele. Corrigendum: Multiprocessing compactifying garbage collection. *Communications of the ACM*, 19(6):354, June 1976.
27. David M. Ungar. Generation scavenging: A non-disruptive high performance storage reclamation algorithm. *ACM SIGPLAN Notices*, 19(5):157–167, April 1984.

Optimizing C Multithreaded Memory Management Using Thread-Local Storage

Yair Sade[1], Mooly Sagiv[2], and Ran Shaham[3]

[1] Tel-Aviv University
{sadeyair, msagiv}@post.tau.ac.il *
[2] Tel-Aviv University
[3] IBM Haifa Laboratories
rans@il.ibm.com

Abstract. Dynamic memory management in C programs can be rather costly. Multithreading introduces additional synchronization overhead of C memory management functions (`malloc`, `free`). In order to reduce this overhead, we extended Hoard — a state of the art memory allocator with the ability to allocate thread-local storage. Experimental results using the tool show runtime saving of up to 44% for a set of memory management benchmarks.

To allow transparent usage of thread-local storage, we develop a compile-time algorithm, which conservatively detects allocation sites that can be replaced by thread-local allocations. Our static analysis is sound, i.e., every detected thread-local storage is indeed so, although we may fail to identify opportunities for allocating thread-local storage. Technically, we reduce the problem of estimating thread-local storage to the problem of escape analysis and provide an efficient escape analysis for C. We solve the problem of escape analysis for C using existing points-to analysis algorithms. Our solution is parameterized by the points-to information. We empirically evaluated the solution with two different methods for computing points-to information. The usage of scalable points-to analysis algorithms and the fact that our reduction is efficient, guarantees that our static analysis technique is scalable.

1 Introduction

This paper addresses the problem of reducing the overhead of memory management functions in multithreaded C applications by combining efficient allocation libraries with compile-time static pointer analysis techniques.

1.1 Multithreaded Memory Management Performance

Memory allocation in C programs can be costly in general; multithreading functions add additional complexity. Memory management implementations in C usually consist of a global heap. The `malloc` function acquires a memory block from the global

* Supported in part by a grant from the Israeli Academy of Science.

R. Bodik (Ed.): CC 2005, LNCS 3443, pp. 137–155, 2005.

heap and the `free` function returns the memory block into the heap. The global heap data-structure is shared among the process threads. In order to protect this shared data-structure from concurrent accesses and race conditions, accesses are synchronized by locking primitives such as mutexes or critical-sections. This synchronization may degrade performance due to the following reasons: (i) on multithreaded environments, threads that call memory management functions concurrently are blocked by the locks; (ii) once a thread is blocked, an expensive context-switch occurs; (iii) the lock primitives can have an overhead even if no block occurs.

On SMP machines the problem can become acute and cause an application performance bottleneck. It can happen when threads that are executed on different processors call memory management functions concurrently. Those threads are blocked by the lock primitives and the blocked processors become unutilized. This reduces the application parallelism and may reduce throughput.

1.2 Existing Solutions

There are two main approaches for improving the performance of memory management routines in multithreaded applications: (i) runtime solutions, and (ii) programmable solutions. Runtime solutions usually provide an alternative multithreaded-efficient memory management implementation [8, 11, 21]. In programmable solutions, the programmer develops or exploits application-specific custom allocators, for example memory-pools or thread-local arenas as in [1].

Runtime approaches only mitigate performance degradation — even the most efficient memory management implementations have a synchronization overhead. In programmable approaches, the programmer has to design the application to work with a custom allocator, which is not an easy task on large-scale applications, and almost impossible on existing systems. Moreover, programmable solutions are error prone and might cause new bugs. Finally, in [9] it is shown that in most cases custom allocators do not improve the performance of the applications at all.

1.3 Our Solution

Thread-Local Storage Allocator. We extended Hoard — a state of the art memory allocator [8] by adding the ability to allocate *thread-local storage*. Thread-local storage is a memory location, which is allocated and freed by a single thread. Therefore, there is no need to synchronize allocation and deallocation of thread-local storage. Specifically, we enhance the memory management functions with two new functions, `tls_malloc` and `tls_free`. The `tls_malloc` function acquires storage from a *thread-local heap*, and the `tls_free` function deallocates storage acquired in a thread-local heap. Both functions manipulate the thread-local heap with no synchronization.

Additional benefit of thread-local storage is better utilization of the processor's cache. Modern processors maintain a cache of the recently used memory. The processor's cache saves accesses to the memory which are relatively expensive operations. When a thread is mainly executed on the same processor, the locality of the thread-local storage allocations improves the processor's cache utilization.

Statically Estimating Thread-Local Storage. Employing thread-local storage by programmers in a language like C is far from trivial. The main difficulty is deciding whether an allocation statement can be replaced by `tls_malloc`. Pointers into shared data can be accessed by multiple threads, thus complicating the task of correctly identifying thread-local storage. Therefore, in this paper, we develop automatic techniques for conservatively estimating thread-local storage. This means that our algorithm may fail to identify certain opportunities for using `tls_malloc`. However, storage detected as `tls_malloc` is guaranteed to be allocated and freed by the same thread. Thus, our solution is fully automatic.

The analysis conservatively detects whether each allocation site can be replaced by `tls_malloc`. This is actually checked by requiring that every location allocated by this statement cannot be accessed by other threads. In particular, it guarantees that all deallocations are performed in the code of this thread. Therefore, our algorithms may be seen as a special case of escape analysis, since thread-local storage identified by our algorithm may not escape its allocating thread. We are unaware of any other escape analysis for C.

Our analysis scales to large code bases. Scalability is achieved by developing a flow- and context-insensitive algorithm. Furthermore, our algorithm performs simple queries on a points-to graph in order to determine which allocation site may be accessed by other threads. Thus, existing flow-insensitive points-to analysis algorithms [7, 27, 30, 14, 15, 18] can be exploited by our analysis. This also simplifies the implementation of our method.

Empirical Evaluation. We have fully implemented our algorithm to handle arbitrary ANSI C programs. Our algorithm is parameterized by the points-to information. Thus the precision of the analysis is directly affected by the precision of the points-to graph. In particular, the way structure fields are handled can affect precision. We therefore integrated our algorithm with two points-to analysis algorithms: Heinze's algorithm [18], which handles fields very conservatively, and GrammaTech's CodeSurfer points-to algorithm [30]. CodeSurfer handles fields in a more precise manner.

We have tested our implementation on a set of 7 memory management benchmarks used by Hoard and other high performance allocators. We verified that on the memory management benchmarks our static analysis precisely determines all opportunities for use of `tls_malloc` instead of `malloc`.

The standard memory management benchmarks are somewhat artificial. Thus, we also applied our static algorithm to work with a multithreaded application that uses `Zlib` [5], the popular compression library. Finally, we applied our algorithm on `OpenSSL-mttest` which is a multithreaded test of the `OpenSSL` cryptographic library [4].

For 3 of the memory management benchmarks, there are no opportunities for replacing `malloc` with `tls_malloc`. On the other 4 memory management benchmarks, we achieve up to 44% speedup due to use of thread-local storage. This is encouraging, given that Hoard is highly optimized for speed.

For the `Zlib` library, our static algorithm detected the opportunities for using `tls_malloc` instead of `malloc`. We achieved a speedup of up to 20% over Hoard by using the thread-local storage allocator. This result shows the potential use of our methods on more realistic applications.

On `OpenSSL-mttest` our static algorithm fails to detect opportunities for thread-local storage. However, inspecting the runtime behavior of this benchmark, we find that only a negligible amount of the allocated memory during the run is actually thread-local. Therefore, even an identification of some thread-local storage for this benchmark is not expected to yield any performance benefits. Nevertheless, the application of our algorithm on `OpenSSL` demonstrates the scalability of our tool for handling large code bases.

1.4 Related Work

Static Analysis. We reduce the problem of thread-local storage detection to the problem of escape analysis for C. In this paper we developed an escape analysis algorithm that uses an existing points-to algorithm. Our analysis uses points-to information generated by any flow-insensitive points-to analysis. Flow-sensitive points-to algorithms are more precise but less suitable for multithreaded programs, due to the thread interaction that needs to be considered. Our analysis can use either context-sensitive or context-insensitive points-to analysis algorithms.

There are two commonly used techniques for performing flow-insensitive points-to analysis: (i) unification-based points-to analysis suggested by Steensgaard [27], (ii) inclusion-based points-to analysis suggested by Andersen [7]. Generally, the unification method is more scalable but less precise. The GOLF algorithm [14, 15] is a unification-based implementation with additional precision improvements.

In our prototype, we used the following points-to analysis algorithms: (i) GrammaTech's CodeSurfer [30], (ii) Heintze's points-to analysis [17, 18]. Both algorithms are context-insensitive algorithms based on Andersen's analysis. A specialized flow- and context-sensitive points-to algorithm that is specialized for multithreaded programs, is that of Rugina and Rinard [24]. The algorithm is used for multithreaded programs written in Cilk, an extension of C. Another efficient context-sensitive points-to analysis is Wilson and Lam analysis [29].

In this paper, we study the problem of thread-local storage identification through escape analysis for C programs and the performance benefits obtained through the use of thread-local storage. Escape analysis for Java has been studied extensively [13, 10, 12, 6, 23, 26] and was employed for thread-local storage in [28]. We note that there are several differences between C and Java, which make our task non-trivial. First, in contrast to Java, C programs may include unsafe casting, pointers into the stack, multilevel pointers, and pointer arithmetic. These features complicate the task of developing sound and useful static analysis algorithms for C programs. Second, explicit memory management is supported in C, whereas Java employs automatic memory management, usually through a garbage collection mechanism. In [11] Boehm observes that a garbage collector may incur less synchronization overhead than in explicit memory management. This is due to the fact that many objects can be deallocated in the same GC cycle, while explicit memory management requires synchronization for every `free`. Our thread-local storage allocator reduces the above synchronization overhead by providing synchronization-free memory management constructs.

Of course it should be noted that our analysis for C is made simpler since it does not need to consider Java aspects such as inheritance, virtual method calls and dynamic thread allocation. The difficulties that rise in escape analysis for C programs are handled by the underlying points-to algorithms. The points-to algorithms for C are rather conservative, but interestingly they provide good empirical results when analyzing the memory management benchmark programs.

In [28] Steensgard describes an algorithm for allocating thread-local storage in Java using the unification-based points-to analysis described in [27]. Our simple static algorithm can use an arbitrary points-to algorithm. Our prototype implementation uses inclusion-based points-to analysis algorithms which are potentially more precise. Indeed, one of the interesting preliminary conclusions from our initial experiments is that in many C programs thread-local storage can be automatically identified despite the fact that C allows more expressive pointer manipulations.

Multithreaded Memory Allocation for C. In [19] Larson studies multithreading support and SMP scalability in memory allocators. Berger's Hoard allocator [8] is an efficient multithreaded allocator. In the paper we extend Hoard to support an efficient thread-local storage allocation. In [21], Maged shows an extension of Hoard with an efficient lock handling based on hardware atomic operations. In [11], Boehm suggests a scalable multithreaded automatic memory management for C programs.

1.5 Contributions

The contributions of this paper can be summarized as follows:

- A new generic and scalable escape analysis algorithm targeted for C. The input to our static algorithm is points-to information obtained by *any* flow-insensitive points-to algorithm.
- Static estimation of thread-local storage allocations.
- Extending an existing allocator with high performance treatment of thread-local storage.
- Empirical evaluation which shows rather precise static analysis algorithms resulting in significant runtime performance improvements.

1.6 Outline of the Rest of This Paper

The remainder of the paper is organized as follows: Section 2 provides an overview of our work. Section 3 describes our thread-local storage allocator. In Section 4 the static analysis algorithm is described. Empirical results are reported in Section 5. Preliminary conclusions and further work are sketched in Section 6.

2 Overview

This section provides an overview of the capabilities of our technique by showing its application to artificial program fragments. These fragments are intended to give a feel of the potential and the limitations of our algorithms.

2.1 Escaped Locations and C Multithreading

C programs consist of three types of memory locations:

Stack Locations. Stack locations are allocated to automatic program variables and by the `alloca` function.
Global Locations. Static and global variables are allocated in global locations.
Heap Locations. Heap locations are the dynamically allocated locations.

Multithreading is not an integral part of the C programming language. In this paper, we follow the `POSIX thread` standard. Inter-thread communication in `pthreads` is performed by `pthread_create` function, which creates a thread and passes an argument to the thread function. The argument may point to memory locations that are accessible by the creator thread. After invoking the `pthread_create` function, these memory locations are also accessible by the new thread. However, our method can also support different thread implementations with other inter-thread communication methods such as *message-passing* or *signals*. Finally, we assume that each thread owns its own stack.

We say that a heap-location *escapes* in a given execution trace when it is accessed by different threads than the one in which it was allocated. A heap-location that does not escape on any execution trace, is accessible only by a single thread. Therefore, it is allocated and freed by the same thread. Hence, the allocation statement can be replaced by `tls_malloc`.

Our static analysis algorithm conservatively estimates whether a location may escape. The estimation is performed by checking the following criteria: (i) global locations as well as locations which may be pointed by global pointers may escape; (ii) locations passed between threads by the operating system's inter-thread-communication functions and locations reachable from these locations may escape. Allocation of locations that do not meet the above criteria are guaranteed to be accessible by a single thread [25], thus are allocated using `tls_malloc`.

Clearly, our algorithm is conservative and may therefore detect a certain location as "may-escape" while there is no program execution in which this location escapes. This may result in missing some opportunities for using thread-local storage.

2.2 Motivating Example

Figure 1 shows a program fragment that uses the `pthread` implementation of threads. This program creates a thread by using the `pthread_create` function, and waits for its termination by using the `pthread_join` function.

Our static algorithm detects the allocation in line 1 as a thread-local storage allocation and replaces it with `tls_malloc`. The location that is pointed by the assigned variable `l` is accessible by a single thread. Specifically, it is allocated and freed by the `foo` thread. In this case, static analysis can trivially detect the latter, since `l` is assigned once. Therefore, this allocation statement can be allocated on the thread-local heap of `foo`. In principle, the free statement in line 2 could be replaced by `tls_free`. However, as explained in Section 3.2 we extend the `free` statement implementation to support the deallocation of thread-local storage with negligible overhead, thus it is also possible to avoid replacements of the `free` statement with `tls_free`.

```
#include <stdio.h>
#include <pthread.h>
char *g;
void foo(void *p){
  char *l;
  1: l = malloc(...); // Is tls_malloc?
  2: free(l);
  3: free(p);
  4: g = malloc(...); // Is tls_malloc?
  5: free(g);
}
int main(int argc, char **argv) {
  char *x, *q;
  pthread_t t;
  6: x = malloc(...); // Is tls_malloc?
  7: q = x;
  8: if (get_input()){
       9: pthread_create(&t, NULL, foo, q);
       10: pthread_join(t, NULL);
  }
  11: else {
        12: free(x);
  }
  13: return 0;
}
```

Fig. 1. A sample C program

One can mistakenly conclude that the `malloc` in line 6 can be replaced by `tls_malloc`. At first glance, it seems that the location allocated in line 6 and freed in line 12 is allocated and freed by the same thread and can therefore be allocated on the thread-local storage. However, if we observe more closely, we can see that in line 7, that location is assigned to the pointer `q`, if the condition in line 8 holds, we execute line 9 on which `q` is passed as a parameter to the thread function `foo`, and then it is finally freed in line 3. Thus, on some executions, the location allocated in line 6 may be freed by a different thread and therefore it *cannot* be allocated on the thread-local storage. Our static algorithm correctly identifies that by observing that `q` is passed as a parameter to another thread, and therefore marks the memory locations that `q` may points-to as accessible by multiple threads. The flow-insensitive points-to analysis tracks the fact that `x` and `p` are aliases to the location that is allocated in line 6. Therefore, that location violates the conditions for thread-local storage allocation. Of course, manually tracking pointer values for complex applications is not a trivial task and it is error prone.

The allocation in line 4 pointed by `g` is allocated and freed by the same thread — the `foo` thread, and can therefore be safely allocated on the thread-local storage and replaced by `tls_malloc`. However, our static algorithm will fail to identify the memory allocated in line 4 as thread-local. This is due to the fact that memory allocated in line 4 is pointed by the global variable `g`, making it accessible by both the `main` and the `foo` threads.

3 Thread-Local Storage Allocator

Our allocator is based on the Hoard [8] allocator which is briefly described in Section 3.1. In Section 3.2 we describe our extensions to allow thread-local storage support in Hoard.

3.1 The Hoard Allocator

Hoard is a scalable memory allocator for multithreaded applications running on multiprocessor machines. It addresses performance issues such as contentions, memory fragmentation, and cache-locality. In particular, it reduces contentions by improving lock implementation and by avoiding global locks. Hoard manages a dedicated heap for each processor. The use of dedicated processor heaps reduces the contention and also improves the processor cache locality.

Hoard maintains two kinds of heaps: (i) a *processor heap* which belongs to a processor, and (ii) a *global heap* which is one heap for the entire process. Each heap is synchronized using locks. The global heap is backed by the operating system memory management routines[4]. The fact that a thread is mostly executed on the same processor helps in synchronization reduction since its processor's heap should be unlocked when it calls the allocator. Contention may occur if the thread is accessing the processor heap from a different processor.

The processor heap and the global heap contain *super-blocks*, where a super-block is a pool of memory blocks of the same size. When a thread attempts to allocate memory, Hoard first tries to acquire it from its thread heap super-blocks, then (if there is no memory available in these blocks), it attempts to allocate a super-block from the global heap and assigns the block to the current processor. As a last resort Hoard attempts to allocate memory from the operating system.

Hoard improves the performance significantly, however, a synchronization contention may still frequently occur for the global heap (and less frequently for the processor heap). Our extensions to Hoard reduce these kinds of synchronization contention.

3.2 Hoard Extensions

We extend Hoard to allow support for thread-local heaps. In particular, we enhance the memory management functions with two new functions, `tls_malloc` and `tls_free`. The `tls_malloc` function acquires storage from the thread-local heap, and the `tls_free` function deallocates storage acquired in a thread-local heap. Both functions manipulate the thread-local heap with no synchronization. In addition, we extend the `free` statement implementation to deallocate thread-local storage. This extension is made to allow a `free` statement to deallocate memory allocated both by a `malloc` statement and a `tls_malloc` statement.

[4] Actually, Hoard uses dlmalloc [2] implementation instead of the standard operating system memory management routines.

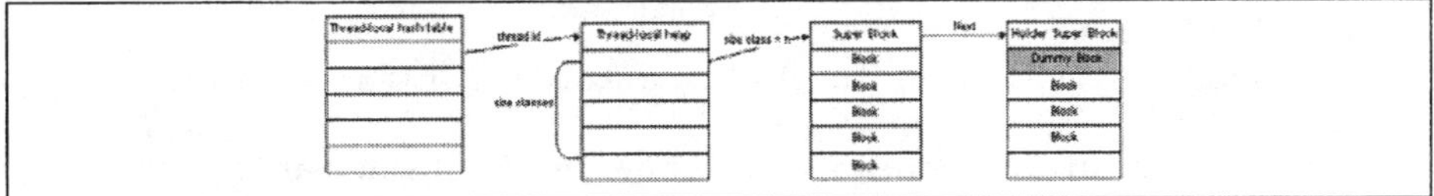

Fig. 2. Thread-local heaps layout

Thread-Local Heaps Implementation. In principle, we could have used the POSIX thread specific functions (`pthread_setspecifc`, `pthread_getspecific`) to allow a thread to access its corresponding thread-local heap. These functions, however, have performance cost as Boehm shows [11]. Thus, Boehm provides a more efficient implementation to allow a thread to access its corresponding thread-specific information. However, Boehm's implementation assumes a garbage-collector environment. We therefore develop a similar implementation for the case of an explicit allocator environment.

We maintain the thread-local heaps in a hash table (denoted further by *thread-local hash table*) as shown in Figure 2. We normalize the unique thread id and use it as a key for that table. Our implementation uses the value for a key as a pointer to a thread-local heap ; thus, a thread accesses its thread-local heap by fetching the value in the hash table entry corresponding to its thread id.

Our implementation assumes the following simplifying assumptions: (i) the number of thread-local heaps is fixed. A thread may thus fail to obtain a thread-local heap. In this case, memory is allocated using `malloc`. Our implementation sets the number of thread-local heaps to 2048. We expect most programs to have a smaller number of threads. (ii) we assume a 1-1 mapping between a thread id and an entry index in the thread-local hash table. This assumption holds for the Linux `pthreads` implementation.

Creation and maintenance of thread-local heaps require some overhead. We therefore create such heaps only upon the first `tls_malloc` request. Thread-local heaps are not backed by the Hoard global heap, but directly by the operating-system heap. We do not use the global heap for simplicity reasons, and because it does not affect performance on the benchmarks we tried. Synchronization is required only when the thread-local heap aqcuires/frees memory from the operating system.

In order to avoid trashing of allocations and deallocations of blocks from the operating-system, we guarantee that a thread-local heap always maintains one super-block for each size class. We call this super-block a *holder super-block*. The latter is enabled by allocation of a *dummy block*, which prevents the deallocation of this holder super-block. The dummy block is freed only when the holder super-block becomes full. Using this method we can help applications that frequently allocate and deallocate small blocks. Upon thread termination, we clean up the thread-local heap, as well as its holder super-blocks.

tls_malloc. Figure 3 shows a pseudo-code of the `tls_malloc` implementation. In order to allow fast access to a thread-local heap, we maintain thread-local heaps in a hash table. Thus, `tls_malloc` first searches the hash table for the thread-local heap corresponding to the allocating thread. We make an optimization, and allocate a thread-

```
tls_malloc(size)
 if no thread-local heap in the hash-table for the current thread
 exists then
   create thread-local heap and store in the hash-table
 if no available super-block exists in thread-local heap then
   if no holder super-block exists then
     allocate a super-block from OS and mark as thread-local
     set super-block as a holder super-block
     allocate dummy block from holder super-block
     insert to thread-local heap super-block list
   else
     free the dummy block back to the super-block
     set holder super-block as regular super-block
 return block from super-block
```

Fig. 3. Pseudo-Code for tls_malloc

local heap only upon the first `tls_malloc` request occurring in a thread; thus, threads that do not make `tls_malloc` requests are not affected.

Next, the `tls_malloc` routine looks at the thread-local heap super-blocks list in order to find a suitable super-block for the allocation. As in Hoard, each heap has super-blocks of various allocation sizes. In case a super-block is not found, we check whether a holder super-block exists, and allocate one if necessary. As mentioned earlier, the holder super-blocks are used to reduce the number of the operating system's memory management functions calls.

Once we mark the super-block as thread-local, we save this super-block in our thread-local hash table. The next step is acquiring a dummy block from the holder super-block, that will prevent deallocation of the latter, even when it becomes empty. The last step is adding this holder super-block as a part of our super-blocks list. In case we have an allocated holder super-block that is out of free blocks, we free our dummy allocated block and transform the holder super-block to a regular super block. Once we have a super-block we return a block from it to the caller.

tls_free. Freeing memory is performed by the `tls_free` function. The function returns the block to its super-block and frees the super-block in case it becomes empty. As already mentioned all the thread-local heap manipulations are performed without synchronization since only a single thread accesses the heap data.

The `tls_free` complements the `tls_malloc` operation, and the programmer invokes it to free thread-local storage objects. In addition, we extend the `free` statement implementation to deallocate thread-local storage. This extension is made to allow a `free` statement to deallocate memory allocated both by a `malloc` statement and a `tls_malloc` statement. In particular, when a block is freed using the `free` function, our allocator first checks whether the allocated block is from the thread-local heap. This information was stored in the super-block of the block. Once we determine that the allocated block is thread-local block we will free it appropriately.

4 Statically Identifying Thread-Local Storage

In this section, we describe our static algorithm for estimating allocation sites that can be replaced by thread-local storage allocation. Our analysis conservatively detects whether each allocation site can be replaced by `tls_malloc`. In particular, it guarantees that all deallocations are performed in the code of this thread.

We reduce the problem of finding thread-local storage to the problem of escape-analysis. In order to determine that an allocation site can be replaced by `tls_malloc`, a static algorithm must ensure that all locations allocated at the allocation site are thread-local storage, i.e., deallocated by the code of the allocating thread. Our algorithm does that by checking stronger property for locations. Our algorithm makes sure that memory locations allocated at an allocation site never *escape* their allocating thread, i.e., all locations allocated at that site are accessed only by the allocating thread in all execution traces. Clearly, locations that do not escape their allocating thread cannot be deallocated by other threads, therefore we conclude that our algorithm indeed yields safe thread-local storage information.

Our algorithm enjoys two characteristics that make it attractive for the "real-world". First, it scales for large code bases. Second, our algorithm is very simple to implement. Scalability is achieved by using flow- and context-insensitive algorithms, based on simple queries on points-to graphs in order to determine allocations sites that do not allocate escaped memory locations. Furthermore, the points-to graph we use may be obtained by applying *as is* any existing flow-insensitive points-to analysis(e.g., [7, 27, 30, 14, 15, 18, 29]). This last fact greatly simplifies the implementation of our algorithm. In fact, we integrated our algorithm with two existing points-to analysis algorithms, as discussed in Section 4.2.

4.1 The Algorithm

Our algorithm partitions the memory locations into two sets, *may-escape* locations and the *non-escaped* locations. A may-escaped location may be accessed by other threads, while a non-escaped location cannot be accessed by threads, other than its allocating thread, on all execution paths. Our algorithm concludes that an allocation site that does not allocate may-escape locations may be replaced by `tls_malloc`.

Our algorithm performs simple queries on a points-to graph generated by a flow-insensitive point-to analysis. This points-to graph is an abstract representation of all memory locations and pointer relations that exist for all program points and for all execution paths. A node in the graph represents an abstract memory location and an edge in that graph represents a points-to relation.

Static analysis of C programs is not trivial. There are difficulties such as casting and pointers arithmetic. These difficulties are tackled during the generation of the points-to graph which is a preceding step to our analysis. Our analysis can simply traverse the graph and bypass the problems of static analysis of C programs.

A pseudo-code of the algorithm for detecting may-escape locations is shown in Figure 4. The algorithm traverses abstract heap locations that represent allocation sites. For each abstract location it performs a query on the points-to graph. The query checks whether the location is pointed by a global abstract location, or whether it is being passed

```
Input: Program points-to flow-insensitive graph
Output: Partition of the locations to may-escape/thread-local
for each abstract heap location l {
  if l is reachable from a global location or
    l is reachable from a thread function argument or
    l is reachable from a location that passed as thread
    function argument
  then
    mark l as may-escape
  else
    mark l as thread-local
}
```

Fig. 4. Thread-local storage detection by an escape analysis for C using points-to information

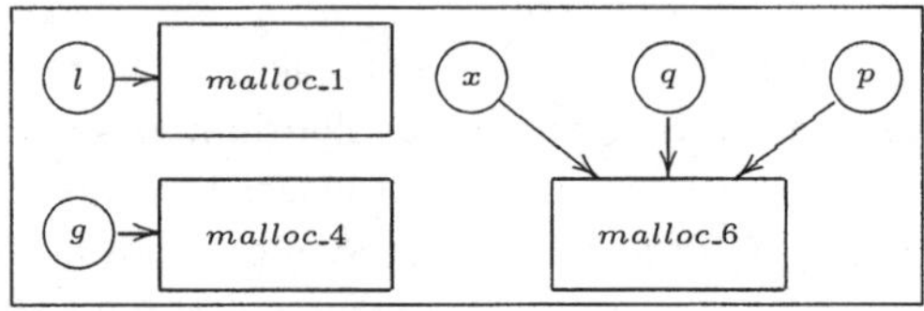

Fig. 5. Flow-insensitive points-to graph for the program shown in Figure 1

as an argument to inter-thread communication functions. Otherwise all runtime locations represented by the abstract heap location, cannot be pointed by any global location or by inter-thread communication function arguments, and thus, the location can be safely allocated using thread-local storage.

We can also detect deallocations of thread-local storage as follows: for each statement of the form `free(x)`, if all the abstract locations which may be pointed by `x` are not may-escape, we can safely replace this statement by `tls_free`. Otherwise we conservatively assume that it may represent a location which is not allocated using thread-local storage. In this case, the runtime implementation checks the status of this location and deallocates it appropriately. Our experience shows that this runtime overhead is marginal. Therefore, we decided not to implement this static optimization and leave `free` statements unchanged.

Let us demonstrate the application of our algorithm by running it on the sample C program shown in Figure 1. In Figure 5 a flow-insensitive points-to graph is shown. The heap abstract location, representing locations allocated by the `malloc` in line 1, is not pointed by any global abstract location nor by inter-thread communication function arguments. Therefore it can be safely allocated on the thread-local heap. The heap abstract location, representing locations allocated by the `malloc` in line 4, is pointed by a global location, and therefore cannot be allocated on the thread-local heap. The abstract heap location in line 6, may be pointed by `q` location which is an argument of the inter-thread communication function, thus the location may-escape and cannot be allocated on the thread-local heap.

The precision of our algorithm is affected directly by the precision of the underlying points-to algorithm. One of the issues that mostly affects the precision of our algorithm is the way the points-to algorithm handles structure fields. There exist three kinds of points-to algorithms that respect: (i) field-insensitive points-to analysis, (ii) field-based points-to analysis, and (iii) field-sensitive points-to analysis.

Field-insensitive points-to analysis [7, 17] ignores structure fields, thus all structure members are abstracted to a single abstract location. Field-based points-to analysis [7, 17] abstracts all instances of the same structure field to a single global abstract location. For our algorithm, this means that all structure fields are considered may-escape, and cannot be considered as thread-local storage; thus it makes little sense to use these kind of algorithms for our purposes. Field-sensitive points-to analysis [30] is more precise than field-insensitive point-to analysis and field-based points-to analysis. It abstracts the fields of an allocated structure to different abstract locations.

4.2 Implementation of the Flow-Insensitive Algorithm

We have implemented our thread-local storage detection algorithm and integrated it with two points-to graphs with varying degrees of precision. The first points-to graph was produced by the CLA (compile-link-analyze) pointer-analysis of [18]. CLA provides field-based or field-insensitive points-to analysis. The second points-to graph was generated by GrammaTech CodeSurfer, which provides field-sensitive points-to analysis.

Our implementation supports the analysis of programs that follow the `POSIX thread` standard. In particular, we model the `pthread_create` function (which creates a thread and passes an argument to it) as an assignment of the thread parameter to a global variable. Thus, memory pointed by the thread parameter is conservatively assumed to be escaping.

The CLA based analysis scales better than the CodeSurfer based analysis, however it provides less precise results. On the small benchmarks we used, both implementations have been able to detect thread-local storage correctly. In general, for larger programs, the precision of field dependent analysis (as in CodeSurfer implementation) is expected to be better. However, we did not observe differences in the benchmarks we performed.

5 Experimental Results

In this section we describe the experimental results of our static analysis tool and our thread-local storage allocator. Our static analysis experimental performance results were produced on 2X2.8GHZ pentium IV processor with 1GB of memory running RedHat enterprise Linux with a kernel version of 2.4.21. Our runtime experimental performance results were produced on 8X700MHZ Pentium III processor with 8GB of memory running a RedHat enterprise Linux with a kernel version of 2.4.9-e3. We compare our allocator with the default Linux *glibc malloc*, and with the Hoard version 2.1.2d [8].

5.1 Benchmarks

Measuring the performance of multithreaded dynamic memory allocation in real life applications is almost impossible. The multithreaded servers are mostly I/O bound and the effect of memory management improvements is hard to measure. Since there are no real

Table 1. Static Analysis results. The points-to time column presents the time that the underlying points-to analysis took. The algorithm time column presents the time that our algorithm ran on the points-to graph. The total mallocs column presents the number of malloc statements in the benchmark. The identified tls_mallocs column presents the number of mallocs that our algorithm actually identified as thread-local storage. The tls opportunities column presents the number of allocation sites that are actually thread-local storage

Benchmark	Description	LOC	points-to time	algorithm time	total mallocs	identified tls_mallocs	tls opportunities
cache-thrash [8]	Cache locality test	144	$< 1s$	$< 1s$	3	2	2
cache-scratch[8]	Cache locality test	144	$< 1s$	$< 1s$	5	3	3
threadtest [8]	Scalability test	155	$< 1s$	$< 1s$	3	3	3
linux-scalability [20]	Scalability test	137	$< 1s$	$< 1s$	1	1	1
sh6bench [3]	Scalability test	557	$< 1s$	$< 1s$	3	3	3
larson [19]	Inter-threadallocations	672	$< 1s$	$< 1s$	5	0	0
consume[8]	Inter-thread allocations	141	$< 1s$	$< 1s$	5	0	0
zlib[5] (field-sensitive)	Use of zlib compression library	$12K$	$9s$	$62s$	12	11	11
zlib[5] (field-insensitive)	Use of zlib compression library	$12K$	$8s$	$1s$	12	11	11
openssl mttest[4] (field-sensitive)	multithreaded sll connections	$140K$	$1565s$	$22449s$	N/A	N/A	N/A
openssl mttest[4] (field-insensitive)	multithreaded sll connections	$140K$	$542s$	$39s$	N/A	N/A	N/A

benchmarks for dynamic memory allocators, we applied the benchmarks used to evaluate the performance of Hoard [8]. These benchmarks have become the standard defacto benchmarks for dynamic memory allocations. They have been used by [8, 11, 19, 21]. We tested the following benchmarks: *cache-trash, linux-scalability, shbench, threadtest, cache-scratch, larson, consume* [5]. The first 5 benchmarks contain allocations that have been detected as thread-local by our static analysis tool, and have been optimized to use `tls_malloc` instead of `malloc`. The last two benchmarks contain no thread-local storage, and as expected, the static algorithm correctly determines it, and these benchmarks have therefore not been optimized.

We have also added benchmarks of more realistic applications. The `Zlib` benchmark tests multithreaded usage of the `Zlib` compression library [5]. Our static analysis algorithm successfully detected allocations as thread-local. Those allocations have been optimized to use `tls_malloc` instead of `malloc`. We also tested `OpenSSL-mttest` a multithreaded test of the `OpenSSL` cryptographic library [4]. Our static algorithm did not find opportunities for optimizing the program using thread-local storage. When we

[5] We took all the open-source multithreaded benchmarks from [8]. There are two additional multithreaded benchmarks (BEMengine, and Barnet-Hut) which we did not take since we did not have their source code.

manually examined the `OpenSSL-mttest` code we verified that there were no thread-local storage opportunities.

5.2 Static Analysis Results

Static analysis results are summarized in Table 1. For the first 7 benchmarks we used Heintze's field-insensitive pointer-analysis [18] as the underlying points-to algorithm. All of these benchmarks are small and artificial memory management benchmarks. The pointer-analysis time was less than a second for all of these and so was the application of our own static algorithm. Some of the benchmarks were originally written in C++. We ported these benchmarks to C, so we can apply our static analysis tool. For the larger programs of `OpenSSL-mttest` and `Zlib` we used CodeSurfer's pointer-analysis as a back-end for our algorithm. From the experimental results we can see that applying field-sensitive pointer-analysis yields to a much longer execution time. The reason for this is that the points-to graph can be exponentially larger in that case. We can also see that the field-sensitivite analysis did not improve the analysis precision for the benchmarks we selected, even though it is theoretically more precise.

5.3 Runtime Speedup

We executed each benchmark with a different number of threads. Each benchmark performs some work that consumes a certain period of time on a single-threaded execution. When we add threads, this work is performed concurrently and we expect the execution time to be shorter. On an optimal allocator, there should be a linear relation between the number of threads and the execution time. For each benchmark we performed the following tests. (i) an execution with *glibc* — the default allocator of the Linux operating system. (ii) an execution with the `Hoard` allocator. (iii) an execution with our allocator, after we have optimized the benchmark to use thread-local storage allocations. Runtime speedups for the benchmarks are shown in Figure 6. The circle line represents `glibc` allocator, the triangle line represents `Hoard` allocator and the box line represents our `tls Hoard` allocator.

The speedup on `threadtest` benchmark (see Figure 6(a)) is between 16% to 29% compared to the `Hoard` allocator. On `linux-scalability` benchmark (see Figure 6(c)) the speedup is between 18% to 44% and in most cases it is around 40%. On `shbench` benchmark (see Figure 6(d)), the speedup is between 2% to 14%. These benchmark programs test pure scalability, without other issues such as processor cache performance and memory fragmentation. As expected, we get a significant performance improvement, since the allocator reduces the global heap contention which directly leads to better scalability. On `cache-thrash` benchmark (see Figure 6(b)) our optimizations do not improve Hoard. This benchmark checks the cache behavior of the allocator and our allocator does not handle cache issues directly, even-though thread-local storage improves locality. However, we discovered that when the amount of computations between allocations is reduced, our optimized version outperforms Hoard, since the frequency of the allocations increases the contention, and our allocator handles it better. In `Zlib` benchmark (see Figure 6(e)) the speedup is between 1% to 20%. `Zlib` benchmark represents a more realistic application that also involves I/O processing and computations.

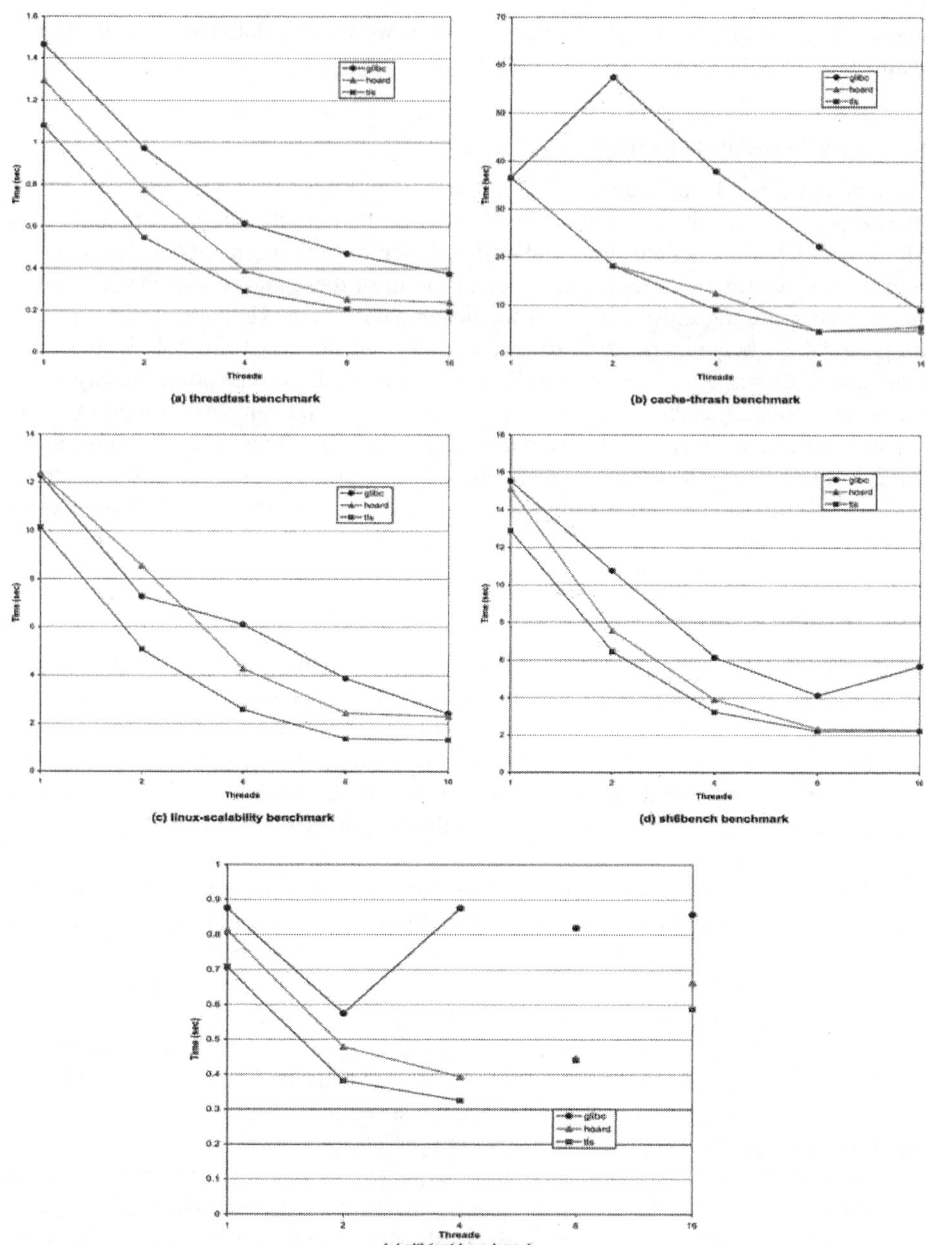

Fig. 6. Thread-local storage allocator benchmark results. The X axis is the number of threads and the Y axis is the runtime in seconds. The lines represent the *glibc* allocator, the *Hoard* allocator, and our allocator. We obtain up to 44% runtime speedup compared to the other allocators

The performance of the `Zlib` benchmark drops when the number of threads increases due to the cost of the I/O processing. However, our allocator still outperforms the others when the number of threads increases.

5.4 Summary

From the static analysis benchmark results shown in Table 1, we can deduce that the static algorithm successfully detects all the opportunities for thread-local storage for the standard memory management benchmarks. The analysis time is less than a second in these benchmarks, and the analysis is precise and identifies all opportunities for using thread-local storage. On the `Zlib` benchmark we also precisely detected all the possible opportunities for using thread-local storage. We proved that our analysis can handle large programs by running it on `OpenSSL-mttest` and `Zlib`. We could also see the significant performance overhead of using field-sensitive analysis.

The runtime benchmark results show that our allocator provides significant multithreaded scalability improvement for thread-local storage allocations. Moreover, our allocator performs better, compared to different allocators, even on a single-threaded environment. There are two potential reasons for this behavior. The first reason is that locks have some overhead even on a single-threaded environment. The second reason is the super-block holder, which we keep for each thread-local heap. These holders avoid trashing between the thread-local heap and the operating system heap and improve the locality and performance of allocation from the thread-local heap. The performance improvements for the `Zlib` benchmark result show the potential benefit of our method on more realistic programs.

6 Conclusions

Dynamic memory management in C for multithreaded applications can become a performance bottleneck. We could see the impact of the synchronization contentions by examining the memory allocation benchmarks suite. This paper shows that a thread-local storage allocator can significantly improve the performance of dynamic memory management. However, manual detection of thread-local storage is almost an infeasible task. Therefore, the paper shows that a simple sound static analysis can successfully detect heap allocation statements that can be replaced by allocating thread-local storage. We reduce the problem of finding thread-local storage to the escape analysis problem for C and solve it by using flow-insensitive points-to algorithms.

References

1. Apache http Server Project. Available at http://httpd.apache.org.
2. D. Lea A Memory Allocator. Available at http://g.oswego.edu/dl/html/malloc.html.
3. Microquill inc. Available at http://www.microquill.com.
4. openssl cryptographic library. Available at http://www.openssl.org.
5. zlib compression library. Available at http://www.zlib.org.
6. J. Aldrich, E. G. Sirer, C. Chambers, and S. J. Eggers. Comprehensive synchronization elimination for Java. Technical Report, University of Washington, Oct. 2000.
7. L. Andersen. *Program Analysis and Specialization for the C Programming Language*. PhD thesis, DIKU Univ. of Copenhagen., Copenhagen, Denmark, 1994.

8. E. Berger. Hoard: AScalable Memory Allocator for Multithreaded Applications. In *Architectural Support for Programming Languages and Operating Systems*, pages 117–128, Cambridge, Massachusetts, US, Nov. 2000.
9. E. D. Berger, B. G. Zorn, and K. S. McKinley. Reconsidering Custom Memory Allocation. In *Conf. on Object-Oriented Prog. Syst., Lang. and Appl.*, pages 1–12, Seattle, Washington, US, Nov. 2002.
10. B. Blanchet. Escape Analysis for Object Oriented Languages. Application to Java. In *Conf. on Object-Oriented Prog. Syst., Lang. and Appl.*, pages 20–34, Denver, Colorado, US, Nov. 1999.
11. H. Boehm. Fast Multiprocessor Memory Allocation and Garbage Collection. Tech Report, HP Labs, Dec. 2000.
12. J. Bogda and U. Hoelzle. Removing unnecessary synchronization in Java. In *Conf. on Object-Oriented Prog. Syst., Lang. and Appl.*, pages 35–46, Denver, Colorado, US, Nov. 1999.
13. J. Choi, M. Gupta, M. Serrano, V. Sreedhar, and S. Midkiff. Escape Analysis for Java. In *Conf. on Object-Oriented Prog. Syst., Lang. and Appl.*, pages 1–19, Denver, Colorado, US, Nov. 1999.
14. M. Das. Unification-based Pointer Analysis with Directional Assignments. In *SIGPLAN Conf. on Prog. Lang. Design and Impl.*, volume 35, pages 35–46, Vancouver, Canada, June 2000.
15. M. Das, B. Liblit, M. Fahndrich, and J. Rehof. Estimating the Impact of Scalable Pointer Analysis on Optimization. In *Static Analysis Symp.*, volume 2126, pages 260–278, Paris, France, July 2001.
16. T. Domani, G. Goldshtein, E. K. Kolodner, E. Lewis, E. Petrank, and D. Sheinwald. Thread-local heaps for java. In *Int. Symp. on Memory Management*, pages 76–87, Berlin, Germany, 2002.
17. N. Heintze. Analysis of Large Code Bases: The Compile-Link-Analyse Model. Unpublished Report, Nov. 1999.
18. N. Heintze and O. Tardieu. Ultra-fast Aliasing Analysis using cla: A Million Lines of C Code in a Second. In *SIGPLAN Conf. on Prog. Lang. Design and Impl.*, pages 254–263, Snowbird, Utah, US, May 2001.
19. P. Larson and M. Krishnan. Memory Allocation for Long-running Server Applications. In *Int. Symp. on Memory Management*, pages 176–185, Vancouver, Canada, Oct. 1998.
20. C. Lever and D. Boreham. malloc() performance in a multithreaded linux environment. In *USENIX, the Advanced Computing System Association*, San Diego, California, US, 2000.
21. M. M. Michael. Scalable Lock-Free Dynamic Memory Allocation. In *SIGPLAN Conf. on Prog. Lang. Design and Impl.*, pages 35–46, Washington, US, June 2004.
22. M. Rinard. Analysis of multithreaded programs. In *Static Analysis Symp.*, pages 1–19, Paris, France, July 2001.
23. E. Ruf. Effective Synchronization Removal for Java. In *SIGPLAN Conf. on Prog. Lang. Design and Impl.*, pages 208–218, Vancouver, Canada, June 2000.
24. R. Rugina and M. Rinard. Pointer Analysis for Multithreaded Programs. In *SIGPLAN Conf. on Prog. Lang. Design and Impl.*, pages 77–90, Atlanta, Georgia, US, May 1999.
25. Y. Sade. Optimizing C Multithreaded Memory Management Using Thread-Local Storage. Master's thesis, Tel-Aviv University, Tel-Aviv, Israel, 2004.
26. A. Salcianu and M. Rinard. Pointer and Escape Analysis for Multithreaded Programs. In *Principles Practice of Parallel Programming*, pages 12–23, Atlanta, Georgia, US, June 2001.
27. B. Steensgaard. Points-to Analysis in Almost Linear Time. In *Symp. on Princ. of Prog. Lang.*, pages 32–41, St. Petersburg Beach, Florida, US, Jan. 1996. ACM Press.

28. B. Steensgaard. Thread-Specific Heaps for Multi-Threaded Programs. In *Int. Symp. on Memory Management*, pages 18–24, Minneapolis, Minnesota, US, Oct. 2000.
29. R. P. Wilson and M. S. Lam. Efficient Context-Sensitive Pointer Analysis for C Programs. In *SIGPLAN Conf. on Prog. Lang. Design and Impl.*, pages 1–12, 1995.
30. S. Yang, S. Horwitz, and T. Reps. Pointer Analysis for Programs with Structures and Casting. In *SIGPLAN Conf. on Prog. Lang. Design and Impl.*, pages 91–103, Atlanta, Georgia, US, May 1999.

An Efficient On-the-Fly Cycle Collection

Harel Paz[1], Erez Petrank[1,*], David F. Bacon[2], Elliot K. Kolodner[3], and V. T. Rajan[2]

[1]Dept. of Computer Science, Technion - Israel Institute of Technology, Haifa 32000, Israel
{erez, pharel}@cs.technion.ac.il
[2]IBM T.J. Watson Research Center
{dfb, vtrajan}@us.ibm.com
[3]IBM Haifa Research Lab
{kolodner}@il.ibm.com

Abstract. A reference-counting garbage collector cannot reclaim unreachable cyclic structures of objects. Therefore, reference-counting collectors either use a backup tracing collector infrequently, or employ a cycle collector to reclaim cyclic structures. We propose a new *concurrent* cycle collector, i.e., one that runs concurrently with the program threads, imposing negligible pauses (of around 1ms) on a multiprocessor.

Our new collector combines the state-of-the-art cycle collector [5] with the sliding-views collectors [20, 2]. The use of sliding views for cycle collection yields two advantages. First, it drastically reduces the *number* of cycle candidates, which in turn, drastically reduces the *work* required to record and trace these candidates. Therefore, a large improvement in cycle collection efficiency is obtained. Second, it eliminates the theoretical termination problem that appeared in the previous concurrent cycle collector. There, a rare race may delay the reclamation of an unreachable cyclic structure forever. The sliding-views cycle collector guarantees reclamation of all unreachable cyclic structures.

The proposed collector was implemented on the Jikes RVM and we provide measurements including a comparison between the use of backup tracing and the use of cycle collection with reference counting. To the best of our knowledge, such a comparison has not been reported before.

1 Introduction

Reference counting is a classical garbage collection algorithm. Systems using reference counting were implemented starting from the sixties [11]. However, reference-counting garbage collectors cannot reclaim cyclic structures of objects. Thus, reference-counting collectors must be either accompanied by a backup mark and sweep collector (run infrequently to collect unreachable cyclic structures) or by a cycle collector.

Trying to avoid developing and maintaining an additional mark and sweep collector on the reference-counting collected system motivated attempts to design a cycle collector [8, 10, 23]. This effort culminated in the state-of-the-art on-the-fly cycle collector of Bacon and Rajan [5].

* Research supported by the Bar-Nir Bergreen Software Technology Center of Excellence and by the IBM Faculty Partnership Award.

R. Bodik (Ed.): CC 2005, LNCS 3443, pp. 156–171, 2005.

1.1 On-the-Fly Garbage Collection

Many garbage collectors were designed to work on a single thread while program threads are stopped, the so-called *stop the world* setting. On multiprocessor platforms, it is not desirable to stop the program and perform the collection in a single thread on one processor, as this leads both to long pause times and poor processor utilization. A concurrent collector runs concurrently with the program threads. The program threads are usually stopped for a short time to initiate and/or finish the collection. An *on-the-fly* collector does not need to stop the program threads simultaneously, not even for the initialization or the completion of the collection cycle.

The study of on-the-fly garbage collectors was initiated by Steele and Dijkstra, et al. [30, 31, 12] and continued in a series of papers culminating in [13, 4, 17, 20, 2]. The advantage of an on-the-fly collector over a parallel collector and other types of concurrent collectors [6, 28, 9, 14, 15, 18] is that it avoids the operation of stopping all the program threads. Such an operation usually increases the pause times. Today, on-the-fly collectors achieve pauses as short as a couple of milliseconds, and sometimes less [17].

1.2 The Challenge

Bacon and Rajan [5] propose two cycle collectors. The simpler *synchronous* collector is the most efficient cycle collector known today. It runs in a stop-the-world context. Their more involved *asynchronous* collector is the only *concurrent* cycle collector known today.

A typical stop-the-world cycle collector traces cycle candidates two or three times to discover which cycles are unreachable. A concurrent cycle collector must deal with concurrent program threads that modify the objects graph during the scan. Thus, a concurrent collector cannot trust a scan to repeat the very same structure that a previous scan has traversed. Furthermore, as modifications occur concurrently with the scan, each specific scan cannot be guaranteed to view a consistent snapshot of the objects graph at any specific point in time. This concurrency problem is the source of the two drawbacks of Bacon and Rajan's on-the-fly cycle collector. A practical drawback is the reduced efficiency: the asynchronous collector employs additional checks (which add substantial additional work) in order to make the collection safe in the presence of concurrent program threads. A theoretical drawback is that completeness cannot be guaranteed[4]. A rare race condition may prevent an unreachable cyclic structure from being ever reclaimed.

1.3 The Solution

We present an on-the-fly cycle collector which solves these drawbacks, by employing the sliding-views techniques [20]. The idea is to obtain a fixed view of the heap (via the sliding-views mechanism), and then run the more efficient *synchronous* (i.e., stop-the-world) cycle collector of [5] on this obtained view. The theoretical completeness problem is immediately solved. Any unreachable cyclic structure generated before the view of

[4] *Completeness* of a concurrent garbage collector stands for the standard *liveness* term in distributed computing. A collector is complete if all unreachable objects are eventually reclaimed.

the heap is created can be identified in the view and reclaimed. From the practical point of view, the use of the simpler and more efficient synchronous algorithm implies a more efficient execution.

But there are more efficiency benefits. All previous cycle collectors required as input a list of all reference-count decrements, in order to reclaim all garbage cycles correctly. However, the sliding-views reference-counting collector keeps track of only a small fraction of reference-count updates (and in particular decrements). This problem is solved by improving the analysis of the cycle collector to show that the small number of decrements recorded by the sliding-views mechanism suffices to reclaim all garbage cycles. Note, that fewer decrements implies recording fewer candidates for cyclic structures, which, in turn, implies less work on traversing these candidates and a reduction in the cycle collector work. Finally, we improve the efficiency of the synchronous algorithm of [5] by employing a better scheduling strategy and new filtering techniques that further reduce the number of traced objects.

In order to check the behavior of the cycle collector in a different environment, we also incorporated it into the age-oriented collector [27]. The age-oriented collector is an efficient variation of generational collection that uses reference counting to collect the old generation and tracing to collect the young generation. Cycle collectors spend a large fraction of their time working on cycle candidates among newly allocated objects. The age-oriented collector eliminates a large fraction of the cycles as well as a large fraction of the cycle collector's work, as it uses mark and sweep on the young objects and it runs the cycle collector only on the older objects.

Organization. An overview of previous cycle collectors and the sliding-views collectors is presented in Section 2. An overview of the new cycle collector appears in Section 3. Results are given in Section 4. Related work is discussed in Section 5 and we conclude in Section 6.

2 Review of Previous Collectors

This section reviews relevant previous work. We start by reviewing the algorithms for cycle collection [23, 21, 5] and then we review the sliding-views collectors [20, 2].

In this paper the term *cycle* or *cyclic structure* refers to a strongly connected component in the objects graph. A strongly connected component is a maximal subgraph of a directed graph such that for every pair of vertices u, v in the subgraph, there exists a directed path from u to v and a directed path from v to u.

2.1 Collecting Cycles in the Stop-the-World Setting

We start with the synchronous cycle collector of [5] (building on [23, 21]) that runs in a stop-the-world manner on a single thread. Garbage cycles can only be created when a reference count is decremented to a non-zero value ([23, 21]). The reference-counting collector records all objects whose reference count is decremented to a non-zero value. The cycle collector uses this list as a set of candidates that may belong to a garbage cycle. Three colors are used to mark the state of objects. The initial color of all objects is black. A possible member of a garbage cycle is marked gray. The white color signifies an object that is identified as part of an unreachable cycle. The cycle collector runs three traversals on all objects reachable from the candidate set as follows.

- **The mark stage:** traces the graph of objects reachable from the candidates, subtracting counts due to internal references and marking traversed nodes gray. At the end of this traversal, all nodes of each unreachable cyclic structure have zero reference counts, whereas each reachable structure has at least one node with positive reference count.
- **The scan stage:** scans the subgraph of (gray) objects reachable from the candidates. All objects reachable from external pointers (objects with positive reference counts and all their descendants) are marked black. Also reference counts are restored to reflect all outgoing pointers from black objects. All other nodes in the subgraph are colored white (these objects are identified as forming a garbage cycle).
- **The collect stage:** scans the subgraph again and reclaims all white objects.

2.2 Collecting Cycles On-the-Fly

The on-the-fly cycle collection algorithm of [5] consists of two phases. In the first phase, a variant of the above synchronous algorithm is used, but instead of reclaiming the white nodes these nodes are recorded as potential unreachable cyclic structures. Due to concurrent mutator activity, some of the white objects may have been incorrectly identified and may actually be reachable. The second phase is executed only at the next (reference-counting) collection. The potential unreachable cycles are re-examined and those found still unreachable are reclaimed.

This collector has a theoretical drawback and a practical drawback. A garbage collector is called *complete* if it eventually collects all unreachable objects. The first problem of this cycle collector is that it is not complete. Rare race conditions may prevent it from collecting garbage cycles. An example appears in [5]. The second (practical) problem is that the algorithm traces the candidate cycles a couple of times in the second phase to ensure that no false garbage cycle is reclaimed. These extra scannings cause a substantial reduction in efficiency, especially for (typical) benchmarks which contain many garbage cycles or many false cycle candidates. Moreover, additional work is required to fix subgraphs that were not recolored black on time due to improper re-traversals.

2.3 The Sliding-Views Reference-Counting Collector

A simple version of the Levanoni-Petrank sliding-views collector is one that allows stopping all program threads (mutators) simultaneously in the beginning of the collection. Using such a halt, it is possible to get a virtual snapshot of the heap using a copy-on-write mechanism. Each object is associated with a dirty bit which is cleared during the halt. Then, whenever a pointer is modified, the dirty bit of the object holding this reference is probed. If the object is dirty (i.e., has been modified previously) then the pointer assignment may proceed with no further action. Otherwise, the object is copied to a thread-local buffer before the assignment is executed.

This allows a reference-counting or a tracing collector to access a view of a heap snapshot as taken during the simultaneous halt. If an object is not dirty, then its value in

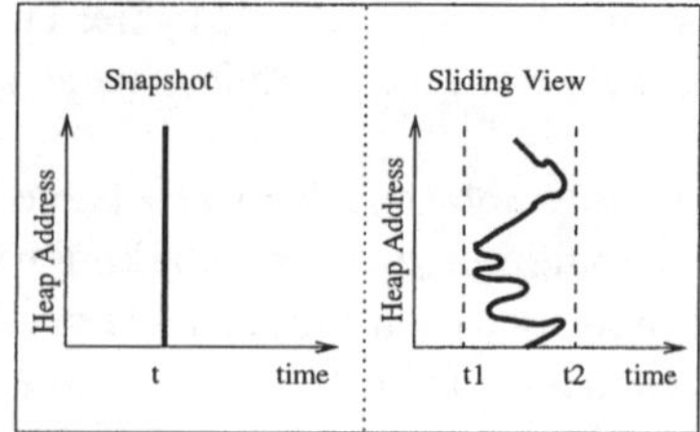

Fig. 1. A snapshot view at time t vs. a sliding view at interval [$t1$,$t2$]

the heap is equal to its value at the snapshot time. The snapshot value of dirty objects may be obtained from the local buffers. To deal with multithreaded programs, a carefully designed write barrier is presented in [20] allowing the above write barrier to operate on concurrent threads without requiring synchronized operations.

The collector in [20] eliminates many of the reference-count updates by updating the reference counts according to the change in pointer values between the previous snapshot to the current one. Consider a pointer slot that, between two garbage collections is assigned the values $o_0, o_1, o_2, \ldots, o_n$. All previous reference-counting collectors execute $2n$ reference-count updates for these assignments: RC(o_0)−−, RC(o_1)++, RC(o_1)−−, RC(o_2)++, ..., RC(o_n)++. However, it is observed that only two are required: RC(o_0)−− and RC(o_n)++, which buys a substantial reduction in the number of required updates. The "o_0" value of a modified slot (previous snapshot value) is exactly the value recorded by the write-barrier when the slot is modified. The "o_n" value of a modified slot (current snapshot value) is obtained according to the dirty flag, as explained above. Note, that for pointers in newly created objects the previous referent o_0 is always null. However, the reference count of current child (o_n) of newly created objects should be incremented.

The algorithm described so far probably obtains short pause times, but in order to get even shorter pause times, the sliding-views mechanism is proposed. Here, the program threads are not halted simultaneously, but one at a time. The obtained view of the heap is not a snapshot but a sliding view. A snapshot of the heap at time t is a copy of the content of each object in the heap at time t. A sliding view of the heap is associated with a time interval [$t1$,$t2$] (rather than a single point in time). It provides the content of each object in the heap at an arbitrary time t, satisfying $t_1 \leq t \leq t_2$. In contrast to a snapshot, objects are not all recorded at the same time. Figure 1 depicts the difference between a sliding view and a snapshot.

As a snapshot view cannot be assumed anymore, correctness considerations dictate a *snooping* mechanism. During the (short) time interval $[t_1, t_2]$ in which the program threads are being halted one by one, the snooping mechanism operates for each modified pointer via the write barrier. For each modified reference, the snooping mechanism records in a local buffer the address of the object that has acquired a new reference. These logged addresses are considered roots for the current collection and so such objects are not reclaimed. The view of the heap used by the collector may be thought of as a view that is sliding in time: the heap objects are viewed at slightly different points in time. The snooping mechanism makes sure that no reachable object is reclaimed. More details appear in [20].

3 Cycle Collector Overview

In this section we provide an overview of the new collector with its main ideas stressed. A full description including the pseudo code is provided in our technical report [26].

We first observe that if we were given a snapshot of the heap with all reference counts updated and a list of all objects whose reference counts have been decremented to a positive value since the last cycle collection, then we would have been able to run the *synchronous* algorithm of [5] on the given snapshot and correctly identify the garbage cycles in the heap as viewed at the snapshot. This is good news because being a garbage cycle is a stable property and such a cycle remains unreachable, no matter how the application behaves, until the collector reclaims its objects. Thus, unreachable cycles can be reclaimed based on a snapshot and a list of decrements.

Next, we explain how we obtain the snapshot and the list of decrements efficiently. We first concentrate on the first issue: obtaining the snapshot. The full list of reference-count decrements cannot be obtained efficiently, but we will show that it is possible to use a partial list and how that partial list can be obtained efficiently.

3.1 Obtaining a Snapshot (or a Sliding View)

The cycle collector uses the heap (or a snapshot of it) by repeatedly traversing several subgraphs of it. To obtain a virtual snapshot of the heap that may be used for such traversals, we use the mechanism of [20] described in Subsection 2.3. Traversing a subgraph is done as follows (following [2]). The write barrier of [20] is employed by the program threads. To traverse an object according to its pointer values at snapshot time, we obtain these values in the following manner. First, the dirty bit of the object is examined. If the object is not dirty (no pointer in the object has been modified since the snapshot was taken), then its current state in the heap is equal to its state during the snapshot and the collector may trace it by reading its pointers from the heap. Otherwise, the object has been modified since the snapshot time and it is marked dirty. In this case, the collector finds its snapshot values in the threads local buffers. After obtaining the snapshot values, objects can be traced according to their state at the snapshot time, and thus, repeated traces are bound to trace the same graph repeatedly.

In terms of completeness, once a garbage cycle is created, it must exist in the next snapshot, and thus it is bound to be reclaimed by the synchronous algorithm of [5]. We also improve efficiency, since we can use the efficient synchronous algorithm of [5] instead of using their less efficient concurrent collector. Inefficiencies originating from the need to insure correctness in spite of program-collector races are eliminated. For example, the entire second phase of the asynchronous algorithm of [5] is redundant: there is no need to *store* identified garbage cycles and there is no need to re-examine them during the next garbage collection by more traversals.

We now extend the discussion to using sliding views instead of snapshots in order to obtain an on-the-fly collector. The on-the-fly collector does not halt all program threads simultaneously, but stops each of them separately to obtain their roots and read their buffers. This creates a sliding view of the heap associated with a short time interval $[t_1, t_2]$ instead of a snapshot.

The cycle collector remains the same, except that it (obliviously) uses a sliding view of the heap rather than a snapshot. A sliding view may incorrectly indicate that an object is unreachable because the view does not represent the heap at a consistent point in time. The snooping mechanism makes sure that such objects are not reclaimed, ensuring the safety property. The snooping mechanism is explained in [20]. Let us review it shortly.

How can objects be seen unreachable in the sliding view while they are actually reachable at all times? Suppose the sliding view is read during the interval $[t_1, t_2]$. If no pointer is written to the heap during this time, the sliding view represents a snapshot of the pointers in the heap taken at the time t_2. However, as pointers are being written in the heap, this snapshot gets distorted, and the view may contain values of pointers that were updated between t_1 and t_2. It can be shown that if such a modified pointer creates a false unreachable garbage cycle in the view, then a pointer must have been written pointing to an object in this cycle during the time interval $[t_1, t_2]$. The snooping mechanism records all objects that acquire a new reference. Thus, the object that falsely seems unreachable in the sliding view must be snooped. Snooped objects are considered roots, and therefore, cyclic structures containing snooped objects cannot be reclaimed.

With respect to completeness, any unreachable cyclic structure formed before the collection begins, must be collected. The reason is that these objects are not modified during the time interval $[t_1, t_2]$ and in particular, no new pointers are being written to objects in this cycle. Thus, none of the objects in the cyclic structure is snooped and the view of all pointers into and in between these objects appears in the sliding view exactly as it would have appeared had we taken a real snapshot at time t_2. Thus, such an unreachable cyclic structure must be reclaimed.

3.2 Obtaining the List of Candidates

It remains to explain how the list of objects whose reference counts was decremented is obtained. All cycle collectors use a candidate set consisting of all newly created objects plus all objects whose reference count is reduced to a positive value by any pointer modification since the previous cycle collection. However, the sliding-views reference-counting collector of Levanoni and Petrank [20] does not maintain such a list. In fact, it is oblivious to most of the pointer updates and this obliviousness is what buys its efficiency. A naive solution is to make the reference-counting collector record all the extra required updates. This solution is unacceptable as it undermine the efficiency of the reference-counting collector. Instead, we improve the analysis of the cycle collector and show that the reduced set of candidates obtained from the Levanoni-Petrank collector suffices. This way, we can preserve the efficiency of the reference-counting collector and also significantly improves the efficiency of the cycle collector as fewer candidates need to be recorded and less work is required to traverse their descendants.

Newly created objects. Taking only reference-count decrements as candidates is not enough when the write barrier is not used with the roots. This is the case with all modern collectors, as a write barrier on the roots is too costly. Since decrements of roots are not accounted for, cycle collectors also include in the set of candidates all objects created since the last collection and all objects referenced directly from the roots during the previous collection.

To see that this is indeed required for all modern collectors, consider two newly created objects that point to each other only (forming a cycle) and a root pointer that references one of them. If the root pointer is modified, then a cycle of garbage is formed, but it cannot be noticed from reference-count decrements. The extended candidate set as above is enough to detect any such garbage cycle.

Obtaining the candidates. The sliding-views reference-counting collector yields almost for free a list of newly created objects and a list of objects that were referenced by the roots during the previous collection. We now concentrate on finding the more problematic set of objects whose reference counts were decremented.

As the sliding-views collector reduces a large fraction of the reference-count updates, we now claim that it is possible to collect all garbage cycles, even though we record and consider much fewer objects as candidates. To be more precise, when a pointer p takes the values $o_0, o_1, o_2, \ldots, o_n$ between two collections, only o_0 is considered as a candidate (if its reference count is decremented to a non-zero value) by the new cycle collector. Previous collectors considered also the objects $o_1, o_2, \ldots, o_{n-1}$ as candidates but are ignored by us. Additional relevant decrements are treated by this collector in the same manner as previous collectors. These are decrements that are executed by the reference-counting collector itself. When an object is reclaimed, the collector decrements the reference counts of all its descendants. These decrements may also produce candidates (if the descendant's reference count is not decremented to zero).

To show that the collector does not miss a garbage cycle, we divide the argument into 2 cases: garbage cycles comprising solely of old objects and garbage cycles containing at least one young object, where a young object is an object that has been created after the previous sliding view (or snapshot). Both cases are properly handled.

The easy case is when an unreachable cycle includes a young object. As mentioned earlier in this section, all young objects (surviving the reference-counting collection) are considered candidates. Thus, this cycle will not be missed.

The more involved case is a garbage cycle containing only old objects (created before the previous sliding view). If this cycle was reachable during the previous sliding view and is unreachable in the current sliding view, then there exists a pointer to one of the cycle's objects in the previous sliding view, but this pointer does not exist in the current sliding view. If this was a root pointer, then the cycle is considered by the fact that all root pointers from previous collection are candidates. Otherwise, this is a heap pointer that has been modified during the time interval between the two sliding views. The pointer modification could originate either from the application modifying a pointer (as in Figure 2), or from a reclamation of the object containing this pointer and the memory manager deleting the pointer. In the first case, the change of this pointer is logged in a local buffer causing a reference-count decrement to the object previously referenced. In the latter case, the delete operation of the collector implies a similar reference-count decrement. In each of these cases, this object becomes a candidate for cycle collection. Hence, cycles containing only old objects are accounted for properly.

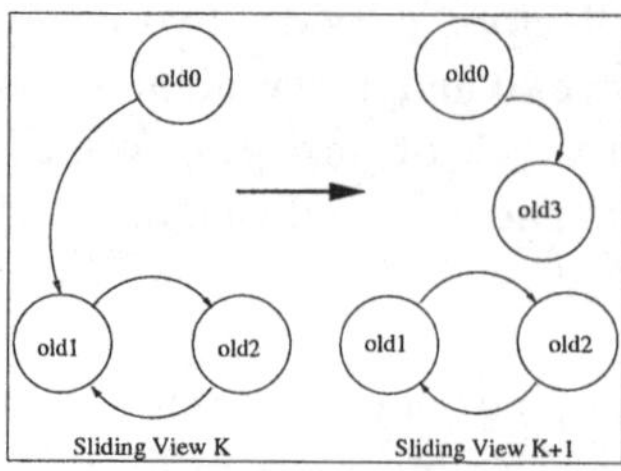

Fig. 2. A garbage cycle comprising solely of old objects created between the Kth and the $K+1^{\text{st}}$ sliding views. The cycle was reachable from *old0* and it became unreachable because *old0* was modified. Since *old0* is modified between the sliding views, *old0* (and its previous value *old1*) must be logged to a local buffer that is later used by reference-counting collector. Therefore, the reference count of *old1* gets decremented in the $K+1^{\text{st}}$ collection, and it is then considered as a candidate

To summarize, even though the Levanoni-Petrank reference-counting collector executes only a small fraction of the reference-count updates, we may collect cycles correctly using as candidates only those objects whose reference counts are decremented by this collector to a non-zero value, plus the roots at the previous sliding view and all newly created objects.

3.3 Checking Behavior with the Age-Oriented Collector

Newly created objects add a substantial burden on the cycle collector. Therefore, we also used the proposed cycle collector with a collector that runs reference counting and cycle collection on the old generation only. We chose the age-oriented collector, a twist on generational collection that is adequate for concurrent collection. Our age-oriented collector runs concurrent reference counting on the old generation and concurrent mark and sweep on the young objects [27]. The age-oriented collector eliminates a large fraction of the cycles as well as a large fraction of the cycle collector's work since it does not need to consider the young objects as candidates. Indeed cycle collection was more effective in this setting. Let us say a few words about the age-oriented collector. For a full description see [27].

The age-oriented collector keeps generations, but it does not run frequent young generation collections. The reason for allowing entire heap collections is that short pauses are obtained by concurrency already and do not need to be obtained by short young collections. The heap is collected only when it gets full. When that happens, the age-oriented collector uses a reference-counting collector to reclaim objects in the old generation and mark and sweep collector to reclaim objects in the young generation. Since these collections always happen together, there is no need to record inter-generational pointers. It is important to note that the age-oriented collector is an efficient collector, in particular, it is more efficient than the reference-counting algorithm as a stand-alone. Therefore, it is relevant to check its performance with a cycle collector.

3.4 Reducing the Number of Traced Objects

New techniques for filtering and reducing the number of traced objects were designed and implemented in the proposed collector. For lack of space, these techniques are omitted. They are described in our technical report [26].

4 Measurements

An Implementation for Java. Our algorithm was implemented in Jikes RVM [1], a research Java virtual machine. The entire system, including the collector itself is written in Java (extended with unsafe primitives available only to the Java Virtual Machine implementation to access raw memory).

Platform and benchmarks. We have taken measurements on a 4-way IBM Netfinity 8500R server with a 550MHz Intel Pentium III Xeon processor and 2GB of physical memory. The benchmarks used were the SPECjvm98 benchmark suite and the SPECjbb2000 benchmark (described in [29]). We feel that the multithreaded SPECjbb-2000 benchmark is more interesting, as the SPECjvm98 are more appropriate for clients and our algorithm is targeted at servers (multi-processors). SPECjbb2000 runs in a single JVM in which threads represent terminals in a warehouse. It is run with one terminal per warehouse, thus, the number of warehouses signifies the number of threads. We also feel that there is a dire need in academic research for more multithreaded benchmarks. In this work, as well as in other recent work ([4, 13]) SPECjbb2000 is the only representative of large multithreaded applications.

Testing procedure. We used the benchmark suite using the test harness, performing standard automated runs of all the benchmarks in the suite. Our standard automated run runs each benchmark five times for each of the JVM's involved (each implementing a different collector). The average of this 5 runs is used. Finally, each JVM was run on varying heap sizes. For the SPECjvm98 suite, we started with a 32MB[5] heap size and extended the sizes by 8MB increments until a final large size of 96MB. For SPECjbb2000 we started from 256MB heap size and extended by 64MB increments until a final large size of 704MB.

The compared collectors. The cycle collection algorithm was incorporated into two collectors: the Levanoni-Petrank reference-counting collector [20], and the more efficient age-oriented collector [27]. Both collectors are also implemented in Jikes and are accompanied by a backup mark and sweep collector which is run infrequently to collect garbage cycles. For performance measurements, we ran both collectors accompanied with our cycle collection algorithm against both collectors when using the backup mark and sweep algorithm. This first ever reported comparison of cycle collection to a backup tracing collector is important since these are the main two options provided to an implementer of a reference-counting algorithm. In addition, we have compared characteristics of our cycle collection algorithm (with both collectors), against the characteristics of the previous on-the-fly cycle collector of Bacon and Rajan [4].

4.1 Performance

SPECjbb2000. Figure 3 depicts the throughput ratio between using the cycle collector and a backup tracing collector when both are used with the Levanoni-Petrank collector. With 1–3 warehouses the collector has a spare processor to run on, since the platform has four processors. In this case, throughput differences occur only when the collector is not efficient enough to free enough space for program threads with on-going allocations.

[5] This is a tight heap for Jikes as it is self-hosted.

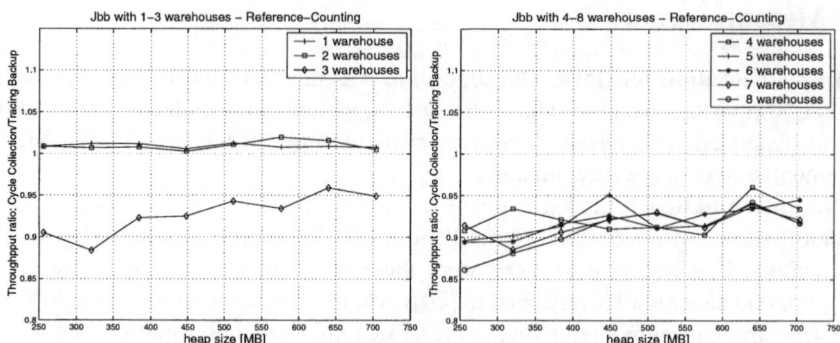

Fig. 3. SPECjbb2000 on a multiprocessor with the reference-counting collector. The higher the ratio, the better the cycle collector performs compared to the backup tracing algorithm

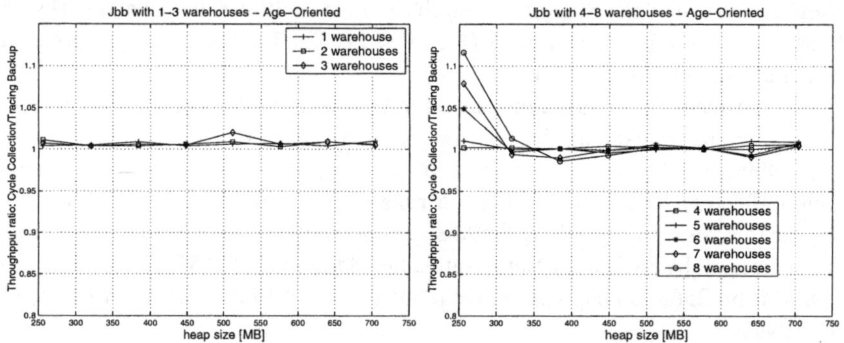

Fig. 4. SPECjbb2000 on a multiprocessor with the age-oriented collector. The higher the ratio, the better the cycle collector performs compared to the backup tracing algorithm

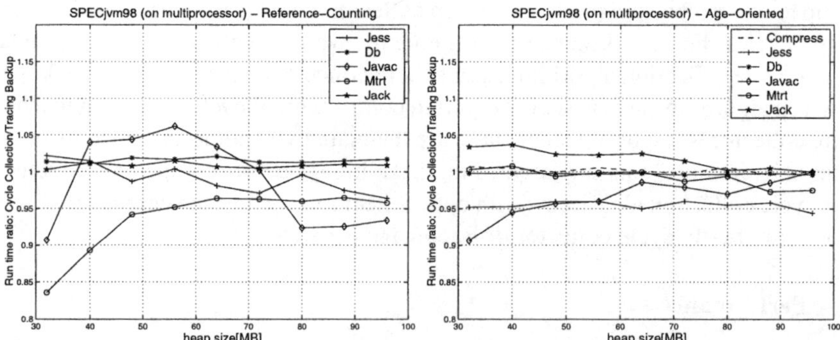

Fig. 5. SPECjvm98 on a multiprocessor. The higher the ratio, the better the cycle collector performs compared to the backup tracing algorithm

This is more noticeable on tight heaps. With 4–8 warehouses, the collector does not have a spare processor and its use of CPU directly affects the throughput. The tracing backup collector outperforms the cycle collector usually by 5%–10%.

The same measurements have been run when the cycle collector and the backup tracing collector were used with the old generation of the age-oriented collector [27], see Figure 4. As only old objects are collected with reference counting and cycle collection, the behavior differs. Here, cycle collection performs usually as good as the backup tracing collector, whereas in tight heaps in which cycle collection wins. As already observed in [2] reference counting has an advantage on tight heaps over tracing. Here it is seen that cycle collection is also preferable on tracing (as an add-on to reference counting) when the heap is tight.

SPECjvm98. When running the SPECjvm98 benchmarks on a multiprocessor the collector runs concurrently with the program thread(s) on a spare processor. Figure 5 depicts the results both with the Levanoni-Petrank reference-counting collector as well as with the age-oriented collector. The results do not point to a clear winner. Each application behaves somewhat differently and most of the differences are below 5%. The only clear noticeable difference is with the _227_mtrt benchmark. In _227_mtrt there exists an initial phase in which many objects are created and kept alive till the end of the run. These newly created objects induce a large amount of work on the cycle collector. During the (single) long collection, the mutators halt waiting for free space. Performance difference on _227_mtrt is not noticeable with the age-oriented collector, where the cycle collector is not run on this pack of young objects.

Discussion. At first glance, it may seem that backup tracing is the right choice. However, it is worth noting that modern platforms and benchmarks also run more efficiently with tracing than with reference counting [2]. Should we give up on reference counting and cycle collection? To our minds, the answer is no. With the direction modern computing is taking, we believe that the cycle collector may become much more effective compared to a backup tracing collector. As heaps grow larger, reference counting may become the preferred method of choice. While tracing must traverse the live objects in the heap, reference counting needs only account for reference-counts updates and reclaiming dead objects [6]. If future benchmarks use a large live heap or even a large old generation, then reference counting may become the best collector, and a companion cycle collector will be required. In that case, the cycle collector proposed here is an effective companion and we expect it to outperform a backup tracing collector. Note also, that the best way to use reference counting today is to run it on the old generation only as proposed in [3, 7, 27]. In that case, running cycle collection with the reference counting is the right choice.

4.2 Pause Times

Table 1 presents the maximum pause times of the Levanoni-Petrank reference-counting collector accompanied by our cycle collection algorithm. Pauses were measured with a 64MB heap for SPECjvm98 benchmarks, and a 256MB heap for SPECjbb2000 with 1, 2, and 3 warehouses. For this number of threads, no thread gets swapped out, and so pauses are due to the garbage collection only. If we run more program threads, large

[6] Actually, when the heap is tight and collections are frequent, reference counting is already winning over tracing the whole heap [2]. But, we don't expect heaps to be tighter in the future.

Table 1. Maximum pause time in milliseconds

Benchmarks	Maximum pause time (ms)
compress	1.0
jess	1.3
db	0.7
javac	1.7
jack	1.0
mtrt	0.9
jbb-1	0.8
jbb-2	0.6
jbb-3	1.1

Table 2. Cyclic garbage collected for each benchmark

	RC		AO	
Bench-marks	cyclic objects reclaimed	cyclic bytes (in MB)	cyclic objects reclaimed	cyclic bytes (in MB)
compress	108	84.08	0	0
jess	24	0.15	0	0
db	16	0.09	0	0
javac	1 M	67.64	0.57 M	37.02
mtrt	66052	5.78	66042	5.66
jack	8976	1.72	3360	0.62
jbb	146	0.88	0	0

pause times (whose lengths depend on the operating system scheduler) appear because threads lose the CPU to other threads.

The maximum pause time measured for all benchmarks was 1.7 ms. The maximum pause time of the Levanoni-Petrank reference-counting collector does not depend on whether it is accompanied by a tracing backup or by a cycle collector. The operation that determines the length of the pause time is the scanning of the roots of a single thread, which occurs in one of the handshakes of the collector with the program threads.

4.3 Collector Characteristics

Amount of Cyclic Garbage. Table 2 provides, for each benchmark, the number of garbage cycle objects reclaimed and the space they consume. As the age-oriented collector only employs cycle collection on old objects, it needs to reclaim a smaller set of garbage cycles than the reference-counting collector.

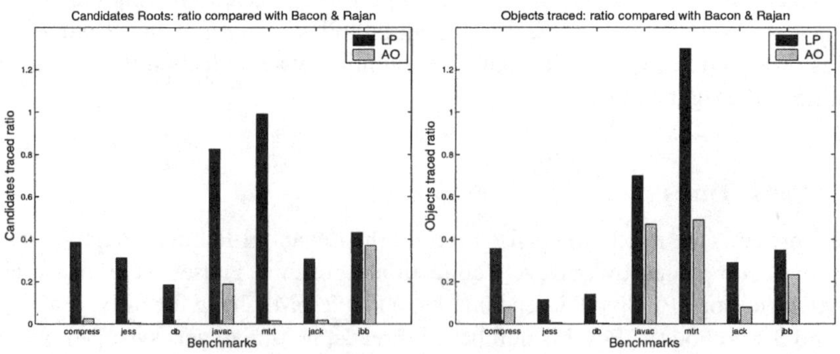

Fig. 6. Comparison between the new collector and the previous cycle collector of Bacon and Rajan. On the left, comparing the number of cycle candidates and on the right the number of traced objects. The lower the ratio, the better the new cycle collector algorithm behaves

The benchmarks producing a substantial amount of garbage cycles space are _213_javac and _201_compress. _201_compress creates dozens of garbage cycles comprised of huge objects, and thus requires only a small amount of tracing. _213_javac however, contains thousands of garbage cycles, thus requiring a large cycle collection work.

Amount of Tracing. Figure 6 reports the *candidates examined* and the *objects traced* ratios when the cycle collector is run with the Levanoni-Petrank collector (LP) and age-oriented collector (AO) compared to these of the cycle collector of Bacon and Rajan [5]. To be extremely conservative we did not include the objects scanned during the additional verification phase of [5] (since in this phase the actual operation on some objects only included work on their colors, i.e., they were not actually *traced*). Thus, the actual advantage of the new collector is even higher than reported.

Figure 6 shows that the new cycle collector with the Levanoni-Petrank collector traces fewer candidates compared to the previous cycle collector (of [5]) over all benchmarks[7]. It usually also traces substantially fewer objects except for one case: the _227_mtrt benchmark (discussed above). The additional saving when the cycle collector is used with the age-oriented collector is substantial for most benchmarks.

5 Related Work

The inability of reference counting to reclaim cyclic garbage structures was first noticed by McBeth [24]. Martinez et al. [23] (inspired by [10]) reclaim cells, which were uniquely referenced when their count drops to zero, while when a pointer to a shared object is deleted, a local depth-first search is applied on it. Lins [21] postponed these traversals while saving the values of the deleted pointer in a buffer (each such value is a candidate to be a root of a garbage cycle) and traversed the buffer at a suitable point. Bacon et al. [5] extended Lins algorithm to a concurrent cycle collection algorithm. They also improved Lins' algorithm by performing the tracing of all candidates simultaneously, reducing the number of traced objects. Lins [22] showed the algorithm can employ 2 graph traversals (instead of 3) per candidate by using an extra data structure.

6 Conclusion

We presented a new non-intrusive, complete, and efficient cycle collector adequate for use with a reference-counting garbage collector. The new cycle collector runs concurrently with the program threads, achieving negligibly short pauses of less than 2ms. It uses the sliding-views reference-counting collector of Levanoni and Petrank [20] with the synchronous cycle collector of Bacon and Rajan [5]. These algorithms do not naturally fit together since the original cycle collector expects to get a list of all reference-count decrements, whereas the original reference-counting collector is oblivious to most of these decrements. However, we provide a finer analysis of cycle collection showing

---

[7] These measurements include the new techniques reducing the number of traced objects, reported in our technical report [26].

that the information gathered by the reference-counting collector is enough to guarantee reclamation of all unreachable cycles.

The use of the sliding-views mechanism yields a drastic improvement in efficiency. Much of the work required to ensure concurrent correctness may be eliminated. We have further added filtering techniques to optimize the collector's performance. An additional theoretical contribution is the completeness of the collector. The resulting cycle collector is guaranteed to reclaim all garbage cycles, whereas the only available previously known concurrent collector [5] had an (extremely rare) sequence of events that prevented it from collecting an unreachable cyclic structure forever.

We implemented the proposed cycle collector and we provide the first direct comparison of running a cycle collector with reference counting against running reference counting with a backup tracing collector. Our results show that with contemporary benchmarks, the backup tracing collector outperforms the cycle collector, although it is the most efficient cycle collector available. However, when the reference-counting collector was run only on the old generation, the cycle collector performed equally to the backup tracing collector, and even better on tight heaps. Thus on today's platforms and benchmarks cycle collection is effective when applied to the old generation only. In the future, as heaps and live data become much larger, the techniques described in this work may become a preferred and most effective method to reclaim garbage.

Acknowledgement. Ram Natahniel initiated our discussion on this problem by suggesting to use algorithms for strongly connected components to efficiently locate garbage cycles. Our attempts to follow this direction failed, but this paper has evolved. We thanks Ram for many interesting discussions.

References

1. Bowen Alpern, C. R. Attanasio, Anthony Cocchi, Derek Lieber, Stephen Smith, Ton Ngo, John J. Barton, Susan Flynn Hummel, Janice C. Sheperd, and Mark Mergen. Implementing Jalapeño in Java. In *OOPSLA'99 ACM Conference on Object-Oriented Systems, Languages and Applications*, volume 34(10) of *ACM SIGPLAN Notices*, pages 314–324, 1999.
2. Hezi Azatchi, Yossi Levanoni, Harel Paz, and Erez Petrank. An on-the-fly mark and sweep garbage collector based on sliding view. In OOPSLA [25].
3. Hezi Azatchi and Erez Petrank. Integrating generations with advanced reference counting garbage collectors. In *Proceedings of the Compiler Construction: 12th International Conference on Compiler Construction*, volume 2622 of *LNCS*, pages 185–199, 2003.
4. David F. Bacon, Clement R. Attanasio, Han B. Lee, V. T. Rajan, and Stephen Smith. Java without the coffee breaks: A nonintrusive multiprocessor garbage collector. In *Proceedings of SIGPLAN 2001 Conference on Programming Languages Design and Implementation*, ACM SIGPLAN Notices, Snowbird, Utah, June 2001.
5. David F. Bacon and V.T. Rajan. Concurrent cycle collection in reference counted systems. In Jørgen Lindskov Knudsen, editor, *Proceedings of 15th European Conference on Object-Oriented Programming, ECOOP 2001*, volume 2072 of *Springer-Verlag*, 2001.
6. Henry G. Baker. List processing in real-time on a serial computer. *Communications of the ACM*, 21(4):280–94, 1978. Also AI Laboratory Working Paper 139, 1977.
7. Stephen M. Blackburn and Kathryn S. McKinley. Ulterior reference counting: Fast garbage collection without a long wait. In OOPSLA [25].

8. Daniel G. Bobrow. Managing re-entrant structures using reference counts. *ACM Transactions on Programming Languages and Systems*, 2(3):269–273, July 1980.
9. Hans-Juergen Boehm, Alan J. Demers, and Scott Shenker. Mostly parallel garbage collection. *ACM SIGPLAN Notices*, 26(6):157–164, 1991.
10. T. W. Christopher. Reference count garbage collection. *Software Practice and Experience*, 14(6):503–507, June 1984.
11. George E. Collins. A method for overlapping and erasure of lists. *Communications of the ACM*, 3(12):655–657, December 1960.
12. Edsgar W. Dijkstra, Leslie Lamport, A. J. Martin, C. S. Scholten, and E. F. M. Steffens. On-the-fly garbage collection: An exercise in cooperation. *Communications of the ACM*, 21(11):965–975, November 1978.
13. Tamar Domani, Elliot Kolodner, and Erez Petrank. A generational on-the-fly garbage collector for Java. In *Proceedings of SIGPLAN 2000 Conference on Programming Languages Design and Implementation*, ACM SIGPLAN Notices, Vancouver, June 2000.
14. Toshio Endo, Kenjiro Taura, and Akinori Yonezawa. A scalable mark-sweep garbage collector on large-scale shared-memory machines. In *Proceedings of High Performance Computing and Networking (SC'97)*, 1997.
15. Christine Flood, Dave Detlefs, Nir Shavit, and Catherine Zhang. Parallel garbage collection for shared memory multiprocessors. In *Usenix Java Virtual Machine Research and Technology Symposium (JVM '01)*, Monterey, CA, April 2001.
16. Tony Hosking, editor. *ISMM 2000 Proceedings of the Second International Symposium on Memory Management*, volume 36(1) of *ACM SIGPLAN Notices*, 2000.
17. Richard L. Hudson and J. Eliot B. Moss. Sapphire: Copying GC without stopping the world. In *Joint ACM Java Grande — ISCOPE 2001 Conference*, Stanford University, CA, 2001.
18. Elliot K. Kolodner and Erez Petrank. Parallel copying garbage collection using delayed allocation. In *Parallel Processing Letters*, volume 14, June 2004.
19. Yossi Levanoni and Erez Petrank. A scalable reference counting garbage collector. Technical Report CS–0967, Technion — Israel Institute of Technology, Haifa, Israel, November 1999.
20. Yossi Levanoni and Erez Petrank. An on-the-fly reference counting garbage collector for Java. In *OOPSLA'01 ACM Conference on Object-Oriented Systems, Languages and Applications*, volume 36(10) of *ACM SIGPLAN Notices*, Tampa, FL, October 2001.
21. Rafael D. Lins. Cyclic reference counting with lazy mark-scan. *IPL*, 44(4):215–220, 1992.
22. Rafael D. Lins. An efficient algorithm for cyclic reference counting. *IPL*, 83:145–150, 2002.
23. A. D. Martinez, R. Wachenchauzer, and Rafael D. Lins. Cyclic reference counting with local mark-scan. *Information Processing Letters*, 34:31–35, 1990.
24. J. Harold McBeth. On the reference counter method. *CACM*, 6(9):575, September 1963.
25. *OOPSLA'03 ACM Conference on Object-Oriented Systems, Languages and Applications*, ACM SIGPLAN Notices, Anaheim, CA, November 2003.
26. Harel Paz, David F. Bacon, Elliot K. Kolodner, Erez Petrank, and V.T. Rajan. Efficient on-the-fly cycle collection. Technical Report CS–2003–10, Technion, 2003.
27. Harel Paz, Erez Petrank, and Stephen M. Blackburn. Age-Oriented Concurrent Garbage Collection. In *Proceedings of the 14th Int. Conference on Compiler Construction*, 2005.
28. Tony Printezis and David Detlefs. A generational mostly-concurrent garbage collector. In Hosking [16].
29. SPEC Benchmarks. Standard Performance Evaluation Corporation. http://www.spec.org/, 1998,2000.
30. Guy L. Steele. Multiprocessing compactifying garbage collection. *Communications of the ACM*, 18(9):495–508, September 1975.
31. Guy L. Steele. Corrigendum: Multiprocessing compactifying garbage collection. *Communications of the ACM*, 19(6):354, June 1976.

Data Slicing: Separating the Heap into Independent Regions

Jeremy Condit and George C. Necula

Department of Electrical Engineering and Computer Science,
University of California, Berkeley
{jcondit, necula}@cs.berkeley.edu

Abstract. In this paper, we present a formal description of *data slicing*, which is a type-directed program transformation technique that separates a program's heap into several independent regions. Pointers within each region mirror the structure of pointers in the original heap; however, each field whose type is a base type (e.g., the integer type) appears in only one of these regions. In addition, we discuss several applications of data slicing. First, data slicing can be used to add extra fields to existing data structures without compromising backward compatibility; the CCured project uses data slicing to preserve library compatibility in instrumented programs at a reasonable performance cost. Data slicing can also be used to improve locality by separating "hot" and "cold" fields in an array of data structures, and it can be used to protect sensitive data by separating "public" and "private" fields. Finally, data slicing can serve as a refactoring tool, allowing the programmer to split data structures while automatically updating the code that manipulates them.

1 Introduction

When maintaining a large software project, a seemingly trivial change to a data structure can be largely intractable due to the amount of code that depends upon that data structure's layout. When programmers wish to modify a data structure, they must weigh the benefits of these modifications against the time required to modify the program and the risk of introducing new bugs. Compilers face a similar challenge; for example, a compiler may wish to alter one of the data structures in the program it is compiling without violating data layout assumptions made by precompiled code. Such changes require a principled approach that can achieve the desired goal automatically and without changing the program's semantics.

This paper introduces *data slicing*, a program transformation technique that addresses this problem. Given an existing program, data slicing produces a new program that computes the same result while splitting its data structures among several memory regions. This transformation allows the programmer or the compiler to factor out portions of a data structure that must reside in a different place in memory.

R. Bodik (Ed.): CC 2005, LNCS 3443, pp. 172–187, 2005.

Data slicing can be used to preserve backward compatibility after a program transformation. For example, a transformation that adds new fields to existing data structures may make the program incompatible with precompiled libraries; data slicing can be used to separate these new fields from the old ones, allowing the original program's data structures to retain their original layout. As the prototypical example of this application, we show how to instantiate data slicing in the context of the CCured project [4] to enable extensive run-time checking of C programs while maintaining compatibility with precompiled libraries.

Data slicing can also be applied to performance optimizations. For example, data slicing can be used to produce an improved implementation of the instance interleaving optimization [13], which interleaves the fields of several objects in order to place frequently-accessed fields in the same cache line.

Finally, data slicing can be applied to security problems. For example, data slicing can move function pointers to a separate memory region to make it more difficult for an attacker to overwrite them. In general, data slicing acts as a refactoring tool that simplifies the task of making global changes to data structures.

This paper offers two main contributions. First, it presents a formal description of the type-directed data slicing transformation on a simple imperative language. Second, it discusses several applications of this technique, including CCured, instance interleaving, and security-related transformations.

2 Data Slicing

Data slicing is a program transformation that separates a program's heap into independent regions. The input to this transformation is a program whose base types (e.g., integer types) have been annotated with region names. The goal of data slicing is to produce a new program that computes the same result as the original program while splitting the data structures in the program's heap into independent regions. Each region must contain only the data that has been annotated for that region, as well as any pointers that are necessary for keeping track of that data. We focus on the case when the regions must be *independent*, in the sense that there are no pointers that cross region boundaries; however, we will show how to relax this requirement in Sections 2.5 and 3.1.

To achieve these goals, data slicing ensures that each region in the program mirrors the structure of the original program's heap. For example, if the original program's heap contains a linked list with data whose fields are annotated with multiple regions, then each region of the transformed program's heap will contain a linked list of the same length containing the list data for that region. More precisely, there is an injective mapping m_i from objects in region R_i to objects in the original program's heap at a given point in execution. An object A in region R_i contains the fields of object $m_i(A)$ whose type is labelled with region R_i. Furthermore, if object A points to object B in region R_i, then object $m_i(A)$ points to object $m_i(B)$ in the original program's heap. Note that base fields (i.e., fields whose type is a base type) will be stored in exactly one region according to the relevant type annotation, whereas each pointer field may be split into several

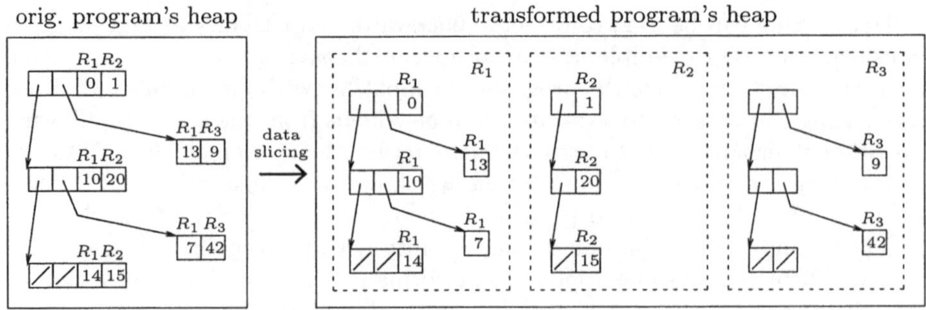

Fig. 1. Illustration of data slicing's effects. The dashed lines delimit the regions within the transformed program's heap

pointer fields, one in each region where it is necessary. Essentially, data slicing *separates* base fields and *replicates* some pointer fields.

Figure 1 illustrates the effects of data slicing. This figure shows a program's heap at a specific point in time before and after data slicing. The base fields in the original heap are annotated with region names R_1, R_2, and R_3. In the transformed heap, each region contains a data structure with the same shape as the original, except that it contains only the base fields for that region as well as any pointers needed to access those fields. Note that we have eliminated entire objects from region R_2; thus, the mapping m_2 is injective but not surjective.

The remainder of this section presents the data slicing transformation formally. First, we introduce a C-like language (Section 2.1), and then we define data slicing on types and programs (Sections 2.2 and 2.3). Then, we discuss first-class functions and partial data slicing (Sections 2.4 and 2.5).

2.1 Language

Figure 2 shows an imperative language that will be the basis for our discussion of data slicing. The types in this language include integer types, pointer types, structure types, and named types (t). We use `void` as a shorthand for `struct{}`. Base types (here, the integer type) have a region qualifier that indicates the region where this data should be placed. Region names are R_1 through R_n; throughout this paper, n will refer to the number of available regions.

The syntax for l-expressions (l) and expressions (e) is based loosely on that of C. Binary operations ("op" in the grammar) include arithmetic and comparison, and they may only be applied to integers in the same region. We permit casts between integers in different regions as well as casts from pointers to integers.

Commands (c) include standard imperative constructs. We will use $l_1, ..., l_k := e_1, ..., e_k$ as syntactic sugar for simultaneous assignment where all right-hand sides are evaluated before any assignments occur. Function calls have no explicit return value; instead, the programmer must pass a pointer to the result variable as an argument. At the top level, a program (p) is a list of definitions (d) of func-

types	$\tau ::= \texttt{int}\ R_i \mid t \mid \tau\ \texttt{ptr} \mid \texttt{struct}\{\ \ldots f_j : \tau_j;\ \ldots\ \}$
l-expressions	$l\ ::= x \mid l.f \mid *e$
expressions	$e ::= n \mid \texttt{null} \mid \texttt{new}\ \tau \mid e_1\ \texttt{op}\ e_2\ \mid \&l \mid l$
	$\mid \texttt{cast}\langle\texttt{int}\ R_j \hookrightarrow \texttt{int}\ R_i\rangle\ e \mid \texttt{cast}\langle\tau\ \texttt{ptr}\ \hookrightarrow \texttt{int}\ R_i\rangle\ e$
commands	$c ::= l := e \mid f(x) \mid \texttt{let}\ x : \tau\ \texttt{in}\ c \mid c_1; c_2$
	$\mid \texttt{if}\ e\ \texttt{then}\ c_1\ \texttt{else}\ c_2 \mid \texttt{while}\ e\ \texttt{do}\ c$
definitions	$d ::= f(x : \tau)\ \{c\} \mid \texttt{type}\ t = \tau$
programs	$p ::= d\ p \mid d$

Fig. 2. A C-like language used as the basis for discussing data slicing

tions and types. Type definitions allow recursive types to be defined. To simplify the presentation, we defer the discussion of function pointers to Section 2.4. The complete static semantics for this language can be found in Appendix A.

Using this language, we can write down the types of the objects in Figure 1. In the original program's heap, there are two types of objects, t and t', as follows:

$$\begin{aligned}
&\texttt{type}\ t\ = \texttt{struct}\{\ p_1 : t\ \texttt{ptr};\ p_2 : t'\ \texttt{ptr};\ f_1 : \texttt{int}\ R_1;\ f_2 : \texttt{int}\ R_2;\ \}\\
&\texttt{type}\ t' = \texttt{struct}\{\ f_1 : \texttt{int}\ R_1;\ f_3 : \texttt{int}\ R_3;\ \}
\end{aligned}$$

To translate a C program to this language, the programmer must add region annotations to each field or variable whose type is a base type. The programmer must either eliminate unsafe pointer casts or limit the use of data slicing to the safe portions of the program using a technique discussed in Section 2.5.

2.2 Transformation of Types

We now define the data slicing transformation on types, which will guide the rest of the transformation. In the previous section, we defined two types, t and t', for the objects on the left-hand side of Figure 1. Data slicing splits each object of type t or t' into three objects, one in each region. The resulting types are:

$$\begin{aligned}
&\texttt{type}\ t_1 = \texttt{struct}\{\ p_1 : t_1\ \texttt{ptr};\ p_2 : t'_1\ \texttt{ptr};\ f_1 : \texttt{int}\ R_1;\ \}\\
&\texttt{type}\ t_2 = \texttt{struct}\{\ p_1 : t_2\ \texttt{ptr};\ f_2 : \texttt{int}\ R_2;\ \}\\
&\texttt{type}\ t_3 = \texttt{struct}\{\ p_1 : t_3\ \texttt{ptr};\ p_2 : t'_3\ \texttt{ptr};\ \}
\end{aligned}$$

$$\begin{aligned}
&\texttt{type}\ t'_1 = \texttt{struct}\{\ f_1 : \texttt{int}\ R_1;\ \}\\
&\texttt{type}\ t'_2 = \texttt{void}\\
&\texttt{type}\ t'_3 = \texttt{struct}\{\ f_3 : \texttt{int}\ R_3;\ \}
\end{aligned}$$

Note that the pointers of type t `ptr` in the original heap have been split into pointers of type t_1 `ptr`, t_2 `ptr`, and t_3 `ptr` in their respective regions. Similarly, the pointers of type t' `ptr` have been split into pointers of type t'_1 `ptr` and t'_3 `ptr` in regions R_1 and R_3. It is unnecessary to have a pointer of type t'_2 `ptr` in region R_2 because t' contains no data labelled with region R_2 (i.e., t'_2 is `void`). Note that integer fields only appear in the region to which they have been assigned.

Formally, we define a mapping TSlice_i from types in the original program to the corresponding types in region R_i of the transformed program (see Figure 3).

$$\mathsf{TSlice}_i(\mathtt{int}\ R_j) = \begin{cases} \mathtt{int}\ R_j & \text{if } i = j \\ \mathtt{void} & \text{otherwise} \end{cases}$$

$$\mathsf{TSlice}_i(\tau\ \mathtt{ptr}) = \begin{cases} \mathsf{TSlice}_i(\tau)\ \mathtt{ptr} & \text{if } \mathsf{TSlice}_i(\tau) \neq \mathtt{void} \\ \mathtt{void} & \text{otherwise} \end{cases}$$

$$\mathsf{TSlice}_i(\mathtt{struct}\{\ \ldots\ f_j : \tau_j;\ \ldots\ \}) = \mathtt{struct}\{\ \ldots\ f_j : \mathsf{TSlice}_i(\tau_j);\ \ldots\ \}$$

$$\mathsf{TSlice}_i(t) = t_i$$

$$\mathsf{VSlice}(\tau) = \mathtt{struct}\{\ \ldots\ r_i : \mathsf{TSlice}_i(\tau);\ \ldots\ \}$$

Fig. 3. Data slicing transformation for types. Note that we omit `void` fields from the resulting structure types

The first rule in this definition says that the sliced type for region R_i contains only those base types that are annotated with region R_i. The rules for structures and pointers recursively apply TSlice_i, and the rule for named types transforms a named type t into its corresponding named type t_i in region R_i. (In Section 2.3, we will define t_i to be $\mathsf{TSlice}_i(\tau)$, where τ is the original definition of t.)

Two optimizations occur during this transformation. First, when the result is a structure type, we omit fields of type `void`. Second, we omit pointers that cannot be used to reach any data in region R_i, as shown in the "otherwise" case for pointer types. For example, $\mathsf{TSlice}_1(\mathtt{int}\ R_2\ \mathtt{ptr}\ \mathtt{ptr}) = \mathtt{void}$ rather than `void ptr ptr`, since this type contains no information from region R_1. Of course, TSlice_2 yields $\mathtt{int}\ R_2\ \mathtt{ptr}\ \mathtt{ptr}$, as desired.

TSlice_i gives the transformation for a specific region; however, at certain points in the program (variables and formal parameters), we must gather the sliced data into one structure containing the data from all regions. In Figure 3, VSlice gives the type of this merged structure. For example, a variable or formal parameter whose type is a pointer type would be transformed into a structure containing one pointer for each region where the pointer's sliced type is not `void`.

2.3 Transformation of Programs

In Figure 4, we show the transformation for the remaining syntactic constructs.

PSlice and DSlice transform programs and definitions. Formal parameters are transformed with VSlice, so they include data from all regions. For type definitions, we create one named type for each region.

CSlice defines data slicing for commands. Function calls are unchanged, since the argument variable's type will have been transformed with VSlice. For conditionals and loops, we transform the guard expression with ESlice_1, which slices an expression with type $\mathtt{int}\ R_1$. (The guard expression must have this type.)

The assignment command is the key part of this transformation: essentially, the transformed program performs the corresponding assignment in each region where the type being assigned is not `void`. Since each region's assignment operation is performed separately, the rules for expressions and l-expressions are

$$
\begin{aligned}
\mathsf{PSlice}(d\ p) &= \mathsf{DSlice}(d)\ \mathsf{PSlice}(p)\\
\mathsf{PSlice}(d) &= \mathsf{DSlice}(d)\\[4pt]
\mathsf{DSlice}(f(x:\tau)\ \{c\}) &= f(x:\mathsf{VSlice}(\tau))\ \{\mathsf{CSlice}(c)\}\\
\mathsf{DSlice}(\mathtt{type}\ t=\tau) &= \mathtt{type}\ t_1=\mathsf{TSlice}_1(\tau)\ \ldots\ \mathtt{type}\ t_n=\mathsf{TSlice}_n(\tau)\\[4pt]
\mathsf{CSlice}(f(x)) &= f(x)\\
\mathsf{CSlice}(\mathtt{if}\ e\ \mathtt{then}\ c_1\ \mathtt{else}\ c_2) &= \mathtt{if}\ \mathsf{ESlice}_1(e)\ \mathtt{then}\ \mathsf{CSlice}(c_1)\ \mathtt{else}\ \mathsf{CSlice}(c_2)\\
\mathsf{CSlice}(\mathtt{while}\ e\ \mathtt{do}\ c) &= \mathtt{while}\ \mathsf{ESlice}_1(e)\ \mathtt{do}\ \mathsf{CSlice}(c)\\
\mathsf{CSlice}(\mathtt{let}\ x:\tau\ \mathtt{in}\ c) &= \mathtt{let}\ x:\mathsf{VSlice}(\tau)\ \mathtt{in}\ \mathsf{CSlice}(c)\\
\mathsf{CSlice}(c_1;c_2) &= \mathsf{CSlice}(c_1);\mathsf{CSlice}(c_2)\\
\mathsf{CSlice}(l:=e) &= \mathsf{LSlice}_{i_1}(l),..,\mathsf{LSlice}_{i_k}(l) := \mathsf{ESlice}_{i_1}(e),..,\mathsf{ESlice}_{i_k}(e)\\
&\quad \text{where } \{i_1,..,i_k\}=\{i\in\{1,..,n\}\mid \mathsf{TSlice}_i(\mathsf{TypeOf}(e))\neq \mathtt{void}\}\\[4pt]
\mathsf{ESlice}_i(n) &= n\\
\mathsf{ESlice}_i(\mathtt{null}) &= \mathtt{null}\\
\mathsf{ESlice}_i(e_1\ \mathtt{op}\ e_2) &= \mathsf{ESlice}_i(e_1)\ \mathtt{op}\ \mathsf{ESlice}_i(e_2)\\
\mathsf{ESlice}_i(\mathtt{cast}\langle\mathtt{int}\ R_j \hookrightarrow \mathtt{int}\ R_i\rangle e) &= \mathtt{cast}\langle\mathtt{int}\ R_j \hookrightarrow \mathtt{int}\ R_i\rangle\ \mathsf{ESlice}_j(e)\\
\mathsf{ESlice}_i(\mathtt{cast}\langle\tau\ \mathtt{ptr} \hookrightarrow \mathtt{int}\ R_i\rangle e) &= \mathtt{cast}\langle\mathsf{TSlice}_i(\tau\ \mathtt{ptr}) \hookrightarrow \mathtt{int}\ R_i\rangle\ \mathsf{ESlice}_i(e)\\
\mathsf{ESlice}_i(\mathtt{new}\ \tau) &= \mathtt{new}\ \mathsf{TSlice}_i(\tau)\\
\mathsf{ESlice}_i(\&l) &= \&\mathsf{LSlice}_i(l)\\
\mathsf{ESlice}_i(l) &= \mathsf{LSlice}_i(l)\\[4pt]
\mathsf{LSlice}_i(x) &= x.r_i\\
\mathsf{LSlice}_i(l.f) &= \mathsf{LSlice}_i(l).f\\
\mathsf{LSlice}_i(*e) &= *\mathsf{ESlice}_i(e)
\end{aligned}
$$

Fig. 4. Data slicing transformation for programs, definitions, commands, expressions, and l-expressions, using n regions

defined with respect to a single region, and they assume that the sliced type of the expression in the given region is not `void`.

For example, suppose we want to transform the command $(*x).p_2 := y$, where x has type t `ptr` and y has type t' `ptr`. (We use the types t and t' defined in Section 2.1.) The rule for assignment yields $\mathsf{CSlice}((*x).p_2 := y) = \mathsf{LSlice}_1((*x).p_2), \mathsf{LSlice}_3((*x).p_2) := \mathsf{ESlice}_1(y), \mathsf{ESlice}_3(y)$. Thus, we will perform the corresponding assignment in regions R_1 and R_3, since $\mathsf{TSlice}_1(t'\ \mathtt{ptr}) \neq \mathtt{void}$ and $\mathsf{TSlice}_3(t'\ \mathtt{ptr}) \neq \mathtt{void}$, but not in region R_2, since $\mathsf{TSlice}_2(t'\ \mathtt{ptr}) = \mathtt{void}$.

Now consider ESlice_i and LSlice_i, the slicing operations for expressions and l-expressions, respectively. Here, we slice with respect to a specific region; for example, when transforming a variable reference, we select the component of that variable corresponding to the region in question. Continuing the example above, we have $\mathsf{LSlice}_1((*x).p_2) = (*x.r_1).p_2$ and $\mathsf{LSlice}_3((*x).p_2) = (*x.r_3).p_2$. Note that this slicing operation could not have been performed in region R_2, since $\mathsf{TSlice}_2(t)$ does not have a field called p_2. However, the assignment rule prevents us from calling ESlice_2 in this case, since $\mathsf{TSlice}_2(t'\ \mathtt{ptr}) = \mathtt{void}$. The final result for the example is $\mathsf{CSlice}((*x).p_2 := y) = (*x.r_1).p_2, (*x.r_3).p_2 := y.r_1, y.r_3$.

The integer cast expression computes a single integer value in region R_j using ESlice_j, casts this integer to region R_i, and completes the computation in region

R_i. Since we only move a single integer value between regions, this operation preserves the invariant that there are no inter-region pointers.

Finally, note that the pointer cast expression targets a specific region, and this choice affects the result of the transformation. For example, the expression $\texttt{cast}\langle t\ \texttt{ptr} \hookrightarrow \texttt{int}\ R_1\rangle\ x$ would be transformed to $\texttt{cast}\langle t\ \texttt{ptr} \hookrightarrow \texttt{int}\ R_1\rangle\ x.r_1$, whereas $\texttt{cast}\langle t\ \texttt{ptr} \hookrightarrow \texttt{int}\ R_3\rangle\ x$ would become $\texttt{cast}\langle t\ \texttt{ptr} \hookrightarrow \texttt{int}\ R_3\rangle\ x.r_3$. After data slicing, these expressions will yield different integers; thus, when comparing two pointers, the programmer must ensure that they were obtained by casting to the same region. In this example, we cannot cast to region R_2 because our typing rules require that we cast to a region where $\mathsf{TSlice}_i(\tau\ \texttt{ptr}) \neq \texttt{void}$.

2.4 Handling First-Class Functions

Since data slicing splits data but not code, we cannot split a function among n different regions in the same way that we can split a pointer. Rather, function types are handled in the same manner as integer types: by adding a region qualifier. To implement this scheme, we add a function type, a function name expression, a function cast expression, and a new function invocation command.

$$\begin{aligned} \tau &::= \ldots \mid \tau\ \texttt{fn}\ R_i \\ e &::= \ldots \mid f \mid \texttt{cast}\langle \tau\ \texttt{fn}\ R_j \hookrightarrow \tau\ \texttt{fn}\ R_i\rangle\ e \\ c &::= \ldots \mid e(x) \end{aligned}$$

In the function type $\tau\ \texttt{fn}\ R_i$, the type τ refers to the type of the argument to the function. Next, we add new rules to our type and program transformations:

$$\begin{aligned} \mathsf{TSlice}_i(\tau\ \texttt{fn}\ R_j) &= \begin{cases} \mathsf{VSlice}(\tau)\ \texttt{fn}\ R_i & \text{if } i = j \\ \texttt{void} & \text{otherwise} \end{cases} \\ \mathsf{ESlice}_i(f) &= f \\ \mathsf{CSlice}(e(x)) &= \mathsf{ESlice}_1(e)(x) \end{aligned}$$

Function argument types are transformed with VSlice. Function names are unchanged, and function invocation retrieves the function from region R_1 as required by our type system. Function casts (not shown) resemble integer casts.

Unfortunately, this approach does not suffice for applications where data slicing is used to preserve backward compatibility. In these applications, we start with a program whose fields are all labelled with region R_1. When we add new fields, we label them with region R_2 so that data slicing will separate these fields from the original data structures, thus preserving the original layout of region R_1. However, the original layout of region R_1 may contain function types. We cannot label these types with region R_2, because data slicing would remove them from region R_1, breaking backward compatibility. However, we cannot keep them in region R_1, because the sliced type in R_1 may differ from the original type.

To solve this problem, we allow the programmer to introduce wrapper functions. These functions have the appropriate type for the original data layout, and they are responsible for calling the transformed function with arguments from all regions. In the above example, we can annotate the function type with region R_2, and then data slicing will place a wrapper function of the appropriate type in region R_1. The wrapper's implementation is application-specific.

For example, function types and expressions may be transformed as follows:

$$\mathsf{TSlice}_i(\tau\ \mathtt{fn}\ R_j) = \begin{cases} \mathsf{VSlice}(\tau)\ \mathtt{fn}\ R_i & \text{if } i = j \\ \mathsf{TSlice}_i(\tau)\ \mathtt{fn}\ R_i & \text{otherwise} \end{cases}$$

$$\mathsf{ESlice}_i(f) = \begin{cases} f & \text{if TypeOf}(f) = \tau\ \mathtt{fn}\ R_i \\ f_i & \text{otherwise} \end{cases}$$

The function f_i is a wrapper for function f in region R_i. This wrapper function takes an argument of type $\mathsf{TSlice}_i(\tau)$, which it uses to call f. Since this data corresponds to only one of the fields that make up $\mathsf{VSlice}(\tau)$, the wrapper function must fill in the rest of the fields in an application-specific manner. We will see an example of this approach in the CCured case study (Section 3.1).

2.5 Partial Data Slicing

The variant of data slicing presented so far splits the base fields of a data structure as well as all objects that directly or indirectly point to these base fields. In many cases, this additional slicing is wasteful; for example, when using data slicing to preserve library compatibility, we need not split objects that will not be shared with a library.

To solve this problem, we introduce an extension that allows pointer and structure types to be given region annotations. A pointer of type τ `ptr` R_1 would be split into as many as n pointers using the original rules, but all of these pointers would be stored in region R_1, despite the fact that they point to other regions. Because all components of this pointer appear in one region, types that contain this pointer do not necessarily need to be split. In a sense, we introduce a limited form of inter-region pointer in exchange for the ability to restrict data slicing to a small portion of the program. In fact, this extension can be used to derive CCured's technique for restricting its compatible metadata representation [4]. Due to space constraints, we omit the remaining details.

3 Case Studies

3.1 CCured

CCured [4, 10] is a program transformation system designed to guarantee memory safety in C programs through a combination of static analysis and run-time checks. To perform its run-time checks, CCured adds metadata to pointers, altering the layout of the program's data structures. Unfortunately, this new layout is incompatible with precompiled libraries, which proved to be a major obstacle when applying CCured to large software systems such as `bind` and `OpenSSH`. To solve this problem, CCured can separate its metadata from the original program's data, placing this metadata in a parallel structure [4]. Data slicing generalizes this technique, as discussed in Section 4. In this section, we show how data slicing can be instantiated for CCured, demonstrating how one can solve data structure backward compatibility problems with data slicing.

CCured classifies pointers into one of several pointer kinds, which determine the metadata required by a given pointer. We will consider three CCured pointer kinds: SAFE pointers, which carry no metadata, SEQ ("sequence") pointers, which carry array bound information, and RTTI ("run-time type information") pointers, which carry an integer identifying the dynamic type of the pointer.

CCured infers these pointer kinds based on pointer usage, and then it implements them by transforming them into C structures, as follows:

$$\begin{array}{ll}
\mathsf{Rep}(\texttt{int}) & = \texttt{int}\ R_D \\
\mathsf{Rep}(\tau\ \texttt{ptr SAFE}) & = \texttt{struct\{}\ p : \mathsf{Rep}(\tau)\ \texttt{ptr;}\ \texttt{\}} \\
\mathsf{Rep}(\tau\ \texttt{ptr SEQ}) & = \texttt{struct\{}\ p : \mathsf{Rep}(\tau)\ \texttt{ptr;}\ b : \texttt{int}\ R_M\texttt{;}\ e : \texttt{int}\ R_M\texttt{;}\ \texttt{\}} \\
\mathsf{Rep}(\tau\ \texttt{ptr RTTI}) & = \texttt{struct\{}\ p : \mathsf{Rep}(\tau)\ \texttt{ptr;}\ t : \texttt{int}\ R_M\texttt{;}\ \texttt{\}} \\
\mathsf{Rep}(\tau\ \texttt{fn}) & = \mathsf{Rep}(\tau)\ \texttt{fn}\ R_M
\end{array}$$

Given a type annotated with CCured pointer kinds, the Rep function gives the representation of that type as a C type. For example, SAFE pointers are represented by a single pointer, whereas SEQ pointers also carry bounds information. Rep adds region qualifiers as appropriate: R_D for data, R_M for metadata.

To make these data structures compatible with existing libraries, we can apply the data slicing transformation after the CCured transformation. In previous work [4], we introduced functions called C and Meta to describe the types of the separated data and metadata structures; the interested reader can verify that $\mathsf{C} = \mathsf{TSlice}_D \circ \mathsf{Rep}$ and that $\mathsf{Meta} = \mathsf{TSlice}_M \circ \mathsf{Rep}$. (Note that in this paper, we use integer types instead of pointer types for the b and e fields.)

For function types, we use the wrapper function scheme from Section 2.4. Since Rep uses region R_M for all function types, the transformed functions (which take both data and metadata as arguments) are always stored in and retrieved from R_M. In region R_D, we place a wrapper whose type matches the original type of the function. This wrapper is responsible for looking up (or generating) appropriate metadata for its arguments before calling the transformed function.

Example of Data Slicing in CCured. The C library functions sendmsg and recvmsg take as a parameter a pointer to a msghdr, which in turn contains an array of iovecs. A simplified declaration for these structures is as follows:

$$\begin{array}{rl}
\texttt{type}\ \mathit{iovec} = & \texttt{struct\{}\ \mathit{iov_base} : \mathit{data}\ \texttt{ptr RTTI;}\ \mathit{iov_len} : \texttt{int;}\texttt{\}} \\
\texttt{type}\ \mathit{msghdr} = & \texttt{struct\{}\ \mathit{msg_iov} : \mathit{iovec}\ \texttt{ptr SEQ;} \\
& \qquad \mathit{msg_iovlen} : \texttt{int;}\ \mathit{msg_flags} : \texttt{int;}\texttt{\}}
\end{array}$$

The type *data* is some unspecified type; for simplicity, we assume it contains no metadata. Figure 5 shows how data slicing separates the CCured metadata from this data structures. Once separated, the data portion can be passed directly to C library functions.

Performance. CCured has been applied to several large systems programs (e.g., OpenSSH, bind, ftpd, sendmail, Apache modules) for which the ability

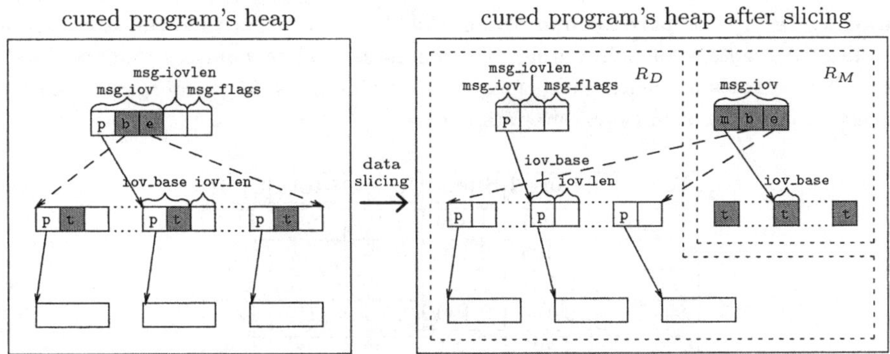

Fig. 5. Illustration of data slicing in CCured. CCured's metadata, shown in gray, is separated into the metadata region, R_M. The base and end fields are integers, not pointers, which is why they are allowed to "point" across region boundaries. These "pointers," which are drawn with dashed lines, are compared but never dereferenced

to maintain compatibility with precompiled libraries was essential. In order to determine the impact of data slicing, we also applied CCured to simple benchmarks (`olden` [2] and `ptrdist` [1]) that can be cured without using data slicing.

These experiments were conducted on a 2.4 GHz Pentium 4 with 1 GB of memory running Linux 2.6.6. The results are reported in Table 1. The second and third columns show the average execution time (in seconds) of five runs of the cured program, with and without data slicing. Standard deviations were negligible in all cases. The third column shows the ratio of the sliced version to the unsliced version. The fourth column shows the percentage of pointers in the program text that required CCured metadata (i.e., were not `SAFE`). The final column indicates the percentage of pointers in the program text that were split into two pointers (i.e., one in each region). These percentages include all pointer types and all variables, since each variable's address is potentially a pointer.

The impact of data slicing on execution time was minimal for most of these benchmarks. The only three cases that had more than a 1% slowdown were `anagram`, `em3d`, and `mst`. The worst performance by far was shown by `em3d`, which had a 63% slowdown. For such cases, it is possible to restrict data slicing to only those portions of the program where it is necessary (see Section 2.5), thus minimizing the overall performance impact.

There is a rough correspondence between the number of pointers needing metadata and the number of pointers that need to be split into two pointers. Recall that a pointer will be split into two pointers if there is CCured metadata reachable from that pointer; thus, these two numbers will be correlated. While these static counts give a rough estimate of the performance impact of data slicing, they are not always reliable (compare `anagram` and `bh`); naturally, data slicing's performance depends significantly on how pointers are used at run time.

Table 1. Results for `ptrdist` and `olden`. We show execution time (in seconds) and the static percentage of pointers needing metadata and of pointers that were split. We omit `ptrdist`'s `bh` benchmark, since it uses CCured's `WILD` pointer, whose current implementation is not amenable to data slicing

Test	Cured	Sliced	Ratio	Meta	Split
anagram	3.001	3.329	1.10	12%	11%
ft	2.164	2.140	0.99	2%	1%
ks	2.617	2.597	0.99	12%	6%
yacr2	0.197	0.199	1.01	11%	12%
bh	3.592	3.572	0.99	20%	13%
bisort	1.906	1.915	1.00	3%	2%
em3d	0.275	0.449	1.63	6%	18%
health	1.305	1.303	1.00	3%	2%
mst	0.651	0.677	1.04	3%	14%
perim	2.106	2.106	1.00	0%	0%
power	3.584	3.583	1.00	2%	4%
treeadd	0.417	0.420	1.01	3%	3%
tsp	2.162	2.160	1.00	0%	0%

3.2 Instance Interleaving

Data slicing can also be used to implement compiler optimizations. To illustrate this application, we consider the instance interleaving optimization described by Truong et al. [13]. Instance interleaving is a data layout technique that clusters frequently-accessed ("hot") fields from a number of instances of a data structure, improving cache performance. Unfortunately, the original implementation required programmer intervention and had significant restrictions on the use of these structures. Data slicing provides an alternative implementation that addresses these problems.

Truong et al. presented instance interleaving using the following structure:

$$\texttt{type}\ t = \texttt{struct}\{\ a : \texttt{int};\ b : \texttt{int};\ c : \texttt{int};\ d : \texttt{int};\ \}$$

Assume that fields `a` and `c` are accessed far more frequently than fields `b` and `d`. To apply instance interleaving using the original approach, we would separate the "hot" fields and add padding (represented by an ellipsis):

$$\texttt{type}\ t = \texttt{struct}\{\ a : \texttt{int};\ c : \texttt{int};\ \ldots\ b : \texttt{int};\ d : \texttt{int};\ \}$$

Now, we allocate these objects from an array that is sized according to the amount of padding. "Hot" fields are stored in the first half of the array, and "cold" fields are stored in the second half. The padding represents the portions of the array that do not belong to this particular instance. The top half of Figure 6 shows how a pointer of type t `ptr` points to an instance of the structure t that is part of an interleaved array. The padding in the structure corresponds

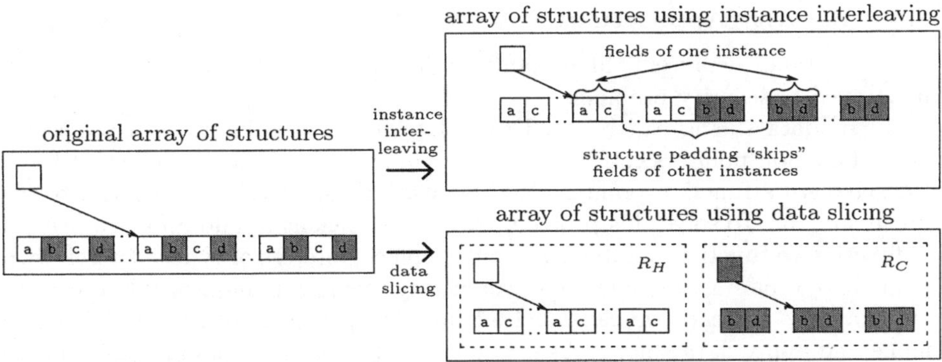

Fig. 6. Two implementations of instance interleaving. "Hot" fields are white, and "cold" fields are gray

to the fields of the other interleaved instances. The programmer allocates from this array by calling *ialloc*, a library function that manages the array.

This implementation requires that the programmer modify only the structure declaration and the allocation sites. However, pointer arithmetic, structure assignment, and static allocation are either prohibited or extremely wasteful.

Data slicing offers an alternative implementation that solves these problems. To use data slicing, we would assign "hot" and "cold" fields to different regions:

$$\texttt{type } t = \texttt{struct\{ } a : \texttt{int } R_H;\ b : \texttt{int } R_C;\ c : \texttt{int } R_H;\ d : \texttt{int } R_C;\ \}$$

After data slicing, the "hot" and "cold" fields will appear in different regions. If we allocate objects from an array, the "hot" fields of several instances will be allocated adjacent to one another, as shown in the bottom half of Figure 6.

The data slicing approach has many advantages. First, there is minimal programmer intervention required, which eliminates an opportunity for introducing bugs. Second, it is possible to use pointer arithmetic, structure assignment, static allocation, and dynamically-sized arrays. Finally, we can have more than two classes of fields; for example, we could group fields that tend to be accessed at the same time and then assign one region to each group.

The primary disadvantage of the data slicing implementation is that in some cases, data slicing introduces an additional pointer. In Figure 6, the pointer into the array has been split into two pointers, one for the "hot" region and one for the "cold" region. This splitting arises because data slicing makes no assumptions about the size of the array. However, if we restrict data slicing using the technique from Section 2.5, then the pointers to the "hot" and "cold" parts of a data structure can be stored in the same region, without splitting the data structure that contains them. Truong et al. report speedups of 1.08 to 2.52 when using instance interleaving and reordering some fields; the overhead of the extra pointer required by data slicing should be comparatively small.

3.3 Security Applications

In this section, we present three examples that demonstrate how data slicing can be applied to security problems.

First, data slicing can be used to isolate function pointers in a program's heap. Function pointers can be a security vulnerability because an errant write that changes a function pointer could allow an attacker can gain control of the processor [15]. To solve this problem, it is not sufficient to add an extra level of indirection to function pointers: we could replace pointers of type τ `fn ptr` with pointers of type τ `fn ptr ptr`, but overwriting this new pointer is still a security vulnerability. Instead, we can label all function pointers with a special region name and apply data slicing. As a result, all function pointers and all pointers that indirectly point to them will be placed in this region, reducing the chances that an attacker can overwrite them.

Second, data slicing can protect sensitive data (such as a password) that is stored in virtual memory. Normally, the programmer must ensure that this data is not paged to disk; otherwise, an attacker who has access to the page file could recover the secret data [8]. If the user annotates sensitive data with a specific region name, then data slicing will separate this data into a region that can be marked as non-pageable. Here, data slicing automates a task that would otherwise be a tedious refactoring exercise.

Finally, suppose the programmer wishes to share portions of an application's data structures with an untrusted party. If the programmer labels public and private fields appropriately, data slicing will separate these fields into independent data structures. Since data slicing disallows inter-region pointers, the user is guaranteed that private data is not accessible from shared public data. Indeed, because the private data is stored in a completely separate memory region, it could be protected by the virtual memory system as well.

In general, data slicing provides the programmer with a refactoring tool. The programmer can label fields that need to be removed from a data structure, and data slicing will automatically make the desired change throughout the program.

4 Related Work

This work originated in the design of CCured's compatible metadata representation [4]. Unfortunately, the design of this compatible representation was largely ad-hoc and would be difficult to adapt for other purposes; in addition, the original presentation only showed how to transform types. Data slicing, as presented in this paper, provides a framework for applying this transformation in a much more general setting. In addition, we improve over previously published work by showing how to handle first-class functions, by allowing the transformation to split the heap into more than two regions, and by providing a detailed discussion of the program transformation itself. Finally, we show how this technique can be applied to other problems.

Structure splitting [3] separates infrequently-accessed fields by adding an extra level of indirection to a data structure. Data slicing provides an alternative approach, as shown in the instance interleaving example. Unfortunately, structure splitting is inappropriate for solving backward compatibility problems, since it adds an extra pointer to the original structure after removing fields.

Intensional polymorphism [5, 6, 7] is an approach to compiling polymorphism that allows type information to be used at run time. This technique allows a compiler to use efficient data representations while preserving type safety. Data slicing solves a similar problem, since it allows the compiler to refactor data structures automatically. Also, many of these approaches to intensional polymorphism represent types as terms in parallel with expressions; data slicing provides such parallel structures for arbitrary data.

One alternative approach to preserving backward compatibility is to use a global splay tree to store metadata [9]. However, this strategy was prohibitively expensive in CCured, since it altered the asymptotic complexity of some simple test cases. Data slicing allows constant-time metadata lookup in most cases; global lookups are only needed by wrapper functions at library boundaries. Another alternative is to factor runtime checks into a "shadow process" that executes on another processor [11]. Data slicing has several advantages over this approach: it is type-directed, handles first-class functions, requires less overhead, and requires only one processor.

Program slicing, which was introduced by Weiser [14] and later surveyed by Tip [12], extracts only those portions of a program that are relevant to computing the value of a particular variable at a particular program point. Data slicing does not discard any code; rather, it separates data in the heap into independent regions. However, there is some similarity: program slicing preserves statements that indirectly affect the value of the specified variable, and data slicing preserves pointers from which data in a given region is reachable.

5 Conclusions

In this paper, we have introduced data slicing, a program transformation that separates the heap into several independent regions. Using this technique, we can add new fields to a data structure without interfering with backward compatibility, and we can also implement compiler optimizations in a principled manner. In addition, we can implement security-related program transformations. Future work includes investigating ways to make data slicing work in the presence of unsafe pointer casts and automating the task of constructing wrapper functions for function pointers.

We believe that the data slicing technique is a promising approach to a number of common software engineering problems. It is particularly useful in combination with other automated program transformations, since it simplifies the task of improving these programs while preserving backward compatibility. As automated program transformations become more popular in practice, we believe that this technique will find a wide range of additional applications.

Acknowledgements

Thanks to Matt Harren, Scott McPeak, and Westley Weimer, whose work on CCured made this work possible. This material is based upon work supported under a National Science Foundation Graduate Research Fellowship.

References

1. Todd M. Austin, Scott E. Breach, and Gurindar S. Sohi. Efficient detection of all pointer and array access errors. In *SIGPLAN Conference on Programming Language Design and Implementation*, pages 290–301, 1994.
2. Martin C. Carlisle. *Olden: Parallelizing Programs with Dynamic Data Structures on Distributed-Memory Machines.* PhD thesis, Princeton University Department of Computer Science, June 1996.
3. Trishul M. Chilimbi, Bob Davidson, and James R. Larus. Cache-conscious structure definition. In *SIGPLAN Conference on Programming Language Design and Implementation*, pages 13–24, 1999.
4. Jeremy Condit, Matthew Harren, Scott McPeak, George C. Necula, and Westley Weimer. CCured in the real world. In *SIGPLAN Conference on Programming Language Design and Implementation*, June 2003.
5. Karl Crary, Stephanie Weirich, and J. Gregory Morrisett. Intensional polymorphism in type-erasure semantics. In *International Conference on Functional Programming*, pages 301–312, 1998.
6. Dominic Duggan. Dynamic typing for distributed programming in polymorphic languages. *ACM Transactions on Programming Languages and Systems*, 21(1):11–45, 1999.
7. Robert Harper and Greg Morrisett. Compiling polymorphism using intensional type analysis. In *SIGPLAN-SIGACT Symposium on Principles of Programming Languages*, pages 130–141, 1995.
8. Michael Howard and David LeBlanc. *Writing Secure Code.* Microsoft, 2002.
9. Richard W. M. Jones and Paul H. J. Kelly. Backwards-compatible bounds checking for arrays and pointers in C programs. *AADEBUG*, 1997.
10. George C. Necula, Scott McPeak, and Westley Weimer. CCured: Type-safe retrofitting of legacy code. In *SIGPLAN–SIGACT Symposium on Principles of Programming Languages*, pages 128–139, 2002.
11. Harish Patil and Charles N. Fischer. Efficient run-time monitoring using shadow processing. In *Automated and Algorithmic Debugging*, pages 119–132, 1995.
12. Frank Tip. A survey of program slicing techniques. *Journal of programming languages*, 3:121–189, 1995.
13. Dan N. Truong, François Bodin, and André Seznec. Improving cache behavior of dynamically allocated data structures. In *IEEE PACT*, pages 322+, 1998.
14. Mark Weiser. Program slicing. *IEEE Transactions on Software Engineering*, 10:352–357, 1984.
15. Suan Hsi Yong and Susan Horwitz. Protecting C programs from attacks via invalid pointer dereferences. In *SIGSOFT International Symposium on Foundations of Software Engineering*, pages 307–316, 2003.

A Static Semantics

This section gives the static semantics for the language presented in this paper, including first-class functions. The environment Γ maps variables to types. A program is well-typed if the body of every function f type-checks with initial environment Γ_f, which maps f's argument to its type. FieldType(τ, f) gives the type of field f in the structure type τ. ArgType(f) gives the type of f's argument. The predicate HasComponent(τ, i) indicates whether there is a base type in region R_i that is reachable from τ, and it holds if and only if $\mathsf{TSlice}_i(\tau) \neq \mathtt{void}$. This latter fact is required by the translation of the pointer-to-integer cast.

Expressions

$$\frac{}{\Gamma \vdash n : \mathtt{int}\ R_i} \quad \frac{}{\Gamma \vdash \mathtt{null} : \tau\ \mathtt{ptr}} \quad \frac{}{\Gamma \vdash \mathtt{new}\ \tau : \tau\ \mathtt{ptr}}$$

$$\frac{\Gamma \vdash l : \tau}{\Gamma \vdash \&l : \tau\ \mathtt{ptr}} \quad \frac{\tau = \mathrm{ArgType}(f)}{\Gamma \vdash f : \tau\ \mathtt{fn}\ R_i} \quad \frac{\Gamma \vdash e_1 : \mathtt{int}\ R_i \quad \Gamma \vdash e_2 : \mathtt{int}\ R_i}{\Gamma \vdash e_1\ \mathtt{op}\ e_2 : \mathtt{int}\ R_i}$$

$$\frac{\Gamma \vdash e : \mathtt{int}\ R_j}{\Gamma \vdash \mathtt{cast}\langle \mathtt{int}\ R_j \hookrightarrow \mathtt{int}\ R_i\rangle\ e : \mathtt{int}\ R_i} \quad \frac{\Gamma \vdash e : \tau\ \mathtt{ptr} \quad \mathrm{HasComponent}(\tau, i)}{\Gamma \vdash \mathtt{cast}\langle \tau\ \mathtt{ptr} \hookrightarrow \mathtt{int}\ R_i\rangle\ e : \mathtt{int}\ R_i}$$

L-Expressions

$$\frac{x \in \mathrm{Dom}(\Gamma)}{\Gamma \vdash x : \Gamma(x)} \quad \frac{\Gamma \vdash l : \tau_1 \quad \tau_2 = \mathrm{FieldType}(\tau_1, f)}{\Gamma \vdash l.f : \tau_2} \quad \frac{\Gamma \vdash e : \tau\ \mathtt{ptr}}{\Gamma \vdash *e : \tau}$$

Commands

$$\frac{\Gamma \vdash l : \tau \quad \Gamma \vdash e : \tau}{\Gamma \vdash l := e} \quad \frac{\Gamma \vdash e : \tau\ \mathtt{fn}\ R_1 \quad \tau = \Gamma(x)}{\Gamma \vdash e(x)} \quad \frac{\Gamma \vdash e : \mathtt{int}\ R_1 \quad \Gamma \vdash c_1 \quad \Gamma \vdash c_2}{\Gamma \vdash \mathtt{if}\ e\ \mathtt{then}\ c_1\ \mathtt{else}\ c_2}$$

$$\frac{\Gamma \vdash e : \mathtt{int}\ R_1 \quad \Gamma \vdash c}{\Gamma \vdash \mathtt{while}\ e\ \mathtt{do}\ c} \quad \frac{\Gamma[x \mapsto \tau] \vdash c}{\Gamma \vdash \mathtt{let}\ x : \tau\ \mathtt{in}\ c} \quad \frac{\Gamma \vdash c_1 \quad \Gamma \vdash c_2}{\Gamma \vdash c_1; c_2}$$

A Compiler-Based Approach to Data Security*

F. Li[1], G. Chen[1], M. Kandemir[1], and R. Brooks[2]

[1] Computer Science and Engineering Department,
The Pennsylvania State University, University Park, PA 16802
{feli, guilchen, kandemir}@cse.psu.edu
[2] Electrical and Computer Engineering Department,
Clemson University, Clemson, SC 29634
rrb@clemson.edu

Abstract. With the proliferation of personal electronic devices and embedded systems, personal and financial data is more easily accessible. As a consequence, we also observe a proliferation of techniques that attempt to illegally access sensitive data without proper authorization. Due to the severe financial and social ramifications of such data leakage, the need for secure memory has become critical. However, working with secure memories can have performance, power, and code size overheads since accessing a secure memory involves additional overheads for encryption/decryption and/or password checks. In addition, an application code may need to be restructured to work under such a memory system. In this paper, we propose a compiler-directed strategy to generate code for a secure memory based embedded architecture. The idea is to let the programmer mark certain data elements, called the seed elements, as secure (i.e., need to be stored in secure memory), and let the compiler determine the remaining secure elements automatically. We also address the problem of code size increase due to our strategy. The experimental results obtained through simulations clearly show that the proposed approach is effective in reducing the total secure memory size. The results also indicate that it is possible to reduce the resulting code size increase by clustering accesses to secure memory.

1 Introduction

Secure memories are those that provide a secure place for the storage of sensitive information to prevent undesired accesses. Such memories are becoming increasingly important in many embedded systems such as smartcards, health-monitoring devices, and PDAs that store vital personal/financial information. There are different ways of implementing secure memories. For example, crypto-memories store data in an encrypted form and require decryption for data access. The password-protected memories, on the other hand, require a handshaking protocol for verifying the identity of the requester.

Secure memories, while effective in providing data protection, have at least two problems associated with them. First, accessing a secure memory takes more execu-

* This work is supported in part by NSF Grants #0444158, #0406340, #0093082, and a grant from GSRC.

R. Bodik (Ed.): CC 2005, LNCS 3443, pp. 188–203, 2005.

tion cycles than accessing a non-secure (conventional) memory. The number of additional cycles for the required security checks depends on the type of the secure memory employed, i.e., whether it is password-protected or crypto-memory. Second, secure memory accesses consume extra energy, which may or may not be tolerated depending on energy budget of the battery-operated embedded system under consideration. Fortunately, in a given embedded application, not all the data elements demand security (or at least the same level of security), and thus, not all the data elements need to be stored in a secure memory. As an example, in an image processing application that manipulates secure images, a certain portion of the frames can contain sensitive data (and need to be stored in a secure memory), whereas the remaining parts can be stored in a conventional (i.e., non-secure) memory. The problem then is to decide, given an embedded program, the set of data elements that need to be stored in the secure memory. Since an error in making this decision can have serious consequences (as it can compromise security of the application), it might be beneficial to automate this decision within an optimizer.

This paper proposes a compiler-directed approach to this problem. The idea is to let the programmer mark certain data elements, called the seed elements, as secure (i.e., need to be stored in the secure memory), and let the compiler determine the remaining secure elements automatically. The programmer can be conservative in determining the seed elements; however, more accurate she is in marking such elements, the smaller the total number of secure elements determined by the approach. It should be noticed that, since the seed elements can be assigned to other data elements in the application, the final set of secure elements determined by our approach is normally larger than the seed elements alone. We use a compiler-directed program analysis that captures such assignments of seed elements and keeps track of the elements that need to be stored in the secure memory. Since our approach determines the minimum set of secure elements, it reduces the secure memory space required by the application. In addition, reducing the number of secure elements both improves execution cycles and reduces memory energy consumption. However, since secure and non-secure memory accesses typically make use of different load/store operations, one needs to be careful in not excessively increasing the size of the generated code. To address this issue, this paper also proposes and evaluates a loop iteration scheduling scheme. The experiments with this scheduler indicate significant savings in the code memory space requirements.

We implemented the proposed approach within an optimizing compiler and performed several experiments with five embedded benchmark codes. Our experimental results obtained through simulations clearly show that the proposed approach is effective in reducing the secure memory size, and the overheads associated with working under secure memories.

The remainder of this paper is structured as follows. The next section gives an overview of secure memories. Section 3 presents the details of our code and data partitioning for secure memories. Section 4 presents results from our experimental evaluation, and Section 5 discusses related work. Finally, Section 6 concludes the paper.

2 Secure Memory Background

The basic secure memory architecture consists primarily of a cryptographic engine and a normal memory unit. The cryptographic engine facilitates the encryption/decryption of the data transmitted between the CPU and the secure memory. Secure memories [5,11] can additionally support mechanisms for password protection and authentication in addition to the encryption functionality. The encryption and decryption are performed based on whether a secure load/store is desired. The instruction set architecture is augmented by special *secure load* and *secure store* operations. These secure memory operations can be implemented through the use of an additional bit in the instruction format, which can be set by the compiler during code generation. If this bit is set, a load operation requires the read data to be decrypted before it is fed to the datapath, and a store operation requires the data to be encrypted before it is written into the memory. However, normal loads and stores incur *no* additional performance penalty as they can identify that the encryption/decryption can be bypassed early in the instruction decode stage. The encryption scheme typically employs block encryption that translates a given plain text to a cipher text of the *same length*. Hence, there are no complexities involved with mapping the encrypted data on to the memory.

Since the data is stored in an encrypted form, the proposed technique counteracts other non-intrusive techniques such as microscope probing, determining electromagnetic flux, and using laser beams [22,8]. Circumventing other unauthorized programs from accessing the data locations is also possible in this technique. The compiler, in addition to marking load/stores as secure, can also generate a *unique encryption key* for use in the program. Consequently, even if another program uses a secure load or store operation on an illegal location, the operation will not be permitted since the keys would not match. The work presented in this paper can be also be defined as the problem of determining the type of each memory operation (secure vs. non-secure).

3 Code and Data Partitioning

The main problem that makes it difficult to generate code for a memory architecture that is composed of both secure and non-secure memories is that one does not want to compromise any security, but at the same time one does not want to incur severe performance or power overheads due to ensured security. In the following discussion, we first list the constraints under which our compiler-driven approach operates. Following that, we give the details for identifying the set of elements that need to be stored in the secure memory, and the details of a scheduling scheme that can be used for minimizing the code size increase.

3.1 Constraints

In restructuring an embedded application code for execution in a secure memory based environment, there are three major constraints that need to be addressed:

- o Security Constraint: All sensitive data elements must be assigned to secure memory. Note that, this is a correctness issue since failing to satisfy this constraint can lead to serious consequences and is not acceptable.
- o Overhead Constraint: The data memory space occupied by the secure data elements must be minimized. In addition, the performance (execution cycles) and energy overheads imposed by the secure accesses must be minimized. In fact, this is one of the main goals of this paper.
- o Code Size Constraint: The size of the generated code should not be excessively large since this can increase the code memory demand. Both this and the previous constraint are important; but, if they are not satisfied, correctness is not affected (unlike the security constraint).

It must be noted that, some of these constraints can conflict with each other. For example, if one keeps the set of secure elements larger than necessary, this can increase overheads but can also reduce the increase in code size (as the accesses to secure and non-secure memories are not excessively interleaved and thus can be clustered in a compact manner), and thus a more compact code can be generated.

3.2 Details

3.2.1 Determining Secure Elements

Our approach tries to reduce performance/energy overheads and code size under the security constraint. That is, without compromising security, we want to reduce the overheads to the greatest extent possible.

Our focus is on array-based embedded applications, where multi-dimensional arrays are operated on using a series of nested loops. Let $seed(U_k)$ be the set of seed elements (as specified by the programmer) from array U_k. Then, the set of secure elements, denoted $secure(.)$, is initially set to $\biguplus_k seed(U_k)$, that is, the union of all $seed(U_k)$ sets. If an element s_i of $secure(.)$ is used on the right-hand-side (RHS) of a statement that assigns a new value to an s_j that does not currently belong to $secure(.)$, then we perform:

$$secure(.) \leftarrow secure(.) \cup s_j.$$

In other words, the set of secure elements is augmented by sj. The main reason for this is the possibility for some malicious entity to determine the value of si by looking at (i.e., observing) the value of sj as well as the values of the other non-secure elements used in the assignment statement in question, if sj is not treated as secure. Therefore, we conservatively add sj to secure(.).

However, the problem of determining whether si is actually used to update sj is not a trivial one. This is because we are dealing with array indices that are expressed in terms of loop iterators (and potentially loop-independent constants), which take multiple values during the course of execution. To identify such assignments carefully, we employ a polyhedral approach that expresses loop based computations and array accesses using Presburger formulas. Consider the following generic loop nest:

$$\text{for } I :: I_s, I_e$$

$$U_j[R_j(I)] \leftarrow \mathcal{H}\{U_k[R_k(I)]\}$$

```
Input:          loop nests L_1, L_2, ... L_n;
                seed(U_k) for each array U_k.
Output:secure(.).

secure(.) = ∪_k seed(U_k);
changed = true;
while (changed) do
        oldsecure = secure(.);
    foreach loop nest L_i do
        foreach statement S_i in L_i
                assume that Ref_l is the LHS reference in S_i;
                foreach reference Ref_r on the RHS of S_i
                        E = the set of elements in secure(.) that can be
                                accessed by Ref_r;
                        L = the set of iterations at which Ref_r accesses
                                elements in E;
                        NewS = elements accessed by Ref_l in iterations L;
                        secure(.) = secure(.) ∪NewS;
                endfor
        endfor
    endfor
    if (oldsecure != secure(.)) then
        changed = true;
    else
        changed = false;
    endif
endwhile
```

Fig. 1. Algorithm for calculating *secure*(.)

In this nest, I represents a vector formed by the loop iterators from top to bottom; I_s and I_e are loop bounds (also expressed as vectors); U_j and U_k are arrays; R_j and R_k are array references to arrays U_j and U_k, respectively (which are functions of I); and $\mathcal{H}$ is a general function. Note that both U_j and U_k can be multi-dimensional.

Suppose now that an element of array U_k, say $U_k[x]$, are in the *secure*(.) set. To determine the corresponding element from array U_j, say $U_j[y]$, that also needs to be placed into the *secure*(.) set, we first determine the loop iteration L that accesses $U_k[x]$. That is, we find an L such that:

$$R_k(L) = x \quad \text{and} \quad I_s \leq L \leq I_e.$$

In the second step, we determine the element from array U_j accessed by L. In mathematical terms, we determine a y such that:

$$R_j(L) = y.$$

Finally, we perform:

$$secure(.) \leftarrow secure(.) \cup U_j[y].$$

Note that, this can easily be extended to the case where we have multiple array references on the RHS. In this way, starting with the seed elements, our approach keeps increasing the *secure*(.) set each time an assignment statement is processed. Therefore, the complexity of the approach is proportional to the number of the assignment statements in the application code being analyzed. It should be noticed that, after *secure*(.) is updated, we might have more secure elements referenced on the RHS. This is because, it is possible that the same array element can be accessed by both the LHS and RHS references within a given loop nest. Therefore, we need to repeat the above process until we cannot add more elements into *secure*(.). We want to emphasize that this approach tries to keep the size of the *secure*(.) set as small as possible. Fig. 1 gives our algorithm for calculating *secure*(.). In the innermost loop of this algorithm, we first calculate the iterations, L, in which the RHS of the statement being considered accesses some elements from the current *secure*(.) set. Then, we add all the elements accessed by the LHS of this statement in iterations L to *secure*(.). It can be seen that if *secure*(.) is changed after all the statements have been processed, which is indicated by a boolean variable *changed*, we repeat the same process again for all the statements until further processing would not add more elements to *secure*(). In our implementation, these elements are determined using a polyhedral tool called the Omega Library [13]. The Omega Library provides a set of routines for manipulating linear constraints over integer variables, Presburger formulas, and integer tuple relations and sets.

3.2.2 Reducing Code Size

It must be noted, though, our approach explained thus far does not do any specific optimization for reducing the code size. In fact, it just determines the smallest set of data elements that need to go to the secure memory (and this also helps reduce the runtime performance overheads of working with secure memory). An important point is that, if the accesses to secure and non-secure memories are interleaved (in the output code generated), this can increase the resulting code size dramatically since these two types of memories are typically accessed using different types of load instructions (distinguished using a bit in the instruction format), as explained in Section 2. As an example, consider a loop nest that accesses five one-dimensional arrays, U_1, U_2, U_3, U_4, and U_5:

for i :: 1, N
... $U_1[i]$, $U_2[i]$, $U_3[i]$, $U_4[i]$, $U_5[i]$ ...

P_i	U_1	U_2	U_3	U_4	U_5
P_1	s	s	s	s	s
P_2	s	s	s	s	n
P_3	s	s	s	n	s
...					
P_{32}	n	n	N	n	n

(a)

Iterations	U_1	U_2	U_3	U_4	U_5
1	s	n	n	s	s
2	n	n	s	s	n
3	n	s	s	s	s
...					
N	s	s	n	n	s

(b)

Fig. 2. (a) Possible load patterns (P_i) for a loop iteration that accesses five arrays. (b) Example load patterns for different iterations. In both (a) and (b), s represents $load_{secure}$, and n represents $load_{nonsecure}$

After our approach has been applied, different loop iterations can have different load instruction patterns from each other (i.e., different combinations of secure and none secure loads). For each array reference, there are two possible load instructions: loadsecure and loadnonsecure. For all the five array references in this example, there are 32 (=25) possible load (instruction) patterns as shown in Fig. 2(a). In each row of this figure, s (or n) means that loadsecure (or loadnonsecure) is used to load the corresponding array element. The original loop nest might not be able to cover such cases due to different load patterns exhibited by the different iterations (i.e., in generating code, we cannot keep the original loop structure). A naïve way that the compiler can generate code is to fully unroll the original loop nest, and use the appropriate load instructions for each iteration. Fig. 2(b) presents such a scenario of complete unrolling. In this figure, each row represents an iteration, and there are a total of N iterations. The last five columns represent accesses to our five arrays, U1, U2, U3, U4, and U5. Each row gives the load pattern for the five array references in the corresponding iteration. In a real environment, iteration number N could be very large, e.g., more than one million. Consequently, the naïve solution leads to considerable code expansion in this case. At this point, one might point out that there could be some regularity in the load patterns across the iterations. But, since the seed sets for these arrays, seed(Uk) (1≤k≤5), are specified by the programmer (i.e., they can exhibit very irregular patterns), the compiler might not be able to extract any regularity from the load patterns and generate simple loop nest(s) to enumerate them. Even if this is possible, the compiler has to unroll all the iterations first before it can analyze the unrolled loop iterations, and this could be a significant overhead for the compiler in terms of both memory space and performance.

An alternative that we employ here is a load pattern centric approach. This approach can be explained as follows. Let us first assume that there is no loop-carried dependence in the original loop nest above. For each load pattern among the 32 possibilities, we calculate the set Gi (1≤i≤32) containing the iterations that have that load

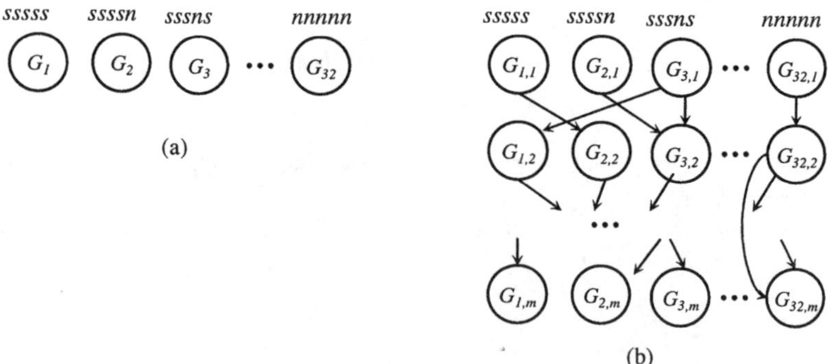

Fig. 3. (a) Sample iteration groups when there is no loop-carried dependence. Each G_i ($1 \leq i \leq 32$) contains the iterations that have the load pattern given above the corresponding node. (b) Example iteration groups when there are loop-carried dependences. The arrows indicate the dependences

pattern. For example, we can obtain the iteration set, G3, for load pattern P3 (sssns), using the Omega Library. That is, using the Omega Library, we build a set that con tains only the iterations that generate the pattern sssns. Fig. 3(a) illustrates this scenario. In this figure, each node represents a set of iterations with the same pattern (written above the node), and there are 32 nodes associated with 32 possible load patterns. Once we obtain all the iteration sets Gi, we make use of the "codegen" utility provided by the Omega Library. Given an iteration set, the Omega Library can generate the corresponding loop nest(s) that enumerates all the loop iterations in that set. Note that, in the ideal case, each node results in a single loop nest. However, if the iterations in a given group could not be enumerated using a single loop nest, the Omega Library can generate multiple nests with the same pattern, and this may lead to an increase in the size of the generated code.

The approach discussed above needs some modifications when there are loop-carried dependences. Fig. 3(b) illustrates such a scenario. In this figure, all the iterations (in the nest for which code is being generated) form a layered dependence graph. Each node G_{ij} represents a subset of G_i, the iterations that have the load pattern P_i given in Fig. 2(a). Note that, each iteration in node G_{ij} (j>1) depends on at least some iteration in $G_{i'j-1}$. The arrows in the graph indicate the dependences between the nodes. It should be emphasized that there cannot be any dependence from G_{ij} to $G_{i'j'}$, where $j' \geq j$. Obtaining such a graph can be done in an iterative way. For each G_i ($1 \leq i \leq 32$), we determine all iterations in G_i that do not depend on any other iteration, and add them to G_{i1}. After all the nodes in layer j have been built, we add $G_{i,j+1}$ the iterations (from the remaining iterations in G_i) that depend only on the iterations in $G_{i'j'}$, where $j' \leq j$. This process is repeated until all the iterations have been assigned to the nodes in the graph. When the entire process is complete, we can schedule the nodes of this graph using any scheduling algorithm (e.g., list scheduling). Then, using the "codegen" utility provided by the Omega Library, we generate code for each node (when we visit that node during scheduling). Fig. 4 gives our scheduling algorithm,

```
Input:          dependence graph G for iteration groups
Output:loop nests that load all the elements in the iteration groups

Ready = all nodes that have no predecessor;
Scheduled = Ø;
while (Ready ≠ Ø)
        remove a node n from Ready;
        codegen(n);
        added n to Scheduled;
        for each successor p of n in G do
                if (all of p's predecessors are in Scheduled) then
                        add p to Ready;
                endif
        endfor
endwhile
```

Fig. 4. Scheduling algorithm for the dependence graph of iteration groups

which is a variant of list scheduling, in the pseudo-code format. In this algorithm, at any scheduling step, we select a node whose all predecessors are already scheduled, so that the dependence requirements can be observed. After selecting a node, we use the "codegen" utility to generate the loop nest(s) that can enumerate the iterations in the group represented by this node. As can be seen, this code generation strategy is oriented towards reducing the number of static load operations in the generated code (through load pattern reuse).

4 Experimental Evaluation

We implemented the proposed strategy within an optimizing compiler built upon SUIF [2], and made experiments with five different embedded benchmark codes. Basically, our compiler reads the input code using SUIF, and fills the Omega Library data structures with necessary information. After this, the Omega Library determines the set of secure elements and secure loop iterations, and the collected information is used by the compiler to construct the dependence graph between the iteration groups. The algorithm given in Fig. 4 is invoked on this dependence graph. Each node of this graph is processed by the Omega Library and the generated enumeration codes are translated into the SUIF internal structures, which in turn is used for emitting the output code. Table 1 shows the five embedded benchmark codes used in this study. The second column gives a brief description of each benchmark, and the third column gives the total data sizes (i.e., the total number of array elements manipulated by the benchmark).

In our experiments, we use the memory access latency values shown in Table 2, which are typical of those memories used in 3.5MHz smartcards [21]. We define the

Table 1. The benchmarks used in this study

Benchmark	Brief Description	Dataset Size
Med-Im04	medical image reconstruction	825.55KB
MxM	triple matrix multiplication	1,173.56KB
Radar	radar imaging	905.28KB
Shape	pattern recognition and shape analysis	1,284.06KB
Track	visual tracking control	744.80KB

Table 2. The latency values used in our experiments

Access Type	Non-secure	Secure
Read	25msec	42msec
Write	50msec	67msec

seed size as follows: (the total number of seed elements marked by the programmer)/(the total number of input elements). We performed experiments with different seed sizes.

The graph in Fig. 5 gives the secure and non-secure memory sizes (percentages) determined by our approach for different sizes of the seed set (as specified by the programmer), namely, seed sizes of 10%, 25%, and 50%. We see from these results that the average secure memory sizes (across all applications) are 29.6%, 55.7%, and 66.9% for the seed sizes of 10%, 25%, and 50%, respectively. Note that, if we conservatively assume that all data elements are secure (i.e., without any compiler analysis), their total sizes (as given in the last column of Table 1) would determine the required capacity

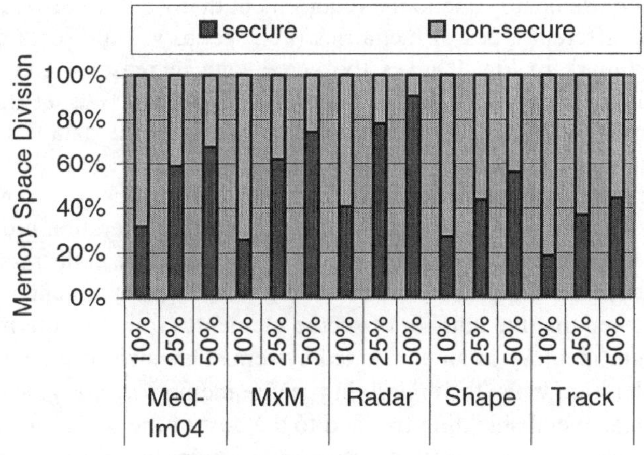

Fig. 5. Memory space division between secure and non-secure components

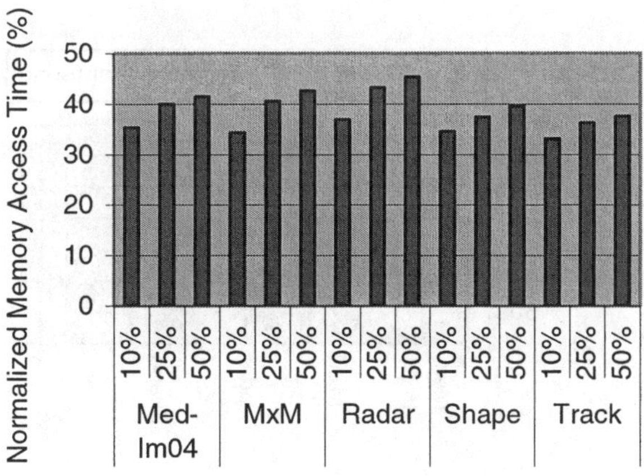

Fig. 6. Memory access time

of the secure memory (i.e., for each bar in Fig. 5, the secure portion would be 100%). In other words, through our compiler-directed approach, we are able to reduce the required secure memory size significantly. The graph in Fig. 6 illustrates how our approach impacts the memory access time. The experiments have been performed in a simulation environment that models a simple five-stage pipelined embedded machine. The values, again given for different seed sizes, are normalized with respect to the case when all data elements are stored in and accessed from the secure memory. We see that our approach reduces the memory access time of this naïve scheme by 64.8%, 60.2%, and 58.7% for the seed sizes of 10%, 25%, and 50%, respectively. Although not quantified here explicitly, one can also expect similar savings in energy consumption as well.

After having presented our secure memory size and performance results, we next focus on the code size increase due to our compiler-based approach. As mentioned earlier, this increase occurs due to the requirement that we have different types of load operations for different types of memories (i.e., secure vs. non-secure). The first bar for each benchmark in Fig. 7 gives the percentage increase in code size when our code re-ordering strategy explained in Section 3.2.2 is used. We see that the code size increase incurred (with respect to the code size where all the data is stored in and accessed from non-secure memory) is about 84% when averaged over all five benchmarks. On the other hand, the second bar for each benchmark represents the code size increase if we use our approach without code reordering (iteration group scheduling). In this case, we observe an average of 243% increase in code size. These results clearly emphasize the importance of our code reordering component.

It is to be noted that the number of secure elements typically determines the capacity of the secure memory in an embedded system. This size of the memory is an important consideration when the underlying secure memory employs additional fabrication steps such as metal shielding that add to the cost of the secure memory. While the approach presented so far is very effective in achieving a reduction in the number of secure elements, one can further reduce the secure memory space needed by considering the lifetimes of secure data elements.

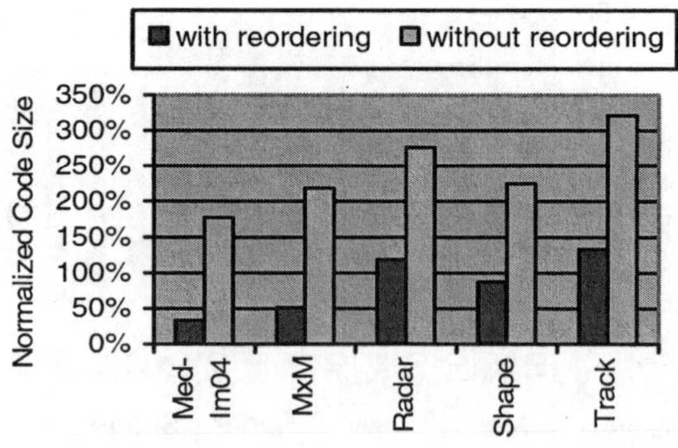

Fig. 7. Impact of code reordering

The main rationale behind the approach studied in this part of the paper is that not all the secure elements are needed for the entire duration of the program execution. In this part of our presentation, we evaluate a framework based on linear algebra to determine (and increase the number of) the cases where the lifetime of two secure array elements do not overlap with each other. When this happens, these two array elements can share the same location in the secure memory, thereby reducing the demand in the secure memory capacity. For array-based embedded applications, in a given loop nest, one can define the lifetime of an array element as the difference (in loop iterations) between the time it is first assigned (written) and the time it is last used (read). For a given array index a (which might be multi-dimensional), the start of its lifetime is referred to as $S(a)$, whereas the end of its lifetime is denoted using $E(a)$ - both in terms of loop iterations. Using these definitions, the lifetime vector for this array element can be given as $s = E(a) - S(a)$, where "-" denotes vector subtraction. Note that the lifetime of a is expressed as a vector as in general there might be multiple loops in the nest, and expressing lifetime as a vector allows the compiler to measure the impact of loop transformations on it. As an example, if an array element (that is accessed in a nest with two loops) is produced in iteration $(2\ \ 2)^T$ and consumed (i.e., last-read) in iteration $(6\ \ 7)^T$, its lifetime vector is $s = (6\ \ 7)^T - (2\ \ 2)^T = (4\ \ 5)^T$. It should be noted that before $S(a)$ and after $E(a)$ the secure memory location allocated to this array element could be used for storing another array element (which belongs to the same array or to a different array). Obviously, the shorter the difference between $E(a)$ and $S(a)$, the better, as it leaves more room for other secure elements.

As stated earlier in Section 3.2.1, the loops in an array-based program surrounding any statement can collectively be represented using a column vector (called the iteration vector) $I = (i_1\ i_2\ \ldots\ i_n)^T$, where n is the number of the enclosing loops. Here, i_k is the kth loop index from top. The loop range or affine bounds of these loops can be described by a system of inequalities, which define a polyhedron. The integer values that can be taken on by I collectively define the iteration space of the nest. In a similar fashion, data (memory) layout of an array can also be represented using a polyhedron. This rectilinear polyhedron, called the index space, is delimited by array bounds, and each integer point in it, called an array index, is represented using an index vector $a = (a_1\ a_2\ \ldots\ a_m)^T$, where m is the number of dimensions of the array. Based on the iteration space and index space (data space) definitions, an array access (i.e., an array reference) can be defined as a mapping from iteration space to index space, and can be described as $GI + o$. Assuming a nest with n loops that accesses an array of m dimensions, in the expression above, I denotes the iteration vector, G is an $m \times n$ matrix (called the access matrix or the reference matrix, and o is an m-entry constant vector (called the offset vector) [26]. As an example, in a nest with two loops (i_1 and i_2) that contains array reference $X_1[i_1+2][i_2-3]$, G is two-by-two identity matrix and $o = (2\ \ -3)^T$.

The application of a loop transformation represented by a square, non-singular matrix T can be accomplished in two steps [26]: (i) re-writing loop body and (ii) re-writing loop bounds. For the first step, assuming that I is the original iteration vector and $J = TI$ is the new (transformed) iteration vector, each occurrence of I in the loop body is replaced by $T^{-1}J$ (note that T is invertible as the transformation must be one-

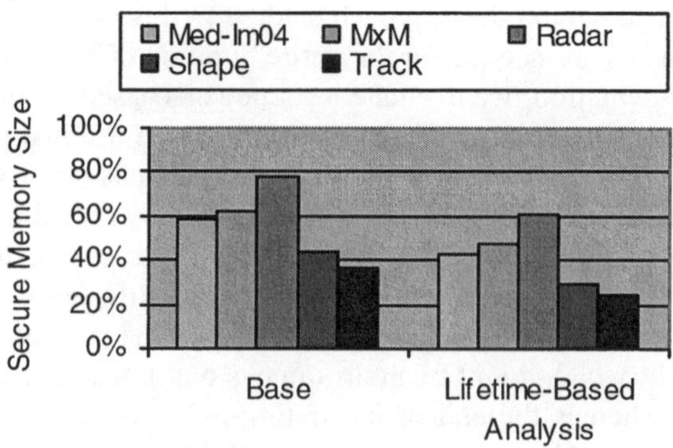

Fig. 8. Impact of lifetime analysis

to-one). In other words, an array reference represented by $GI+o$ is transformed to $GT^{-1}J+o$. Determining the new loop bounds, however, is more complicated and, in general, may require the use of complex methods such as Fourier-Motzkin elimination (a method for solving an affine system of inequalities [26, 3]). One can see that application of a loop transformation changes the execution order of loop iterations and, consequently, the order in which array elements are accessed. As a result, a loop transformation T changes the lifetime vectors as well.

In more technical terms, let $s = I_e - I_s$ be the original lifetime vector for an array element, where I_s is the first iteration that accesses the array element, and I_e the last access. After applying T, we have $I_e' = TI_e$ and $I_s' = TI_s$. Now, we have:

$$s' = I_e' - I_s' = TI_e - TI_s = T(I_e - I_s).$$

That is, if s is the original lifetime vector, s' is the transformed lifetime vector. Our objective is then to select a suitable T such that $s' = (0\ 0\ 0\ \ldots\ 0\ 0\ 1)^T$ for as many array references that access secure elements as possible. In other words, we want to achieve the minimum lifetime vector. Note that, while a more sophisticated implementation can try other lifetime vectors as well (for s') – as long as they are smaller than the original lifetime vector s – in this paper we restrict ourselves to $s' = (0\ 0\ 0\ \ldots\ 0\ 0\ 1)^T$. Obviously, a loop transformation (T) must also preserve the data dependences in the code. In our approach, when we determine a candidate loop transformation, we check whether it preserves data dependences in the code; if it does not, we drop it from consideration.

The memory space results with the lifetime analysis are presented in Fig. 8. All the applications in our experimental suite show significant improvements when the lifetime analysis for secure array elements explained above is used. That is, when applicable, the lifetime analysis of secure elements can be very effective in practice. On an average, using lifetime analysis reduces the secure memory size by 15.3% over our base approach that does not employ any lifetime analysis.

5 Related Work

Several prior efforts address the problem of secure remote execution using a circuit based model as part of the general problem of confidentiality [1,9,27,28]. The integrity of the computation is the ability of the circuit owner to verify the correctness of the execution of the circuit. This problem has been widely studied from the general reliability angle but not from the viewpoint of a malicious server. In a framework proposed by [23,24], the privacy of a function is assured by an encrypting transformation on that function. Yee [29] suggested proof-based techniques in which the untrusted host has to forward a proof of correctness of execution together with the result. In [17,18], a function is encrypted using error coding and sent to the untrusted host that provides the cleartext input. The enciphered output generated by the host is then sent back to the original host, where it is decrypted and the result is verified. The decrypted result matches the result which would have been obtained if the original function had been directly applied to the cleartext input. The authors argue for the need of tamper proof hardware (TPH) to store and provide the control flow between the numerous functions that make up a program. Control flow is located on the TPH and is supplied to the untrusted host. In contrast to these studies, our work is more oriented towards using secure memory in an embedded system. Techniques similar to our use of the Omega Library have been suggested in [19] and [20] in an entirely different context (optimizing data cache locality and interprocessor communication). Slicing [25] is a well-studied program analysis technique that can be used for different optimization goals. In comparison to these studies, our approach targets secure access to data with minimal performance and power overheads.

6 Conclusions

The need for protecting sensitive data from illegal access has resulted in the adoption of secure memories in embedded systems such as smartcards. It is anticipated that securing data will become important for other embedded systems and applications as well. This is because ensuring data security can impose overheads such as increased memory cost, code size, reduced performance or higher power consumption. This work focuses on transforming code structures, with the help of a polyhedral tool, to minimize these overheads when selectively protecting sensitive data identified by the programmer. Experimental results demonstrate that the proposed approach provides required data security by keeping the performance and code size overheads under control.

References

[1] M. Abadi and J. Feigenbaum. Secure circuit evaluation. Journal of Cryptology, 2(1):112, 1990.

[2] S. P. Amarasinghe, J. M. Anderson, C. S. Wilson, S.-W. Liao, B. R. Murphy, R. S. French, M. S. Lam and M. W. Hall. Multiprocessors from a Software Perspective, IEEE Micro, June 1996.

[3] C. Ancourt and F. Irigoin. Scanning polyhedra with DO loops. In Proceedings of the 3rd ACM SIGPLAN Symposium on Principles and Practice of Parallel Programming, pp. 39-50, 1991.
[4] R. J. Anderson, M. G. Kuhn. Low Cost Attacks on Tamper Resistant Devices. In M. Lomas, et al. (eds.), Security Protocols, In Proceedings of the 5th International Workshop, LNCS 1361, pp. 125-136, Springer-Verlag, 1997.
[5] Atmel Secure Memories. http://www.atmel.com/products/SecureMem/.
[6] C. Collberg, C. Thomborson, and D. Low, A Taxonomy of obfuscating transformations. Technical Report #148, Department of Computer Science, University of Auckland, July 1997.
[7] C. Collberg, C. Thomborson, and D. Low. Manufacturing cheap, resilient, and stealthy opaque constructs. In Proceedings of the 25th ACM Symposium on Principles of Programming Languages, pages 184-196, January 1998.
[8] J.-F. Dhem and E. Faber. Built-in hardware security: smart cards and crypto-processors. Embedded tutorial. In Proceedings of International Conference on Computer Design, 2001.
[9] O. Goldreich, S. Micali, and A. Wigderson. How to play any mental game or a completeness theorem for protocols with honest majority. In Proceedings of the 19th Annual ACM Symposium on Theory of Computing,} pages 218--229, New York City, May 1987.
[10] F. Hohl. An approach to solve the problem of malicious hosts. Universitaet Stuttgart Fakultaet Informatik, Bericht Nr. 1997/03, 1997.
[11] Infineon Technologies. Security Chips and ICs. http://www. infineon.com/products
[12] W. Jansen and T. Karygiannis. Mobile agent security. NIST Special Publication, 800-19, http://csrc.nist.gov/mobileagents/publication/sp800-19.pdf, August 1999.
[13] W. Kelly and W. Pugh. *A* Framework for Unifying Reordering Transformations. Technical Report, University of Maryland Institute for Advanced Computer Studies. Dept. of Computer Science, Univ. of Maryland, April 1993.
[14] P. Kilpatrick, D. Crookes, and M. Owens. Program slicing: A computer aided programming technique. In Proceedings of the Second IEEE / BCS Conference on Software Engineering, pp. 602-604, 1988.
[15] C. Linn and S. Debray. Obfuscation of wxecutable code to improve resistance to static disassembly. In Proceedings of the 10th ACM Conference on Computer and Communication Security, October 2003.
[16] S. Loureiro. Mobile Code Protection, Ph. D.Dissertation, Institut Eurecom, 2001.
[17] S. Loureiro, L. Bussard, and Y. Roudier. Extending tamper-proof hardware security to untrusted execution environments. In Proceedings of CARDIS, 2002.
[18] S. Loureiro and R. Molva. Function hiding based on error correcting codes. In Proceedings of the International Workshop on Cryptographic Techniques and Electronic Commerce, pages 92--98, City University of Hong-Kong, July 1999.
[19] W. Pugh and E. Rosser. Iteration space slicing and its application to communication optimization. In Proceedings of the International Conference on Supercomputing, 1997.
[20] W. Pugh and E. Rosser. Iteration space slicing for locality. In Proceedings of Languages and Compilers for Parallel Computing, 1999.
[21] W. Rankl and W. Effing. Smart Card Handbook. pp.71,421. John Wiley and Sons, 1997.
[22] J. Quisquater and D. Samyde. Electromagnetic Analysis: Measures and Countermeasures for smart cards. E-Smart 2001, LNCS 2140, pp. 200-210, 2001.
[23] T. Sander and C. F. Tschudin. Towards mobile cryptography. In Proceedings of the 1998 IEEE Symposium on Security and Privacy, pp. 215--224, Oakland, California, May 1998.

[24] T. Sander and C. Tschudin. On software protection via function hiding. In Proceedings of the Second Workshop on Information Hiding, Portland, Oregon, USA, April 1998.

[25] M. Weiser. Program slicing. IEEE Transactions on Software Engineering, pages 352-357, July 1984.

[26] M. Wolfe. High Performance Compilers for Parallel Computing, Addison-Wesley Publishing Company, 1996.

[27] A. C. Yao. Protocols for secure computations. In Proceedings of the IEEE Symposium on Foundations of Computer Science, pages 160--164, Chicago, 1982.

[28] A. C. Yao. How to generate and exchange secrets. In Proceedings of the IEEE Symposium on Foundations of Computer Science, pages 162--167, Toronto, 1986.

[29] B. Yee. A sanctuary for mobile agents. Technical Report CS97-537, Department of Computer Science and Engineering, UCSD, April 1997.

[30] X. Zhang and R. Gupta. Hiding Program Slices for Software Security. First Annual IEEE/ACM Symposium on Code Generation and Optimization, pp. 325-336, San Francisco, CA, March 2003.

Composing Source-to-Source Data-Flow Transformations with Rewriting Strategies and Dependent Dynamic Rewrite Rules

Karina Olmos and Eelco Visser

Institute of Information and Computing Sciences, Utrecht University,
P.O. Box 80089, 3508 TB Utrecht, The Netherlands
karina@cs.uu.nl, visser@acm.org

Abstract. Data-flow transformations used in optimizing compilers are also useful in other programming tools such as code generators, aspect weavers, domain-specific optimizers, and refactoring tools. These applications require source-to-source transformations rather than transformations on a low-level intermediate representation. In this paper we describe the composition of source-to-source data-flow transformations in the program transformation language Stratego. The language supports the high-level specification of transformations by means of rewriting strategy combinators that allow a natural modeling of data- and control-flow without committing to a specific source language. Data-flow facts are propagated using dynamic rewriting rules. In particular, we introduce the concept of dependent dynamic rewrite rules for modeling the dependencies of data-flow facts on program entities such as variables. The approach supports the combination of analysis and transformation, the combination of multiple transformations, the combination with other types of transformations, and the correct treatment of variable binding constructs and lexical scope to avoid free variable capture.

1 Introduction

Optimizing compilers rely on data-flow facts to perform optimizations [1, 12]. Data-flow optimizations such as constant propagation, copy propagation, and dead code elimination transform or eliminate statements or expressions based on data-flow information that is propagated along the control-flow paths of the program. The implementation of these optimizations is hidden from programmers using the compiler. Data-flow transformations are useful outside the core of compilers as well. In generative programming, high-level and model-driven code generation, refactoring, aspect weaving, open compilers, and domain- and application-specific optimization, transformations are an essential part of program development. While data-flow optimizations in compilers are usually implemented to work on fixed low-level intermediate representations, these applications require transformations on source code in high-level programming languages. Furthermore, compiler optimizations are traditionally implemented in general purpose languages, optimizing for speed of the transformations rather than productivity of the transformation writer. Higher productivity can be achieved using a language and environment that provides more support for the domain of program transformation. For

R. Bodik (Ed.): CC 2005, LNCS 3443, pp. 204–220, 2005.

such an environment for source-to-source transformations to be widely applicable it should cover a wide spectrum of transformational tasks. That is, it should not be specific to one source language and should not restrict support to one type of transformation. Rather, it should provide high-level abstractions for modeling control- and data-flow of the language under consideration, and it should support combination of data-flow transformations with other types of program manipulation such as template based code generation. Also, the environment should not require abstraction from details of program representation and should for instance support handling issues of scope of variables and help to avoid problems such as free variable capture.

In this paper we describe the composition of source-to-source data-flow transformations in the program transformation language Stratego [19]. The language is not restricted to data-flow transformations nor is it restricted to transformations on a specific source language. Instead of building-in knowledge about data-flow, Stratego provides high-level ingredients for composing data-flow transformations on abstract syntax trees. These ingredients are *rewrite rules* for definition of basic transformations, *programmable rewriting and traversal strategies* for the composition of tree traversals and controlling the application of rewrite rules, *dynamic rewrite rules* for propagation of context-sensitive information such as data-flow facts, and *dynamic rule combinators* for modeling control-flow (forks in data-flow). In particular, we introduce the concept of *dependent dynamic rewrite rules* for modeling dependencies of data-flow facts on program entities such as variables. Together these techniques support:

- An abstract interpretation style of data-flow transformation that allows the combination of data-flow analysis and transformation in the same traversal.
- The correct treatment of variable binding constructs and lexical scope to avoid free variable capture and to restrict the application of transformation rules to the scope where they are valid.
- The definition of generic data-flow strategies, which allow concise specifications of data-flow transformations, and the concise combination of multiple transformations into 'super-optimizers'.
- The combination of data-flow transformations with other types of transformations, reuse of elements of a transformation in other transformations, and easy experimentation with alternative transformation strategies.

We proceed as follows. In the next section we describe rewrite rules, strategies, and dynamic rules and illustrate their use in a specification of constant propagation. In Section 3 we motivate the need for *dependent* dynamic rules and illustrate their use in a specification of copy propagation. In Section 4 we generalize the strategies for constant propagation and copy propagation into a generic strategy for forward data-flow propagation and instantiate the strategy to common-subexpression elimination. We also show how, using the same generic strategy, the components of these transformations can be combined in a single super-optimizer. In Section 5 we discuss previous, related, and future work.

2 Rewriting Strategies and Dynamic Rules

In this section we show how rewriting strategies in combination with dynamic rewrite rules can be used to compose data-flow transformations on abstract syntax trees, using constant propagation as running example. Throughout the paper we use a subset of Appel's Tiger language [2] as the source language for transformations. The abstract syntax of this subset is defined in **Fig. 1** However, none of the techniques we present are specific to this language. We assume the reader to be familiar with the basic notions and infrastructure for source-to-source transformations on abstract syntax trees, including parsing, tree representation, and pretty-printing. For an overview of the specific infrastructure used in the Stratego/XT framework we refer to [19].

2.1 Local Transformations with Rewrite Rules

Basic transformations on abstract syntax trees can be defined using *tree* or *term rewriting*. A *rewrite rule* (p_1 `->` p_2) defines the transformation of a tree that matches the left-hand side p_1 of the rule to the instantiation of the right-hand side p_2 of the rule. Term rewriting is the *normalization* of a tree by exhaustively applying a set of rewrite rules. **Fig. 2** shows some typical rewrite rules for constant folding and unreachable code elimination. Note that we use *concrete syntax* [18] to describe the abstract syntax tree patterns in the left-hand side and right-hand side of the rules. That is, a phrase such as `|[ if i then e1 else e2 ]|` denotes a tree pattern `If(Int(i),e1,e2)` where *i*, *e1*, and *e2* are meta-variables. Using the rules from **Fig. 2** the arithmetic expression `2 + 3 + 7` rewrites to `12` and the conditional expression `if 0 then x := 1 else x := 2` reduces to `x := 2`.

```
d ::= var x := e
e ::= x | str | i | e1 ⊕ e2 | f(e*,) | x := e | (e*;) | if e1 then e2 else e3
    | while e1 do e2 | let d* in e*; end
```

Fig. 1. Abstract syntax for a subset of Tiger with $\oplus$ the usual arithmetic, relational, and Boolean operators. The non-terminals x, f, str, and i denote variables, functions, string, and integer constants, respectively. $e^*_;$ denotes a list of zero or more expressions separated by semicolons

```
EvalBinOp  : |[ i + j ]| -> |[ k ]| where <add>(i, j) => k
EvalBinOp  : |[ i * j ]| -> |[ k ]| where <mul>(i, j) => k
EvalWhile  : |[ while 0 do e ]| -> |[ () ]|
EvalIf     : |[ if 0 then e1 else e2 ]| -> |[ e2 ]|
EvalIf     : |[ if i then e1 else e2 ]| -> |[ e1 ]| where <not(eq)>(i,|[0]|)
```

Fig. 2. Some rewrite rules for constant folding and unreachable code elimination

Term rewriting is declarative since rewrite rules can be defined independently and are automatically applied by a rewriting engine. The correctness of the combined transformation can be established by the correctness of the individual rules. However, static rewrite rules are not sufficient for defining data-flow transformations. A rewrite rule can only use information from the term to which it is applied, not from its parents or siblings in the abstract syntax tree. Data-flow transformations typically need information from assignments and variable declarations that are higher-up in the tree. For example, consider the constant folding and propagation transformation in **Fig. 3** The fact that the variable `x` is constant allows constant folding in many of the subsequent expressions. However, this requires the propagation of the initial constant value of `x` to its uses; e.g., folding the expression `x + 1` is only possible after replacing `x` with its value.

2.2 Context-Sensitive Transformations with Dynamic Rewrite Rules

To extend rewriting to propagation of context-sensitive information requires (1) the dynamic (run-time) definition of rewrite rules and (2) the careful control of their application. We first consider the use of dynamic rewrite rules to propagate data-flow information in a control-flow graph and then argue that this approach can also be applied to abstract syntax trees. In the next subsection we then show how this transformation on abstract syntax trees is realized in Stratego.

The left diagram in **Fig. 4** depicts the control-flow graph of the example program in **Fig. 3** The nodes correspond to the assignments and conditionals in the program before and after transformation. The traversal of the graph follows the control-flow of the program, which corresponds to following the direction of the arrows from entry to exit. At nodes with more than one outgoing edge, the traversal subsequently visits each branch and synchronizes at the merge point. Data-flow facts are represented by a set of dynamic rewrite rules `(x -> i)` that rewrite an occurrence of a variable to its constant value. Since the set of propagation rules can be different at each point in the program, the edges of the graph are annotated with the rules that are valid at that point of the traversal.

At each node of the graph, first the right-hand side of the assignment is transformed by rewriting variables in the expression to constant values, if applicable, and attempting to apply constant folding rules such as in **Fig. 2** For example, `y := x + 1` is transformed to `y := 3 + 1` by application of the rule `x -> 3` and then reduced to `y := 4` by constant folding. Next, an assignment x `:=` e causes the undefinition of any rules with x as left-hand side, since these are no longer valid. Finally, if the assignment has a constant value as right-hand side (x `:=` i), a new rewrite rule x `->` i is defined.

Multiple propagation rules for *different variables* can be defined at the same time. For example, after the `y := x + 1` assignment both rules `x -> 3` and `y -> 4` are valid.

```
(x := 3; y := x + 1;                        (x := 3; y := 4;
 if foo(x)                                    if foo(3)
 then (y := 2 * x; x := y - 2)      ⇒         then (y := 6; x := 4)
 else (x := y; y := 23);                      else (x := 4; y := 23);
 z := x + y)                                  z := 4 + y)
```

Fig. 3. Example of constant propagation

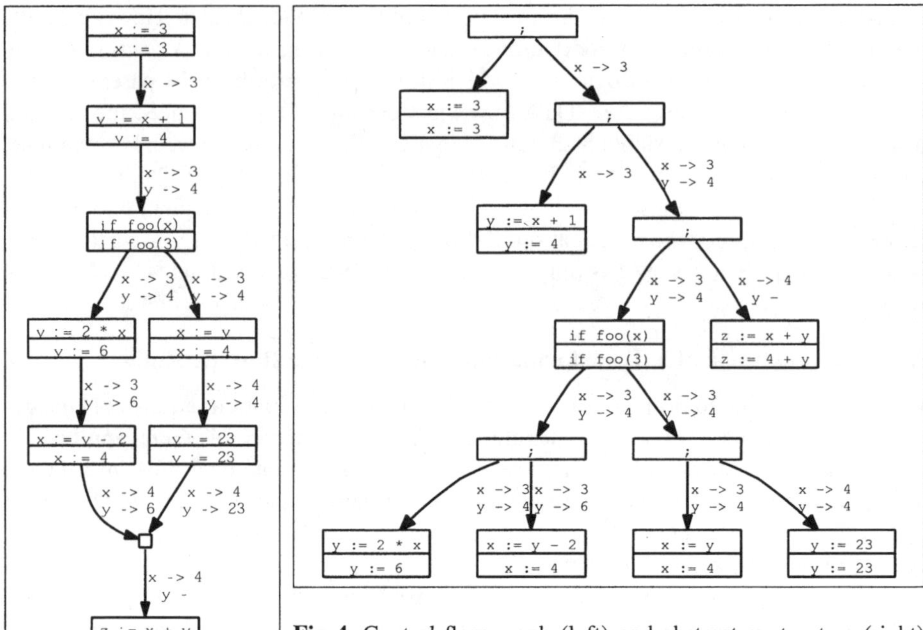

Fig. 4. Control-flow graph (left) and abstract syntax tree (right) annotated with propagation rules

However, only one rule can be defined with the same left-hand side. For example, The assignment `x := y` replaces the rule `x -> 3` with the rule `x -> 4`. At a fork in the control-flow, that is at a node with more than one outgoing edge, each branch starts with the rule-set valid at the branching node. That is, each edge is annotated with a clone of that rule-set. At the merge point only those rules that are consistent in all branches are maintained. In the example, the rules for y are inconsistent at the merge point and are undefined. In the case of loops this process should be repeated until a stable set of rules is obtained.

A control-flow graph traversal of a program can also be realized by traversing its abstract syntax tree. This requires visiting the nodes of the tree in the order that they would be visited in a traversal of the graph. The right diagram in **Fig. 4** depicts the abstract syntax tree of the example program. Simulation of the traversal corresponds basically to a depth-first left-to-right traversal of the syntax tree. Realization of the constant propagation transformation on abstract syntax trees thus requires

- traversal of the abstract syntax tree to visit expressions in the right order
- dynamic definition of rules to reflect the constant assignments
- application of dynamic propagation rules and static constant folding rules
- forking and combining rule-sets to model forks in data-flow

2.3 Realization in Stratego

The Stratego program in **Fig. 5** defines a constant propagation transformation strategy implementing the propagation of dynamic rules as described above. In the rest of this

```
prop-const =
  PropConst <+ prop-const-assign <+ prop-const-declare
  <+ prop-const-let <+ prop-const-if <+ prop-const-while
  <+ (all(prop-const); try(EvalBinOp))

prop-const-assign =
  |[ x := <prop-const => e> ]|
  ; if <is-value> e then rules( PropConst.x :  |[ x ]| -> |[ e ]| )
                    else rules( PropConst.x :- |[ x ]| ) end

prop-const-declare =
  |[ var x := <prop-const => e> ]|
  ; if <is-value> e then rules( PropConst+x :  |[ x ]| -> |[ e ]| )
                    else rules( PropConst+x :- |[ x ]| ) end

prop-const-let =
  ?|[ let d* in e* end ]|; {| PropConst : all(prop-const) |}

prop-const-if =
  |[ if <prop-const> then <id> else <id> ]|
  ; (EvalIf; prop-const
     <+ (|[ if <id> then <prop-const> else <id> ]|
          /PropConst\ |[ if <id> then <id> else <prop-const> ]|))

prop-const-while =
  ?|[ while e1 do e2 ]|
  ; (|[ while <prop-const> do <id> ]|; EvalWhile
     <+ (/PropConst\* |[ while <prop-const> do <prop-const> ]|))
```

Fig. 5. Constant propagation transformation strategy

```
        program P ::= (rules | strategies) d*
     definition d ::= h = s | h : r
         header h ::= f(f*, | x*,) | f(f*,) | f
           rule r ::= p1 -> p2 (where s)?
        pattern p ::= str | i | r | x | c(p*,) | (p*,) | [p*, | p] | [p*,] | <s> p | <s>
       strategy s ::= ?p | !p | {x*,: s} | <s> p | s => p
                    | s1 ; s2 | f(s*, | p*,) | f(s*,) | f
                    | s1 <+ s2 | s1 < s2 + s3 | if s1 then s2 (else s3)?
                    | fail | id | not(s) | where(s) | let d* in s end
                    | rules(drd*) | {| f*,: s |} | s1 /f*,\ s2 | /f*,\* s
dyn. rule def. drd ::= h((.|+)p)? :(+)? dr  | h((.|+)p)? :- p
      dyn.rule dr ::= r | r depends on p
```

Fig. 6. Abstract syntax of a subset of Stratego. The following additional non-terminals are used: *str*, i and r denote string, integer, and real constants; x a pattern variable, c a constructor, f a strategy operator. Operators are listed in the order of precedence; in particular ; has precedence over <+. Note that the use of concrete syntax for patterns and congruence strategies is not covered by this abstract syntax definition

section we examine the components of this definition and informally introduce the Stratego constructs that they use. The definition of a subset of the abstract syntax of Stratego in **Fig. 6** should be helpful in understanding the structure of Stratego programs. A full description of the language is beyond the scope of this paper; see [4, 19].

Rules and Strategies. Rewrite rules as described in Section 2.1 are the basic entities of Stratego programs. A named rule f : p_1 -> p_2 transforms a term matching pattern p_1 to the instantiation of pattern p_2. Some example rewrite rules are shown in **Fig. 2** using *concrete syntax* for the term patterns. Stratego extends the basic notion of term rewriting with programmable strategies for the controlled application of rewrite rules. A rule with name f defines a transformation from terms to terms. A rule may fail to apply to a term, e.g., when its left-hand side does not match the term it is applied to. Strategies combine rules into more complex transformations using a number of *strategy combinators*. Since rules can fail, strategies can fail to apply to a term as well. Strategy *definitions* of the form f = s name a strategy expression. Thus, **Fig. 5** introduces six, mutually recursive, definitions that compose the constant propagation strategy `prop-const`.

The basic strategy combinators are sequential composition s_1; s_2 (first apply s_1 and then s_2) and deterministic choice s_1 <+ s_2 (first apply s_1, if that fails apply s_2). Note that sequential composition has higher precedence than deterministic choice. Thus, the `prop-const` strategy defines a choice between seven cases, which are tried in turn until one succeeds.

Term Traversal. In order to transform sub-terms of a term, a strategy needs to *traverse* the term. While in conventional languages traversal requires a tedious enumeration of all elements of the data structure and their traversal, Stratego supports *generic* traversal through *one-level traversal combinators* [20]. One of these combinators is `all`(s), which applies s to each direct sub-term of the subject term. Thus, the basic schema of the `prop-const` strategy is

```
prop-const = PropConst <+ (all(prop-const); try(EvalBinOp))
```

which either applies the `PropConst` dynamic rule to replace a variable by a constant value or recursively visits the direct sub-terms with a recursive call to the `prop-const` strategy (`all(prop-const)`) and then tries to apply a constant folding rule. The other cases in the definition of `prop-const` introduce exceptions to the generic traversal. For example, only the right-hand side of an assignment should be visited, and the branching of the conditional statement requires special care.

In addition to generic traversal, Stratego supports data-type specific traversal by means of *congruence operators*. For each constructor c with arity n in the abstract syntax tree format, a corresponding strategy $c(s_1, ..., s_n)$ is defined that applies only to c terms, applying the s_i strategies to the corresponding sub-terms. For example, the strategy expression `If(prop-const,id,id)` applies the `prop-const` strategy only to the first argument of `If` terms. Note that `id` is the *identity* strategy that always succeeds. We can write such congruences again using the concrete syntax of the source language, where we enclose the argument strategies in `<.>`. For instance, the strategy `|[if <prop-const> then <id> else <id>]|` denotes `If(prop-const,id,id)`.

Pattern Matching. While the prop-const-if definition **Fig. 5** uses a congruence to recognize a conditional statement, the prop-const-let and prop-const-while definitions use a *pattern match* strategy for this purpose. A pattern match ?p matches the subject term against the pattern p, binding the meta-variables in the pattern. The construct s => p is syntactic sugar for s; ?p, i.e., first applying strategy s and then match the result against p. The concrete syntax congruence operators in prop-const-assign and prop-const-declare are combinations between traversal and matching; the use of a meta-variable in a congruence denotes matching that variable. Thus, the strategy |[x := <prop-const => e>]| denotes Assign(Var(?x), prop-const => e); it entails application of the prop-const strategy only to the right-hand side of an assignment and binding the result to the meta-variable e.

Dynamic Rules. The elements we have examined so far concern the traversal order of the abstract syntax tree. The next aspect is the definition of dynamic rules for propagation of constant assignments. The prop-const-assign and prop-const-declare strategies examine the right-hand side expression e of an assignment and variable declaration, respectively, after these have been transformed. If the expression is a constant value, a new dynamic rule is defined with as left-hand side the variable x from the left-hand side of the assignment and as right-hand side the constant value e. Thus for an assignment |[a := 3]| the rule |[a]| -> |[3]| is defined. In general, a dynamic rule definition rules(f : p_1 -> p_2) defines a new rule f : p'_1 -> p'_2 with p'_1 and p'_2 the original patterns in which variable bindings from the context of the definition are substituted.

If the right-hand side expression is *not* a constant value, the prop-const-assign and prop-const-declare strategies *undefine* the PropConst rule with x as left-hand side. This is necessary in constant propagation since an assignment invalidates earlier assignments to the same variable. For example an assignment |[a := b + 4]| after |[a := 3]| invalidates the |[a]| -> |[3]| rule.

Dynamic Rule Scope. Dynamic rules are usually related to elements of the source program such as variables. Therefore, rules should only be applied to those parts of the tree, where they are 'in scope'. This is managed using the dynamic rule scope construct {| R : s |}, which limits the scope of R rules to the strategy s. That is, all R rules defined during the execution of s are removed when leaving the scope. This is necessary in a case such as the following:

```
let var x := 17
 in let var y := x + 1
     in let var x := y+1 in () end
    end; print(x)
end
```

⇒

```
let var x := 17
 in let var y := 18
     in let var x := 19 in () end
    end; print(17)
end
```

Without scoping the dynamic rule produced from the assignment x := 19 in the inner scope would be used for the print(x) call, and produce print(19) instead.

In fact, not all rules defined within s are removed on leaving the scope. Rules can be defined relative to a named dynamic rule scope. For this purpose prop-const-declare *labels* the current scope with the name of the declared variable (notation: PropConst+x). The dynamic rule definitions by prop-const-assign are relative to the scope of the variable (notation: PropConst.x) to ensure that the rule is still visible when later scopes are exited. Therefore, the rule for x defined in the scope for y is not removed when leaving that scope.

Dynamic Rule Intersection. As discussed above, when encountering a fork in the control-flow the current rule-set should be distributed over the branches and merged afterwards. For this purpose, Stratego provides dynamic rule intersection and union operators. The intersection operator s_1 /PropConst\ s_2 applies both strategies s_1 and s_2 to the current term in sequence, but distributes the same rule-set to both strategies. Afterwards the rule-sets are merged into one by keeping only those rules that are consistent in both sets. The union operator s_1 \PropConst/ s_2 is similar, but keeps all rules instead. Thus, the traversal of the branches of the conditional statement is defined as

```
|[ if <id> then <prop-const> else <id> ]|
   /PropConst\ |[ if <id> then <id> else <prop-const> ]|
```

first visiting the left branch and then the right branch, keeping only the propagation rules that are valid after both branches.

The fixed-point version /PropConst* s of the intersection operator repeats the application of s until a stable rule-set is obtained. The transformation is applied each time using the *original term*; only the result of the last application is used to replace the term. Thus, the traversal of while statements is defined as

```
/PropConst\* |[ while <prop-const> do <prop-const> ]|
```

In fact, in the implementation of dynamic rules the rule-sets are not actually cloned. Instead, changes to the rule-set are stored in a fresh ‘change-set’ for each branch. These changesets are merged at the meet-point. Thus, the effort of merging two rule-sets is proportional to the number of rules in the change-sets rather than the number of rules in the rule-set.

Combining Analysis and Transformation. The constant propagation strategy defined in **Fig. 5** combines analysis and transformation; the analysis of which variables are constant and the actual substitution of these constant values interact. This combination is strictly more expressive than the conventional approach of performing separate analysis and transformation phases. The application of constant folding may enable new constant propagations and the application of unreachable code elimination through the EvalIf and EvalWhile rules may discard entire sub-terms that an analysis would have to consider. This phenomenon is illustrated by the following example from [8]:

```
(x := 10;
 while A do
   if x = 10 then dosomething()
   else (dosomethingelse(); x := x + 1);
 y := x)
```

⇒

```
(x := 10;
 while A do
   dosomething();
 y := 10)
```

Since the assignment to x in the loop is never reached, the conditional statement can be reduced to its first branch.

3 Dependent Dynamic Rewrite Rules

While dynamic rules as presented in the previous section can be used to implement constant propagation, they cannot be used for all data-flow transformations without changes. In constant propagation a propagation rule maps a variable to a constant expression. Propagation rules are undefined when an assignment to the variable is encountered. However, in optimizations such as copy propagation and common-subexpression elimination there are multiple variables that affect a propagation rule. We illustrate the problems using copy propagation. An assignment of a variable to a variable introduces a copy. In copy propagation these copies are replaced by their original. For example, the occurrence of a in the second assignment of (`a := b; c := d + a`) is replaced by the variable b to produce (`a := b; c := d + b`). The following dynamic rule definition for copy propagation follows naturally from the constant propagation approach:

```
copy-prop-assign = ?|[ x := y ]|;
  if <not(eq)>(x,y) then rules( CopyProp.x : |[ x ]| -> |[ y ]| )
                    else rules( CopyProp.x :- |[ x ]| ) end
```

Here we assume that the definition is embedded in a similar traversal strategy as that for constant propagation. However, it is incorrect in a number of ways.

(1) Insufficient Dependencies. The rule is not undefined when the variable in its right-hand side changes. For example, in the program (`a := b; b := foo(); c := d + a`) the variable a in the last statement will be replaced by b even though its value changed in the second statement. Thus, a `CopyProp` rule should be undefined when any of its variables is assigned.

(2) Free Variable Capture. The rule is not undefined when the local variable shadows the variable in the right-hand side. For example, in the program

```
let var a := bar() var b := baz()
 in a := b; let var b := foo() in print(a) end end
```

the occurrence of a in the call to `print` will be replaced with b, which now refers to the variable in the inner scope. Thus, a `CopyProp` rule should be undefined in a local scope when the local variable is used in the rule.

(3) Escaping Variables. The rule is not undefined when its target is going out of scope. For example, in the following program

```
let var a := bar() in let var b := foo() in a := b end; print(a) end
```

the assignment `a := b` causes the definition of a dynamic rule `a -> b`, which replaces the variable a in `print(a)` by b, which is then used outside its scope. This suggests that a `CopyProp` rule should be defined in the local scope, i.e., the scope in which the assignment lives. However, in the following variant of the program

```
let var a := bar() var c := baz()
 in let var b := foo() in a := b; a := c end; print(a) end
```

the assignment `a := c` leads to a copy propagation rules which *can* be applied in the outer scope, since neither a nor c are declared in the inner scope. Thus, a `CopyProp` rule should be defined in the *innermost* scope of the variables involved, but not necessarily the innermost scope.

```
copy-prop-declare = ?|[ var x := e ]|
  ; where( new-CopyProp(|x,x) )
  ; where( try(<copy-prop-assign-aux> |[ x := e ]|) )

copy-prop-assign = ?|[ x := e ]|
  ; where( undefine-CopyProp(|x) )
  ; where( try(copy-prop-assign-aux) )

copy-prop-assign-aux = ?|[ x := y ]|
  ; where( <not(eq)>(x,y) )
  ; where( innermost-scope-CopyProp => z )
  ; rules( CopyProp.z : |[ x ]| -> |[ y ]| depends on [(x,x), (y,y)] )

innermost-scope-CopyProp =
  get-var-names => vars; innermost-scope-CopyProp(elem-of(|vars))
```

Fig. 7. Specification of copy propagation with dependent dynamic rules

This sums up the problems with the extrapolation of the use of dynamic rules for constant propagation to transformations involving variables in the right-hand sides of rules. The first two problems are solved by means of *dependent* dynamic rules, the last problem is solved by defining rules in the innermost scope of all variables involved. A correct definition of copy propagation using these techniques is presented in **Fig. 7** Note that the traversal part of the specification is similar to the one of constant propagation and is omitted.

A *dependent dynamic rule* is a dynamic rule that declares its dependencies on program entities such as variables. The `depends on` clause of a dependent rule declares a list of pairs of the scope and value of the dependencies. For example, a copy propagation rule `|[ a ]| -> |[ b ]|` depends on the object variables `a` and `b`, entailing the dependency list `[(a,a),(b,b)]`. In the case of the Tiger transformations in this paper, variable names are used as scope labels and as dependencies. However, this is not necessarily the case in general, which motivates the distinction. Rule dependencies are used to undefine or shadow a dynamic rule when one of its dependencies is changed. For example, if the object variable `b` is assigned to, all copy propagation rules in which that variable is involved become invalid. For this purpose, a mapping from dependencies to the rules they affect is maintained. For a dependent dynamic rule R, the strategies `undefine-`R, `new-`R, and `innermost-scope-`R solve the problems discussed above.

(1) The `undefine-`R`(|`*dep*`)` strategy undefines all rules depending on *dep*. It should be used when the meaning of *dep* has changed, e.g. in `copy-prop-assign`.

(2) The `new-`R`(|`*l*`,`*dep*`)` strategy labels the current scope with *l* and *locally* undefines any rules that depend on *dep*. This strategy is typically used when encountering a local declaration for dependency *dep* with scope label *l*, e.g., in `copy-prop-declare`, and avoids rules depending on dep living in external scopes from being applied, which would result in free variable capture.

(3) The `innermost-scope-`R`(`*s*`)` strategy examines the labels in the scopes for R starting with the most recent one, producing the first for which s succeeds. This is

used in the definition of `innermost-scope-CopyProp` to obtain the innermost scope label for the set of variables in an expression. Thus, in `copy-prop-assign-aux`, new `CopyProp` rules are defined in the innermost scope z, which is the innermost scope of x and y. This ensures that the rule is removed as soon as one of its dependencies goes out of scope. As a consequence rules are only applied to those parts of the tree where both variables are in scope, avoiding variables to escape from their scope.

Dependent dynamic rules are a generative extension of basic dynamic rules. Thus, the effect of dependent dynamic rules can be achieved using only basic dynamic rules, but the implementation of the administration of dependencies and their mapping is rather tedious. The language feature supports the reuse of this code pattern by means of a code generator in the compiler, which can also exploit the internal representation of dynamic rules.

4 Generic Data-Flow Transformation Strategies

The definition of copy propagation in **Fig. 7** is very similar to the definition of constant propagation in **Fig. 5** The difference between the two transformations is restricted to the optimization specific strategies for handling declarations and assignments. Control flow constructs for forking and iteration share a common strategy with the dynamic rule name as only difference. The generic forward propagation strategy for Tiger (`forward-prop`) in **Fig. 9** allows individual optimizations to focus on their essential elements by reusing the code for the common parts of the transformation. A dual strategy for backwards propagation is defined in similar fashion [14].

The `forward-prop` strategy is parameterized with strategies that are applied at certain stages of the transformation of a language construct. The strategies `transform`, `before` and `after` are local rewrites of a construct and can be used to tune the transformation. Further parameters are the names of rules to be intersected (*Rs1*) and unified (*Rs2*) at fork and join points, and rule names (*Rs3*) that are part of the transformation, but do not require a dynamic rule operation at confluence points.

Common-Subexpresson Elimination. **Fig. 10** presents an instantiation of `forward-prop` for common-subexpression elimination (CSE). CSE is a transformation that replaces common expressions with a variable that already contains the value of the expression. For example, CSE transforms `(a := b + c; d := b + c)` to `(a := b + c; d := a)`. By instantiating `forward-prop`, we can focus on the definition of the conditions that enable the propagation of non-trivial expressions by defining `CSE` rules. Scoping and undefining of dynamic rules are handled in the `forward-prop` strategy. This is a

```
super-opt =
  forward-prop(prop-const-transform, bvr-before,
    bvr-after; copy-prop-after; prop-const-after; cse-after
    | ["PropConst", "CopyProp", "CSE"], [], ["RenameVar"])
```

Fig. 8. 'Super' transformation combining constant propagation, copy propagation, common-subexpression elimination, and bound variable renaming

```
forward-prop(transform, before, after | Rs1 , Rs2, Rs3) =
<conc>(Rs1, Rs2, Rs3) => RsSc; <conc>(Rs1, Rs2) => RsDf;
let
  fp = prop-assign <+ prop-declare <+ prop-let <+ prop-if <+ prop-while
       <+ transform(fp) <+ (before; all(fp); after)

  prop-assign =
    |[ <id> := <fp> ]|
    ; (transform(fp)
       <+ before; ?|[ x := e ]|; undefine-dynamic-rules(|RsDf,x); after)

  prop-declare =
    |[ var <id> := <fp> ]|
    ; (transform(fp)
       <+ before; ?|[ var x := e ]|; new-dynamic-rules(|RsSc,x,x);after)

  prop-let =
    ?|[ let d* in e* end ]|
    ; (transform(fp) <+ {|~RsSc : before; all(fp); after |})

  prop-if =
    |[ if <fp> then <id> else <id> ]|
    ; (transform(fp)
       <+ before ; (|[ if <id> then <fp> else <id> ]| /~Rs1\~Rs2/
                    |[ if <id> then <id> else <fp> ]|); after)
  prop-while =
    ?|[ while e1 do e2 ]|
    ; (transform(fp)
       <+ before; /~Rs1\~Rs2/* |[ while <fp> do <fp> ]|; after)
 in fp
end
```

Fig. 9. A generic strategy for forward propagation transformations

```
cse = forward-prop(cse-transform, id, cse-after | ["CSE"], [], [])

cse-transform(recur) = fail

cse-after = try(cse-assign <+ cse-declare <+ CSE)

cse-declare = ?|[ var x := e ]|; where( <cse-assign> |[ x := e ]| )

cse-assign = ?|[ x := e ]|
  ; where( <pure-and-not-trivial(|x)> |[ e ]| )
  ; where( get-var-dependencies => xs )
  ; where( innermost-scope-CSE => z )
  ; rules( CSE.z : |[ e ]| -> |[ x ]| depends on xs )
```

Fig. 10. Common-subexpression elimination using generic forward propagation strategy

major simplification of the implementation of CSE, since we do not have to handle all the control-flow constructs separately in this specific optimization.

Combining Transformations. The `forward-prop` strategy uses generalized versions of the dynamic rule combinators to deal with multiple rules. The `new-dynamic-rules` and `undefine-dynamic-rules` strategies apply the `new-R` and `undefine-R` rules for all parameter rules. Similarly, the `/Rs1\Rs2/` and `/Rs1\Rs2/*` operators generalize the intersection and union operators to a single combined operator, which performs intersection over the first set of rules and union over the second. Thus, the generic forward propagation strategy can apply different analyses and transformations at the same time by combining elements from several one issue transformations. As an example, **Fig. 8** shows a strategy that combines constant propagation, copy propagation, common-subexpression elimination, unreachable code elimination and bound-variable renaming. We have included bound-variable renaming on the fly in this combined transformation to avoid dynamic rules from being unnecessarily undefined/shadowed.

5 Discussion

Previous Work. Scoped dynamic rules were introduced in [17] to overcome the limitations of the context-free nature of static rewrite rules with applications to bound variable renaming, function inlining, and dead code elimination. A first version of constant propagation based on that design is described in [13]. Scoped dynamic rules have been extended, improved, and formalized in [4], introducing labeling of scopes to provide more fine-grained control over the definition and removal of dynamic rules, and introducing the fork, intersection, union and fixed-point operations on sets of dynamic rules. The contributions of this paper with respect to that work are the introduction of dependent dynamic rules, the definition of generic data-flow transformation strategies, and the combination of data-flow transformations. In the technical report version of this paper [14] we also present a generic backwards propagation strategy, the other instantiations of the generic forward propagation strategy used in the combined optimizer and a specification of partial redundancy elimination, illustrating how two separate analyses (backwards and forwards) can communicate via annotations.

Related Work. A discussion of techniques for data-flow transformations is beyond the scope of this paper. Rather, we focus on languages and tools that automate part of the effort of producing program data-flow transformations.

Program analyzer generators such as Sharlit [16] and PAG [11] produce analyzers from a specification of the flow values and flow functions for the problem at hand. In Sharlit [16] these have to be implemented in C++ following the conventions of the tool. PAG provides a dedicated domain-specific language for all aspects of the specification. These tools do not support combined super-analyses, nor the specification of transformations; applications of analysis and transformation are alternated.

Graph transformation tools such as OPTIMIX [3] and the tools of De Moor et al. [7, 6] provide a transformation-oriented approach, aiming at declarative specification of individual transformations, in contrast to the global approach of data-flow analyses.

An OPTIMIX program consists of a set of rewrite rules on a graph representation of a program. The graph can be extended with additional edges to express analysis results. Transformation is by exhaustive application of rules. Lacey and De Moor [7] use graph rewrite rules with temporal logic conditions to check properties of the control-flow graph; that is, enabling conditions are checked from the point of view of the node that is transformed, rather than as a global analysis. Path logic programming [6] is a variation on this approach using path patterns, regular expressions over paths through the control-flow graph of a program that express the properties that should hold on all or some paths to the node subject to transformation. The drawback of these approaches is that pattern matching requires performing a global program analysis and a search for graph nodes that match a certain pattern. After applying a transformation, the analysis needs to be redone. Obtaining efficient optimizers requires *incrementally* updating the analysis information after applying transformations. There is some progress in this area [15] with a technique for compositional analysis based on path expressions. Our approach provides effective procedures for finding data-flow redices in abstract syntax trees.

Combination of analysis and transformation is not only desirable from the point of view of performance, but can also produce better results. Wegman and Zadek introduced conditional constant propagation, a combination of constant propagation and unreachable code elimination [21], which produces better results than applying the two transformations in sequence. Click and Cooper [5] formally defined in which cases integrating two data-flow analyses results in better results than a sequential application of the individual analyses, and they combined constant propagation, unreachable code elimination and value numbering. Rather than implementing such combined transformations in dedicated algorithms, we provide high-level constructs for the composition of such combined transformations. In this sense our work is most related to that of Lerner et al. who have developed a series of frameworks [8, 9, 10] for the composition of data-flow transformations in a modular way. Similarly to our approach they combine analysis and the application of transformations as long as they share the same direction. There is a difference in perspective, though; while we model program analysis by dynamic transformation rules, they let the analysis framework *simulate* transformations. Another difference is that their frameworks operate on fixed control-flow graph representations. In contrast, Stratego is not specifically designed for data-flow transformations. Rewrite rules, strategy combinators, and dynamic rules are useful in a wide variety of transformations. In addition, our approach handles variable bindings correctly.

Conclusion. We have presented a language for the concise specification of source-to-source data-flow transformations. The generic high-level constructs allow adaptation of the approach to other programming languages with little effort; we have used the approach to implement optimizations in a compiler for the Octave language. Transfer functions are elegantly captured by dynamic rewrite rules and confluence operators for intersection or fixed-point applications are used to specify program analysis and transformation. The language supports combination of analysis and transformation in one traversal and the combination of multiple transformations in the same traversal.

The techniques presented in this paper are supported by Stratego/XT 0.14, which is available from `http://www.stratego-language.org/`.

Acknowledgments. We thank Martin Bravenboer for his help with the preparation of this paper, Tom de Vries and the anonymous referees for their comments on a previous version of this paper, and Oege de Moor and Ganesh Sittampalam for the discussions of specification of optimizers.

References

1. A. Aho, R. Sethi, and J. Ullman. *Compilers: Principles, Techniques, and Tools.* Addison-Wesley, 1986.
2. A. Appel. *Modern compiler implementation in ML.* Cambridge University Press, 1998.
3. U. Assmann. How To Uniformly Specify Program Analysis and Transformation. In T. Gyimóthy, editor, *Internationational Conference on Compiler Construction (CC'96)*, volume 1060 of *LNCS*, pages 121–135, Linköping, Sweden, 1996. Springer.
4. M. Bravenboer, A. van Dam, K. Olmos, and E. Visser. Program transformation with scoped dynamic rewrite rules. Technical Report UU-CS-2005-005, Institute of Information and Computing Sciences, Utrecht University, 2005.
5. C. Click and K. D. Cooper. Combining analyses, combining optimizations. *ACM Transactions on Programming Languages and Systems*, 17(2):181–196, March 1995.
6. S. Drape, O. de Moor, and G. Sittampalam. Transforming the .NET intermediate language using path logic programming. In C. Kirchner, editor, *Proceedings of the Fourth ACM SIGPLAN Conference on Principles and Practice of Declarative Programming (PPDP'02)*, pages 133–144, Pittsburgh, Pensylvania, USA, October 2002. ACM.
7. D. Lacey and O. de Moor. Imperative program transformation by rewriting. In R. Wilhelm, editor, *Proceedings of the 10th International Conference on Compiler Construction*, volume 2027 of *LNCS*, pages 52–68. Springer Verlag, 2001.
8. S. Lerner, D. Grove, and C. Chambers. Combining dataflow analyses and transformations. In *SIGPLAN Symposium on Principles of Programming Languages (POPL'02)*, pages 270–282, Portland, Oregon, January 2002.
9. S. Lerner, T. Millstein, and C. Chambers. Automatically proving the correctness of compiler optimizations. In *Programming Language Design and Implementation (PLDI'03)*, pages 220 – 231. ACM SIGPLAN, June 2003.
10. S. Lerner, T. Millstein, E. Rice, and C. Chambers. Automated soundness proofs for dataflow analyses and transformations via local rules. In *Principles of Programming Languages (POPL'05)*, pages 364–377. ACM SIGPLAN, January 2005.
11. F. Martin. PAG an efficient program analyzer generator. *International Journal on Software Tools for Technology Transfer STTT*, 2(1):46–67, November 1998.
12. S. Muchnick. *Advanced compiler design and implementation.* Morgan Kaufmann, 1997.
13. K. Olmos and E. Visser. Strategies for source-to-source constant propagation. In B. Gramlich and S. Lucas, editors, *Workshop on Reduction Strategies (WRS'02)*, volume 70 of *ENTCS*, page 20, Copenhagen, Denmark, July 2002. Elsevier Science Publishers.
14. K. Olmos and E. Visser. Composing source-to-source data-flow transformations with rewriting strategies and dependent dynamic rewrite rules. Technical Report UU-CS-2005-006, Institute of Information and Computing Sciences, Utrecht University, 2005.
15. G. Sittampalam, O. de Moor, and K. F. Larsen. Incremental execution of transformation specifications. In *SIGPLAN Symposium on Principles of Programming Languages (POPL'04)*, pages 26–38. ACM, January 2004.
16. S. W. K. Tjiang and J. L. Hennessy. Sharlit—A tool for building optimizers. In *ACM SIGPLAN '92 Conference on Programming Language Design and Implementation*, July 1992.

17. E. Visser. Scoped dynamic rewrite rules. In M. van den Brand and R. Verma, editors, *Rule Based Programming (RULE'01)*, volume 59/4 of *ENTCS*. Elsevier Science Publishers, September 2001.
18. E. Visser. Meta-programming with concrete object syntax. In D. Batory, C. Consel, and W. Taha, editors, *Generative Programming and Component Engineering (GPCE'02)*, volume 2487 of *LNCS*, pages 299–315, Pittsburgh, PA, USA, October 2002. Springer-Verlag.
19. E. Visser. Program transformation with Stratego/XT: Rules, strategies, tools, and systems in StrategoXT-0.9. In C. Lengauer et al., editors, *Domain-Specific Program Generation*, volume 3016 of *LNCS*, pages 216–238. Spinger-Verlag, June 2004.
20. E. Visser, Z.-e.-A. Benaissa, and A. Tolmach. Building program optimizers with rewriting strategies. In *Proceedings of the third ACM SIGPLAN International Conference on Functional Programming (ICFP'98)*, pages 13–26. ACM Press, September 1998.
21. M. Wegman and F. Zadeck. Constant propagation with conditional branches. *ACM Transactions on Programming Languages and Systems*, 13:181–210, April 1991.

Verification of Source Code Transformations by Program Equivalence Checking

K.C. Shashidhar[1,2], Maurice Bruynooghe[2], Francky Catthoor[1,3], and Gerda Janssens[2]

[1] Interuniversitair Micro-Elektronica Centrum (IMEC) vzw, Leuven, Belgium
[2] Departement Computerwetenschappen, Katholieke Universiteit Leuven, Belgium
[3] Departement Elektrotechniek (ESAT), Katholieke Universiteit Leuven, Belgium
{kodambal, catthoor}@imec.be, {maurice, gerda}@cs.kuleuven.ac.be

Abstract. Typically, a combination of manual and automated transformations is applied when algorithms for digital signal processing are adapted for energy and performance-efficient embedded systems. This poses severe verification problems. Verification becomes easier after converting the code into dynamic single-assignment form (DSA). This paper describes a method to prove equivalence between two programs in DSA where subscripts to array variables and loop bounds are (piecewise) affine expressions. For such programs, geometric modeling can be used and it can be shown, for groups of elements at once, that the outputs in both programs are the same function of the inputs.

1 Introduction

In the recent years, embedded processor systems have emerged as pervasive platforms for multimedia and telecom systems. They are highly resource-constrained and there is an increasing stress on rigorous optimization of the software that runs on them. Current compiler optimizations, though powerful, are insufficient to meet the resource constraints. Designers apply domain specific optimizations to obtain programs with a better performance/energy consumption trade-off.

Accesses to the data memory hierarchy are the most time and energy consuming operations in data-intensive applications. Globally applied loop transformations, expression propagations and algebraic transformations can reduce their cost. Guided by elaborate cost models, experienced designers apply them manually or use ad-hoc tools in a transformation phase prior to compilation. The process is error prone and testing hampers designer's productivity. We present a formal and automated method for the verification of such transformations.

Fig. 1 shows an artificial example where program (b) has been derived from (a) through expression propagations, loop and algebraic transformations. The functions, when executed, take inputs `A[]` and `B[]`, and assign the computed values to the elements of the output array `C[]`. Ignoring possible overflow, integer addition is both associative and commutative. Hence, both programs compute

R. Bodik (Ed.): CC 2005, LNCS 3443, pp. 221–236, 2005.

```
void foo(int A[], int B[], int C[])
{
  int k, tmp1[256], tmp2[266], tmp3[256];

    for(k=0; k<256; k++)
s1:     tmp1[k] = A[2*k] + f(B[k+1]);
    for(k=10; k<138; k++)
s2:     tmp2[k] = B[k-8];
    for(k=10; k<266; k++){
        if(k >= 138)
s3:         tmp2[k] = B[k-8];
s4:     tmp3[k-10] = f(A[2*k-19]) + tmp2[k];
    }
    for(k=255; k>=0; k--)
s5:     C[3*k] = tmp1[k] + tmp3[k];
}
```
a

```
void foo(int A[], int B[], int C[])
{
 int k, tmp4[256], tmp5[256];

    for(k=0; k<256; k++){
t1:     tmp4[k] = f(A[2*k+1]) + A[2*k];
t2:     tmp5[k] = B[k+2] + tmp4[k];
t3:     C[3*k] = f(B[k+1]) + tmp5[k];
    }

}
```
b

Fig. 1. Example of an original (a) and transformed (b) program function pair

the same outputs for the same inputs, i.e., they are *input-output equivalent.* Our method automates the checking of their input-output equivalence.

The method handles a decidable subset of structured, imperative programs that are in dynamic single-assignment form, have only piecewise-affine expressions as subscripts to array variables and bounds of `for`-loops, and have static control-flow free from side-effects. It relies on code pre-processing methods to convert programs commonly seen in practice into the subset. For programs in this subset, we introduce a representation that captures both computation and the *true* data dependencies (Sec. 2). This representation exposes the invariant properties for the transformations and can deal with algebraic transformations (Sec. 3). Equivalence is shown by checking that a one-to-one correspondence exists between the two programs in their computation and in the data dependencies between the individual elements of their observable array variables (Sec. 4). It neither relies on any information about the particular instances of the transformations that were applied nor on the order of their application. It scales well for larger problem sizes (Sec. 5). Prior work outlines our method and discusses its application in embedded systems design [13]. This paper formally presents the method and explains how recurrences in data dependencies are handled. In Sec. 6, we situate our work with respect to other approaches.

2 Program Representation

We assume an imperative programming language that has array data structures and has a form of `for`-loops to control iteration. Our current tools are focused on C. The analysis is intra-procedural and the equivalence is checked between two procedures (functions). They can call other functions (common to both) to the extent that those functions can be considered as side effect free operators.

2.1 Class of Allowed Programs

Programs we can handle have the following properties:

1. *Dynamic single-assignment:* Every memory location is written only once. Optimizing compilers use the *static single-assignment* (SSA) form [6] to facilitate optimizations which still can write the same array element several times. This is not the case with *dynamic single-assignment* (DSA) form; it eliminates all false dependencies. Methods for conversion to DSA are described in [7, 16]. We also require that functions are free from side-effects.
2. *Piecewise-affine expressions:* Subscripts in the arrays and expressions in the bounds of the `for`-loops are all piece-wise affine in the iterator variables of the enclosing `for`-loops. Additionally, the expressions can also include operators like `mod`, `div`, `max`, `min`, `floor` and `ceil`. This allows representing the addressing relationships between elements of arrays as affine inequalities in integers and makes it possible to use well-understood dependence tests (for example, the Omega test [12]) to solve those systems.
3. *Static control-flow:* There are no data-dependent `while`-loops in the programs. We assume that data-dependent `while`-loops have been converted to `for`-loops with worst-case bounds and a global if-condition on its body; and the data-dependent if-conditions in the program have been converted into data dependencies by using if-conversion [1].
4. *No pointer references:* Programs are free from pointer references. Pointer-to-array conversion methods (for example, [15]) can be used here.

The class is not unduly restrictive for the application domain. In fact, it is advantageous to bring programs into such a form before applying global transformations as this form creates more freedom for the transformations and the tools used for guiding the transformations can do a better job [5].

2.2 Array Data Dependence Graphs

Scalars can be considered as one element arrays. Hence, which element is assigned by a (assignment) statement depends on the instantiation of the subscripts of the assigned array. The subscripts can depend on the values of the surrounding iterators when the statement appears inside a nest of `for`-loops. Which values the subscripts take during execution can be described in closed form as an integer domain in a multi-dimensional geometrical space. Such descriptions which record a variety of information related to the statements and dependencies among them are together referred to as the geometrical or polyhedral representation. This representation is commonly used for dependence analysis by optimizing compilers [2, 3, 17]. Here we briefly review the main elements.

Let us consider a statement s of the form

$$\texttt{s:}\quad \texttt{v[}f_{i_1}(\vec{k}_d)\texttt{]...[}f_{i_n}(\vec{k}_d)\texttt{]} = \texttt{exp(}\cdots,\ \texttt{u[}f_{j_1}(\vec{k}_d)\texttt{]...[}f_{j_m}(\vec{k}_d)\texttt{]},\cdots\texttt{);}$$

where $\vec{k}_d = (k_1, \ldots, k_r, \ldots, k_d)$ is the vector of iterator variables of the surrounding `for`-loops. Let $l_r(\vec{k}_{r-1})$, $u_r(\vec{k}_{r-1})$ and $s_r(\vec{k}_{r-1})$ be affine functions defining respectively the lower and upper bounds, and the stride of iterator k_r. Finally, assume execution of the for-loops is controlled by affine expressions $c_r(\vec{k}_{r-1})$ and execution of the statement s by $c_{d+1}(\vec{k}_d)$. Then we can define the following:

Definition 1 (Iteration Domain, D). *Integer domain in which each point* $[k_1, \ldots, k_d]$ *represents exactly one execution of the statement* s*:*

$$\mathrm{D} := \{[k_1, \ldots, k_d] \mid (\bigwedge_{r=1}^{d} k_r \in \mathbb{Z} \wedge (l_r(\vec{k}_{r-1}) \leq k_r \leq u_r(\vec{k}_{r-1})) \wedge c_r(\vec{k}_{r-1}) \wedge (\exists \alpha_r \in \mathbb{Z} \mid k_r = \alpha_r s_r(\vec{k}_{r-1}) + l_r(\vec{k}_{r-1}))) \wedge c_{d+1}(\vec{k}_d)\}.$$

Definition 2 (Definition Domain, $\mathrm{W_v}$). *Integer domain in which each point* $[i_1, \ldots, i_n]$ *represents exactly one* write *to* v[i_1]...[i_n]*, an element of the array* v *defined by the statement* s *with iteration domain* D*:*

$$\mathrm{W_v} := \{[i_1, \ldots, i_n] \mid (\bigwedge_{r=1}^{n} i_r = f_{i_r}(\vec{k})) \wedge \vec{k} \in \mathrm{D}\}.$$

Definition 3 (Operand Domain, $\mathrm{R_u}$). *Integer domain in which each point* $[j_1, \ldots, j_m]$ *represents exactly one* read *from an element* u[j_1]...[j_m]*, of an operand array* u *in statement* s *with iteration domain* D*:*

$$\mathrm{R_u} := \{[j_1, \ldots, j_m] \mid (\bigwedge_{r=1}^{m} j_r = f_{j_r}(\vec{k})) \wedge \vec{k} \in \mathrm{D}\}.$$

Definition 4 (Dependency Mapping, $\mathrm{M_{v,u}}$). *A mapping associated with a statement, between a defined array* v *and an operand array* u*. Each instance* $[i_1, \ldots, i_n] \rightarrow [j_1, \ldots, j_m]$ *in the mapping indicates that element* u[j_1]...[j_m] *is read when the element* v[i_1]...[i_n] *is written by the statement* s *with iteration domain* D*:*

$$\mathrm{M_{v,u}} := \{[i_1, \ldots, i_n] \rightarrow [j_1, \ldots, j_m] \mid (\bigwedge_{r=1}^{n} i_r = f_{i_r}(\vec{k})) \wedge (\bigwedge_{r=1}^{m} j_r = f_{j_r}(\vec{k})) \wedge \vec{k} \in \mathrm{D}\}.$$

For example, the definitions given above for statement s4 in the original function in Fig. 1 are:

<table>
<tr><td colspan="2">$\mathrm{D} := \{[k] \mid 10 \leq k < 266 \wedge k \in \mathbb{Z}\}$</td></tr>
<tr><td>$\mathrm{W_{tmp3}} := \{[d] \mid d = k - 10 \wedge k \in \mathrm{D}\}$</td><td>$\mathrm{R_A} := \{[d] \mid d = 2 * k - 19 \wedge k \in \mathrm{D}\}$
$\mathrm{R_{tmp2}} := \{[d] \mid d = k \wedge k \in \mathrm{D}\}$</td></tr>
<tr><td colspan="2">$\mathrm{M_{tmp3,A}} := \{[d_1] \rightarrow [d_2] \mid d_1 = k - 10 \wedge d_2 = 2 * k - 19 \wedge k \in \mathrm{D}\}$
$\mathrm{M_{tmp3,tmp2}} := \{[d_1] \rightarrow [d_2] \mid d_1 = k - 10 \wedge d_2 = k \wedge k \in \mathrm{D}\}$</td></tr>
</table>

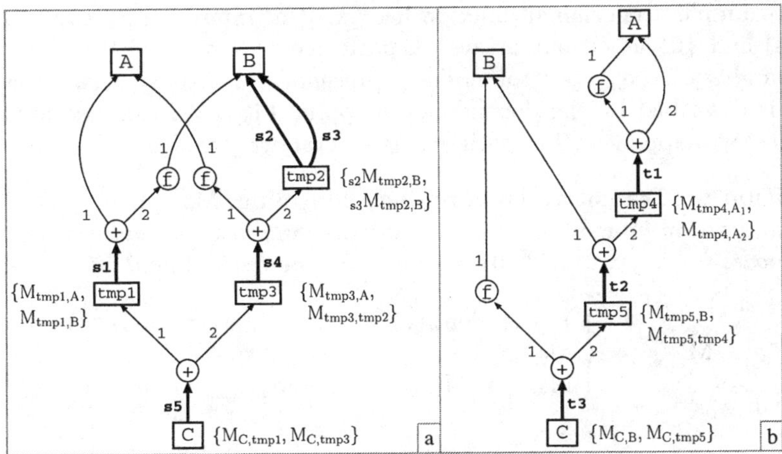

Fig. 2. The ADDGs of program functions in Fig. 1. Array A_1 and A_2 in the dependency mapping of `tmp4` in (b) refer to different occurrences of `A` in statement `t1`

A data dependence exists between two statements s and t when s produces values and t consumes them, i.e., s has definition domain $\mathrm{W_v}$, t has operand domain $\mathrm{R_v}$ and $\mathrm{W_v} \cap \mathrm{R_v} \neq \emptyset$. Dependencies are represented at a fine grained level. The assigned array depends either on the consumed array or on the main operator of the rhs. In the latter case, the operator in turn depends on its arguments which are either other operators or arrays. The set of all dependencies can be represented as an array data dependence graph (ADDG).

Definition 5 (Array Data Dependence Graph, ADDG). *The* ADDG *of a program is a directed graph $G = (V, E)$, where the node set V is the union of arrays used in the program (array nodes) and the operator occurrences (operator nodes) of the statements and the edge set E represents the dependencies. An edge with operator node as source is labeled by the operand position of its destination; an edge with an array as source is labeled with the statement identifier of the assignment. Array nodes of defined arrays are annotated with the dependency mappings of the statement.*

Whereas standard data dependence graphs used in high-performance compilers represent dependencies at the statement level, we use more detailed dependencies. Also, a data dependence (*reverse flow*), denoted by a directed edge, refers not just to a single value, but to a *set of values*. A dependency mapping (Def. 4) corresponds to a path with the defined array as source and the operand array as destination (paths that pass through zero or more operators). Fig. 2 shows the ADDG representations of the programs of Fig. 1.

An array v is an *internal array* if $\bigcup \mathrm{W_v} = \bigcup \mathrm{R_v}$, i.e. each produced element is consumed; it is an *input array* if $\bigcup \mathrm{W_v} = \emptyset$, i.e., no element is produced; and an *output array* if $\bigcup \mathrm{R_v} \subset \bigcup \mathrm{W_v}$, i.e. some of its elements are not consumed.

In the example, the original function has {A, B} as input, {tmp1, tmp2, tmp3} as internal and {C} as output arrays. A path $u, o_1, \ldots, o_n, v$ with u and v array nodes and $o_1, \ldots, o_n$ operator nodes represents a data-flow between v and u which is described by the dependency mapping $\mathrm{M}_{\mathtt{u,v}}$. We can also associate a dependency mapping with a path across several array nodes.

Definition 6 (Transitive Dependency Mapping, $\mathrm{M}^*_{\mathtt{v_0,v_n}}$). *Let p be a path in an* ADDG *starting in array node v_o, ending in array node v_n and passing through array nodes $v_1, \ldots, v_{n-1}$ ($n \geq 0$). Using $\bowtie$ for the natural join*[4] *of two relations:*

$$\mathrm{M}^*_{\mathtt{v_0,v_n}} := \begin{cases} I \text{ (the identity)} & n = 0 \\ \mathrm{M}_{\mathtt{v_0,v_1}} & n = 1 \\ \mathrm{M}_{\mathtt{v_0,v_1}} \bowtie \mathrm{M}_{\mathtt{v_1,v_2}} \bowtie \ldots \bowtie \mathrm{M}_{\mathtt{v_{n-1},v_n}} & \text{otherwise} \end{cases}$$

Definition 7 (Data Dependence Path). *A path between two array nodes is a data dependence path iff its transitive dependency mapping is non-empty.*

The transitive dependency mapping from an output to an input node is called the *output-to-input mapping.* The set of output-to-input mappings characterizes the data-flow of the computation.

For example, in the ADDG of the original function in Fig. 2 the output-to-input mapping from C to B on the rightmost path is given by

$$\begin{aligned} \mathrm{M}^*_{\mathtt{C,B}} &:= \mathrm{M}_{\mathtt{C,tmp3}} \bowtie \mathrm{M}_{\mathtt{tmp3,tmp2}} \bowtie \mathrm{M}_{\mathtt{tmp2,B}} \\ &:= \{[d_1] \rightarrow [d_2] \mid d_1 = 3 * k \wedge d_2 = k + 2 \wedge 128 \leq k < 256 \wedge k \in \mathbb{Z}\}. \end{aligned}$$

The data dependence paths from a node v can be used to identify the program slices contributing to the computation of the elements of v. The outgoing edges of v partition the elements of the array and different paths correspond to different slices of the computation. Also an operator node has different outgoing edges. They correspond to different operands of the operator; they all contribute to the computation by the operator and hence belong to the same slice.

An ADDG can have cycles, in which case it has cyclic paths. A cyclic data dependence path indicates the presence of a *recurrence* in the computation: arrays in a cyclic path have elements whose value depend on other elements of the same array. While an ADDG with a cycle has infinite paths, all data dependence paths are finite as the program is composed of terminating `for`-loops. We return to recurrences in Sec. 4.2.

An internal array node acts as a buffer and can be eliminated from a given path (because the program is in DSA).

Operation 1 (Internal Array Node Elimination). *Let the outgoing edges of an internal array node w be $(w, x_1), \ldots, (w, x_k)$ with labels $s_1, \ldots, s_k$ and let $\mathrm{M}_{\mathtt{w,t_1}}, \ldots, \mathrm{M}_{\mathtt{w,t_k}}$ be the corresponding dependency mappings. Let p be a path*

[4] $x \rightarrow z \in F \bowtie G \Leftrightarrow \exists y$ s.t. $x \rightarrow y \in F \wedge y \rightarrow z \in G$.

(possibly including operators) from an array node u to w and s be the label of the outgoing edge of u on p and $\mathrm{M_{u,w}}$ *the associated dependency mapping. Let the incoming edge on w on p be (v, w) with the label l. The node w is eliminated on the path p from u as follows:*

- $\forall i, 1 \leq i \leq k$: *add the edge (v, x_i) and if $u = v$, label it as $s.s_i$, else label it as l*
- *Replace* $\mathrm{M_{u,w}}$ *by the transitive dependency mappings* $\mathrm{M^*_{u,t_1}}, \ldots, \mathrm{M^*_{u,t_k}}$
- *Remove the edge (v, w).*

In the above operation, when v is an operator node and $k > 1$, v has multiple operands with the same position label. Such operands correspond to disjunct slices of the computation.

3 Transformations and Their Effect

In this section, we discuss three categories of transformations that we allow and their effect on the ADDG representation of the program function.

Global Loop Transformations. Loop transformations are usually classified into *structure preserving* and *structure modifying* categories. The former category includes such transformations as loop permutation, interchange, skewing, reversal and bumping, and those that can be derived from combining them. The latter includes loop distribution, fission, splitting, merging, folding, fusion, strip-mining, tiling and unrolling. Structure preserving transformations only affect the iteration domains of statements. While the graph structure of the ADDG remains, the associated dependency mappings are affected. A transformation preserves correctness when the output-to-input mappings for the paths of the same computation on the transformed ADDG is identical to the output-to-input mappings in the original ADDG. Structure modifying transformations can result in a re-distribution of definition domains of the involved arrays. For example, in the original function, the rightmost path splits at array node tmp2 and partitions the output-to-input mappings from the output array C to input array B for the same computation. Therefore, the invariant for the correctness of these transformations is that, the union of output-to-input mappings for the paths of the same computation on the transformed ADDG must be identical to a similar union of mappings in the original ADDG.

Expression Propagations. Expression propagation involves both introduction and elimination of intermediate arrays for partial computations in the program function. For example, a statement with a summation of three terms on the right-hand side can be converted into two statements with summation of two terms each, by the introduction of an intermediate array. Another possibility is that a set of values are recomputed, instead of reused. The effect of expression propagation on the ADDG of the program function is insertion/elimination of array nodes on the paths of the ADDG and/or duplication of sub-ADDGs. The invariant for the correctness of the propagation transformations is the same as for

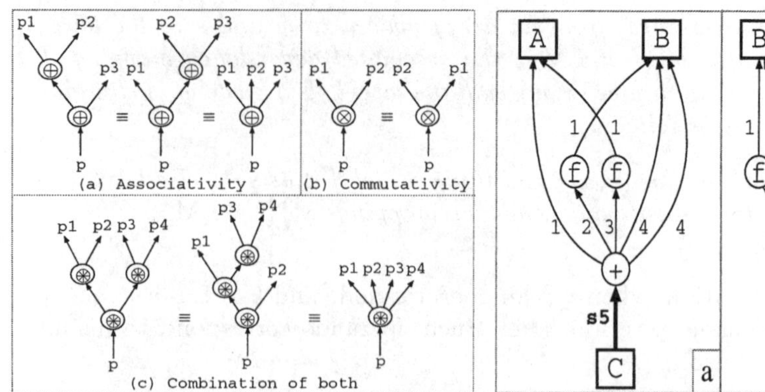

Fig. 3. AC transformations

Fig. 4. ADDGs after flattening

loop transformations. That is, the output-to-input mappings for the paths of the same computation on the transformed ADDG is identical to the output-to-input mappings in the original ADDG.

Global Algebraic Transformations. Algebraic transformations exploit properties of operators and user-defined functions and modify the data-flow in order to improve efficiency or to enable the other transformations. Several statements can be involved as can be seen in Fig. 1, where these transformations have been applied across expressions of multiple statements. The ADDGs of the two functions, as shown in Fig. 2, also reflect this. Most of these transformations just rely on the associativity and/or commutativity properties of the operators like addition and multiplication on a data-type such as integer. We distinguish:

Associativity. Let $\oplus$ be an associative operator. Fig. 3(a) shows two computations that are equivalent due to associativity. To integrate associativity in our method, we replace the graph fragment by its normal form: A single $\oplus$ operator with a variable number of arguments as shown on the right of Fig. 3(a). This does not affect the output-to-input mappings of the ADDG. In addition, internal array nodes receiving input from another $\oplus$ operator can be eliminated. This results in the following operator:

Operation 2 (Flattening). *Process all successor nodes of an associative $\oplus$-node p as follows: if it is an internal array node, apply internal array node elimination. If it is another $\oplus$-node o, eliminate it: let l be the label of the edge (p, o) and let $(o, s_0), \ldots, (o, s_n)$ be the outgoing edges. For all the outgoing edges of p with label $(k > l)$, replace the label k by $k + n$ and add edges (p, s_i) with labels $l + i$. Remove the edge (p, o). Repeat flattening on p until all its successor nodes are either input nodes or operator nodes other than $\oplus$.*

Note that elimination of a node adds new children to the root node, which are in turn processed and that the order of the nodes is preserved. Fig. 4 shows the effect on the ADDGs of Fig. 2. On the left, note the two outgoing edges with the same label, they correspond to disjunct slices of the computation.

Commutativity. A commutative operator allows to permute the arguments as shown in Fig. 3(b). As a consequence, one cannot use the labels on the edges to find corresponding arguments for operators that should perform the same computation. E.g., the +-nodes of Fig. 4 are commutative. To find the correspondence between their arguments, a matching operation is needed.

Operation 3 (Matching). *Given a pair of commutative operators in two different* ADDGs *matching selects pairs of corresponding edges. To do so, it has to look-ahead in the subtrees of the edges, using information about operator labels and transitive dependency mappings to eliminate candidates. This boils down to a recursive application of the method described in Sec. 4.*

Consider the two addition operators in the two ADDGs of Fig. 4. Edge 1 in the left ADDG pairs with edge 4 in the right ADDG, as they are the only ones leading to the input array A. Both +-nodes haves two edges leading to an operator labeled f, so further look-ahead is needed. In both cases, one of the operator nodes leads to input array A and the other to B, hence the correct pairing is $(2, 1)$ and $(3, 3)$. Finally, the left ADDG has two edges labeled 4, leading to input array B, also edge 2 of the right ADDG leads to B, resulting in two pairs $(4, 2)$.

Combination of associativity and commutativity. Operators can be both associative and commutative, increasing the number of equivalent forms, as illustrated in Fig. 3(c) for the $\circledast$-operator. As already explained on our example, the flattening operation has to be followed by a matching operation.

Other Properties. Operations for handling other properties (distributivity, inverse of an operator, identity element of an operator, evaluation of constant values) can be developed in a similar way by a combination of reduction to a suitable normal form and matching.

4 Equivalence Checking Method

We start by introducing a sufficient condition for equivalence between programs. Next, in Sec. 4.1, we explain a traversal based method to check the condition. Finally, in Sec. 4.2 we discuss how recurrences are tackled.

Two programs are equivalent when they have identical outputs for identical inputs. Assuming they have the same input and output arrays, we distinguish the following two conditions. For each output element in both programs:

COND-A: The set of output-to-input mappings is the same; and
COND-B: The computation is the same.

Together, they ensure that each output element is obtained by applying the same function on the same input elements, i.e., that both programs are equivalent. The ADDG is an abstraction of the computation that allows one to do the verification for groups of elements at once. The verification is based on a synchronous traversal of the ADDGs from output to input. Using the structure of the ADDGs, the dependency mappings and the operators, it is verified whether both programs perform the same computation.

4.1 Synchronized Traversal of Two ADDGs

Starting with a proof obligation about the equality of the outputs we try to reduce it to proof obligations about equality of inputs that are trivially satisfied.

Definition 8 (Proof Obligation). *Given two ADDGs, G_1 and G_2. A* primitive proof obligation *is of the form $(v_1, v_2, M^*_{0,v_1}, M^*_{0,v_2})$, where v_1 and v_2 are arrays from G_1 and G_2, respectively, and M^*_{0,v_1} and M^*_{0,v_2} are transitive dependency mappings with identical domains, i.e., $dom(M^*_{0,v_1}) = dom(M^*_{0,v_2})$. A* proof obligation *is a conjunction of primitive proof obligations.*

Definition 9 (Truth of Proof Obligation). *A proof obligation is true if each of its primitive proof obligations is true. A primitive proof obligation $(v_1, v_2, M^*_{0,v_1}, M^*_{0,v_2})$ is true if $v_1[M^*_{0,v_1}(i)] = v_2[M^*_{0,v_2}(i)]$ for all i in $dom(M^*_{0,v_1})$ for any execution of the program.*

Operation 4 (Proof Initialization). *A first requirement is that the data-flow is correct, i.e., each read element is either input or has been written before. A second requirement is that both programs output the same set of elements. These requirements need to be checked before the actual verification by inspecting definition and operand domains of statements.*

For each output array O_i in both G_1 and G_2, let W_i be the total definition domain of O_i (the union of the definition domains of the defining statements). Let p_i be the primitive proof obligation $(O_i, O_i, M^*_{0_i,0_i}, M^*_{0_i,0_i})$ with $dom(M^*_{0_i,0_i}) = W_i$. The initial proof obligation is the conjunction of all p_i.

Obviously, the initial proof obligation implies equivalence of both programs.

Definition 10 (Terminal Proof Obligation). *A primitive proof obligation $p = (v_1, v_2, M^*_{0,v_1}, M^*_{0,v_2})$ is terminal iff v_1 and v_2 are input arrays.*

A terminal proof obligation is true according to Def. 9 iff $v_1 = v_2$ and $M^*_{0,v_1} = M^*_{0,v_2}$, i.e., the output-to-input mappings select the same elements in the same input arrays.

The following reduction introduces primitive proof obligations where the nodes are not arrays; such obligations are auxiliary obligations, which have not been given a formal meaning. They are further reduced in subsequent reductions.

Operation 5 (Reduction of Primitive Proof Obligation). *Let the primitive proof obligation to be reduced be $p = (v_1, v_2, M^*_{0,v_1}, M^*_{0,v_2})$. The reduction generates a set (conjunction) of new primitive proof obligations that replaces p.*

Case 1. v_1 *is an array node. For each successor node of* v_1 *that is an array node an* array-array reduction *is applied and for each successor node of* v_1 *that is an operator node an* array-operator reduction *is applied.*

- Array–array reduction. *Suppose that the successor node is the array node* a. *For every dependency mapping* $\mathtt{M_{v_1,a}}$, $\mathtt{M^*_{0,a}} := \mathtt{M^*_{0,v_1}} \bowtie \mathtt{M_{v_1,a}}$ *is computed, and the proof obligation* $(a, v_2, \mathtt{M^*_{0,a}}, \text{restrict}(\mathtt{M^*_{0,v_2}}))$ *is added, where* $\text{restrict}(\mathtt{M^*_{0,v_2}})$ *is the projection of* $\mathtt{M^*_{0,v_2}}$ *on* $dom(\mathtt{M^*_{0,a}})$.
- Array–operator reduction. *Suppose that the successor node is the operator node* f. *The proof obligation* $(f, v_2, \mathtt{M^*_{0,v_1}}, \mathtt{M^*_{0,v_2}})$ *is added.*

Case 2. v_2 *is an array node: this case is similar to* **Case 1**.

Case 3. v_1 *and* v_2 *are both operator nodes* $v_1 = v_2 = \odot$. *If* $\odot$ *is associative, apply flattening on* $\odot$*-node on both sides. Let* $x_1, \ldots, x_{k'}$ *and* $y_1, \ldots, y_{l'}$ *be the successor nodes of* v_1 *and* v_2, *with labels* $\{1, \ldots, k\}$ *and* $\{1, \ldots, l\}$ *respectively, for edges between them (where* $k \leq k'$ *and* $l \leq l'$*). If* $\odot$ *is commutative, apply matching. Let* x_i *be matched with* $y_{m(w_i)}$, *where* $w_i = label(v, x_i)$. *If* $\odot$ *is neither associative nor commutative, then* $m(w_i) = w_i$. *For each pair* $(x_i, y_{m(w_i)})$, $\forall i, 1 \leq i \leq k'$, $(x_i, y_{m(w_i)}, M_1, M_2)$ *is added, such that, if* x_i *(resp.* $y_{m(w_i)}$*) is an operator node, then* $M_1 = \mathtt{M^*_{0,v_1}}$ *(resp.* $M_2 = \mathtt{M^*_{0,v_2}}$*), else* $M_1 := \mathtt{M^*_{0,v_1}} \bowtie \mathtt{M_{v_1,x_i}}$ *(resp.* $M_2 := \mathtt{M^*_{0,v_2}} \bowtie \mathtt{M_{v_2,y_{m(w_i)}}}$*).*

The method is summarized in Algorithm 1. The actual implementation uses the proof obligations and reasons over the program representation without manipulating its initial structure.

Algorithm 1: Outline of the equivalence checker.

```
Input: ADDGs G1 and G2 of the two functions.
Output: If they are equivalent, return True, else return False, with diagnostics.
P ⟵ ProofInitialization()
while P ≠ ∅ do
    p ⟵ SelectObligation()
    if TerminalObligation(p) then
        if not TrueObligation(p) then
            return (False, errorDiagnostics)
    else
        newObligations ⟵ ReduceObligation(p)
        if newObligations = ∅ then
            return (False, errorDiagnostics)
        else
            P ⟵ (P \ {p}) ∪ newObligations
return True
```

4.2 Handling Recurrences in the ADDG

Recurrences are detected when reduction leads to an array node that has already been visited. Clearly, it is inefficient to step through each instance of a recurrence.

```
foo(int A[], int B[]){
 int k, tmp[256];
 tmp[0] = f2(A[0]);
 for(k=1; k<256; k++)
  tmp[k] = tmp[k-1];
 B[0] = f1(tmp[255]);
}
```
a

```
foo(int A[], int B[]){
 int k, c[256];
 c[0] = f2(A[0]);
 for(k=1; k<256; k++)
  c[k] = f2(f1(c[k-1]));
 B[0] = f1(c[255]);
}
```
b

```
foo(int A[], int B[]){
 int k, r[256];
 r[0] = f1(f2(A[0]));
 for(k=1; k<256; k++)
  r[k] = f1(f2(r[k-1]));
 B[0] = r[255];
}
```
c

Fig. 5. Example program functions with recurrences

In most practical cases it can be avoided by computing the relation with the set of values at the end of the coil of recurrence, called the *across-recurrence mapping*. The key operation that enables such a computation is the positive *transitive closure* of an integer tuple relation.

Definition 11 (Across-recurrence Mapping). *Suppose we have a recurrence with* $\mathtt{v}, \mathtt{w}_1, \ldots, \mathtt{w}_k, \mathtt{v}$ *as the internal array nodes in the cycle that is entered on a path from array* $\mathtt{u}$. *Then the transitive dependency mapping for the cycle from* $\mathtt{v}$ *back to* $\mathtt{v}$ *is given by,* $\mathrm{M}^*_{\mathtt{v},\mathtt{v}} := \mathrm{M}_{\mathtt{v},\mathtt{w}_1} \bowtie \mathrm{M}_{\mathtt{w}_1,\mathtt{w}_2} \bowtie \cdots \bowtie \mathrm{M}_{\mathtt{w}_k,\mathtt{v}}$. *The across-recurrence mapping between* $\mathtt{u}$ *and* $\mathtt{v}$ *is the transitive dependency mapping between* $\mathtt{u}$ *and* $\mathtt{v}$ *that is across the recurrence on* $\mathtt{v}$ *and it relates the elements of* $\mathtt{u}$ *to the elements of* $\mathtt{v}$ *that are assigned outside the cycle on the same path. It is defined as,* $\mathrm{M}^R_{\mathtt{u},\mathtt{v}} = \mathrm{M}_{\mathtt{u},\mathtt{v}} \bowtie \mathrm{M}'_{\mathtt{v},\mathtt{v}}$, *where* $\mathrm{M}'_{\mathtt{v},\mathtt{v}}$ *is calculated as follows:*
- *Compute positive transitive closure of the recurrent mapping:* $m := (\mathrm{M}^*_{\mathtt{v},\mathtt{v}})^+$
- *Get domain and range of the computed closure:* $d := \mathrm{domain}(m)$; $r := \mathrm{range}(m)$
- *Get domain and range of the end-to-end mapping:* $d' := (d - r)$; $r' := (r - d)$
- *Restrict the closure to the tuples in the end-to-end mapping:* $\mathrm{M}'_{\mathtt{v},\mathtt{v}} := \{x \to y \,|\, x \to y \in m \wedge x \in d' \wedge y \in r'\}$.

For a tuple relation F, its positive transitive closure F^+, is a tuple relation defined as $x \to z \in F^+ \Leftrightarrow x \to z \in F \vee \exists y \text{ s.t. } x \to y \in F \wedge y \to z \in F^+$. A remark here is that exact transitive closure of a relation in closed form is not computable in the general case. A sufficient condition [9] for its computation is that, if the tuple of the relation is $[\vec{k_1}] \to [\vec{k_2}]$, then $\vec{k_2} = \vec{k_1} + \vec{c}$, where $\vec{c}$ is a vector of integer constants.

Depending on the nodes that appear in the cycle of recurrence, we distinguish two possible cases of recurrences in an ADDG.

Recurrence without computation. In this case, no operator nodes are present in the recurrence cycle. Fig. 5(a) shows an example program having such a recurrence without computation. During traversal (or during array node elimination), if such a recurrence is encountered on a given path, the across-recurrence mapping is computed and this essentially eliminates the cycle on the path. This is illustrated in the Fig. 6(a), where $\mathtt{v}$ is the array at the entry to the cycle and no operator nodes exist on the path p.

Recurrence with computation. In this case, operator nodes are present in the recurrence cycle. Fig. 5(b) and (c) show an example of equivalent program pair

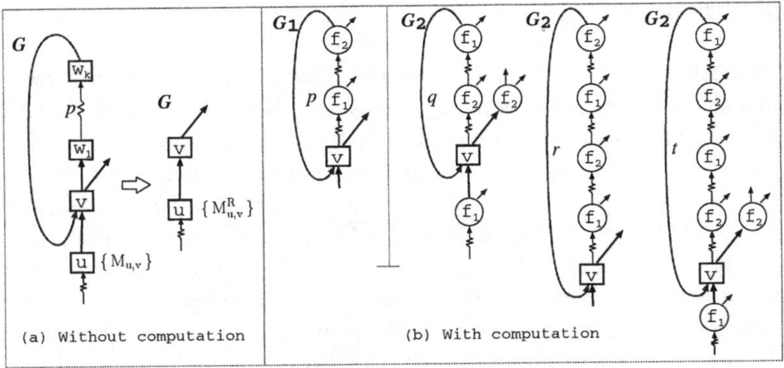

Fig. 6. Two cases of recurrence

that have such a recurrence with computation. When confronted with this recurrence, it is required that the across-recurrence mapping be computed on the two corresponding ADDGs in a synchronized way. That is, we need to ensure that the new dependency mappings computed account for the same computation. In order to be able to do that we first have to get identical sequence of operators on the recurrence cycles on both the ADDGs. This is achieved by *unfolding*.

Operation 6 (Unfolding). *Suppose G_1 and G_2 are the* ADDGs *being traversed in synchronization and we detect a recurrence on one of them, say, G_1, with $(f_1, \ldots, f_k, f_1)$ as operator nodes on the cycle. The traversal ensures that the corresponding nodes traversed on G_2 are also $(f_1, \ldots, f_k, f_1)$. If a recurrence is also detected at this point on G_2, we are done. Otherwise, we unfold G_1, by stepping through the recurrence along with G_2 as many times as it takes to reveal a cycle with identical sequence of operators on G_2.*

Fig. 6(b) shows G_1 with cycle p and G_2 with the basic possibilities for a cycle, viz,, operators shifted by one (q), unfolded once completely (r) and both unfolded once and shifted by one (t). In the example pair in Fig. 5(b) and (c), the operator is shifted by one in the transformed program.

Once we have established matching cycles on the two sides by unfolding, we have transitive dependency mappings for the two corresponding cycles, $M_1 := \{[\vec{a_1}] \rightarrow [\vec{a_2}] \mid C_1\}$ and $M_2 := \{[\vec{c_1}] \rightarrow [\vec{c_2}] \mid C_2\}$, where C_1 and C_2 are affine constraint expressions. Now, in order to compute the across-recurrence mapping that ensures same computation on both sides we combine the two transitive dependency mappings and use the *combined mapping* M as the dependency mapping for the cycle, given by, $M := \{[\vec{a_1}, \vec{c_1}] \rightarrow [\vec{a_2}, \vec{c_2}] \mid C_1 \wedge C_2\}$, where the vector variables in the formulae describing M_1 and M_2 are made distinct by renaming. This mapping is used for the computation of the mapping M' as described in the Def. 11. M' is then split into M'_1 and M'_2 along the same dimensions that were combined earlier. These mappings are used in calculating the across-recurrence mappings on the respective ADDGs.

5 Discussion

As we described, the method is a synchronized traversal on the two ADDGs. Our method traverses corresponding paths only once and tables all established equivalences. Therefore, if we assume that the number of maximal slices of computation in the ADDGs is very small compared to their sizes, the complexity of the traversal is linear in the size of the larger of the two ADDGs, i.e., $O(\max(|V_1| + |E_1|, |V_2| + |E_2|))$. The operations on the integer domains and relations, that our method calls, are based on checking the validity of Presburger formulae, whose best known upper bound has triple-exponential complexity in the length of the constraint expressions. However, the expressions are usually small enough in practice and the operations are feasibly computed with a dependence test like Omega Test [12]. Therefore, we can assume the time for these operations to be bounded by a constant. Hence, the overall complexity is still in the order of the traversal.

With a prototype implementation of the method, we have been able to check equivalences of real-life program pairs efficiently. For programs with 1000 lines of uncommented C code, with control and data-flow complexity comparable to real-life signal processing algorithm kernels, the tool took less than 100 seconds on a standard desktop [14].

Typically, as can be expected, the original and the transformed program pairs seen in practice do not fall in the class that we have assumed for our method, at least not in all respects. But as discussed in Sec. 2.1, some restrictions can be relaxed by using code-preprocessing tools. They are used to pre-process the initial and the transformed programs separately, before passing them to our equivalence checker. For instance, using tools that are available to us in-house, we are able to handle programs that are not in DSA and also not having static control-flow (because of data-dependent if-conditions). Additionally, since ours is an intra-procedural method, by inlining functions in both programs using a function-inlining tool, we are able to verify correctness of inter-procedural code transformations from the categories that we handle.

6 Related Work

Undecidability of the program equivalence problem implies that any effort start with the definition of a decidable class of programs that is of interest. Hence, the problem has been addressed by various researchers for different program classes with different applications in mind. The problem we address is distinct by its central requirement to represent and maintain the relationships among elements of the arrays in the programs in closed form. Unrolling deeply nested loops with large bounds is clearly infeasible for real-life signal processing programs. To add to this, algebraic transformations will require an infeasible search for normalization on a combination of the unrolled statements. Hence, we restrict our discussion of related work to methods that do not propose loop unrolling.

Translation validation [8, 11] and fractal symbolic analysis [10], both present methods which show semantic equivalence of two versions of programs. In the case of the former, the comparison is between the source and the target code. These methods are distinct from ours in that they essentially try to heuristically *infer* a sequence of legal transformations that can relate the two programs. Instead, we are able to directly check for equivalence of programs that are in a suitable language class. Also, their methods do not handle algebraic transformations. The work most related to ours, because we address the same class of programs, is the algorithm recognition method presented in [4]. Again, algebraic transformations are not handled by them. Another distinction is that, all these methods do not pay attention to debugging support which is very important in the context of source code transformations.

7 Conclusions

We have presented a program equivalence checking method that enables verification of global source code transformations. The transformations considered are the ones that are widely reported in current practice relating to development of data-intensive software for high-performance and low-power systems. The program class handled is also the one that is often referred to in the literature relevant to the application domain of the transformations. The method is fully automatic and efficient. Hence, we believe that it provides a practical addition to the toolbox used by programmers applying source code transformations.

References

1. J. R. Allen, K. Kennedy, C. Porterfield, and J. D. Warren. Conversion of control dependence to data dependence. In *POPL*, pp. 177–189. ACM, 1983.
2. R. Allen and K. Kennedy. *Optimizing Compilers for Modern Architectures*. Morgan Kaufmann Publishers, 2001.
3. U. Banerjee. *Dependence Analysis for Supercomputing*. Kluwer Publishers, 1988.
4. D. Barthou, P. Feautrier, and X. Redon. On the equivalence of two systems of affine recurrence equations. In *8th Euro-Par*, pp. 309–313. Springer, 2002.
5. F. Catthoor, S. Wuytack, E. de Greef, F. Balasa, L. Nachtergaele, and A. Vandecappelle. *Custom Memory Management Methodology: Exploration of Memory Organization for Embedded Multimedia System Design*. Kluwer Publishers, 1998.
6. R. Cytron, J. Ferrante, B. K. Rosen, M. N. Wegman, and F. K. Zadeck. Efficiently computing static single assignment form and the control dependence graph. *ACM Transactions on Programming Languages and Systems*, 13(4):451–490, 1991.
7. P. Feautrier. Array expansion. In *ICS*, pp 429–441. ACM, 1988.
8. B. Goldberg, L. Zuck, and C. Barrett. Into the loops: Practical issues in translation validation for optimizing compilers. In *International Workshop on Compiler Optimization Meets Compiler Verification*, ENTCS. Elsevier, 2004.
9. W. Kelly, W. Pugh, E. Rosser, and T. Shpeisman. Transitive closure of infinite graphs and its applications. *Intl. Journ. of Parallel Prog.*, 24(6):579–598, 1996.

10. N. Mateev, V. Menon, and K. Pingali. Fractal symbolic analysis. *ACM Transactions on Programming Languages and Systems*, 25(6):776–813, 2003.
11. G. C. Necula. Translation validation for an optimizing compiler. In *SIGPLAN Programming Language Design and Implementation*, pp. 83–95. ACM, 2000.
12. W. Pugh. A practical algorithm for exact array dependence analysis. *Communications of the ACM*, 35(8):102–114, 1992.
13. K. C. Shashidhar, M. Bruynooghe, F. Catthoor, and G. Janssens. Functional equivalence checking for verification of algebraic transformations on array-intensive source code. In *Design, Automation and Test in Europe*. IEEE, 2005.
14. K. C. Shashidhar, M. Bruynooghe, F. Catthoor, and G. Janssens. Automatic Verification of Source Code Transformations on Array-Intensive Programs: Demonstration with Real-life Examples. Tech. Rep. CW 401, Dept. of Computer Science, Katholieke Universiteit Leuven, Belgium, 2005.
15. R. A. van Engelen and K. A. Gallivan. An efficient algorithm for pointer-to-array access conversion for compiling and optimizing DSP applications. In *International Workshop on Innovative Architectures for Future Generation High-Performance Processors and Systems*, pp. 80–89. IEEE, 2001.
16. P. Vanbroekhoven, G. Janssens, M. Bruynooghe, H. Corporaal, and F. Catthoor. A step towards a scalable dynamic single assignment conversion. Tech. Rep. CW 360, Dept. of Computer Science, Katholieke Universiteit Leuven, Belgium, 2003.
17. M. Wolfe. *High Performance Compilers for Parallel Computing*. Addison-Wesley Publishing Company, 1996.

Hob: A Tool for Verifying Data Structure Consistency

Patrick Lam, Viktor Kuncak, and Martin Rinard

Computer Science and Artificial Intelligence Laboratory,
Massachusetts Institute of Technology
{plam, vkuncak, rinard}@csail.mit.edu

Abstract. This tool demonstration presents Hob, a system for verifying data structure consistency for programs written in a general-purpose programming language. Our tool enables the focused application of multiple communicating static analyses to different modules in the same program. Using our tool throughout the program development process, we have successfully identified several bugs in both specifications and implementations of programs.

1 Introduction

Hob is a static analysis framework that verifies that program implementations satisfy their specifications. Using Hob, developers can apply multiple pluggable analyses to different parts of a program, applying each analysis to the modules for which it is most appropriate. Each Hob analysis plugin verifies that program modules 1) properly implement their specifications; and 2) respect the preconditions of the procedures that they call. Program modules often encapsulate data structures, and many data structures maintain a dynamically changing set of objects as their primary purpose; we have therefore found that set specifications allow developers to express crucial data structure interface properties, including in particular, the preconditions needed by typical data structure operations to successfully execute. Hob's common set specification language therefore enables different analyses to effectively communicate with each other.

The Hob project addresses the program verification problem [1, 5]. Our tool supports assume/guarantee reasoning and data refinement. The techniques embodied in the Hob tool are particularly suited for expressing and verifying data structure consistency properties: Hob allows static analysis plugins to verify that data structure preconditions hold upon entry to a data structure, that data structure operations preserve data structure invariants, and that data structure operations conform to their specifications.

Our technique is designed to support programs that encapsulate the implementations of complex data structures in instantiatable leaf modules, with these modules analyzed once by very precise, potentially expensive analyses (such as shape analyses or even analyses that generate verification conditions that must be manually discharged using a theorem prover or proof checker). The rest of the program uses these modules but does not directly manipulate the encapsulated data structures. These modules can then be analyzed by more efficient analyses that operate primarily at the level of the common set abstraction. Given the scalability issues associated with precise data structure verification techniques, this kind of approach is the only way to make these analyses viable in practice.

R. Bodik (Ed.): CC 2005, LNCS 3443, pp. 237–241, 2005.

We have implemented our analysis framework and populated this framework with three analysis plugins: 1) the flags plugin, which is designed to analyze modules that use a flag field to indicate the typestate of the objects that they manipulate [3]; 2) the PALE plugin, which implements a shape analysis for linked data structures (we integrated the Pointer Analysis Logic Engine analysis tool [4] into our system); and 3) the theorem proving plugin, which generates verification conditions designed to be discharged manually using the Isabelle interactive theorem prover [6]. We have used our analysis framework to analyze several programs; our experience shows that it can effectively 1) verify the consistency of data structures encapsulated within a single module and 2) combine analysis results from different analysis plugins to verify properties involving objects shared by multiple modules analyzed by different analyses. We have observed that our approach reduces the program annotation effort, improves the performance of the resulting analysis, and extends the range of programs to which each component analysis is applicable in isolation.

2 The Hob Approach

We next describe how developers write implementations and specifications for Hob. A program to be analyzed contains a number of modules. Each module is analyzed by an analysis plugin; plugins ensure that the module's implementation conforms to its specification and that the module satisfies all preconditions for the calls that it makes.

2.1 How Analysis Plugins Work

The basic task of an analysis plugin is to certify that the implementation for a module conforms to its specification and that the module meets all preconditions for calls that it makes. Implementation sections for modules in our system are written in a standard Java-like memory-safe imperative language supporting arrays and dynamic object allocation. Module specification sections give preconditions and postconditions for procedures in the boolean algebra of sets; these conditions are augmented with a `modifies` clause, which states the frame condition for the procedure. Specification modules may also name global boolean predicates to be tracked by the analysis. Finally, since modules may implement their specifications in a variety of ways, the abstraction section of a module describes the relationship between the module's implementation and its specification; each analysis plugin has a specialized syntax for abstraction settings, suitable for the type of properties checked by that plugin. An abstraction section may additionally state representation invariants applicable to the data structure implemented in that module.

In general, the Hob system analyzes individual modules as follows. For each module, Hob examines the implementation, specification, and abstraction sections of that module, as well as the specifications of all procedures that the module invokes. Hob first uses the abstraction function (from the abstraction section) to translate the `requires` and `ensures` clauses into the internal representation of the specialized analysis that will analyze the module (as specified in the abstraction section). Hob then conjoins the representation invariant to the translated `requires` and `ensures` clauses. Finally,

Hob invokes the specified analysis plugin to verify that each procedure conforms to its translated `requires` and `ensures` clauses.

2.2 Verifying Cross-Module Properties and Simplifying Specifications

Modules may belong to analysis scopes [2]. A scope encloses a number of program modules and designates a subset of these modules as exported modules; it also states scope invariants that always hold outside the scope. Scopes serve two purposes: they enable the specification and verification of cross-module invariants by identifying the subset of a program in which an invariant is expected to hold, and they combat annotation aggregation by hiding irrelevant sets from callers. Scopes are key to our system's verification of invariants containing sets from different modules: by designating the exported modules as external access points, and because scope invariants are preserved outside a scope, it is sufficient to check the scope invariants upon exit from a scope, therefore reducing the annotation and analysis burden which would otherwise be associated with scope invariants. Scopes also shield callers from irrelevant detail: only sets from exported modules may occur as free variables in specifications for modules in different scopes. This serves to bound the detail required in procedure specifications: the specification of procedure p belonging to scope $\mathcal{C}$ need only contain the effects of procedures on sets in $\mathcal{C}$ and sets belonging to exported modules outside $\mathcal{C}$.

Hob specification sections may also use defaults to simplify procedure preconditions and postconditions. A default is a clause that is automatically conjoined to procedure preconditions and postconditions across a specified program pointcut, unless explicitly suspended. In our example applications, we use defaults for ensuring that initialization predicates hold everywhere in a program except in the initial state; these defaults free the developer from the burden of manually conjoining the initialization predicate to a substantial portion of the program's specifications.

3 Hob in Practice

We have coded up several benchmark programs, using our system during the development of the programs. Our benchmarks include the water scientific computation benchmark, a minesweeper game, and programs with computational patterns from operating-system schedulers, air-traffic control, and program transformation passes. These benchmarks use a variety of data structures, and we have therefore implemented and verified sets, set iterators, queues, stacks, and priority queues. Our implementations range from singly-linked and doubly-linked lists and tree insertion (all verified using the PALE plugin) through array data structures (verified using the theorem proving plugin with the Isabelle theorem prover used to discharge verification conditions); our largest benchmark (water) contains approximately 2000 lines of implementation and 500 lines of specification. The Hob project homepage is

```
http://cag.csail.mit.edu/~plam/hob/
```

This homepage links to the O'Caml source tarball and publicly readable Subversion repository, further explains our example applications, and includes past presentations about Hob. Hob is distributed under the GNU General Public License.

The Hob infrastructure contains several general components that perform tasks required by all analyses. The implementation language component can parse and type-check implementation sections. It produces an abstract syntax tree and methods that allow analyses to conveniently access this representation. The specification component can parse and type check specification sections and provides access to the resulting abstract syntax tree. Large parts of abstraction sections are expressed in a language that is specific to each analysis. The abstraction section component parses those parts of the abstraction section syntax that are common to all analyses and uses uninterpreted strings to pass along the analysis-specific parts. Using these components, it is fairly simple to create new analysis plugins and apply them to analyze more types of data structures. Our implementation consists of approximately 10,000 lines of O'Caml code, to which the flag plugin contributes 2000 lines, the PALE plugin another 700 lines, and the theorem proving plugin 1000 lines; the rest of the code is shared analysis infrastructure.

We next present an example of a client code that Hob successfully verifies.

```
impl module UseList {
  format Node {}
  proc use() {
    Node n1;
    Node n2;
    n1 = new Node();
    n2 = new Node();
    List.add(n1);
    List.add(n2);
    List.remove(n2);
    List.remove(n1); } }
```

```
spec module UseList {
  proc use1()
    requires List.Content = {}
    modifies List.Content
    calls List
    ensures List.Content' = {}; }

abst module UseList {
  use plugin "flags"; }
```

This `UseList` example is analyzed by the flags plugin; it uses a `List` module, which is verified by the PALE plugin. Note that the `UseList` module does not define any sets itself; it relies on the `List` module to store its `Node` objects in a linked list. The flags plugin verifies the `use` procedure by propagating boolean formulas; upon procedure entry, the `Content` set from list is assumed to be empty (this condition is verified in all callers of `use`.) After the pair of `List.add` operations completes, the `Content` set is known to contain the elements {`n1, n2`} (by incorporating the postcondition of `List.add`). Finally, the pair of `List.remove` operations ensures that `Content` is empty at the end of the procedure, ensuring the stated procedure postcondition.

4 Conclusion

The program analysis community has produced many precise analyses that are capable of extracting or verifying quite sophisticated data structure properties. Issues associated with using these analyses include scalability limitations and the diversity of important data structure properties, some of which will inevitably elude any single analysis.

The Hob tool can apply a full range of analyses to programs composed of multiple modules. The key elements of the Hob approach include modules that encapsulate object fields and data structure implementations, specifications based on membership in abstract sets, and invariants that use these sets to express (and enable the verification of) properties that involve multiple data structures in multiple modules analyzed by different analyses. We anticipate that our techniques will enable the productive application of a variety of precise analyses to verify important data structure consistency properties and check important typestate properties in programs built out of multiple modules.

References

1. C. A. R. Hoare. The verifying compiler: still a Grand Challenge for computing research. ETAPS Invited Lecture, April 2003.
2. P. Lam, V. Kuncak, and M. Rinard. Crosscutting techniques in program specification and analysis. In P. Tarr, editor, *Proceedings of the Fourth Conference on Aspect-Oriented Software Development*, 2005.
3. P. Lam, V. Kuncak, and M. Rinard. Generalized typestate checking for data structure consistency. In *6th International Conference on Verification, Model Checking and Abstract Interpretation*, 2005.
4. A. Møller and M. I. Schwartzbach. The Pointer Assertion Logic Engine. In *Proc. PLDI*, 2001.
5. G. Nelson. Techniques for program verification. Technical report, XEROX Palo Alto Research Center, 1981.
6. K. Zee, P. Lam, V. Kuncak, and M. Rinard. Combining theorem proving with static analysis for data structure consistency. In *International Workshop on Software Verification and Validation (SVV 2004)*, Seattle, November 2004.

Jazz: A Tool for Demand-Driven Structural Testing

Jonathan Misurda[1], Jim Clause[1], Juliya Reed[1], Bruce R. Childers[1], and Mary Lou Soffa[2]

[1] University of Pittsburgh, Pittsburgh PA 15260, USA
{jmisurda, clausej, juliya, childers}@cs.pitt.edu
[2] University of Virginia, Charlottesville VA 22904, USA
soffa@cs.virginia.edu

Abstract. Software testing to produce reliable and robust software has become vitally important. Testing is a process by which quality can be assured through the collection of information about software. While testing can improve software quality, current tools typically are inflexible and have high overheads, making it a challenge to test large projects. We describe a new scalable and flexible tool, called Jazz, that uses a demand-driven structural testing approach. Jazz has a low overhead of only 17.6% for branch testing.

1 Introduction

In the last several years, the importance of producing high quality and robust software has become paramount. Testing is an important process to support quality assurance by gathering information about the software being developed or modified. It is, in general, extremely labor and resource intensive, accounting for 50-60% of the total cost of software development [1]. The increased emphasis on software quality and robustness mandates improved testing methodologies.

To test software, a number of techniques can be applied. One class of techniques is structural testing, which checks that a given coverage criterion is satisfied. For example, branch testing checks that a certain percentage of branches are executed. Other structural tests include def-use testing in which pairs of variable definitions and uses are checked for coverage and node testing in which nodes in a program's control flow graph are checked.

Unfortunately, structural testing is often hindered by the lack of scalable and flexible tools. Current tools are not scalable in terms of both time and memory, limiting the number and scope of the tests that can be applied to large programs. These tools often modify the software binary to insert instrumentation for testing. In this case, the tested version of the application is not the same version that is shipped to customers and errors may remain. Testing tools are usually inflexible and only implement certain types of testing. For example, many tools implement branch testing, but do not implement node or def-use testing.

In this paper, we describe a new tool for structural testing, called Jazz, that addresses these problems. Jazz uses a novel demand-driven technique to apply

R. Bodik (Ed.): CC 2005, LNCS 3443, pp. 242–245, 2005.

different testing strategies in an efficient and automatic way. Our method relies on test plans that describe what test instrumentation should be inserted and removed on-demand in executing code to carry out testing strategies. A test plan is a "recipe" that describes how and where a test should be performed. The approach is path specific and uses execution paths of an application to drive the instrumentation and testing. Once a test site is covered, the instrumentation is dynamically removed to avoid performance overhead.

Jazz uses a specification language to describe what to test. From the specification, a test plan can be automatically generated by a test planner. The test specification describes what tests to apply and under what conditions to apply them. The specification language can be described with a GUI or through a textual representation. Jazz implements a GUI, a test planner, and a dynamic instrumenter for demand-driven testing. Jazz is incorporated as a plug-in in Eclipse and the IBM Jikes Java Research Virtual Machine. It supports branch, node and def-use testing over code regions in a program.

2 Testing Java Programs

To carry out a test with Jazz, a user constructs a test specification with a GUI. Next, the graphical specification is converted into a textual form in a language called *testspec*. A testspec specification includes the relevant code segments to be tested and the actions needed in the testing process. Once the user is ready to test the program, the specification is passed to a test planner. This step translates the specification into a test plan. In the next step, the test plan is used by the dynamic instrumenter to instrument the program and determine coverage. Finally, the test results are displayed by the GUI.

2.1 Test Specification

In testing a software application, a developer may wish to apply different tests to various code regions. The tests are also often applied with different coverage criteria. The Jazz GUI can specify the tests to apply, where to apply them, and under what conditions. A coverage criterion can also be specified for each region. As shown in Figure 1, the GUI lets an user create and apply a test specification. To illustrate user interaction with the tool, the figure shows several steps. The figure shows that the user has selected several source lines in the Eclipse source editor (step 1). The selected lines are used to build a test specification. In this case, lines 343-356 in the file Compress.java have been selected as a test region for branch testing. When a region is selected, a test specification is created and displayed by the GUI. Test specifications are shown in a "specification viewer" window (step 2). A specification may be changed or deleted from this window.

To run the current tests, the user clicks a button on the toolbar (step 3). Jazz automatically invokes the test planner, Jikes and the dynamic instrumenter. When the program completes, the test results are displayed as a bar graph in the specification viewer (step 4). The GUI also highlights covered and uncovered source lines in the Eclipse editor window.

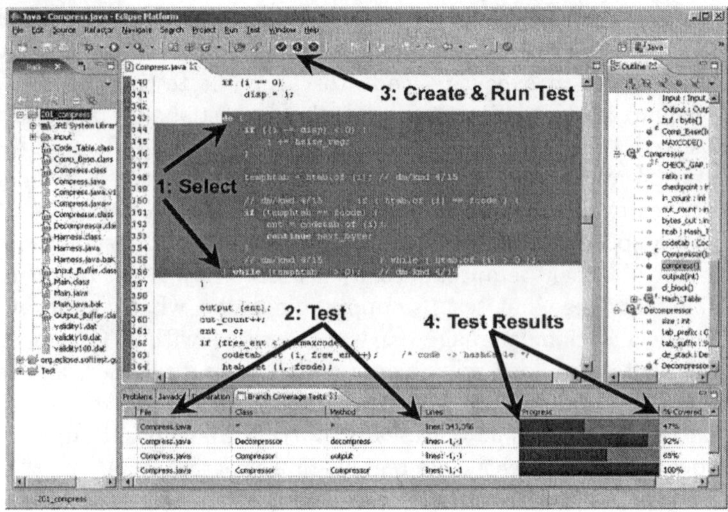

Fig. 1. Branch coverage GUI for Jazz

2.2 Test Planner

Using the test specification, the test planner decides how to test Java methods. The test planner is invoked every time a method is loaded by Jikes' Just-in-Time compiler. The planner checks whether there is a test specification for any portion of the method. If a specification exists, then the planner generates a test plan for the relevant code in the method. Thus, only methods that are actually loaded and executed are tested.

The main function of the test planner is to produce a test plan that determines where and how to instrument a method to do the test actions. The test plan describes how best to dynamically instrument a method to determine coverage. To generate a test plan, the planner identifies the locations where to instrument a test region, when to insert and remove instrumentation at each location, and what to do at each location. Typically, instrumentation locations correspond to basic blocks where coverage information is collected. For example, in def-use testing, there is instrumentation at each variable definition and all uses reachable from a definition.

Instrumentation is inserted and removed on-demand as the program executes. For example, in node testing, when a particular basic block is executed, instrumentation is inserted in successor blocks. Once a block is hit, its instrumentation can be removed because the block is covered. In branch and def-use testing, the planner ensures that instrumentation remains until all edges or all uses of a definition are covered.

Finally, the planner determines what actions to perform at each location. The actions are encoded in a "payload" that is executed at each location. In node testing, the payload updates coverage information, inserts instrumentation at successor blocks, and removes the instrumentation in the current block. The payloads for branch and def-use testing are similar, except they check whether all edges or def-use pairs are covered.

2.3 Dynamic Instrumenter

With the test plan from the planner, the dynamic instrumenter provides the functionality to insert and remove instrumentation at run-time. This interface is targeted by the test planner. Dynamic instrumentation (that can be removed/ inserted at run-time) is implemented with fast breakpoints[2]. A fast breakpoint replaces an instruction in the target machine code generated with a jump to a breakpoint handler that invokes the test instrumentation payload from the test planner.

3 Experimental Results

We investigated Jazz's performance and compared it to a traditional approach based on static instrumentation. To ensure a fair comparison, we implemented a separate tool that uses static instrumentation in our framework. This tool instruments a method's binary code before run time and does not remove instrumentation. It is similar to IBM Rational PurifyPlus and JCover. Jazz and the static tool differ only in on-demand versus static instrumentation. In the experiments, all loaded methods were covered and the benchmarks were run on a Linux 2.4 GHz Pentium IV with 1 GB RAM.

We measured run-time when the benchmarks were run directly in Jikes without testing, with Jazz and with the static tool. For brevity, we summarize the run-times only for branch testing. When run without testing, the benchmarks take 13.8-44.7 seconds. With the static branch testing tool, run-time is increased dramatically. It varies from 20.7-96.1 seconds and incurs an overhead of 11.7-241% (average 89.9%) over native execution. Jazz has much lower run-times than the static tool. Its run-time is 20.6-43.9 seconds and the performance overhead is only 0.3% to 7.8% (average 17.6%). Jazz has less overhead than the static tool because instrumentation is inserted and removed on-demand.

4 Summary

This paper described a new tool, called Jazz, for software testing of Java programs that relies on a novel scheme for dynamically inserting and removing instrumentation on-demand. The performance results with Jazz are very encouraging: The average overhead for branch testing with Jazz was only 17.6%.

References

1. W. Perry: Effective Methods for Software Testing. John Wiley and Sons, Inc., New York, 1996.
2. P. Kessler: Fast breakpoints: Design and implementation. ACM SIGPLAN Conference on Programming Languages, Design and Implementation, 1990.

Tiger – An Interpreter Generation Tool

Kevin Casey[1], David Gregg[1], and M. Anton Ertl[2]

[1] Department of Computer Science, Trinity College, Dublin 2, Ireland
{Kevin.Casey, David.Gregg}@cs.tcd.ie
[2] Institut für Computersprachen, TU Wien, A-1040 Wien, Austria
anton@complang.tuwien.ac.at

Abstract. Tiger (Trinity Interpreter GEneratoR) is a new interpreter generator tool along the lines of vmgen, but with significant improvements in flexibility and feedback. Support for important new features such as instruction specialisation, replication and improved analysis of code at runtime are presented. A simple 'C' virtual machine imported into Tiger is used for demonstration purposes. Various realistic benchmarks (such as sorting and Davis-Putnam backtracking algorithms) are used to show the utility of these new features in Tiger.

1 Introduction

Tiger is a new interpreter generator tool along the lines of vmgen[1], but with significant improvements in flexibility and feedback. Some of these features which are to be demonstrated are outlined briefly in the remainder of this document.

2 Input Language

A typical opcode defined in Tiger is depicted as follows:

```
ADD SP( int a, int b - int c )
    IP( - next);
    c=a+b;
```

The first token is the opcode name, then followed either by the stack behaviour (SP) or the instruction stream behaviour (IP). The stack behaviour specifies what types and instances needs to be popped off the stack before the core of the opcode is to be executed and what is to be pushed onto the stack after the core of the instruction has completed. The '-' symbol represents the separator between what is to be popped and what is to be pushed in the stack descriptor. The instruction stream behaviour allows us to specify what operands are to be loaded from the instruction stream (none in this case). The '-' symbol represents the end of the current instruction. The keyword next indicates that another instruction will follow in the instruction stream. Tiger uses the stack and instruction stream descriptors supplied and the code core specified to generate 'C' code for the instruction.

R. Bodik (Ed.): CC 2005, LNCS 3443, pp. 246–249, 2005.

3 Instruction Specialisation

Often in a compiler we find that certain operands occur in combination with particular opcodes quite frequently. For example, if we find that a large number of `PUSHINT 0` instructions occur in our interpreter, we might consider replacing it with a single instruction `PUSHINT_0`. The advantage of this is that the `PUSHINT_0` instruction no longer requires an extra read from the instruction stream (to retrieve the operand), since the operand is 'hardwired' into the instruction. For example:

```
+SPECIAL PUSHINT 0;
```

generates code for the `PUSHINT` instruction seen above, but where the operand `a` is specialised to 0 (#defined to 0). This eliminates the instruction stream read. `Tiger` provides support for a translation-time specialisation of opcodes in the form of a variable argument `vm_specialise` macro. For example, when translating an opcode with a single operand:

```
OPCODE'=vm_specialise(OPCODE,OPERAND);
```

This macro will attempt to find a specialised version of `OPCODE,OPERAND` and will return the original opcode if no specialisation has been found, or the specialised version if one has been found. For unspecialised opcodes, the application of the macro has no computational cost.

4 Instruction Replication

One strategy to improve branch prediction accuracy in interpreters is to create copies of commonly occurring opcodes. The idea here is that using multiple copies of an opcode increases the number of entries in the Branch Target Buffer (BTB) due to the extra dispatches in the code. `Tiger` supports the creation of replications in the following manner.

```
+ALIAS OPCODE COUNT;
```

This creates `COUNT` copies (in addition to the original) of `OPCODE`. `Tiger` also creates a macro `vm_alias` and supporting data structures to facilitate the inclusion of these aliases into the instruction stream (replacing the original). During the code-translation phase this macro can be used to replace original versions of opcodes with their copies in the following way:

```
OPCODE'=vm_alias(OPCODE)
```

If the opcode is not replicated at all, then `OPCODE'=OPCODE` (and there is no computational cost associated with the macro). For replicated instructions however, each successive call to `vm_alias` yields the next copy of the opcode in a cyclical order. `Tiger` maintains an array of counters and replication counts to support this approach.

5 Superinstructions

The generation of compound instructions, or superinstructions is quite straightforward in `Tiger`. If one finds that the sequence of instructions `PUSHINT ADD` occur quite frequently, one could define a superinstruction `PUSHINT_ADD` as follows:

```
PUSHINT_ADD = PUSHINT ADD;
```

Superinstruction parsing routines for greedy parsing and optimal parsing are also supplied with `Tiger`. The parse tables for all superinstructions are combined into a large compressed Deterministic Finite-state Automata which is accessed via the supplied routines. The actual implementation of the DFA is as a number of overlapping hashtables, one hashtable for each set of transitions from a particular state.

6 Specialised Superinstructions

`Tiger` also allows the creation of specialised superinstructions. In the example above, we came across the `PUSHINT_ADD` superinstruction. If we encountered the instruction sequence `PUSHINT 1 ADD` sequence, we could decide to create a specialised superinstruction such as:

```
PUSHINT1_ADD = PUSHINT 1 ADD;
```

`Tiger` will then generate the superinstruction and modify the parsing tables so that this instruction will be added automatically when applicable.

7 Other Optimizations

Early Loading: On some architectures it is advantageous to retrieve the address of the next instruction as early in the current instruction as possible. In opcodes where the keyword `next` appears in the instruction stream specifier, `Tiger` will automatically retrieve the address of the next instruction from that slot in the instruction stream. This will happen at the beginning of the current instruction. This optimisation can be turned on or off easily, making a determination of its utility relatively straightforward.

Deferred Reading/Writing allows the reading or writing of an item in the stack/instruction stream descriptors to be deferred until the programmer wishes it to happen. This mechanism is accomplished by the use of the `+DEFER` directive which is used in combination with automatically generated macros. For example, a `+DEFER` might be useful in a conditional branch where we do not want to load the target address from the instruction stream unless we have tested the condition and are sure the branch is to take place.

8 Diagnostics

Histogram: Turning on the histogram option creates a logfile containing a frequencies of all opcode calls. A tool is provided that interprets this data and generates a Scaled Vector Graphic (SVG) file containing a histogram that can be viewed in a web-browser.

Indirect Branch Data: Virtual machine interpreters execute an indirect branch for each VM instruction executed. The prediction accuracy of these branches has a huge impact on running time. Tiger generates data and graphs which allow us to visualize the order in which instructions are executed, and estimate the indirect branch prediction accuracies. Figure 1 depicts a sample output of this tool, showing the transitions between VM instructions, along with their frequency and an estimate of their indirect branch misprediction rate.

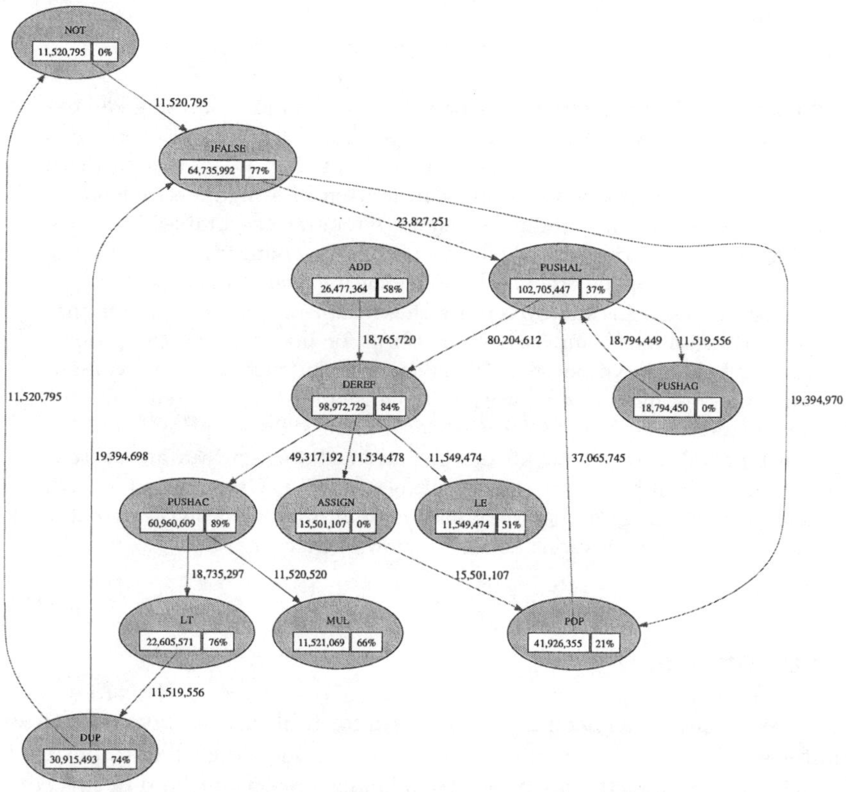

Fig. 1. Automatically generated instruction-transition graph

Reference

1. M. A. Ertl, D. Gregg, A. Krall, and B. Paysan. vmgen — A generator of efficient virtual machine interpreters. *Software—Practice and Experience*, 32(3):265–294, 2002.

CodeSurfer/x86—A Platform for Analyzing x86 Executables*

Gogul Balakrishnan[1], Radu Gruian[2], Thomas Reps[1,2], and Tim Teitelbaum[2]

[1] Comp. Sci. Dept., University of Wisconsin
{bgogul, reps}@cs.wisc.edu
[2] GrammaTech, Inc.
{radu, tt}@grammatech.com

Abstract. CodeSurfer/x86 is a prototype system for analyzing x86 executables. It uses a static-analysis algorithm called *value-set analysis* (VSA) to recover intermediate representations that are similar to those that a compiler creates for a program written in a high-level language. A major challenge in building an analysis tool for executables is in providing useful information about operations involving memory. This is difficult when symbol-table and debugging information is absent or untrusted. CodeSurfer/x86 overcomes these challenges to provide an analyst with a powerful and flexible platform for investigating the properties and behaviors of potentially malicious code (such as COTS components, plugins, mobile code, worms, Trojans, and virus-infected code) using (i) CodeSurfer/x86's GUI, (ii) CodeSurfer/x86's scripting language, which provides access to all of the intermediate representations that CodeSurfer/x86 builds for the executable, and (iii) GrammaTech's Path Inspector, which is a tool that uses a sophisticated pattern-matching engine to answer questions about the flow of execution in a program.

1 Introduction

In recent years, there has been a growing need for tools that analyze executables. Computer-security issues provide one motivation: one would like to ensure that third-party applications do not perform malicious operations, and in this context it is important for analysts to be able to decipher the behavior of Trojans, worms, and virus-infected code. Static analysis provides techniques that can help with such problems; however, there are several obstacles that must be overcome:

– For potentially malicious programs, symbol-table and debugging information is either entirely absent, or cannot be relied upon if present.

* Supported by Air Force (AFRL/Rome) SBIR contracts F30602-01-{C-0112, C-0051}, ONR contracts N00014-{02-C-0188, 03-C-0502, 01-1-0708, 01-1-0796}, and NSF grant CCR-9986308.

R. Bodik (Ed.): CC 2005, LNCS 3443, pp. 250–254, 2005.

- Instructions that perform memory operations use explicit memory addresses and indirect addressing, which complicates the task of understanding the overall behavior of the code.

Several others [3, 2, 10, 5, 12] have proposed algorithms for statically analyzing executables. However, existing tools assume the presence of symbol-table and/or debugging information, or ignore instructions with memory operands altogether, or assume that an instruction with memory operands can write-to/read-from any part of memory. None of these solutions are satisfactory in terms of understanding how an x86 executable works. Recently, Balakrishnan and Reps developed a static-analysis algorithm, called *value-set analysis* (VSA), to recover information about the contents of memory locations and how they are manipulated by an executable [1]. By combining VSA with facilities provided by the IDAPro and CodeSurfer toolkits, we have created CodeSurfer/x86, a prototype tool for browsing, inspecting, and analyzing x86 executables. From an x86 executable, CodeSurfer/x86 recovers an intermediate representation that is similar to what would be created by a compiler for a program written in a high-level language. In this document, we emphasize the facilities of CodeSurfer/x86 that provide an analyst with a powerful and flexible platform for investigating the properties and behaviors of an x86 executable.

Because CodeSurfer/x86 works on the actual executable code that is run on the machine, it automatically takes into account platform-specific aspects of the code, such as the positions (i.e., offsets) of variables in the run-time stack's activation records. This is a key ability, because many security exploits depend on platform-specific features, such as the structure of activation records. In this sense, CodeSurfer/x86 is a "higher fidelity" tool than most tools that analyze source code.

2 CodeSurfer/x86

CodeSurfer/x86 is the outcome of a joint project between the Univ. of Wisconsin and GrammaTech, Inc. CodeSurfer/x86 makes use of both IDAPro [9], a disassembly toolkit, and GrammaTech's CodeSurfer system [4], a toolkit for building program-analysis and inspection tools. Fig. 1 shows the various components of CodeSurfer/x86. This section sketches how these components are combined in CodeSurfer/x86.

An x86 executable is first disassembled using IDAPro. In addition to the disassembly listing and control-flow graphs, IDAPro also provides access to the following information: (1) procedure boundaries, (2) calls to library functions (identified using an algorithm called the Fast Library Identification and Recognition Technology (FLIRT) [7]), and (3) statically known memory addresses and offsets.

IDAPro provides access to its internal resources via an API that allows users to create plug-ins to be executed by IDAPro. We created a plug-in to IDAPro, called the Connector, that creates data structures to represent the information obtained from IDAPro. The IDAPro/Connector combination is also able to create the same data structures for dynamically linked libraries, and to link them into the data structures that represent the program itself. This infrastructure permits whole-program analysis to be carried out—*including analysis of the code for all library functions that are called.*

Based on the data structures in the Connector, we implemented a static analysis algorithm called *value-set analysis* (VSA) [1]. VSA does not assume the presence of symbol-table and debugging information.[3] Hence, as a first step, a set of data objects called a-locs (for "abstract locations") is determined based on the static memory addresses and offsets provided by IDAPro. VSA is a combined numeric and pointer-analysis algorithm that determines an over-approximation of the set of numeric values or addresses that each a-loc holds at each program point. The set of addresses and numeric values is referred to as a *value-set.* A key feature of VSA is that it tracks integer-valued and address-valued quantities simultaneously. This is crucial for analyzing executables because numeric values and addresses are indistinguishable in an executable.

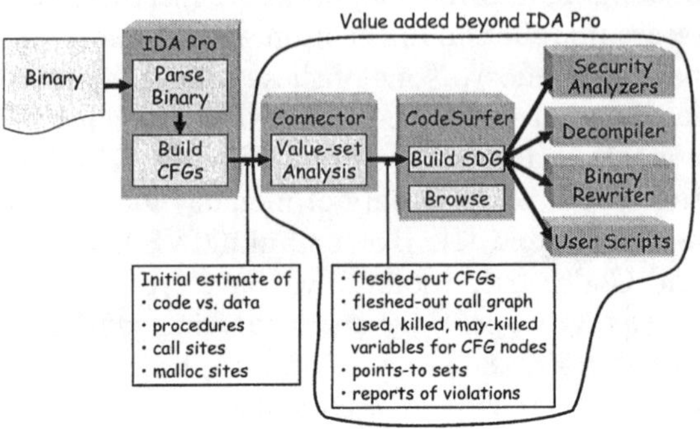

Fig. 1. Organization of CodeSurfer/x86

Note that IDAPro does not identify the targets of all indirect jumps and indirect calls, and therefore the call graph and control-flow graphs that it constructs are not complete. However, the information computed during VSA can be used to augment the call graph and control-flow graphs on-the-fly to account for indirect jumps and indirect calls. In fact, the relationship between VSA and the preliminary IRs created by IDAPro is similar to the relationship between a points-to-analysis algorithm in a C compiler and the preliminary IRs created by the C compiler's front end. In both cases, the preliminary IRs are fleshed out during the course of analysis.

Once VSA completes, the value-sets for the a-locs at each program point are used to determine each point's sets of used, killed, and possibly-killed a-locs; these are emitted in a format that is suitable for input to CodeSurfer. CodeSurfer takes in this information and builds a collection of IRs, consisting of abstract-syntax trees, control-flow graphs (CFGs), a call graph, and a system dependence graph (SDG). An SDG consists of a set of program dependence graphs (PDGs), one for each procedure in the program. A vertex in a PDG corresponds to a construct in the program, such as a statement or instruction,

[3] Although VSA does not need debugging/symbol-table information, in principle, it would be possible to extend VSA to use such information.

a call to a procedure, an actual parameter of a call, or a formal parameter of a procedure. The edges correspond to data and control dependences between the vertices [6]. The PDGs are connected together with interprocedural edges that represent control dependences between procedure calls and entries, and data dependences between actual parameters and formal parameters/return values.

Dependence graphs are invaluable for many applications, because they highlight chains of dependent instructions that may be widely scattered through the program. For example, given a instruction, it is often useful to know its *data-dependence predecessors* (instructions that write to locations read by that instruction) and its *control-dependence predecessors* (control points that may affect whether a given instruction gets executed). Similarly, it may be useful to know for a given instruction its *data-dependence successors* (instructions that read locations written by that instruction) and *control-dependence* successors (instructions whose execution depends on the decision made at a given control point).

3 CodeSurfer/x86 Facilities

As described in the Section 2, given an executable as input, CodeSurfer/x86 builds a collection of IRs for it. In addition to building the IRs, CodeSurfer/x86 also checks whether the executable conforms to a "standard" compilation model—i.e., a runtime stack is maintained; activation records (ARs) are pushed onto the stack on procedure entry and popped from the stack on procedure exit; a procedure does not modify the return address on the stack; the program's instructions occupy a fixed area of memory, are not self-modifying, and are separate from the program's data. If it cannot be confirmed that the executable conforms to the model, then the IR is possibly incorrect. For example, the call-graph will be incorrect if a procedure modifies the return address on the stack. Consequently, CodeSurfer/x86 issues error reports if it finds one or more violations of the "standard" compilation model. The analyst can go over these reports and determine whether they are false alarms or real violations.

CodeSurfer's GUI supports browsing ("surfing") of an SDG, along with a variety of operations for making queries about the SDG—such as slicing [8] and chopping [11].[4] The GUI allows a user to navigate through the assembly code using these dependences in a manner analogous to navigating the World Wide Web. CodeSurfer's API provides a programmatic interface to these operations, as well as to lower-level information, such as the individual nodes and edges of the program's SDG, call graph, and control-flow graph, and a node's sets of used,

[4] A backward slice of a program with respect to a set of program points S is the set of all program points that might affect the computations performed at S; a forward slice with respect to S is the set of all program points that might be affected by the computations performed at members of S [8]. A program chop between a set of source program points S and a set of target program points T shows how S can affect the points in T [11]. Chopping is a key operation in information-flow analysis.

killed, and possibly-killed a-locs. By writing programs that traverse CodeSurfer's IRs to implement additional program analyses, the API can be used to extend CodeSurfer's capabilities.

CodeSurfer/x86 can be used in conjunction with GrammaTech's Path Inspector, which is a tool that uses a sophisticated pattern-matching engine to answer questions about the flow of execution in a program. The Path Inspector checks *sequencing properties* of events in a program, which—in the context of security analysis, for example—can be used to answer such questions as "Is it possible for the program to bypass the authentication routine?" (which indicates that the program may contain a trapdoor).

With the Path Inspector, such questions are posed as questions about the existence of problematic event sequences; after checking the query, if a problematic path exists, it is displayed in the Path Explorer tool. This lists all of the program points that may occur along the problematic path. These items are linked to the disassembly; the analyst can navigate from a point in the path to the corresponding assembly-code element. In addition, the Path Inspector allows the analyst to step forward and backward through the path, while simultaneously stepping through the assembly code. (The code-stepping operations are similar to the single-stepping operations in a traditional debugger.)

References

1. G. Balakrishnan and T. Reps. Analyzing memory accesses in x86 executables. In *Comp. Construct.*, pages 5–23, 2004.
2. C. Cifuentes and A. Fraboulet. Interprocedural data flow recovery of high-level language code from assembly. Technical Report 421, Univ. Queensland, 1997.
3. C. Cifuentes, D. Simon, and A. Fraboulet. Assembly to high-level language translation. In *Int. Conf. on Softw. Maint.*, pages 228–237, 1998.
4. CodeSurfer, GrammaTech, Inc., http://www.grammatech.com/products/codesurfer/.
5. S.K. Debray, R. Muth, and M. Weippert. Alias analysis of executable code. In *Princ. of Prog. Lang.*, pages 12–24, 1998.
6. J. Ferrante, K. Ottenstein, and J. Warren. The program dependence graph and its use in optimization. *Trans. on Prog. Lang. and Syst.*, 3(9):319–349, 1987.
7. Fast library identification and recognition technology, DataRescue sa/nv, Liège, Belgium, http://www.datarescue.com/idabase/flirt.htm.
8. S. Horwitz, T. Reps, and D. Binkley. Interprocedural slicing using dependence graphs. *Trans. on Prog. Lang. and Syst.*, 12(1):26–60, January 1990.
9. IDAPro disassembler, http://www.datarescue.com/idabase/.
10. A. Mycroft. Type-based decompilation. In *European Symp. on Programming*, 1999.
11. T. Reps and G. Rosay. Precise interprocedural chopping. In *Found. of Softw. Eng.*, 1995.
12. X. Rival. Abstract interpretation based certification of assembly code. In *Int. Conf. on Verif., Model Checking, and Abs. Int.*, 2003.

A Study of Type Analysis for Speculative Method Inlining in a JIT Environment

Feng Qian* and Laurie Hendren
{fqian, hendren}@sable.mcgill.ca

School of Computer Science, McGill University

Abstract. Method inlining is one of the most important optimizations for JIT compilers in Java virtual machines. In order to increase the number of inlining opportunities, a type analysis can be used to identify monomorphic virtual calls. In a JIT environment, the compiler and type analysis must also handle dynamic class loading properly because class loading can invalidate previous analysis results and invalidate some speculative inlining decisions. To date, a very simple type analysis, class hierarchy analysis (CHA), has been used successfully in JIT compilers for speculative inlining with invalidation techniques as backup.
This paper seeks to determine if more powerful dynamic type analyses could further improve inlining opportunities in a JIT compiler. To achieve this goal we developed a general *dynamic* type analysis framework which we have used for designing and implementing dynamic versions of several well-known static type analyses, including CHA, RTA, XTA and VTA. Surprisingly, the simple dynamic CHA is nearly as good as an ideal type analysis for inlining **virtual method** calls. There is little room for further improvement. On the other hand, only a reachability-based interprocedural type analysis (VTA) is able to capture the majority of monomorphic **interface** calls.

1 Introduction

The Java programming language [3] encourages programmers to write compact classes and small methods to obtain great engineering benefits. However, using small methods requires frequent method calls. A high performance Java virtual machine heavily relies on JIT compilers to reduce calling overhead.

Even though the direct overhead of virtual calls is low, further performance improvement is often obtained from method inlining and optimizations on inlined code. Inlining creates larger code blocks for program analyses and improves the accuracy of intraprocedural analyses which must often handle method calls conservatively. Thus, method inlining is a very important part of a Java optimizer because it further reduces method call overhead and also increases other opportunities for optimizations.

* The author is currently affiliated with Goolge Inc., 1600 Amphitheatre Parkway, Mountain View, CA 94043, USA. This research was done while the author was at McGill University.

R. Bodik (Ed.): CC 2005, LNCS 3443, pp. 255–270, 2005.

A key step of method inlining is to decide which method(s) can be inlined at a call site. This can be achieved by using information conveyed via language constructs such as *final* and *private* declarations (which provide restrictions on which methods could be called), or the information can be gathered using a type analysis which determines which runtime types may be associated with a receiver, and hence which methods may be called. Another alternative is to profile targets of call sites. Inlining based on language constructs and type analyses results is conservative at analysis time and it supports direct inlining that maximizes optimization opportunities. In this paper, we study method inlining using type analysis results.

Static type analyses for Java programs [8,5,19,20] are not directly applicable to JIT compilers because of dynamic features of Java virtual machines. The type set of a variable might have new members as new classes are loaded and thus optimizations based on old results could be invalidated. Various techniques have been devised to use dynamic class hierarchy analysis for directly inlining in the presence of dynamic class loading and JIT compilation.

In this paper we evaluate the effectiveness of several dynamic type analyses for method inlining in a Java virtual machine (Jikes RVM [1]). We built a common type analysis framework for expressing dynamic type analyses and used the results of these analyses for speculative inlining with invalidations. We then used this framework to perform a study of how many method calls can be inlined for the different varieties of type analyses.

We were also interested in finding the upper bound on how many calls that can be inlined, to determine if more accurate type analyses are required. To gather this information we used an efficient call graph profiling mechanism [16] to log call targets of each virtual call site. The logged information is used as an ideal type analysis for re-executing the benchmark. We compare the inlining results of other type analyses to the ideal one. In order to measure the maximum inlining potential of a type analysis, we also relaxed the size limit on inlining targets.

Our results were quite surprising. The simple CHA is nearly as good as the ideal type analysis for inlining virtual method calls and leaves little room for improvement. On the other hand, CHA is less effective for inlining interface calls. Further, we found that the majority of interface invocations are from a small number of hot call sites which are used in a very simple pattern.

In order to capture the monomorphic interface calls we developed *dynamic VTA*, which is a whole-program analysis. We analyzed the effectiveness and costs of this whole-program approach. We found that the main difficulty of such a dynamic whole-program analysis is that it requires large data structures which must co-exist with application data in the heap.

Our objective is to understand how well a dynamic type analysis can perform with respect to method inlining in a JIT compiler, and what opportunities there are for improvement. In this study, we made following contributions:

– a limit study of method inlining using dynamic type analyses on a set of standard Java benchmarks;

– development and experience of an interprocedural reachability-based type analysis in a JIT environment; and
– interesting observations in speculative inlining.

We introduce the necessary background in Section 2. In Section 3, we describe the design of a common type analysis framework for speculative inlining. The limit study results are also presented in this section. The whole-program VTA type analysis is described in Section 4 with experimental results. Related work is discussed in Section 5. Finally, in Section 6, we conclude with some observations and plans for future work.

2 Background

Java methods can be categorized into two types: *non-virtual* and *virtual. Static* and *instance initialization* methods are non-virtual, and the rest of the methods are virtual. A JIT compiler can bind a non-virtual call and its target at compile time, if the callee method has been resolved. Static binding enables efficient implementation of non-virtual calls. For example, a resolved non-virtual call takes two instructions in Jikes RVM [13].

The beauty of object-oriented programming languages comes from supporting virtual methods. In the Java programming language, a virtual call has the form of <`x, A.m()`> where `x` is a variable pointing to objects of type `A` or its subtypes, and `m()` is the method signature. The real target of each invocation depends on the type of object pointed to by the variable `x` at runtime. The object pointed to by `x` is called the *receiver* of the call, and `m()` is a *callee method signature.*

In the Java virtual machine specification, virtual methods are invoked by *invokevirtual* or *invokeinterface* instructions, depending on whether the declaring class of the callee method is a class or interface. A virtual call is slightly more expensive than a non-virtual one since it requires method lookup. By taking advantage of single inheritance, the *invokevirtual* bytecode is implemented by three instructions in Jikes RVM. The implementation of *invokeinterface* is much more expensive than *invokevirtual* due to multiple inheritance. Alpern et al. [2] give an excellent introduction and provide an efficient solution to the problem.

Due to polymorphism, a virtual call may invoke several different methods in the course of program execution. Compilers can use a static type analysis or profiling information to devirtualize the call to a set of possible target methods and inline one or several of them into the caller. The Java execution model allows dynamic class loading which loads classes only on first use, and lazy compilation which compiles methods only on first execution. A new challenge of type analyses in a JIT environment is to handle these dynamic features properly.

An easy solution to dynamic class loading is to guard inlined code with runtime checks. Detlefs and Agesen [9] pioneered this technique in Sun's JVM. Given a virtual call site <`x, A.m()`>, a type analysis (e.g. CHA) might be able to prove the call site is monomorphic at compile time and the target is `A.m()`. If a JIT compiler chooses to inline the call site, it generates a *class test* instruction comparing x's type to A. The inlined A.m() is executed only if the runtime check succeeds, otherwise a normal virtual call is made.

The drawback of the *class test* is that it only covers the case when an object type is A. If the object type is a subclass B which does not override A.m(), the control falls to the normal virtual call, even though the target is still A.m(). *Method tests* fix the problem by testing the target method address instead of the receiver's type. After instructions loading x's type information (A or B), the compiler generates one more instruction to obtain the target address of m() from the type information (A.m() even if the type is B). The inlined code is protected by a test of the target address to the address of A.m(). A single method test can cover more classes than a class test with the cost of one load instruction in the fast path.

Method and class tests have direct runtime overhead and optimizations on inlined code are limited by conditional test instructions. Detlefs and Agesen [9] pointed out that, in a Java virtual machine, a compiler can directly inline currently *monomorphic* call sites induced by CHA. When dynamic class loading makes an inlined monomorphic call site be polymorphic, the class loader must invalidate the compiled method which directly inlined the call site. The next invocation of an invalidated method triggers recompilation using the new, correct CHA results. To ensure the approach is safe for compiled methods running on threads, it requires a static analysis (*invariant argument analysis* [9]) to prove the preexistence of receiver variables of inlined calls.

The invariant argument analysis may not always succeed in removing method and class tests for inlined monomorphic calls. Ishizaki et al. [12] presented a code patching technique to remove the direct overhead of all method and class tests for *monomorphic* call sites in the presence of dynamic class loading. Code patching uses CHA to identify monomorphic calls at compile time. Each inlined call site has a backup path which does normal virtual invocation. The compiler records the addresses at the beginning of inlined code and the start of backup path. It also registers a dependency of the inlined site on the assumption that the call is monomorphic. When dynamic class loading happens and invalidates the assumption, the compiler patches the code at the beginning of inlined code by a direct jump instruction to the address of the backup path. The virtual machine can optionally reset the invalidated method's entry in the virtual method table.

A static type analysis calculates conservative type sets for variables in object-oriented programs. Class hierarchy analysis (CHA) [8] assumes all subtypes of a variable's declaring type are in the runtime type set of the variable. Rapid type analysis (RTA) [5] performs a one pass scan of the program and prunes the CHA results by removing types that do not have an allocation site in the program. XTA [20] is a simple interprocedural type analysis. It uses one set to represent all variables in a method, and propagates type sets along call edges. Variable type analysis (VTA) [19] is a fast reachability-based interprocedural type analysis. Each variable has a type set and the analysis uses intraprocedural data-flow. More advanced analyses have higher costs. One focus in our study is to show how to adopt these static type analyses to a JIT environment and to study their effectiveness on speculative method inlining.

3 A Type Analysis Framework Supporting Speculative Inlining

A *static* analysis is performed at compile-time and must make conservative assumptions that include all possible runtime executions. A static type analysis answers a basic question: what is the set of all possible runtime types of variable v at program point P. A *dynamic* type analysis is performed in a JIT environment, and therefore it is *time-sensitive.* It answers a query similar to a static one, except the answer is not for *all executions*, but for execution prior the time of answering the query. The results may change over program's execution. In order to use type analysis results for optimizations in a JIT environment, there are a few requirements we set for the analysis:

`dynamic`: it has to handle Java's dynamic features seamlessly, such as dynamic class loading, reference resolution, and JIT compilation;
`conservative`: analysis results must be correct at analysis time with respect to the executed part of the program;
`just-in-time`: the analysis should be able to notify clients when previous analysis results are about to change during execution.

A *dynamic* type analysis fits into a Java virtual machine without changing the lazy strategy of handling class loading and compilation. The *conservativeness* ensures optimizations based on analysis results are correct at the analysis time (it might be invalidated in the future). If the analysis can update its results *just-in-time*, it can be used for speculative optimizations with some invalidation mechanisms. Our objective is to design a type analysis framework supporting speculative inlining in a JIT compiler.

3.1 Framework Structure

We designed a type analysis interface shown in Figure 1. In a Java method, a call site is uniquely identified by the method and a bytecode index. Given the method and bytecode index, the `getNodeId` method returns a node ID for further queries. The node ID allocation decides the granularity of different type analyses. For example, CHA and RTA use a single ID for all call sites, XTA allocates a node ID for all call sites in the same method, and VTA assigns different IDs to different call sites. The `lookupTargets` method returns an array of targets resolved by using reaching types of the node with a given callee method signature. The detailed lookup procedure is the same as virtual method lookup, defined by the JVM specification [14]. An inline oracle makes inline decisions according to the lookup results.

If the type analysis finds a monomorphic call site (with only one target), then the oracle decides to perform speculative inlining (using preexistence or code patching). It must register a dependency via the `checkAndRegisterDependency` method. A dependency says that, given a node and a callee method signature, a compiled method (*cm*) is valid only when the lookup results have one target that is the same as the parameter *target*.

After registering the dependency successfully, any change in the type set of the node causes verification of dependencies on this node. The `verifyDependency` method is called by the type analysis when the node has a new reaching type. For each dependency of the node, the verification procedure performs method lookup using the new reaching type and the callee method signature. If the lookup result is different from the target method of the dependency, the compiled method must be invalidated immediately.

```
public interface TypeAnalysis {
  public int getNodeId(VM_Method caller, int bcindex);
  public VM_Method[] lookupTargets(int nodeid, VM_Method callee);
  public boolean checkAndRegisterDependency(int nodeid,
                                            VM_Method callee,
                                            VM_CompiledMethod cm,
                                            VM_Method target);

  protected void verifyDependency(int nodeid, VM_Class newKls);
}
```

Fig. 1. TypeAnalaysis interface

A *TypeAnalysis* implementation has to monitor system events such as class loading, method compilation, etc. We have implemented several type analyses as depicted in Figure 2. We used JikesRVM v2.3.0 with the *FastAdaptiveCopyMS* configuration. JikesRVM implemented dynamic CHA, and we re-implemented it in our framework. CHA and RTA only differentiate classes that participate in the reaching type sets. We made a new variation of CHA, called ITA, to only allow classes with instances to participate in reaching types. XTA and VTA share many components. A special class, `IdealTypeAnalysis`, uses profiled results for the purpose of our limit study. All implementations satisfy the requirements defined at the beginning of this section. A client, `StaticInlineOracle`, uses the analysis results for speculative inlining.

3.2 A Limit Study of Method Inlining Using Dynamic Type Analyses

An Ideal Type Analysis. To measure how precise a type analysis could be, we need an ideal type analysis for comparison. If a benchmark runs deterministically, we can profile targets in the first run, and then use the profiled targets as faked analysis results for the second run. We use an inexpensive call graph profiling mechanism [16] to gather call targets. An *IdealTypeAnalysis* parses the profiled targets for call sites, and the *lookupTargets* method returns profiled target(s) for a call site.

Experimental Approach. An inline oracle has to balance the benefits and costs of inlining. Excessive inlining may blow up code size and slow down the execution. Therefore, a JIT compiler usually sets a size limit on inlined targets

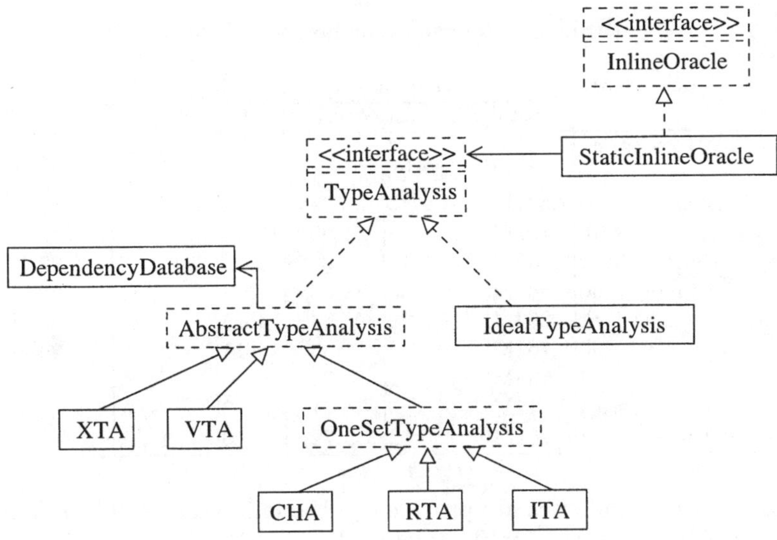

Fig. 2. Type analysis framework diagram

using some heuristics. Hazelwood and Grove [11] described the size heuristic used in Jikes RVM. For the purpose of our study, we would like to measure the maximum potential of a type analysis for method inlining without a size limit. However, inlining all call sites is not feasible. Instead, we only inline the most frequently invoked call sites, without a size limit.

Benchmarks. Our benchmark set includes the SpecJVM98 suite [18], SpecJBB2000 [17], a CFS subset evaluator from a data mining package Weka [22], a simulator of certificate revocation schemes [6], and a variation of the simulator interwoven with AspectJ code for detecting calls that return `null` on error conditions.

Table 1 summarizes dynamic characteristics of benchmark executions. We ignored call sites in the RVM code and Java libraries compiled into the boot image. Virtual and interface calls are measured separately. Columns labeled *total* report the total counts of invocations in each category. Columns labeled *#hottest* are numbers of hottest call sites, ranked in the top 100, whose invocations are more than 1% of *total* in Columns 2 and 5. Columns labeled *coverage* are percentages of invocations contributed by these hottest call sites.

It is interesting to point out that, for most of the benchmarks, the majority of invocations are from a small number of hot call sites. Fewer than 25 call sites exceed the 1% threshold. Only about half of the benchmarks have more than 1M interface invocations. These benchmarks have fewer than 11 hot interface call sites that contribute to more than 92% of invocations.

The `_213_javac` benchmark includes a large amount of auto-generated code. Invocation counts are spread over many call sites. `SpecJBB2000` has a large code base as well, and it runs much longer than other benchmarks. Hot call sites selected by our 1% threshold contribute only about 34% of total invocations.

Table 1. Coverage of the hottest call sites

benchmark	invokevirtual			invokeinterface		
	total	#hottest	coverage	total	#hottest	coverage
_201_compress	2,191M	7	89%	0	N/A	N/A
_202_jess	964M	25	71%	0	N/A	N/A
_205_raytrace	2,837M	16	29%	0	N/A	N/A
_209_db	762M	8	99%	149M	5	99%
_213_javac	688M	10	20%	34M	5	92%
_222_mpegaudio	846M	25	80%	2M	11	98%
_228_jack	264M	22	74%	46M	11	93%
SpecJBB2000	8,162M	9	34%	146M	7	99%
CFS	639M	15	92%	0	N/A	N/A
simulator(orig)	44M	5	71%	0	N/A	N/A
simulator(aspects)	162M	13	72%	0	N/A	N/A

A list of hottest call sites are provided to the inline oracle. The size limit is removed for call sites in the list. Thus, the inline oracle can exploit the potential of a type analysis as much as possible.

As we discussed in Section 5, a virtual call site can be inlined using different techniques:

- *direct*: direct inlining if the called method is *private* or *final*;
- *preex*: direct inlining with invalidation checks if the receiver can be proved to be preexistent prior method calls;
- *cp*: guarded inlining with code patching;
- *mt* or *ct*: guarded inlining with method or class tests.

If a call site is currently monomorphic according to the analysis results, guards are chosen as a command line option. It can be code patching or method/-class tests. For our experiment we used code patching since it has less runtime overhead.

Monomorphic interface calls can be directly inlined if the receiver is preexistent, or inlined with guards. We found that, in our benchmark set, receivers of nearly all hot interface calls cannot be proven to be preexistent by an invariant argument analysis. Thus, in our results, we omit the *preex* category for interface calls. We also performed another experiment where the inline oracle inlined polymorphic call sites (guarded by method or class tests) that had 1 or 2 targets resolved using type analysis results. However, this did not lead to significantly more inlined calls (only `_213_javac` has a 2% increase). Thus, we do not inline polymorphic calls in our experiment reported here.

Limit Study Results. Table 2 compares the results of dynamic *CHA* and *IdealTypeAnalysis*. Each benchmark has two rows: `ideal` and `cha`, showing dynamic counts of inlined calls using different type analyses. Virtual and interface calls are presented separately. Column *total* is the count of invocations in each category. In the *virtual* category, dynamic CHA did nearly as perfect a job as the ideal type analysis in most benchmarks, except `_213_javac` and `simulator(aspects)`. On these benchmarks, the majority of dynamic invocations are contributed by monomorphic call sites. The sum of *direct*, *preex* and *cp* is close to the coverage in Table 1. `_213_javac` leaves a small gap between *cha* and *ideal* (5% of virtual calls could not be solved by CHA), and CHA does not resolve 19% monomorphic virtual calls of `simulator(aspects)` that were proven to be preexistent by the *ideal* type analysis. In the *interface* category, column 8 shows that a large portion of interface invocations are from monomorphic call sites as well. Dynamic CHA is ineffective on inlining interface calls. Furthermore, the other two simple type analyses, RTA and ITA, did not improve the results of inlining interface calls because common interfaces are implemented by different classes that are likely to be instantiated.

Table 2. Limit study of method inlining using type analyses

		virtual				interface		
		total	direct	preex	cp	total	cp	mt
_201_compress	ideal	2,191M	99%	0	0	0	0	0
	cha	2,191M	99%	0	0	0	0	0
_202_jess	ideal	994M	58%	6%	21%	7M	0	0
	cha	994M	58%	6%	21%	7M	0	0
_205_raytrace	ideal	2,837M	0	50%	41%	0	0	0
	cha	2,837M	0	50%	41%	0	0	0
_209_db	ideal	762M	31%	0	67%	150M	99%	0
	cha	762M	31%	0	67%	150M	0	0
_213_javac	ideal	701M	28%	7%	15%	35M	95%	0
	cha	701M	27%	7%	10%	35M	0	0
_222_mpegaudio	ideal	846M	73%	3%	0	2M	57%	0
	cha	846M	73%	3%	0	2M	57%	0
_228_jack	ideal	258M	13%	16%	39%	46M	86%	0
	cha	258M	12%	15%	39%	46M	25%	8%
SpecJBB2000	ideal	8,250M	32%	29%	11%	148M	99%	0
	cha	8,119M	32%	29%	12%	146M	0	0
CFS	ideal	639M	38%	6%	52%	0	0	0
	cha	639M	38%	6%	52%	0	0	0
simulator	ideal	44M	99%	0	0	0	0	0
(original)	cha	44M	99%	0	0	0	0	0
simulator	ideal	162M	11%	19%	53%	0	0	0
(aspects)	cha	162M	11%	0	53%	0	0	0

Discussion. `Simulator(aspects)` is an interesting benchmark. Injecting AspectJ advice code increases the number of invocations and changes inlining behaviors dramatically. In the original benchmark, nearly all virtual calls are monomorphic and can be directly inlined. With aspects, dynamic CHA misses all monomorphic calls in the *preex* category. After looking at the benchmark closely, we found this is due to the generic implementation of pointcuts.

The pointcut implementation boxes primitive values in objects and passes them to AspectJ libraries. The value is then unboxed after the library call. The original code for unboxing looks like

```
int intValue(Object v) {
  if (v instanceof Number)
    return ((Number)v).intValue();
  ......
}
```

The single call site of `((Number)v).intValue()` contributes 19% *preex* invocations. Dynamic CHA failed to inline this call site because the `Number` class has several subclasses, `Integer`, `Double`, and `Long`, and the call site is identified as polymorphic.

This particular problem can be solved in two ways: 1) use a context-sensitive reachability-based type analysis, or 2) change the implementation of unboxing to facilitate the type analysis. We changed the method to use a tighter type, `Integer`, in the type cast expression, then the call site becomes directly inlineable.

Since the number of hot interface call sites is small, we investigated them one by one. It turns out these hot interface calls are used in a similar pattern:

```
// <TYPE> is java.util.Vector, java.util.Hashtable, etc.
Enumeration e = <TYPE>.elements();
......
while (e.hasMoreElements())
  index[i++] = (Entry)e.nextElement();
```

`Enumeration` is an interface in `java.util` package. The *while* loop makes two or more interface calls for enumerating elements of underlying data structures. Dynamic CHA assumes all implementations of the interface are in the runtime type set of `e`, although each `<TYPE>` class returns a specific implementation. Without interprocedural information or inlining the `<TYPE>.elements()` method, a type analysis cannot produce precise type information of `e`. Therefore, these interface call sites cannot be inlined by using dynamic CHA.

From this limit study, we conclude that:

- most virtual calls in standard Java benchmarks are monomorphic;
- dynamic CHA is nearly perfect for inlining virtual calls;
- dynamic CHA is ineffective on inlining interface calls;
- to assist compiler optimizations, a programmer should use precise types when it does not sacrifice other engineering benefits;
- a large percentage of interface calls are monomorphic and used in a simple pattern, but it requires an interprocedural analysis to discover the precise type of the receiver.

4 Dynamic Interprocedural Type Analysis

In Section 3, we presented a type analysis framework for supporting speculative inlining. We also presented the results of our limit study of method inlining which showed that dynamic CHA is not strong enough for inlining interface calls. In this section, we present an interprocedural, reachability-based, type analysis that is suitable for inlining interface calls.

There are two different approaches to performing a dynamic interprocedural analysis in a Java virtual machine. A whole-program analysis analyzes all classes and methods that can participate the program execution. A demand-driven analysis only analyzes the part of code related to a request. In this paper we focus on the whole-program approach.

We designed and implemented a dynamic version XTA in our previous work [16] as an example of how to deal with dynamic class loading and reference resolution. However, due to lack of intraprocedural data-flow information, XTA results are very coarse. Although the computed type sets are smaller than ones from CHA, it still could not recognize important monomorphic interface call sites. From the method inlining study, we found XTA results were no better than dynamic CHA.

4.1 Dynamic Variable Type Analysis (VTA)

Design. VTA [19] uses intraprocedural data flow information to propagate type sets. Given a Java program (all application and library classes), static VTA constructs a directed type flow graph $G = (V, E, \tau)$ where:

- V is a set of nodes, representing local variables, method formals and returns, static and instance fields, and array elements;
- E is a set of directed edges between nodes, an edge $a \rightarrow b$ represents an assignment of a's value to b;
- $\tau : V \rightarrow T$ is a map from a node to a set of types (classes).

We use the same approach outlined in [16] to adopt the static VTA to a JIT compiler. In the whole-program approach, the constraint collector monitors method compilation events at runtime. Before a method is compiled, the constraint collector parses the bytecode and creates VTA edges. The collector uses the front-end of the optimizing compiler in Jikes RVM, which converts bytecode to a three address intermediate representation, HIR. Several optimizations are performed during translation. An HIR operand has a declaring type.

Dynamic VTA analysis is driven by events from JIT compilers and class loaders. Figure 3 shows the flow of events. In the dotted box are the three modules of dynamic VTA analysis: VTA graphs, the analysis (include constraint collector), and dependency databases.

Many system events can change the VTA graph. Whenever the graph is changed (either the graph has an new edge, or a node has a new reaching type), a propagator propagates type sets of nodes (related to changes) until no further change occurs. Whenever the reaching type set of a node has a new member, the analysis verifies dependencies on this node registered by inlining oracles (see Section 3). The oracle has a chance to perform invalidation if inlining assumptions are violated.

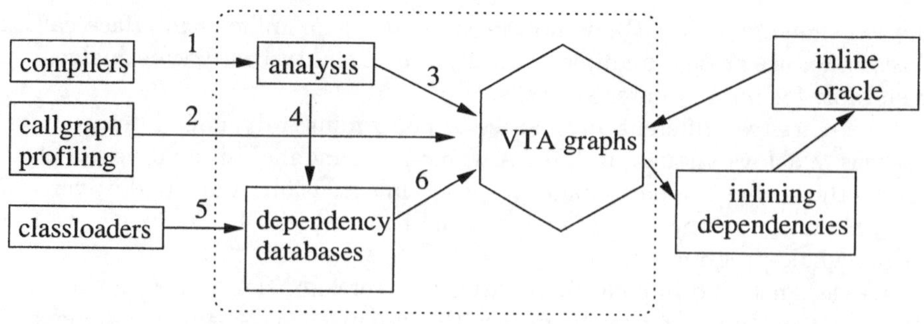

Fig. 3. Model of VTA events

Propagations. To support speculative optimizations, the analysis must keep the results up-to-date whenever a client makes queries. An *eager* approach propagates new types whenever the VTA graph is changed. The second approach is to cache graph changes when collecting constraints of a method, and *batch* propagations at the end of constraint collection. The third approach, as suggested in [15], performs depth-first search (DFS) on nodes that a client makes queries on. Whenever the graph changes, it has to perform DFS on all nodes whose types were used for speculative optimizations to verify that the optimizations are not invalidated by new changes. In our study, we found both eager and batch propagations are efficient, with respect to the total execution time of each benchmark. `_213_javac` takes up to 1.7 seconds and other benchmarks take less than 1 second.

Effectiveness of dynamic VTA. Not surprisingly, VTA is able to handle the simple pattern of interface calls in our benchmarks set. Table 3 compares dynamic counts of inlined interface calls. We omitted benchmarks with few interface calls. Dynamic VTA is able to catch all monomorphic interface calls and allows them to be inlined by using code patching.

Table 3. Comparison of VTA and IdealTypeAnalysis for inlining interface calls

benchmark	Ideal(cp)	VTA(cp)
_209_db	99%	99%
_213_javac	95%	95%
_228_jack	86%	86%
SpecJBB2000	99%	99%

Our preliminary performance measurement shows *Ideal* type analysis yields a small performance improvement over *CHA*. Due to heavier GC workload introduced by VTA graphs, `_213_javac` and `SpecJBB2000` slowed down when using the *copying mark-sweep* collector. Recently we switched to a *generational mark-sweep* collector, which promotes most of VTA graph objects to old generations. The impact of GC has been reduced. Table 4 compares the best run of 10 runs of two benchmarks. Unfortunately, both `_209_db` and `SpecJBB2000` trigger bugs in the *generational mark-sweep* collector in the version of JikesRVM that we are using for our implementation.[1]

Table 4. Performance comparison using VTA and CHA (GenMS)

benchmark	CHA	VTA	speedups
_213_javac	3.924s	3.900s	0.6%
_228_jack	2.514s	2.460s	2.1%

Memory overhead of whole-program VTA. Although dynamic VTA allows the JIT compiler to utilize maximum inlining opportunities, the cost of whole-program VTA is also high. Using `_213_javac` as an example, VTA analysis increases the live data by 60%. It is clear that the whole-program interprocedural analysis has a very high memory overhead.

5 Related Work

We discussed some related work of method inlining while introducing the background in Section 2. The section discusses additional related work on the topic.

Ishizaki et al. [12] conducted an extensive study of dynamic devirtualization techniques for Java programs. In their experiments, size limits were put on inlined targets, and techniques using dynamic CHA were shown to inline about 46% of virtual calls (execution counts). Our study answers the question of what is the limit of method inlining using different type analyses. By lifting the size limit on hottest call sites, we were able to understand the maximum inlining potential using a type analysis. Our limit study shows that CHA performs nearly as well as an ideal type analysis for inlining.

Pechtchanski and Sarkar [15] presented a framework for dynamic optimistic interprocedural analysis (DOIT) in a JIT environment. For each method, the DOIT analysis builds a value graph similar to a VTA graph. However, due to lack of a complete dynamic call graph, DOIT does not track type flow between method calls (parameters and returns). Instead, it uses conservative subtypes of declaring types of method parameters and returns. DOIT is good at obtaining precise type information for fields whose values are assigned in one method and used by another method. Our work focused on limit study of method inlining using type analyses, including online interprocedural analyses based on dynamic call graphs. Our results independently confirms that dynamic CHA is effective for inlining virtual calls in Java programs.

Profiled-directed inlining is effective to identify profitable inlining targets at polymorphic call sites. However, profile-directed inlining requires runtime tests to guard the inlining target. Our focus is on exploiting unguarded inlining opportunities exposed by type analyses.

[1] It is possible that this issue will be resolved when we upgrade our implementation to the lastest version of JikesRVM.

6 Conclusions, Observations and Future Work

In this paper we have presented a study on the limits of speculative inlining. Somewhat to our surprise we found that using dynamic CHA for speculative inlining is almost as good as using an "ideal" analysis, for inlining virtual method calls. However, for even simple uses of interface calls, none of dynamic CHA, RTA, ITA or XTA gives enough information for determining that interface calls are monomorphic. Rather, to detect these opportunities, one requires a stronger type analysis and we presented a dynamic version of VTA for this purpose.

Our experiments with our dynamic VTA do show that it provides detailed enough type information to identify inlining opportunities for interface calls in our benchmark set. However, we also note that the memory overhead of our whole program approach to dynamic VTA is quite large, and we plan to investigate an alternative demand-driven approach.

In addition to these main contributions of the paper, we also made several other general observations about speculative method inlining.

Observation 1. The conventional wisdom is that inlining increases optimization opportunities. However, in the presence of speculative optimizations, inlining may reduce optimization opportunities as well. Figure 4 shows such an example. In Figure 4(a), the method `Foo.m()` is declared as *virtual*, but not overridden. Thus the call site in the `child` method is a candidate of direct inlining based on the receiver's preexistence prior method call (Figure 4(b)). However, if a compiler inlines `child()` into `parent()`, and the receiver of `foo.m()` is not preexistent prior the `parent()`, the call site can only be inlined with a guard as in Figure 4(c). Since the frequency of calling `foo.m()` is much more than calling `child()`, the performance of `parent()` might not be maximized. This pattern did happen in the `_213_javac` benchmark.

(a) source	(b) inline *Foo.m* only	(c) inline *child*, then *Foo.m*

<pre>parent() {
 Foo f = getfield
 this.child(f);
}
 	
child(Foo foo) {
 while(cond)
   foo.m()
}</pre>
	<pre>parent() {
	  Foo f = getfield
	  this.child(f);
	}
	
	child(Foo foo) {
	 while (cond)
	  inlined Foo.m(foo)
	}</pre>
		<pre>parent(){
		 Foo f = getfield
		 while(cond)
		   if (Foo.m is currently final)
		    inlined Foo.m(f)
		   else
		    Foo.m(f)
		}</pre>

Fig. 4. An example where inlining can reduce optimization opportunities

The above dilemma could be resolved by using on-stack replacement technology [10,21] or thin guards [4]. Indeed, method invalidation performs on-stack replacement at method entries. A compiler can insert a general on-stack replacement point after the statement *Foo f = getfield* with a condition that *Foo.m* is currently final. The compiler can directly inline the body of *Foo.m* into the loop.

Observation 2. Our second observation is that inlining decisions may be affected by library implementations. A Java virtual machine is bundled with a specific implementation of Java class library. For example, the GNU classpath [7] is an open-source implementation of Java libraries and used by many open source Java virtual machines, including Jikes RVM. The implementation of `Hashtable.elements()` in the GNU classpath (version 0.07) returns objects of a single type `Hashtable$Enumerator`. The implementation in Sun's JDK 1.4.2_04, however, may return objects of `Hashtable$EmptyEnumerator` and `Hashtable$Enumerator`. Several hot interface call sites in our benchmark set would not be directly inlined if using Sun's JDK.

Future Work. Based on this study we have concluded that a type analysis for invokeinterfaces is an important area of research, and we are currently working on a demand-driven analysis and compact graph representation to reduce the costs of dynamic VTA. We are also looking at more applications of dynamic interprocedural analysis in JIT compilers. A new research topic is to investigate the effectiveness of compiler optimizations on different design patterns.

Acknowledgments. This work was supported, in part, by NSERC. We would like to thank Navindra Umanee for his proofreading of this paper. We also appreciated anonymous reviewers' constructive comments.

References

1. B. Alpern, C. R. Attanasio, J. J. Barton, M. G. Burke, P. Cheng, J.-D. Choi, A. Cocchi, S. J. Fink, D. Grove, M. Hind, S. F. Hummel, D. Lieber, V. Litvinov, M. F. Mergen, T. Ngo, J. R. Russell, V. Sarkar, M. J. Serrano, J. C. Shepherd, S. E. Smith, V. C. Sreedhar, H. Srinivasan, and J. Whaley. The Jalapeño Virtual Machine. *IBM Systems Journal*, 39(1):211–238, February 2000.
2. B. Alpern, A. Cocchi, S. J. Fink, D. Grove, and D. Lieber. Efficient Implementation of Java Interfaces: Invokeinterface Considered Harmless. In *Proceedings of the Conference on Object-Oriented Programming Systems, Languages, and Applications (OOPSLA'01)*, pages 108–124, 2001.
3. K. Arnold, J. Gosling, and D. Holmes. *The Java Programming Language (Third Edition)*. Addison-Wesley, 2000.
4. M. Arnold and B. G. Ryder. Thin Guards: A Simple and Effective Technique for Reducing the Penalty of Dynamic Class Loading. In *16th European Conference for Object-Oriented Programming (ECOOP'02)*, pages 498 – 524, 2002.
5. D. F. Bacon and P. F. Sweeney. Fast Static Analysis of C++ Virtual Function Calls. In *Proceedings of the Conference on Object-Oriented Programming Systems, Languages, and Applications (OOPSLA'96)*, pages 324 – 341, Oct. 1996.
6. Certrevsim. `http://www.pvv.ntnu.no/ andrearn/certrev/sim.html`.

7. Gnu classpath. http://www.gnu.org/classpath.
8. J. Dean, D. Grove, and C. Chambers. Optimization of Object-Oriented Programs Using Static Class Hierarchy Analysis. In *9th European Conference on Object-Oriented Programming (ECOOP'95)*, pages 77 – 101, Aug. 1995.
9. D. Detlefs and O. Agesen. Inlining of Virtual Methods. In *13th European Conference on Object-Oriented Programming (ECOOP'99)*, pages 258 – 278, June 1999.
10. S. J. Fink and F. Qian. Design, Implementation and Evaluation of Adaptive Recompilation with On-Stack Replacement. In *International Symposium on Code Generation and Optimization (CGO'03)*, pages 241 – 252, March 2003.
11. K. Hazelwood and D. Grove. Adaptive Online Context-Sentitive Inlining. In *International Symposium on Code Generation and Optimization (CGO'03)*, pages 253 – 264, March 2003.
12. K. Ishizaki, M. Kawahito, T. Yasue, H. Komatsu, and T. Nakatani. A Study of Devirtualization Techniques for a Java Just-In-Time Compiler. In *Proceedings of the Conference on Object-Oriented Programming, Systems, Languages, and Applications (OOPSLA'00)*, pages 294–310, 2000.
13. Jikes^{TM} Research Virtual Machine. http://www-124.ibm.com/developerworks/-oss/jikesrvm/.
14. T. Lindholm and F. Yellin. *The Java Virtual Machine Specification.* Addison-Wesley, 1996.
15. I. Pechtchanski and V. Sarkar. Dynamic optimistic interprocedural analysis: A framework and an application. In *Proceedings of the Conference on Object-Oriented Programming Systems, Languages, and Applications*, pages 195 – 210, 2001.
16. F. Qian and L. Hendren. Towards Dynamic Interprocedural Analysis in JVMs. In *3rd Virtual Machine Research and Technology Symposium (VM'04)*, pages 139 – 150, May 2004.
17. Spec JBB2000 benchmark. http://www.spec.org/jbb2000/.
18. Spec JVM98 benchmarks. http://www.spec.org/osg/jvm98/index.html.
19. V. Sundaresan, L. J. Hendren, C. Razafimahefa, R. Vallée-Rai, P. Lam, E. Gagnon, and C. Godin. Practical Virtual Method Call Resolution for Java. In *Proceedings of the Conference on Object-Oriented Programming, Systems, Languages, and Applications (OOPSLA'00)*, pages 264–280, 2000.
20. F. Tip and J. Palsberg. Scalable Propagation-based Call Graph Construction Algorithms. In *Proceedings of the Conference on Object-Oriented Programming Systems, Languages, and Applications (OOPSLA'00)*, pages 281–293, Oct. 2000.
21. Urs Hölzle and Craig Chambers and David Ungar. Debugging Optimized Code with Dynamic Deoptimization. In *Proceedings of the Conference on Programming Language Design and Implementation*, pages 32 – 43, 1992.
22. Weka 3: Data Mining Software in Java. http://www.cs.waikato.ac.nz/ml/weka/.

Completeness Analysis for Incomplete Object-Oriented Programs

Jingling Xue and Phung Hua Nguyen

Programming Languages and Compilers Group,
School of Computer Science and Engineering,
University of New South Wales, NSW 2032, Sydney, Australia

Abstract. We introduce a new approach, called completeness analysis, to computing points-to sets for incomplete Java programs such as library modules or applications in the presence of dynamic class loading. One distinctive feature of this work is that the access and modification properties of fields are taken into account. By combining with a whole-program points-to analysis, completeness analysis yields not only the required points-to sets but also determines which points-to sets and call sites are complete (when the pointed-to objects and target methods are statically resolvable) or not. Such a compositional approach yields more precise points-to sets than those computed by the points-to analysis alone. In addition, our technique also determines (for the first time) which objects may be incompletely detectable, i.e., may be missing in some statically computed points-to sets. We provide experimental evidence to demonstrate that better analysis precision in benchmarks is obtained when the field access and modification properties are exploited. In particular, we are able to find significantly more complete and mono call sites in an incomplete program, which is useful in devirtualisation and inlining. Our analysis is simple since it is flow- and context-insensitive and achieves these improvements at reasonably small analysis costs.

1 Introduction

For object-oriented languages such as Java and C♯, points-to analysis finds many applications in compilers and software engineering. However, most existing points-to analysis methods [9, 13] require the whole program to be available. Their inadequacies are being recognised as modern applications rely increasingly more on component programming and software libraries. When applied to components or library modules alone, whole-program methods may yield incomplete points-to sets (i.e. the ones that may not contain all the pointed-to objects at run time), and consequently, incomplete call sites (i.e., the ones whose sets of target methods resolved statically may not contain all methods invoked at run time). In addition, these methods cannot tell whether or not a points-to set or call site is complete or not, making their results hardly useful. The situation is further aggravated by some features in Java and C♯. Due to the presence of dynamic class loading and/or native methods, an application written in these languages may be incomplete in its entirety at analysis time.

R. Bodik (Ed.): CC 2005, LNCS 3443, pp. 271–286, 2005.

This work addresses the problem of computing the points-to sets for an incomplete object-oriented program and also determining at the same time whether these sets and call sites are complete or not. There are some existing methods that are proposed (intentionally or otherwise) to solve this problem. The extant analysis (EA) [16] is developed mainly to support devirtualisation and inlining. For that reason, EA takes as input the points-to sets for a program and produces as output the set of runtime types in the analysed program for each reference. As a by-product of this process, one can deduce that the point-to set of a reference is complete iff all its runtime types are guaranteed to be known in the analysed program. Several techniques reported in [20, 21] combine points-to analysis and escape analysis [2, 4]. Their results can be used to determine the completeness of points-to sets and call sites.

A common problem with these earlier efforts is that they do not exploit the access and modification properties of fields although similar properties for methods are considered somewhat. As a result, they do not provide sufficient precision about the completeness of points-to sets and call sites. Given an incomplete program, applying whole-program analysis alone is inadequate because the reciprocal modification effects between the program and unknown code are not accounted for. In the presence of unknown code, some points-to sets are inevitably incomplete. As a result, some alias relations cannot be determined based on the computed points-to sets alone. In order to obtain better analysis precision, we believe that the reciprocal modification effects between an incomplete program (i.e., the analysed code) and the unknown (i.e., unanalysed) code must be taken into account as accurately as possible. In this work, we exploit the access and modification properties of fields (static or instance) to improve analysis precision. To substantiate this claim, we present a flow- and context-insensitive analysis, called *completeness analysis (CA)*, for incomplete Java programs and demonstrate its benefits in increasing analysis precision in benchmark programs.

The contributions of this work are summarised as follows:

- We present a new compositional approach to conducting points-to analysis for incomplete Java program. By composing with a whole-program points-to analysis, we obtain not only the points-to sets for the program but also determine which point-to sets and call sites are complete or not.
- We exploit the access and modification properties of fields in our analysis. To the best of our knowledge, this is the first work using these properties to compute the points-to sets for incomplete object-oriented programs. As a result, our points-to sets are more precise than those computed by the points-to analysis alone.
- We introduce for the first time the notion of object detectability, which played an important role in completeness analysis. A compile-time object created in an analysed program is *incompletely detectable* if it may be pointed to by a reference at run time but is missing in its statically computed points-to set and *(completely) detectable* otherwise. Since the access and modification properties of fields are considered, object detectability is different from object reachability used in escape analysis [2, 4, 20, 21]. If an object escapes from a function or thread, so are all the reachable objects. If an object is in-

completely detectable, a directly or indirectly reachable object may be either completely or incompletely detectable.

– We have implemented our complete analysis in Soot [19]. When the access and modification properties of fields are exploited, we obtain better analysis precision in benchmarks, in particular, significantly more mono call sites, i.e., more opportunities for devirtualisation and inlining.

The rest of this paper is organised as follows. Section 2 introduces the language model used. Section 3 presents our completeness analysis. Section 4 discusses our experimental results. Section 5 reviews the related work. Section 6 concludes the paper and discusses some future work.

2 Language Model

For simplicity, we describe our approach for a subset of Java with the features most relevant to points-to analysis. The points-to analysis for a Java program is carried out in an intermediate representation (IR) of the program. As our approach is flow- and context-insensitive, IR consists of only the seven kinds of statements listed in Table 1. Furthermore, the features such as multi-inheritance interface and multi-threading do not pose any problems. Of the seven statements, the first and last are explained below and the other five are self-explanatory.

In Java, objects can be created either explicitly via `new` or implicitly, say, via a Java reflection method `newInstance`. In the latter case, the object creation statement can be replaced by $\ell = \texttt{new}\ C$ if C is detected statically to be the class name of the implicitly created object. Otherwise, the object creation statement used is $\ell = \texttt{new}\ \mathit{Unknown}$, where *Unknown* can be any class in the analysed program or any new class that may be loaded dynamically at run time.

For notational convenience, each method is denoted $op(p_0, \ldots, p_n, r)$, where $p_0, \ldots, p_n$ are its $n+1$ formal input parameters and r its formal output parameter. As is clear in Table 1, the return statements in a method are not explicitly represented. Instead, every return statement in a method is replaced by an assignment to the formal output parameter of that method. Correspondingly, a call site has the form $op(a_0, \ldots, a_n, \ell)$, where $a_0, \ldots, a_n$ are the $n+1$ actual input

Table 1. Instruction set for the IR on which points-to analysis is conducted, where ℓ and r are reference variables, f a field, op a method name, and C a class name

Syntax	Semantics
$\ell = \texttt{new}\ C$	Object Creation
$\ell = r$	Assignment
$\ell = C.f$	Static Field Load
$C.f = r$	Static Field Store
$\ell = r.f$	Instance Field Load
$\ell.f = r$	Instance Field Store
$op(a_0, \ldots, a_n, \ell)$	Call Site

parameters and ℓ is the actual output parameter. If *op* is an instance method, then a_0 denotes the receiver of the call. Otherwise, *op* is static and can be conveniently regarded as an instance method if a_0 is set to be the name of the class in which *op* is declared. In Java, parameter passing is call by value.

Accesses to arrays are handled similarly to instance field accesses by introducing a special field, say, *sf*. We do not distinguish accesses to different components of an array. For example, `x[i]` and `x[j]` are both represented by `x.`*sf*.

The term *fixed call site* is used to denote (1) an `invokestatic`, (2) an `invokespecial`, (3) a call site whose (unique) target is declared to be `final` or in a `final` class, or (4) a sealed call site [22]. All other kinds of call sites are called *non-fixed*. In a fixed call site, all target methods that may be invoked are known at compile time. This is obvious in the first three cases. The target methods of a sealed call site are confined to be in the underlying sealed package.

The term *reference* is used to denote all kinds of accesses such as variable accesses, static field accesses and instance field accesses.

The semantics of the following field and method modifiers in Java are exploited in our analysis: `private`, `protected`, `public` and `final`. In the absence of the first three modifiers, the *default* (i.e., *package*) access is assumed.

3 Completeness Analysis for Incomplete Programs

The whole-program points-to analysis requires the entire program, i.e. all its classes and methods, to be available at analysis time. An incomplete program includes only a subset of these classes. In addition, some methods in a class (e.g., native methods) may be unavailable to participate in static analysis.

3.1 Incomplete Programs

Definition 1. An incomplete program, F, is a triple $F = \langle \mathbb{L}_F, \mathbb{M}_F, \mathbb{F}_F \rangle$, where $\mathbb{L}_F$ is the set of classes in F, $\mathbb{M}_F$ the set of methods in $\mathbb{L}_F$ and $\mathbb{F}_F$ the set of fields declared in $\mathbb{L}_F$ such that (1) all classes in $\mathbb{L}_F$ except the root class `java.lang.Object` have all their superclasses in $\mathbb{L}_F$, (2) there is not a reference in $\mathbb{M}_F$ whose type is not in $\mathbb{L}_F$, (3) there is not a read/write to a field not in $\mathbb{F}_F$, and finally, (4) there is not an access (i.e., a call) to a method not in $\mathbb{M}_F$.

According to this definition, our work is applicable to library modules or applications supporting native methods and dynamic class loading.

We use $IM_F \subseteq \mathbb{M}_F$ to denote the set of all *analysed* methods whose code is available for static analysis and define $EM_F = \mathbb{M}_F \setminus IM_F$. Although the methods in EM_F are *unanalysed*, their signatures are always available by Definition 1.

$\mathbb{S}_F$ denotes the set of statements and $\mathbb{O}_F$ the set of compile-time objects created in IM_F, respectively. Let V_F be the set of references in $\mathbb{S}_F$.

Let $\mathbb{U}_F$ symbolise the unknown code, i.e., the code in EM_F and outside F.

Let us define the (in)accessibility of the fields and methods in IM_F with respect to $\mathbb{U}_F$. A method in IM_F is *accessible* if it can be invoked in $\mathbb{U}_F$ and *inaccessible* otherwise. A field in F is *accessible* if it can be accessed by some statements in $\mathbb{U}_F$ and *inaccessible* otherwise. For example, a `private` field is inaccessible if there does not exist any unanalysed method in the class in which the field is declared. $\mathbb{F}_F^i$ denotes the set of all inaccessible fields in F.

Let $\mathbb{F}_F^f$ be the set of all `final` fields in F. In Java, `final` fields are initialised only once in the initialisers or constructors in analysed methods.

3.2 Applying Whole-Program Analysis to F

We use an Andersen-style analysis [1, 9] because of its reasonable precision and efficiency. Let $PT_F(\ell)$ be the points-to-set of a reference ℓ in V_F. By convention, we assume that $PT_F(\ell) = \emptyset$ if $\ell \notin V_F$. The points-to analysis requires an approximation of the call graph for F. A call graph is the relation $\mathbb{C}_F \subseteq \mathbb{S}_F \times \mathbb{M}_F$ such that $(s, op) \in \mathbb{C}_F$ iff s is a call site statement and op is a method that may be a target of the call site. We use CHA (Class Hierarchy Analysis) [5] to construct such a call graph. A more precise alternative [17] is to construct the call graph on-the-fly as the points-to sets of call site receivers are being computed. However, the improved precision may not justify the computational cost [9].

An analysed program F consists of only the seven different kinds of statements given in Table 1. The rules for computing the points-to sets of F are:

Rule P1. *If* $\exists\ s{:}[\ell = \texttt{new}\ C] \in \mathbb{S}_F$, *then* $\{o_s\} \subseteq PT_F(\ell)$.

Rule P2. *If* $\exists\ s{:}[\ell = r] \in \mathbb{S}_F$, *then* $PT_F(r) \subseteq PT_F(\ell)$.

Rule P3. *If* $\exists\ s{:}[\ell = C.f] \in \mathbb{S}_F$ *then* $PT_F(C.f) \subseteq PT_F(\ell)$.

Rule P4. *If* $\exists\ s{:}[C.f = r] \in \mathbb{S}_F$ *then* $PT_F(r) \subseteq PT_F(C.f)$.

Rule P5. *If* $\exists\ s{:}[\ell = r.f] \in \mathbb{S}_F$ *then* $PT_F(r.f) \subseteq PT_F(\ell)$.

Rule P6. *If* $\exists\ s{:}[\ell.f = r] \in \mathbb{S}_F \wedge\ \exists\ \ell'.f \in V_F$ *s.t.* $PT_F(\ell) \cap PT_F(\ell') \neq \emptyset$, *i.e.,* ℓ *and* ℓ' *are aliases (with nonempty points-to sets), then* $PT_F(r) \subseteq PT_F(\ell'.f)$

Rule P7. *If* $\exists\ s{:}[op(a_0, \ldots, a_n, \ell)] \in \mathbb{S}_F \wedge \exists\ op(p_0, \ldots, p_n, r) \in \mathbb{M}_F$ *s.t.* $(s, op) \in \mathbb{C}_F$, *then* $PT_F(a_0) \subseteq PT_F(p_0), \ldots, PT_F(a_n) \subseteq PT_F(p_n)$ *and* $PT_F(r) \subseteq PT_F(\ell)$.

The points-to analysis for F consists of solving the constraints for all its statements to determine the points-to sets of all references in the program.

3.3 Inadequacies of Whole-Program Analysis

When a whole-program points-to analysis technique is applied to an incomplete program F, the following two assumptions are conventionally made:

- All methods in EM_F are considered to have an empty body.
- The points-to sets of all formal input parameters of all methods that are accessible (in the unknown code $\mathbb{U}_F$) are initialised to be empty.

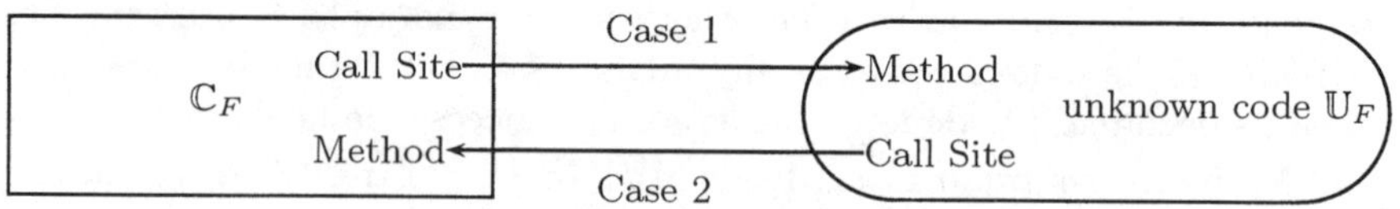

Fig. 1. Two kinds of troublesome missing caller-callee relations in $\mathbb{C}_F$

Due to the lack of knowledge about $\mathbb{U}_F$, a reference (inside F or outside) is said to be incomplete if its statically computed points-to set may not contain some object pointed to at run time – such an object can be created either inside F or outside. In addition, a call site in F may be incomplete when the set of target methods that are statically resolved may not contain a method that is invoked at run time – such a method is declared in the unknown code outside F. (The methods in EM_F cannot be missing since their declarations are available.)

There are several reasons why a points-to sets can be incomplete. First, while the call graph $\mathbb{C}_F$ constructed using CHA over-approximates all caller-callee relations within F, some relations that happen during program execution can be missing if F is incomplete. As illustrated in Figure 1, there are two kinds of troublesome missing caller-callee relations in $\mathbb{C}_F$. In Case 1, the objects passed to an unknown method in $\mathbb{U}_F$ can be used in an unknown way. In addition, the type of the returned object is unknown. In Case 2, the situation is reversed. Second, static fields can be accessed by the unknown code $\mathbb{U}_F$. Third, due to the first two reasons, instance fields can also be accessed indirectly in $\mathbb{U}_F$.

Finally, if some points-to sets are incomplete, the alias relations captured by Rule P6 may also be incomplete. This is because ℓ and ℓ' can still be aliases even if $PT_F(\ell) \cap PT_F(\ell') = \emptyset$. So Rule P6 needs to be augmented later by Rule C6.

3.4 Completeness Analysis (CA)

In the previous section, we argued that whole-program analysis is inadequate if the analysed program is incomplete. In this section, we present a technique, called *completeness analysis (CA)*, to detect which points-to sets and call sites may be incomplete and which compile-time objects may be missing (i.e., incompletely detectable) in some points-to sets. Our approach is compositional. By combining with a whole-program points-to analysis technique, our completeness analysis also produces at the same time the points-to sets with better precision (Theorem 1).

Our approach is flow- and context-insensitive. If an analysed program F is not incomplete, Rules P1 – P7 given in Section 3.2 are sufficient. Otherwise, we rely on Rules C1 – C9, which are introduced in Section 3.4, to carry out the so-called completeness analysis. By applying both sets of rules to an incomplete program F and solving the derived constraints for all the statements in F iteratively, the desired results are found as a fixed point to these constraints.

3.4.1 Completeness; Detectability; Aliases

Let $\mathcal{P}(F)$ be the set of all possible programs that include F as a subset. Let $W \in \mathcal{P}(F)$. Let $\mathbb{M}_W$ be the set of methods in the program W and V_W the set of the reference variables in $\mathbb{M}_W$. The following two concepts are defined conceptually (but not physically constructed). Let $PT_W(\ell)$ be the points-to set of $\ell \in V_W$ observed during program execution. Let $\mathbb{C}_W$ be the call graph of W also observed during program execution.

To determine which objects may be missing in some points-to sets and which references may have such points-to sets, the following notions are introduced.

Definition 2. An object $o \in \mathbb{O}_F$ is *incompletely detectable* if $\exists\, W \in \mathcal{P}(F)$ such that

- $\exists\, \ell \in V_F : o \in PT_W(\ell) \setminus PT_F(\ell)$, or
- $\exists\, \ell \in V_W \setminus V_F : o \in PT_W(\ell)$.

and *(completely) detectable* otherwise. A reference $\ell \in V_F$ is *incomplete* if $\exists\, W \in \mathcal{P}(F)$ such that $PT_W(\ell) \setminus PT_F(\ell) \neq \emptyset$ and *complete* otherwise. Every reference $\ell \in V_W \setminus V_F$ in every program $W \in \mathcal{P}(F)$ is *incomplete*, i.e., every reference $\ell \notin V_F$ is *incomplete.*

Recall the convention that $PT_F(\ell) = \emptyset$ if $\ell \notin V_F$. Therefore, an object in $\mathbb{O}_F$ is incompletely detectable if it may be pointed to by a reference (inside F or outside) at run time but is missing in its statically computed points-to set. A reference (inside F or outside) is incomplete if it may point to an object at run time such that the object is missing in its points-to set. Note that a complete reference may or may not include incompletely detectable objects in its points-to set.

To find out the missing caller-callee pairs (s, op) in the call graph $\mathbb{C}_F \subseteq \mathbb{S}_F \times \mathbb{M}_F$ (built statically), the notion of incomplete call site is introduced below. Essentially, a call site in F is incomplete if its set of statically resolved target methods does not include a method that may be invoked at run time.

Definition 3. If $\exists\, W \in \mathcal{P}(F) \wedge \exists\, s \in \mathbb{S}_F \wedge \exists\, op \in \mathbb{M}_W$ s.t. $(s, op) \in (\mathbb{C}_W \setminus \mathbb{C}_F)$, then s is said to be an *incomplete* call site and *complete* otherwise.

We discussed earlier that the points-to sets computed for an incomplete program is insufficient to determine all the alias relations. The notions of reference completeness and object detectability are used below to provide an over-approximation of all missing aliases.

Definition 4. Let ℓ and ℓ' be two references in $W \in \mathcal{P}(F)$. Both are aliases, denoted *C-Alias*(ℓ, ℓ'), if ℓ is incomplete and ℓ' is either incomplete or complete with its points-to set containing at least one incompletely detectable object, or vice versa.

According to the above definition, *C-Alias*(ℓ, ℓ) is true iff ℓ is incomplete.

3.4.2 Rules

Let O^i, R^i and S^i be the set of incompletely detectable objects, incomplete references and incomplete call sites in an incomplete program F, respectively. Rules C1 – C9 for computing these sets are introduced below. In each rule, the statements or field accesses (among others) to which the rule is applied is indicated. There are no extra rules for object creation statements $\ell = \texttt{new}\ C$, where C is a known class in F, and for assignment statements since they are covered by Rules P1 and P2.

Rule C1 (s:[$\ell = \texttt{new}\ \mathit{Unknown}$]). $o_s \in O^i$, where o_s is the object created at s.

In the following two rules for static fields, the corresponding access and modification properties are used to determine whether they are applicable.

Rule C2 ($C.f = r$). If $f \notin \mathbb{F}^i_F$, then $PT_F(r) \subseteq O^i$.

As $f \notin \mathbb{F}^i_F$, there may exist a static load $\ell = C.f$ in the unknown code $\mathbb{U}_F$, where $\ell \notin V_F$, i.e., $\ell \in V_W \setminus V_F$ for some $W \in \mathcal{P}(F)$. By Rule P4, $C.f$ will point to the objects pointed to by r. But these objects may be assigned to ℓ in $\mathbb{U}_F$. By Definition 2, the objects that r points to are marked as incompletely detectable.

Rule C3 ($C.f$). If $f \notin (\mathbb{F}^i_F \cup \mathbb{F}^f_F)$, then $C.f \in R^i$.

If $f \notin (\mathbb{F}^i_F \cup \mathbb{F}^f_F)$, there may exist a static store $C.f = r$ in the unknown code $\mathbb{U}_F$, where $r \notin V_F$. The objects pointed to by r may not appear in the points-to set of $C.f$ when F is analysed. By Definition 2, $C.f$ is incomplete.

If the access and modification properties of instance fields were ignored, the following two rules would be sufficient for handling instance field loads and stores. We discuss them first in order to motivate Rules C4 – C6 used in our analysis.

Rule S1 ($\ell.f$). *If* $\ell \in R^i \vee PT_F(\ell) \cap O^i \neq \emptyset$, *then* $\ell.f \in R^i$.

Rule S2 ($\ell.f = r$). *If* $\ell \in R^i \vee PT_F(\ell) \cap O^i \neq \emptyset$, *then* $PT_F(r) \subseteq O^i$.

If the access and modification properties of f are ignored, we must assume conservatively the existence of an instance field access $\ell'.f$ in the unknown code $\mathbb{U}_F$, where $\ell' \notin V_F$. If $\ell \in R^i \vee PT_F(\ell) \cap O^i \neq \emptyset$, then $C\text{-}Alias(\ell, \ell')$ may hold, i.e., ℓ and ℓ' are potentially aliases. However, when F is analysed as a whole program, $PT_F(\ell) \cap PT_F(\ell') = \emptyset$ is possible. In this case, Rule P6 will not be applied. We need Rule S1 for the following reason. If there exists a store $\ell'.f = r$ in $\mathbb{U}_F$, the pointed-to objects by r may not belong to the points-to set of $\ell.f$. By Definition 2, $\ell.f$ is incomplete. We need Rule S2, because if there exists a load into $\ell'.f$ in $\mathbb{U}_F$, then all the objects pointed by r may be incompletely detectable.

By exploiting the access and modification properties of instance fields, we have relaxed the assumption about the always existence of of a field access $\ell'.f$ in the unknown code $\mathbb{U}_F$. Rules S1 and S2 are replaced by Rules C4 – C6.

Rule C4 ($\ell.f$). If $f \notin (\mathbb{F}^i_F \cup \mathbb{F}^f_F) \wedge (\ell \in R^i \vee PT_F(\ell) \cap O^i \neq \emptyset)$, then $\ell.f \in R^i$.

Rule C5 $(\ell.f = r)$**.** If $f \notin \mathbb{F}^i_F \wedge (\ell \in R^i \vee PT_F(\ell) \cap O^i \neq \emptyset)$, then $PT_F(r) \subseteq O^i$.

Rule C6 $(\ell.f = r)$**.** If $f \in (\mathbb{F}^i_F \cup \mathbb{F}^f_F) \wedge \exists\, \ell'.f \in V_F$ s.t. *C-Alias*(ℓ, ℓ') holds, then $PT_F(r) \subseteq PT_F(\ell'.f)$.

Rule C4 is refined from Rule S1 since it is applied only when there may be an instance field store $\ell'.f = r$ in the unknown code $\mathbb{U}_F$. Rule C5 is refined from Rule S2 since it is applied only when there may be an instance field access $\ell'.f$ in $\mathbb{U}_F$. In this case, the objects pointed to by $\ell'.f$ may be incompletely detectable since they can be assigned to a reference in $\mathbb{U}_F$. Rule C6 is applied only when $\ell'.f \in V_F$ holds. In this case, there cannot be any store of the form $\ell'.f = r$ in $\mathbb{U}_F$. If ℓ and ℓ' are aliases, then a store to $\ell'.f$ is also a store to $\ell.f$ in disguise. Rule C6 is the rule in completeness analysis that enables better points-to sets to be computed. In this rule, $\ell = \ell'$ is possible. So the rule will be applied if ℓ is incomplete, since by Definition 4, *C-Alias*(ℓ, ℓ) is true iff ℓ is incomplete.

Rule C7 $(s : [op(a_0, \ldots, a_n, \ell)]$ **for Case 1 in Figure 1).** There are three parts:

1. Suppose s is a non-fixed call site. If $a_0 \in R^i \vee (PT_F(a_0)$ includes an instance of *Unknown*), then $s \in S^i$.
2. If $s \in S^i$, then $PT_F(a_1), \ldots, PT_F(a_n) \subseteq O^i$ and $\ell \in R^i$.
3. If there exists $(s, op) \in \mathbb{C}_F$ such that $op \in EM_F$, then
   (a) $PT_F(a_1), \ldots, PT_F(a_n) \subseteq O^i$ and $\ell \in R^i$, and
   (b) $A_0 \subseteq O^i$, where A_0 is the set of all receiver objects in $PT_F(a_0)$ on which op is invoked at s (A_0 can be statically determined from $PT_F(a_0)$).

Part 1 determines whether a call site is incomplete or not. As discussed in Section 2, a fixed call site is complete since its set of target methods can be statically resolved. Under the stated conditions, an overriding method in a class outside F may be invokable at s. Such a caller-callee relation is not available in the call graph $\mathbb{C}_F$. Thus, s is incomplete by Definition 3. Clearly, s is incomplete if a_0 is incomplete or complete but may point to an instance of *Unknown*.

Part 2 applies to a call site at which an unknown method op outside F may be invoked. The objects pointed to by $a_1, \ldots, a_n$ may be missing in the points-to sets of the corresponding formal input parameters of op, and thus, are incompletely detectable. The receiver a_0 is excluded since it is the incompleteness of a_0 rather than the nature of its pointed-to objects that causes op to be invoked at s. The actual output parameter ℓ is incomplete since its points-to set may not include the object returned by the unknown method op.

Part 3 applies to a call site at which an unknown method op in EM_F may be invoked. Therefore, Part 3(a) is exactly the same as Part 2. In Part 3(b), the receiver objects that cause op to be invoked are marked as incompletely detectable since they may be assigned to some unknown references in op.

Rule C8 $(op(p_0, p_1, \ldots, p_n, r) \in \mathbb{M}_F$ **for Case 2 in Figure 1).** If op is accessible (i.e., invokable) in $\mathbb{U}_F$, then $p_0, , \ldots, p_n \in R^i$ and $PT_F(r) \subseteq O^i$.

If *op* is accessible, there may exist a call site $s : [op(a_0, \ldots, a_n, \ell)]$ in $\mathbb{U}_F$. The effect of the assignments due to parameter and result passing cannot be considered when F is analysed. Thus, the points-to sets of p_i and ℓ cannot contain the objects in the points-to sets of a_i and r, respectively. Hence, $p_0, \ldots, p_n$ are incomplete and all objects pointed to by r are incompletely detectable.

Rule C9 ($PT_F(r) \subseteq PT_F(r')$ Created by Rules P1 – P7 and C6). If $r \in R^i$, then $r' \in R^i$.

The incompleteness of points-to sets is propagated during the points-to analysis. If r is incomplete, a missing object in its points-to set is also missing in the points-to set of r' when $PT_F(r) \subseteq PT_F(r')$. So r' is incomplete by Definition 2.

As explained in Section 3.4, we combine Rules P1 – P7 and C1 – C9 to compute not only the points-to sets of all references but also the information about the completeness of references and call sites as well as object detectability.

Thanks to Rule C6, such a compositional approach enables better points-to sets to be computed. Essentially, a reference may be accurately identified as being complete even though it is incomplete if Rule C6 is not used.

Theorem 1. *Let r be a reference in F. Let $PT_F(r)$ be the points-to set of r computed according to CA. Let $PT'_F(r)$ be computed according to CA′, i.e., a version of CA in which C4 – C6 are replaced by S1 and S2. The following two statements are true: (a) if r is complete in CA′, then r is also complete in CA, and in addition, $PT_F(r) = PT'_F(r)$, (b) if r is incomplete in CA′, then r may be complete or incomplete in CA, and in addition, $PT_F(r) \supseteq PT'_F(r)$.*

4 Experiments

In this section, we provide experimental evidence that completeness analysis can yield better precision when the field access and modification properties are exploited. We have implemented our completeness analysis in Soot [19], a bytecode to bytecode optimiser. In Soot, only whole-program analyses and optimisations are supported. A preprocessing translator converts Java bytecode into a three-address IR called *Jimple*. The points-to sets for an analysed program are computed using the points-to analysis pass in Soot [9]. We have implemented our completeness analysis by composing it with this existing points-to analysis.

Due to the space limitation, we discuss briefly how we have handled some other Java language features not present in Table 1. Java exceptions are dealt with as follows. All formal input parameters of a `catch` statement are initialised to be incomplete. All objects that may be thrown by a `throw` statement are marked as incompletely detectable objects. Reflection methods are treated as native ones with some extra rules. For example, all fields that may be accessed by `get` or `set` are considered as accessible fields. We do not address the Java class reloading since it may potentially modify code on-the-fly and so could affect our assumptions about the analysed program. We also assume that all native methods respect the access and modification properties of fields and methods.

In our experiments, three approaches are compared: CA, CA0 and EA. CA denotes our complete analysis technique. CA0 is the version of CA when the field modifiers are ignored. Precisely, the following changes are made to our rules. Rules C4 – C6 are replaced by Rules S1 and S2 and Rule C2 – C3 by:

Rule S3 $(C.f = r)$. $PT_F(r) \subseteq O^i$.

Rule S4 $(C.f)$. If $f \notin \mathbb{F}^f_F$, then $C.f \in R^i$.

The extant analysis[1] (EA) [16] can be used for completeness analysis even though it was originally designed for inlining and devirtualisation. EA is chosen because it is applicable to incomplete Java programs and can also be carried out based on the same kind of points-to analysis, i.e., flow- and context-insensitive Andersen-style points-to analysis. In EA, an extant reference is complete while a non-extant reference is incomplete. A call site is complete if its receiver is complete and incomplete otherwise. EA cannot handle object detectability since their extant or non-extant objects can be completely or incompletely detectable.

4.1 Benchmarks

Table 2 gives some statistics about the 12 benchmarks used in our experiments. The first seven are from SPECjvm98, `jbb` is from SPECjbb2000, `jlex` is a Java scanner generator from Princeton University, `jtar` is GNU's `tar` ported to Java (version 1.21), `jtb` is a Java tree builder from Purdue University (version 1.2.2), and finally, `soot` (version 2.0.1) is the Java bytecode-to-bytecode optimiser [19], in which our completeness analysis is implemented.

In our experiments, the analysed program for a benchmark consists of all classes in the application and the classes in Java library reachable statically from the application. The analysis starts with the methods in these classes that may be invoked from outside and continues to analyse the methods that may be reachable statically from these methods. All packages in a benchmark are assumed to be sealed [18]. For each benchmark (including application and library code), Columns 2 – 4 give the total number of its classes, methods and fields and Columns 5 – 8 summarise the access and modification information about its fields. These statistics show convincingly the existence of opportunities for completeness analysis to exploit the field modifiers for better analysis precision.

4.2 Analysis Precision

Table 3 compares CA, CA0 and EA in finding complete points-to sets, call sites and detectable objects in the application part of a benchmark. In all the benchmarks, CA is more precise than CA0, which is more precise than EA.

CA performs better than CA0 because CA fully exploits the field modifiers in Rules C2 – C6 while CA0 considers only the `final` modifier in Rule S4. As

[1] We do not make the optimistic assumptions as in [16] and ignore all fixed call sites (defined in Section 2) in Tables 3 and 4 since they can all be resolved statically.

Table 2. Java Applications

Benchmark	Classes	Methods	Fields				
			Total	Inaccessible		Final	
				Static	Instance	Static	Instance
compress	2059	21563	5245	730	1647	1865	491
jess	2201	22226	5314	732	1699	1862	488
db	2051	21563	5229	727	1634	1862	488
javac	2225	22764	5491	730	1799	1928	488
mpegaudio	2104	21896	5364	770	1724	1896	488
mtrt	2073	21699	5265	728	1669	1862	488
jack	2104	21844	5301	731	1666	1864	490
jbb	2158	22677	5736	913	1888	1989	491
jlex	652	6345	1571	325	662	492	142
jtar	2132	22092	5560	911	1746	2035	495
jtb	785	7926	2012	361	723	540	141
soot	2459	20062	3842	374	2290	644	491
total	23003	232657	55930	8032	19147	18839	5181

Table 3. Benefits from exploiting field access and modification modifiers

Benchmark	Points-to sets				Objects			Non-fixed call sites			
	Total	Complete			Total	Completely detectable		Total	Complete		
		EA	CA0	CA		CA0	CA		EA	CA0	CA
compress	205	4	46	106	24	5	23	11	3	3	3
jess	4685	152	1176	1679	458	37	78	677	23	92	235
db	353	29	91	164	23	8	13	140	36	38	84
javac	9437	123	1604	2045	808	44	109	1932	40	143	288
mpegaudio	2876	4	1435	2404	1040	1	1013	37	0	0	3
mtrt	1330	75	284	516	128	22	35	868	118	156	195
jack	2848	49	938	1469	218	16	41	851	13	98	498
jbb	10222	522	2341	3389	577	166	266	2521	152	222	629
jlex	2532	1633	2038	2169	184	77	91	553	452	484	486
jtar	3123	273	1177	1770	272	45	73	483	66	197	303
jtb	11780	176	2888	3192	820	25	77	2676	253	609	772
soot	81762	2501	13011	21369	5631	484	1080	25987	1080	2313	6176
total	131153	5541	27029	40272	10183	930	2899	36736	2236	4355	9672

shown in Table 2, a benchmark typically has a significant number of fields that are inaccessible by the unknown code and/or that embrace the `final` modifier. Taking advantage of their existence has resulted in more accurate analysis. Compared to CA0, CA has found 49.0% more complete points-to sets, 122.1% more complete call sites and 211.7% more detectable objects overall.

In EA, all the field modifiers are ignored. CA0 performs better than EA mainly due to the fact that CA0 distinguishes completely from incompletely detectable objects while EA does not. As a result, CA0 has succeeded in classifying many non-extant references as complete references. The exploitation of

Table 4. A comparison of analysis techniques in determining mono call sites

Benchmark	EA	CA0	CA		
				Increase over EA(%)	Increase over CA0 (%)
compress	3	3	3	0.0	0.0
jess	23	92	235	921.7	155.4
db	36	38	83	130.6	118.4
javac	40	143	243	507.5	69.9
mpegaudio	0	0	3	*n/a*	*n/a*
mtrt	118	156	195	65.3	25.0
jack	10	95	489	4790.0	414.7
jbb	152	220	623	309.9	183.2
jlex	452	484	484	7.1	0.0
jtar	66	197	303	359.1	53.8
jtb	253	609	772	205.1	26.8
soot	1080	2295	5928	448.9	158.3
total	2233	4332	9361	319.2	116.1

the `final` modifier in Rule S4 contributes about 4.0% and 0.1% to the improved precisions of CA0 in determining complete points-to sets and call sites, respectively. The concept of object detectability has other applications. For example, it has helped us in developing an interprocedural side-effect analysis for incomplete programs, which cannot be discussed here due to the space limitation.

The knowledge about whether a call site is complete or not can be exploited in a number of ways. A complete call site is a call site whose targets are guaranteed to be in the analysed program. Some compiler optimisations can be applied to complete call sites. A complete call site that has a unique target can be devirtualised or inlined without any test (Section 4.3). In addition, some complete call sites such as `invokeinterface` can be virtualised or annotated to eliminate unnecessary dynamic type checks associated with them.

4.3 Mono Call Sites

A call site is a *mono* call site if it has a unique target method. These call sites can be devirtualised or inlined safely without any runtime tests. Table 4 compares CA, CA0 and EA in detecting the mono call sites from among the set of the non-fixed call sites in the application part of each benchmark. CA has detected significantly more mono call sites than CA0 and EA. CA improves EA by 319.2% overall. By exploiting the field modifiers, CA performs as well as CA0 in `compress` and `jlex` and outperforms CA0 in all the remaining benchmarks, resulting in a total increase of 116.1% in analysis precision.

4.4 Analysis Costs

Our experiments are conducted on a 2.4GHz Intel Xeon PC with 2GB memory. Figure 2 gives both the time and memory overheads of the points-to analysis and completeness analysis combined relative to the points-to analysis alone. The

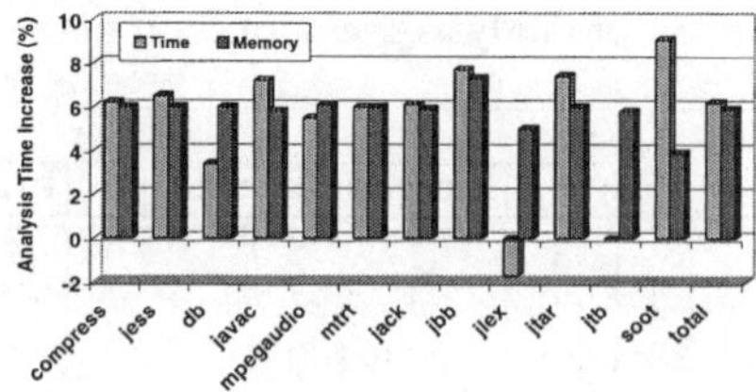

Fig. 2. Analysis costs of completeness analysis relative to the points-to analysis alone

analysis time for `jlex` has decreased slightly and that for `jtb` remains unchanged. The analysis times for the remaining benchmarks range from 3.4% (for `db`) to 9.1% (for `soot`). The overall time increase for all the benchmarks is 6.2%. Due to Rule C6, the number of iterations required for constructing some point-set sets can be reduced. The memory overheads for all the benchmarks are small, ranging from 3.9% and 7.3%. The overall memory increase is only 5.9%.

5 Related Work

Many points-to analysis techniques exist for object-oriented programs but there is little work done when these programs are incomplete. However, points-to analysis for incomplete programs in imperative languages has been studied [7, 15].

Rountev et al. [14] study points-to analysis for incomplete Java programs in order to detect receiver types. Their approach works by creating *placeholders* that serve as representatives for unknown code. A limitation of this work is that dynamic class loading is not permitted. Chatterjee et al. [3] present a points-to analysis for library modules in order to find def-use relations. The analysis evaluates a parameterised points-to solution for each method and propagates conservative assumptions about the clients of the library in a top-down manner. A limitation of this approach is that it does not examine the effects of threads.

Extant analysis [16] is designed for the purposes of specialising Java programs in the presence of dynamic class loading. The technique partitions the references of a program into two categories: *(unconditionally) extant references* when they only point to the objects whose runtime types are in the analysed program and *conditionally extant (i.e., non-extant) references* otherwise. Our experimental results show that our completeness analysis yields more precise information about the completeness of points-to sets and call sites.

Escape analysis [2, 4, 20, 21] detects the objects that never escape out of a method or thread. An object escapes a method if its lifetime may exceed the lifetime of that method. An object that does not escape a method can be possibly allocated on the method's stack frame. If an object does not escape a thread, no other threads can access the object. The synchronisation operations associated with the object can be eliminated. For these reasons, if o is an escaped object, so will the objects pointed to by $o.f$. This facilitates the above two optimisations. However, in completeness analysis, if o is incompletely detectable, the objects pointed to by $o.f$ may be completely or incompletely detectable. Therefore, an incompletely detectable object is an escaped object but the converse is not true. So our object detectability analysis is different from escape analysis.

Some dynamic points-to analysis techniques for Java [8, 10, 12] restrict themselves only to the classes loaded during program execution. They do not determine the completeness of points-to sets. As a result, the analysis and optimisation techniques that make use of the points-to information may require runtime invalidation and recompilation mechanisms, which can hurt performance.

None of these above approaches exploit the access and modification properties of fields when computing points-to sets. These properties are, however, exploited in other kinds of analyses. Immutability analysis [11] is a technique for detecting mutability of fields and classes in a Java program. Field analysis [6] exploits the declared access restrictions placed on fields in order to determine such useful properties of these fields as `exact_type`, `nonnull`, `may_leak` and `only_init`.

6 Conclusion

In this paper, we describe a framework for points-to analysis and optimisation for incomplete object-oriented programs. As an analysed program is incomplete, some of its points-to sets and call sites may be incomplete. We present an completeness analysis technique combined with a whole-program points-to analysis to determine which points-to sets (call sites) may be incomplete in the sense that their pointed-to objects (target methods) are not statically resolvable. We introduce the notion of object detectability and show how such an information can be obtained as part of the completeness analysis. To the best of our knowledge, this is the first work that exploits the field access and modification properties in performing completeness analysis for incomplete object-oriented Java programs. We demonstrate by experiments that such an exploitation leads to better analysis precision. Our approach is compositional, which enables better points-to sets to be computed than those obtained when the points-to analysis is applied alone.

In this paper, completeness analysis is combined with a flow- and context-insensitive points-to analysis. One future work is to extend our approach to accommodate other kinds of points-to analyses. Another future work is to exploit type-based alias analysis to improve the precision of the results.

References

1. Lars Ole Andersen. *Program Analysis and Specialization for the C Programming Language.* PhD thesis, DIKU, University of Copenhagen, May 1994.
2. Bruno Blanchet. Escape analysis: Correctness proof, implementation and experimental results. In *25th Annual ACM Symposium on Principles of Programming Languages*, pages 25–37, January 1998.
3. Ramkrishna Chatterjee and Barbara G.Ryder. Data-flow-based testing of object-oriented libraries. Technical Report 433, Rutgers University, 2001.
4. Jong-Deok Choi, Manish Gupta, Mauricio J. Serrano, Vugranam C. Sreedhar, and Samuel P. Midkiff. Escape analysis for Java. In *14th ACM SIGPLAN Conference on Object-Oriented Programming, Systems, Languages and Applications*, pages 1–19, November 1999.

5. Jeffrey Dean, David Grove, and Craig Chamber. Optimization of object-oriented programs using static class hierarchy analysis. In *5th European Conference on Object-Oriented Programming*, volume 952, pages 77–101. Springer, Aug. 1995.
6. Sanjay Ghemawat, Keith H. Randall, and Daniel J. Scales. Field analysis: Getting useful and low-cost interprocedural information. In *ACM SIGPLAN '00 Conference on Programming Language Design and Implementation*, June 2000.
7. Mary Jean Harrold and Gregg Rothermel. Separate computation of alias information for reuse. *IEEE Transaction on Software Engineering*, 22(7):442–460, 1996.
8. Martin Hirzel, Amer Diwan, and Michael Hind. Pointer analysis in the presence of dynamic class loading. In *18th European Conference on Object-Oriented Programming*, June 2004.
9. Ondřej Lhoták and Laurie Hendren. Scaling Java points-to analysis using Spark. In *12th International Conference on Compiler Construction*, volume 2622 of *LNCS*, pages 153–169, Warsaw, Poland, April 2003. Springer.
10. Igor Pechtchanski and Vivek Sarkar. Dynamic optimistic interprocedural analysis: a framework and an application. In *16th ACM SIGPLAN Conference on Object-Oriented Programming, Systems, Languages and Applications*, October 2001.
11. S. Porat, M. Biberstein, L. Koved, and B. Mendelson. Automatic detection of immutable fields in Java. In *Proceedings of CASCON 2000*, 2000.
12. Feng Qian and Laurie Hendren. Towards dynamic interprocedural analysis in JVMs. In *3rd ACM SIGPLAN Symposium on Virtual Machine Research and Technology*, May 2004.
13. Atanas Rountev, Ana Milanova, and Barbara G. Ryder. Points-to analysis for Java based on annotated constraints. Technical Report DCS-TR-424, Rutgers University, November 2000.
14. Atanas Rountev, Ana Milanova, and Barbara G. Ryder. Fragment class analysis for testing of polymorphism in java software. In *25th International Conference on Software Engineering*, May 2003.
15. Atanas Rountev and Barbare G. Ryder. Practical points-to analysis for programs built with libraries. Technical Report 410, Rutgers University, February 2000.
16. Vugranam C. Sreedhar, Michael Burke, and Jong-Deok Choi. A framework for interprocedural optimization in the presence of dynamic class loading. In *ACM SIGPLAN '00 Conference on Programming Language Design and Implementation*, pages 196–207, June 2000.
17. M. Streckenbach and G. Snelting. Points-to for Java: A general framework and an empirical comparison. Technical report, University Passau, November 2000.
18. Sun Microsystems. Java 2 software development kit version 1.2.2, July 1999.
19. Raja Vallée-Rai, Laurie Hendren, Vijay Sundaresan, Patrick Lam, Etienne Gagnon, and Phong Co. Soot: a java optimization framework. `http://www.sable.mcgill.ca/soot`, 1999.
20. Frédéric Vivien and Martin C. Rinard. Incrementalized pointer and escape analysis. In *ACM SIGPLAN '01 Conference on Programming Language Design and Implementation*, pages 35–46, June 2001.
21. John Whaley and Martin Rinard. Compositional pointer and escape analysis for Java programs. In *14th ACM SIGPLAN Conference on Object-Oriented Programming, Systems, Languages and Applications*, pages 187–206, November 1999.
22. Ayal Zaks, Vitaly Feldman, and Nava Aizikowitz. Sealed calls in Java packages. In *15th ACM SIGPLAN Conference on Object-Oriented Programming, Systems, Languages and Applications*, October 2000.

Using Inter-Procedural Side-Effect Information in JIT Optimizations*

Anatole Le, Ondřej Lhoták, and Laurie Hendren

Sable Research Group, McGill University, Montreal, Canada
{ale44,olhotak,hendren}@sable.mcgill.ca

Abstract. Inter-procedural analyses such as side-effect analysis can provide information useful for performing aggressive optimizations. We present a study of whether side-effect information improves performance in just-in-time (JIT) compilers, and if so, what level of analysis precision is needed.

We used SPARK, the inter-procedural analysis component of the SOOT Java analysis and optimization framework, to compute side-effect information and encode it in class files. We modified Jikes RVM, a research JIT, to make use of side-effect analysis in local common sub-expression elimination, heap SSA, redundant load elimination and loop-invariant code motion. On the SpecJVM98 benchmarks, we measured the static number of memory operations removed, the dynamic counts of memory reads eliminated, and the execution time.

Our results show that the use of side-effect analysis increases the number of static opportunities for load elimination by up to 98%, and reduces dynamic field read instructions by up to 27%. Side-effect information enabled speedups in the range of 1.08x to 1.20x for some benchmarks. Finally, among the different levels of precision of side-effect information, a simple side-effect analysis is usually sufficient to obtain most of these speedups.

1 Introduction

Over the past several years, just-in-time (JIT) compilers have enabled impressive improvements in the execution of Java code, mainly through local and intra-procedural optimizations, speculative inter-procedural optimizations, and efficient implementation techniques. However, JITs do not generally make use of whole-program analysis information, such as conservative call graphs, points-to information, or side-effect information, because it is too costly to compute it each time a program is executed. However, all non-trivial data types in Java are objects always accessed through indirect references (pointers), so one would expect optimizations using side-effect information to enable significant further improvements in performance of Java programs.

The purpose of the study presented in this paper is to answer two key questions. First, is side-effect information useful for the optimizations performed in a modern JIT, and can it significantly improve performance? Second, what level of precision of the side-effect information and the underlying analyses used to compute it is required to obtain these performance improvements?

* This work was supported, in part, by NSERC and FQRNT.

R. Bodik (Ed.): CC 2005, LNCS 3443, pp. 287–304, 2005.

To study these questions, we implemented a system consisting of an ahead-of-time inter-procedural side-effect analysis, whose result is communicated to a modified JIT containing optimizations that we adapted to take advantage of the side-effect information.

We implemented the side-effect analyses using the SPARK [16, 15] points-to analysis framework, a part of the SOOT [29] bytecode analysis, optimization, and annotation framework. The side-effect analysis makes use of points-to and call graph information computed by SPARK. The resulting side-effect information is encoded in class file attributes for use by the JIT using the annotation framework [21] included in SOOT.

We chose Jikes RVM [2] as the JIT for our study, and made several modifications to it. First, we added code to read in the side-effect information produced in our analysis. We then modified several analyses and optimizations to take advantage of the information, including local common subexpression elimination, heap array SSA construction, redundant load elimination, and loop-invariant code motion. Finally, we instrumented Jikes RVM both to count the static opportunities for performing optimizations, and to insert instrumentation code to measure the dynamic effects of the improved optimizations.

The contributions of this paper are the following:

- This is the first published presentation of the side-effect analysis that we have implemented in SOOT using points-to and call graph information computed by SPARK.
- To our knowledge, this is the first study of the run-time performance improvements obtainable by taking advantage of side-effect information in a range of optimizations in a Java JIT.
- We present empirical evidence that the availability of side-effect information in a Java JIT can enable significant performance improvements of up to 20%.
- We show that although precise analyses provide significantly more optimization opportunities when counted statically, most of the dynamic improvement is obtainable even with relatively simple, imprecise analyses. In particular, a side-effect analysis based on a call graph constructed using an inexpensive Class Hierarchy Analysis (CHA) already provides a very significant improvement over not having any side-effect information at all. This confirms what has been observed on other languages such as Modula-3 and C.

The remainder of this paper is organized as follows. Section 2 is devoted to our side-effect analysis in SOOT, the call graph and points-to analyses that it depends on, issues with encoding its result in class file attributes, and the precision variations with which we experimented. In Section 3, we describe how we modified the optimizations in Jikes RVM to take advantage of side-effect information. In Section 4, we present the benchmarks that we used, our experiments, and our empirical results. We discuss related work in Section 5, and we conclude with Section 6.

2 Side-Effect Analysis in Soot

We implemented side-effect analysis in SOOT [29], a framework for analyzing, optimizing, and annotating Java bytecode. The side-effect analysis depends on two other inter-procedural analyses, call graph construction and points-to analysis. We describe how we construct a call graph in Section 2.1. An important difference from most other work on call graph construction is that to obtain a conservative side-effect analysis, we need to ensure that our call graph includes all methods invoked, including those invoked implicitly by the Java VM. In Section 2.2, we briefly explain the output of SPARK, our points-to analysis framework [16, 15]. Section 2.3 explains how we put the information from these two analyses together and produce side-effect information. In Section 2.4, we briefly note some issues with encoding the side-effect analysis results in class file attributes to communicate them to the JIT. Finally, in Section 2.5, we describe how variations in the precision of the call graph and points-to analyses affect the side-effect information.

2.1 Call Graph Construction

To perform an inter-procedural analysis on a Java program, information about the possible targets of method calls is required. This information is approximated by a call graph, which maps each statement s to a set $cg(s)$ containing every method that may be called from s. Constructing a call graph for a Java program is complicated by the fact that most calls in Java are virtual, so the target method of the call depends on the run-time type of the receiver object.

In our study, we compared two different methods of computing call graphs. First, we computed call graphs using Class Hierarchy Analysis (CHA) [8], an inexpensive method which considers only the static type of each receiver object, and does not require any inter-procedural analysis. Second, we used a points-to analysis (discussed in the next section) to compute the run-time types of the objects that the receiver of each call site could point to, and we determined the target method that would be invoked for each run-time receiver type.

Several important, but subtle, details of the Java virtual machine (VM) complicate the construction of a conservative call graph suitable for side-effect analysis. In a Java program, methods may be invoked not only due to explicit invoke instructions, but also implicitly due to various events in the VM. Whenever a new class is first used, the VM implicitly calls its static initialization method. The set of events that may cause a static initialization method to be called is specified in [17, section 2.17.4]. In our analysis, we assume that any of these events could cause the corresponding static initialization method to be invoked. Each static initialization method is executed at most once in a given run of a Java program. Therefore, we use an intra-procedural flow-sensitive analysis to eliminate spurious calls to static initialization methods which must have already been called on every path from the beginning of the method. In addition, the standard class library often invokes methods using the `doPrivileged` methods of `java.security.AccessController`. Our analysis models these with calls of the `run` method of the argument passed to `doPrivileged`. Methods may also be invoked using reflection. In general, it is not possible to determine statically which methods will be invoked reflectively, and our analysis only issues a warning if it finds a reachable call to one of the reflection methods. However, calls to the `newInstance` method of `java.lang.Class` are so common that they merit special treatment. This method creates a new object and calls its constructor. In our analysis, we conservatively assume that any object could be created, and therefore any constructor with no parameters could be invoked.

To partially verify the correctness of the computed call graph, we instrumented the code to ensure that all methods that are executed at run time were included in the call graph and reachable from the entry points. To do this, we computed the set of methods that are not reachable from the entry points through the call graph, and modified them to abort the execution of the benchmark if they do get invoked at run time. Although this does not prove that every possible run-time call edge is included in the computed call graph, it does guarantee that every executed method is considered in call graph construction. To further check that our overall optimizations were conservative on the benchmarks studied, we verified that the benchmarks produced identical output in all configurations, including with the optimizations disabled.

2.2 Points-to Analysis

We use the SPARK [16, 15] points-to analysis framework to compute points-to information. For each *pointer p* in the program, it computes a set $pt(p)$ of *objects* to which it may point. The most common kind of *pointer* is a local variable of reference type in the Jimple representation of the code. Local variables appear in field read and write instructions as pointers to the object whose field is to be read or written, and in method invocation instructions as the receiver of the method call, which determines the method to be invoked. In addition, *pointers* are introduced to represent method arguments and return values, static fields, and special values needed in simulating the effects on pointers of native methods in the standard class library. Typically, an *object* is an allocation site; we model all run-time objects created at a given allocation site as a single entity. In addition, we must include special *objects* for run-time objects without an allocation site, such as objects created by the VM (the argument array to the main method, the main thread, the default class loader) and objects created using reflection. For some of these special *objects*, we may not know the exact run-time type. Therefore, we conservatively assume that their run-time type may be any subtype of their declared type.

SPARK performs a flow-insensitive, context-insensitive, subset-based points-to analysis by propagating *objects* from their allocation sites through all *pointers* through which they may flow. SPARK has many parameters for experimenting with variations of the analysis that affect analysis efficiency and precision. In this study, we experimented with four points-to analysis variations. We explain the variations in more detail in Section 2.5.

2.3 Side-Effect Analysis

The side-effect analysis consists of two steps, which are discussed in this section. First, we compute a read and write set for each statement. Second, we use the read and write sets to compute dependencies between all pairs of statements within each method.

For each statement s, we compute sets $read(s)$ and $write(s)$ containing every static field sf read (written) by s, and a pair (o, f) for every field f of *object* o that may be read (written) by s. These sets also include fields read (written) by all code executed during execution of s, including any other methods that may be called, directly or transitively. The read and write sets are computed in two steps. In the first step, we compute only the direct read and write sets for each statement in the program, ignoring any code that may be called from the statement. The result of the points-to analysis is used to determine the possible objects being pointed to by the pointer in each field read or write instruction. In the second step, we continually aggregate the read and write sets of each method and propagate them to all call sites of the method, until a fixed-point is reached. During the propagation, the call graph is used to determine the call sites of each method.

Once the read and write sets for all statements have been computed, for each method, we compute an interference relation between all the read and write sets in the method. Two sets interfere if they have a non-empty intersection. From the interference relation on read and write sets, we construct four dependence relations between statements (read-read dependence, read-write dependence, write-read dependence, write-write dependence). For example, there is a read-write dependence between statements s_1 and s_2 if the read set of s_1 and the write set of s_2 interfere. It is the dependences between statements that we encode in class files for the JIT to use in performing optimizations.

2.4 Encoding Side-Effects in Class File Attributes

All of the analyses described in the preceding sections are performed on Jimple, the three-address intermediate representation (IR) used in SOOT. In order to communicate the analysis results to a JIT, we must convert them to refer to bytecode instructions during the translation of Jimple to bytecode. SOOT includes a universal tagging framework [21] that propagates analysis information through its various IRs, and encodes it in class file attributes. An important complication in this process is that one Jimple statement may be converted to multiple bytecode instructions. However, Jimple is low-level enough that whenever a Jimple instruction has side-effects, exactly one of the bytecode instructions generated for it has those side-effects. Therefore, for each type of Jimple instruction, we identify the relevant bytecode instruction to the tagging framework, and it attaches the side-effect information to that instruction.

Another complication in communicating the side-effect information is that some methods have a large number of statements with side-effects. Since the dependence relations may have size quadratic in the number of instructions with side-effects, a naive encoding of the dependence relations is sometimes unacceptably large. However, we have observed in those cases, many of the read and write sets in the method are identical. Therefore, we add a level of indirection. Instead of expressing the dependence relations in terms of statements, we enumerate all distinct read and write sets, and express the dependence relations between those sets. For each statement, we indicate which set it reads and writes. The resulting encoding has size $\Theta(m^2+n)$, where n is the number of statements, and m is the number of unique sets. In an earlier study [15, Sections 6.2.2 and 6.2.6], we observed that this encoding limits the annotation size to acceptable levels.

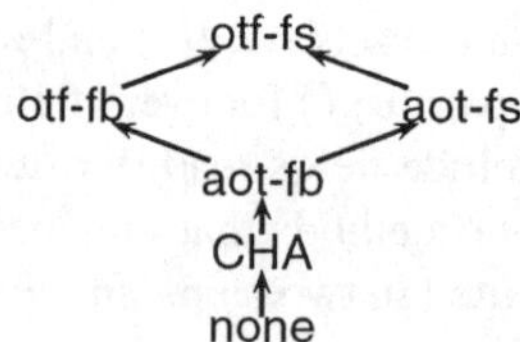

Fig. 1. Relative Precision of Analysis Variations

2.5 Analysis Variations

In this section, we briefly explain the differences between the analysis variations that we compare in our empirical study in Section 4. Figure 1 gives an overview of the relative precision of the variations, with precision increasing from bottom to top.

For the first variation, none, we compute no side-effect information at all, and rely only on the internal analysis in the Jikes RVM JIT for optimizations. This means that any method call in the code is conservatively assumed to read and write anything in the heap.

Our second variation, CHA, is to compute side-effects using a call graph, but without performing any points-to analysis. We construct the call graph using CHA, as described in Section 2.1. In this case, the side-effect information contains a list of all fields possibly read and written at each call site; the JIT takes advantage of the knowledge that no other fields will be accessed. However, this analysis does not distinguish between the same field of different objects.

The remaining variations all take advantage of points-to information of different levels of precision to distinguish different objects. We describe these differences only briefly, because although they do affect the analysis precision measured statically, we found their effect on the dynamic behaviour of real benchmarks to be negligible.

In a field-based analysis (fb), a single points-to set is used for each field regardless of which object it is a field of. On the other hand, a field-sensitive analysis (fs) computes a separate points-to set for each pair (*object*, *field*). Therefore, if an *object* is written to `b1.a` and a different *object* is written to `b2.a`, and if `b1` and `b2` are known to not be aliases, then a field-sensitive analysis determines that `b1.a` and `b2.a` point to different *objects*. In contrast, a field-based analysis does not make this distinction because it considers only the field `a`, and ignores the *objects* (`b1` and `b2`).

To propagate points-to sets inter-procedurally, a points-to analysis requires an approximation of the call graph, but we use the points-to information to build the call graph. We resolve this circular dependency by either building an imprecise initial CHA call graph only for the use of the points-to analysis (aot), or by constructing the call graph on-the-fly as the points-to analysis proceeds (otf): as points-to sets grow, we add edges to the call graph.

3 Optimizations Enabled in Jikes RVM

The JIT compiler that we modified to make use of side-effect information is the Jikes Research Virtual Machine (RVM) [2]. Jikes RVM is an open source research platform for executing Java bytecode. It includes three levels of JIT optimizations (0, 1 and 2).

We adapted three optimizations in Jikes RVM to make use of side-effect information: local common sub-expression elimination (CSE), redundant load elimination (RLE) and loop-invariant code motion (LICM). Sections 3.1 to 3.3 describe each of these optimizations and the changes that we made. Because side-effect information refers to the original bytecode of a method, bytecodes that come from an inlined method need to be treated specially. Section 3.4 describes how we dealt with this case.

3.1 Local Common Sub-expression Elimination

The first optimization in Jikes RVM that we modified to make use of side-effect information is local CSE. This optimization is only performed within a basic block. The algorithm for performing CSE on fields is described in Figure 2(a). A cache is used to store the available field expressions. The algorithm iterates over all instructions in a basic block, and processes them. There are two parts in this process. The first is to try to replace each *getfield* or *getstatic* instruction encountered by an available expression. If one is available, it is assigned to a temporary variable and the *getfield* or *getstatic* instruction is replaced by a copy of the temporary. If none is available, a field expression is added to the cache for the *getfield* or *getstatic* instruction. For every *putfield* and *putstatic* instruction, an associated field expression is also added to the cache. The second part is to update the cache according to which expressions the current instruction kills. A call or synchronization instruction kills all expressions in the cache. A *putfield* or *putstatic* of some field X will remove any expression in the cache associated with field X.

In this algorithm, we used side-effect information to reduce the set of expressions killed (lines 13 and 15 in Figure 2(a)). When the current instruction is a field store

(a)

```
 1: for each basic block bb do
 2:    cache = createNewEmptyCache();
 3:    for each instruction s in bb do
 4:       if isVolatileFieldLoadOrStore( s ) then
 5:          continue
 6:       if isGetField( s ) or isGetStatic( s ) then
 7:          if cache.availableExpression( s ) then
 8:             T = findOrCreateTemporary( expression( s ) )
 9:             replace s by copyTemporaryInstruction( T )
10:          else
11:             add expression( s ) to cache
12:       else if isPutField( s ) or isPutStatic( s ) then
13:          add expression( s ) to cache
14:       if isPutField( s ) or isPutStatic( s ) of field X then
15:          remove all expressions with field X from cache
            (excluding expression( s ))
16:       else if s is a call or synchronization then
17:          remove all expressions from cache
```

(b)

```
A obj1 = new A();
A obj2 = new A();
i = obj1.x;
obj2.x = 10;
nothing();
j = obj1.x;
```

Fig. 2. Local common sub-expression (a) original algorithm (b) example

or a call, we only remove from the cache entries that have a read-write or write-write dependence with the current instruction in the side-effect analysis.

An example is shown in Figure 2(b). Without side-effect information, the compiler would conservatively assume that statement `obj2.x = 10` could write to memory location `obj1.x` and that the call to `nothing()` could write to any memory locations. In contrast, the side-effect analysis would specify that there is no dependence between these instructions, and thus enable the replacement of the load of `obj1.x` on line 6 by an available expression (line 3).

3.2 Redundant Load Elimination

The redundant load elimination algorithm relies on extended Array SSA (also known as Heap Array SSA or Heap SSA) [10] and Global Value Numbering [3]. We explain the general idea of the algorithm below. For a detailed description, please refer to [10].

The algorithm transforms the IR into heap SSA form. A heap array is created for each object field. The object reference is used as the index into this heap array. For example, line 2 of Figure 3(a) would be represented as "heap array X[`a`] = 2" meaning that a store is performed in heap array X at index `a` (the object reference).

After the transformation to heap SSA form is completed, global value numbers are computed. The global value numbering computes definitely-different (*DD*) and definitely-same (*DS*) relations for object references. The *DD* relation distinguishes two object references coming from different allocation sites, or when one is a method parameter and the other one is the result of a new statement. The *DS* relation returns true when two object references have the same value number (one is a copy of the other).

Once global value numbers are computed, index propagation is performed. The index propagation solution holds the available indices into heap arrays at each use of a heap array. Scalar replacement is performed using the sets of available indices. Note that in the algorithm, these sets actually contain value numbers of available indices. For simplicity, we consider sets of available indices.

For increasing the number of opportunities for load elimination, we used side-effect information during the heap SSA transformation and in the *DD* relation. During the heap SSA construction, without side-effect information, each call instruction is annotated with a definition and a use of every heap array. With side-effect information we annotate a call with a definition of a heap array, say X, only if there is a write-read or write-write dependence between the call and the instruction using heap array X. Similarly we annotate a call with a use of a heap array if there is a read-read or read-write dependence. We also use side-effect information when the *DD* relation returns false. Two instructions having no data dependence is equivalent to *DD*(`a`, `b`) = true, where `a` and `b` are the object references used in the instructions.

In Figure 3(a), without side-effect information, since `a` and `b` are method parameters, *DD*(`a`, `b`) = false. Thus, only {`b`} is available after line 3. This allows the load of `b.x` on line 9 to be eliminated. Since it is conservatively assumed that calls can write to any memory location, the available index set after `nothing()` on line 10 is the empty set. Line 12 represents a merge point of the available index sets after line 7 and 10. The intersection of these two sets is the empty set. After the load of `a.x` on line 14, {`a`} is available. Since *DS*(`a`, `b`) = false, the load of `b.x` on line 15 cannot be eliminated.

(a)

```
1  int foo( A a, A b, int n ) {
2    a.x = 2;
3    b.x = 3;
4
5    int i;
6    if( n > 0 ) {
7      i = a.x;
8    } else {
9      i = b.x;
10     nothing();
11   }
12   // Merging point: a phi is
13   // placed here in heap SSA
14   int j = a.x;
15   int k = b.x;
16   return i + j + k;
17 }
18
19 public static void
20     main( String[] args ) {
21   foo( new A(), new A(), 1 );
22 }
```

(b)

```
int foo( A a, A b, int n ) {
  t1 = 2;
  a.x = t1;
  t2 = 3;
  b.x = t2;

  int i;
  if( n > 0 ) {
    i = t1;
  } else {
    i = t2;
    nothing();
  }
  // Merging point: a phi is
  // placed here in heap SSA
  int j = t1;
  int k = t2;
  return i + j + k;
}

public static void
    main( String[] args ) {
  foo( new A(), new A(), 1 );
}
```

Fig. 3. Redundant load elimination example (a) before (b) after

Using side-effect analysis, since `a.x` has no dependence with `b.x` (line 2 and 3) the available index set after line 3 is {`a`, `b`}. Thus, loads of `a.x` and `b.x` on line 7 and 9 can be eliminated. The available index set after line 7 is {`a`, `b`}, and after line 10, it is also {`a`, `b`}, since `nothing()` has no side-effect. The intersection at the merge point (line 12) results in the set {`a`, `b`}. The load of `a.x` can then be removed on line 14. The available index set after line 14 is {`a`, `b`}, allowing load elimination of `b.x` on line 15. The resulting code after performing load elimination is shown in Figure 3(b).

3.3 Loop-Invariant Code Motion

The LICM algorithm in Jikes RVM is an implementation of the Global Code Motion algorithm introduced by Click [7] and is adapted to handle memory operations. As such, it requires the IR to be in heap SSA form. We provide the basic idea of the algorithm below. For more details, see [7].

The algorithm schedules each intruction early, i.e. finds the earliest legal basic block that an instruction could be moved to (all of the instruction's inputs must dominate this basic block). Similarly, it finds the latest legal basic block for each instruction (this block must dominate all uses of the instruction's result). Instructions such as `phi`, `branch` or `return` cannot be moved due to control dependences. Between the earliest and latest legal basic blocks, the heuristic is to place instructions in the basic block with the smallest loop depth. Global Code Motion differs from standard loop-invariant code motion techniques in that it moves instructions after, as well as before, loops.

In Figure 4(a), the compiler first transforms the code into heap SSA form and without side-effect information assumes that method `nothing()` can read and write any memory location. As a result, the compiler will be unable to move the loads of

(a)

```
do {
  i = i + a.x;
  j = i + a.y;
  nothing();
} while( i < n );
```

(b)

```
t = a.x;
do {
  i = i + t;
  nothing();
} while( i < n );
j = i + a.y;
```

Fig. 4. Loop-invariant code motion example (a) before (b) after

(a)

```
Offset  main() {
0 main    b0
1 main    invoke foo
        }
        foo() {
0 foo     b1
1 foo     invoke bar
        }
        bar() {
0 bar     b2
1 bar     b3
        }
```

(b)

```
Offset
            main() {
0 main        b0
0 foo         b1
0 bar         b2
1 bar         b3
            }
```

Fig. 5. Inlining example (a) before (b) after

`a.x` and `a.y` outside of the loop. With side-effect information, knowing that method `nothing()` does not read or write to `a.x` or `a.y`, the loads of `a.x` and `a.y` will be moved before and after the loop respectively, resulting in the code in Figure 4(b).

3.4 Using Side-Effect Information for Inlined Bytecode

The side-effect attribute provides information about data dependences between instructions and refers to a bytecode by using its offset. Since the side-effect analysis is computed ahead-of-time, and thus is not aware of the JIT inlining decisions, the side-effect attribute does not have entries for inlined bytecodes. In Figure 5(a), let's assume that calls to `foo()` and `bar()` are inlined, resulting in the code in Figure 5(b). Since an inlined bytecode is associated with its original offset in the IR, it is, in general, incorrect to retrieve side-effect information for an inlined bytecode in the current method. For example, in the side-effect attribute of method `main()` in Figure 5(b), information about offset `0` is associated with bytecode `b0`, not `b1` or `b2`, which are from other methods.

To handle this case, we keep track of inlining sequences for each instruction. When comparing two bytecodes, we retrieve the least common method ancestor of the two bytecode inlining sequences, and use the side-effect information associated with that method. If a bytecode originally comes from that common method, we use its offset. Otherwise, we retrieve the *invoke* bytecode that it comes from in the common method, and use the offset associated with this *invoke* bytecode.

For example, in Figure 5(b), the least common method ancestor for bytecodes `b0` and `b1` is `main()`. Since `b0` originally comes from `main()`, we use its offset (i.e. 0). Since `b1` was not originally part of `main()`, we retrieve the *invoke* bytecode that it comes from in `main()`, i.e. *invoke* `foo`. We then use the offset associated with this *invoke* bytecode (i.e. `1`). Thus, when inquiring about data dependences between bytecodes `b0` and `b1`, we lookup information for offsets `0` and `1` in the side-effect attribute for method `main()`. Similarly, for bytecodes `b1` and `b2` we lookup offsets `0` and `1` in the side-effect attribute of method `foo()` (same result for `b1` and `b3`). For bytecodes `b2` and `b3`, we lookup offsets `0` and `1` in the side-effect attribute of `bar()`.

4 Experiments

4.1 Environment and Benchmarks

We modified Jikes RVM version 2.3.0.1 to use side-effect information in the optimizations described in the previous section. We used the production configuration (namely FastAdaptiveCopyMS) in Jikes RVM with the JIT-only option (every method is compiled on first invocation and no recompilation occurs thereafter). We ran the SpecJVM98 [1] benchmarks (size 100) with Jikes RVM at optimization level 1 and 2 using the six side-effect variations described in section 2. A description of the benchmarks is given in Table 1. For each benchmark and at each optimization level, we show the number of memory reads per second performed (load density). This shows how important memory operations are in each benchmark. We expect the benchmarks with high load densities, compress, raytrace, mtrt and mpegaudio, to benefit most from side-effect analysis. We computed side-effect information using the development version of SOOT, revision 1621.

Table 1. Benchmark description and load density property

Benchmark	Description	Load density 1000's	
		Level 1	Level 2
compress	Lempel-Ziv compressor/uncompressor	207383	138570
jess	A Java expert shell system based on NASA's CLIPS system	56371	68353
raytrace	Ray tracer application	106271	127806
db	Performs several database functions on a memory-resident database	7140	11776
javac	JDK 1.0.2 Java compiler	21645	19208
mpegaudio	MPEG-3 audio file compression application	82137	179070
mtrt	Dual-threaded version of raytrace	92599	122821
jack	A Java parser generator with lexical analyzers (now Java CC)	14632	15240

We ran our benchmarks on two different architectures to see whether we would get similar trends in our results. The first system that we used runs Linux Debian on an Intel Pentium 4 1.80GHz CPU with 512Mb of RAM. The second one also runs Linux Debian on an dual processor AMD Athlon MP 2000+ 1.66GHz CPU with 2Gb of RAM. For our experiment, Jikes RVM was configured to run on a single processor machine.

4.2 Results

Our primary goal for this study was to see whether side-effect information could improve performance in JITs, and if so, our secondary objective was to determine the level of precision of side-effect information required. To obtain accurate answers to these questions, we measured for each run the static number of loads removed in local CSE and in the redundant load elimination optimization, and the static number of instructions moved in the loop-invariant code motion phase. These numbers provide us details on how much improvement each optimization achieves statically using side-effect information. We also measured dynamic counts of memory load operations eliminated and execution times (best of four runs, not including compilation time). The architecture-independent dynamic counts help us see whether a direct correlation exists between a reduction in memory operations performed and speedups.

It should be noted that although we used the JIT-only option in Jikes RVM where no method recompilation is expected, some optimizations such as inlining can cause invalidation and recompilation. In this case, for our static numbers, we only counted the number of static loads eliminated (in local CSE or load elimination) or instructions moved (in LICM) in the last method compilation before execution.

To examine the effect of side-effect analysis in both local and global optimizations, we ran our benchmarks using Jikes RVM at optimization level 1 and 2. For level 1, only local CSE uses side-effect information. For level 2, local CSE, redundant load elimination and loop-invariant code motion use side-effect analysis. We present in the next two sections our results for level 1 and level 2 optimizations.

Optimization Level 1. Level 1 optimizations in Jikes RVM include standard optimizations such as local copy propagation, local constant propagation, local common sub-expression elimination, null check elimination, type propagation, constant folding, dead code elimination, inlining, etc. Among these, only local CSE uses our side-effect analysis for eliminating *getfield* and *getstatic* instructions.

When running our benchmarks with Jikes RVM at optimization level 1 (which also includes all level 0 optimizations), the use of the five side-effect variations (CHA, aot-

Table 2. Level 1 results

benchmark	side-effect	static counts getfield	static counts getstatic	dynamic counts getfield	dynamic counts getstatic	Intel time(s)	Intel speedup	AMD time(s)	AMD speedup
compress	none	108	1	1 871 398 009	33 418 641	9.215		9.185	
	any	112 (3.7 %)	2	1 871 397 929 (0.0 %)	33 418 641	9.395	0.98x	9.184	1.00x
jess	none	229	0	209 404 162	2 326 905	4.583		3.756	
	any	245 (7.0 %)	1	209 402 840 (0.0 %)	2 326 905	4.615	0.99x	3.77	1.00x
raytrace	none	166	0	287 993 152	1 359	4.276		2.71	
	any	188 (13.3 %)	1	287 979 508 (0.0 %)	1 359	4.198	1.02x	2.662	1.02x
db	none	130	0	160 088 294	96 012	22.023		22.434	
	any	133 (2.3 %)	3	160 087 709 (0.0 %)	96 012	22.054	1.00x	22.453	1.00x
javac	none	415	0	149 595 624	4 028 976	11.047		7.097	
	any	431 (3.9 %)	1	149 407 295 (0.1 %)	4 028 946	11.215	0.99x	7.177	0.99x
mpegaudio	none	340	174	456 136 442	52 215 347	8.874		6.189	
	any	347 (2.1 %)	176	455 026 631 (0.2 %)	52 215 346	8.219	1.08x	5.85	1.06x
mtrt	none	166	0	291 501 667	2 063	4.744		3.148	
	any	188 (13.3 %)	1	291 474 379 (0.0 %)	2 063	4.727	1.00x	3.087	1.02x
jack	none	470	1	50 029 731	1 534 965	6.095		3.524	
	any	663 (41.1 %)	2	49 579 043 (0.9 %)	1 534 977	6.108	1.00x	3.509	1.00x

fb, aot-fs, otf-fb and otf-fs) produced identical static and dynamic counts, and similar runtimes. To avoid repeating identical results, we grouped these five side-effect variations under the name any in the side-effect column of Table 2, and the time reported is the average execution times of runs using these five side-effect variations. The values in brackets denote the percentage increase in static opportunities or the percentage decrease in dynamic counts when compared with the none side-effect variation.

Table 2 shows that using side-effect information in local CSE increased the number of static opportunities for *getfield* elimination by 2% to 41%, but only resulted in a decrease of up to 0.9% dynamically (*getstatic* instructions are almost unaffected). As a result, most benchmarks have similar execution times with or without side-effect analysis. However, the use of side-effect information produced speedups of 1.08x and 1.06x for mpegaudio on our Intel and AMD systems, and 1.02x for raytrace on both systems. Although the dynamic counts show a reduction in load instructions, we note small slowdowns for compress and jess on our Intel system, and javac on both Intel and AMD machines. These slowdowns were reproducible, and are possibly due to secondary effects such as register pressure or cache behaviour.

These results show that the simplest side-effect analysis, CHA, is sufficient for level 1 optimizations in Jikes RVM. Only local CSE uses side-effect analysis, and since it is only performed on basic blocks (typically small in Java programs), the effect is minimal.

Optimization Level 2. The more advanced and expensive analyses and optimizations in Jikes RVM are level 2 optimizations. They include redundant branch elimination, heap SSA, redundant load elimination, coalescing after heap SSA, expression folding, loop-invariant code motion, global CSE, and transforming while into until loops. As described in section 3, we made use of side-effect information in the heap SSA construction, redundant load elimination, and loop-invariant code motion.

Our benchmarks were run at optimization level 2 in Jikes RVM (all level 0 and 1 optimizations are also performed), and produced identical counts and similar runtimes for the side-effect variations aot-fb, aot-fs, otf-fb and otf-fs (except for one case in compress where the static number of loads eliminated is 388 for aot-fb and aot-fs, and 389 for otf-fb and otf-fs). Thus, we grouped these four variations of side-effect analysis that are based on points-to analysis under the name PTA in Tables 3 and 4. In Table 4, the time under PTA is the average runtime of these four variations.

The first part of Table 3 shows that using side-effect information in RLE increased static opportunities for *getfield* removal by 8% to 79%. There were very few improvements for removing *getstatic* instructions, but the increase was large for *aload* (array load) instructions for some benchmarks (jess, raytrace, mpegaudio and mtrt). For raytrace and mtrt, the total load increase when combining these three bytecode instructions is 98%. Interestingly, PTA improved over CHA for all benchmarks except jack.

The second part of Table 3 shows static counts of instructions moved during LICM. The last two columns are the total instructions moved when LICM is performed on high-level (HIR) and low-level (LIR) intermediate representation in Jikes RVM. Note that memory operations are not moved during LICM on LIR; interestingly, the use of side-effect information in HIR optimizations enabled some other transformations that allowed some instructions to be moved during LICM on LIR. We see that side-effect analysis enabled an increase in the number of moved *getfield* by up to 19%,

Table 3. Level 2 static results

benchmark	side-effect	redundant load elimination (RLE) getfield	getstatic	aload	loop-invariant code motion (LICM) getfield	total HIR	total LIR
compress	none	359	4	0	87	118	29
	CHA	386 (7.5 %)	5 (25.0 %)	0	90 (3.5 %)	122 (3.4 %)	29
	PTA	388 (8.1 %)	5 (25.0 %)	0	90 (3.5 %)	122 (3.4 %)	29
jess	none	722	1	129	139	280	250
	CHA	1050 (45.4 %)	2 (100.0 %)	149 (15.5 %)	144 (3.6 %)	287 (2.5 %)	251 (0.4 %)
	PTA	1106 (53.2 %)	3 (200.0 %)	196 (51.9 %)	161 (15.8 %)	309 (10.4 %)	255 (2.0 %)
raytrace	none	342	1	32	87	184	54
	CHA	613 (79.2 %)	2 (100.0 %)	84 (162.5 %)	96 (10.3 %)	210 (14.1 %)	56 (3.7 %)
	PTA	613 (79.2 %)	2 (100.0 %)	127 (296.9 %)	96 (10.3 %)	210 (14.1 %)	56 (3.7 %)
db	none	243	1	2	61	88	31
	CHA	274 (12.8 %)	4 (300.0 %)	2	64 (4.9 %)	92 (4.6 %)	32 (3.2 %)
	PTA	274 (12.8 %)	4 (300.0 %)	3 (50.0 %)	64 (4.9 %)	92 (4.6 %)	32 (3.2 %)
javac	none	1519	26	90	44	116	479
	CHA	1842 (21.3 %)	30 (15.4 %)	101 (12.2 %)	48 (9.1 %)	121 (4.3 %)	479
	PTA	1847 (21.6 %)	30 (15.4 %)	108 (20.0 %)	48 (9.1 %)	121 (4.3 %)	479
mpegaudio	none	706	212	367	128	299	98
	CHA	804 (13.9 %)	216 (1.9 %)	370 (0.8 %)	152 (18.8 %)	327 (9.4 %)	102 (4.1 %)
	PTA	804 (13.9 %)	216 (1.9 %)	426 (16.1 %)	152 (18.8 %)	327 (9.4 %)	102 (4.1 %)
mtrt	none	342	1	32	87	184	55
	CHA	613 (79.2 %)	2 (100.0 %)	84 (162.5 %)	96 (10.3 %)	210 (14.1 %)	57 (3.6 %)
	PTA	613 (79.2 %)	2 (100.0 %)	127 (296.9 %)	96 (10.3 %)	210 (14.1 %)	57 (3.6 %)
jack	none	678	2	69	23	39	58
	CHA	999 (47.4 %)	16 (700.0 %)	69	23	39	58
	PTA	999 (47.4 %)	16 (700.0 %)	69	23	39	58

and the total instructions during HIR by up to 14%. For only one benchmark (jess), using PTA side-effect information allowed more instructions to be moved than CHA. There were no *putstatic*, *aload* or *astore* instructions moved, and only one additional *putfield* moved for javac (not shown). Note that since RLE is performed before LICM, improved side-effect information can cause loads that would have been moved in LICM to be removed in RLE. Therefore, to measure the impact of side-effect information on LICM, we disabled RLE when collecting the static LICM counts. We do not show static counts for local CSE, which are minimal because redundant load elimination is performed before local CSE.

In the first part of Table 4, we see that side-effect analysis enabled a reduction in dynamic *getfield* operations by up to 27%, but only reduced *getstatic* and *aload* instructions by up to 3%. For compress and jess, using PTA side-effect information allowed a larger reduction of *getfield* than CHA. For mpegaudio, it improved the removal of *aload* instructions. The second part of the table shows speedups achieved for compress, raytrace, mtrt and mpegaudio. The speedups vary from 1.08x to 1.17x on our Intel system, and from 1.02x to 1.20x on AMD. On both systems, mpegaudio has the largest speedup. These benchmarks are the ones with the highest load densities (Table 1), and the ones that we expected would benefit the most from side-effect information.

A higher level of precision of side-effect information made a difference in performance for compress and mpegaudio. Using PTA side-effect analysis vs CHA increased the speedup of compress from 1.08x to 1.11x on Intel, and 1.02x to 1.05x on AMD. For mpegaudio, it went from 1.11x to 1.17x on Intel and from 1.15x to 1.20x on AMD.

These results show that using side-effect analysis in global optimizations improved opportunities for load elimination and moving instructions, reduced dynamic load

Table 4. Level 2 dynamic results

benchmark	side-effect	dynamic counts getfield	getstatic	aload	Intel time(s)	Intel speedup	AMD time(s)	AMD speedup
compress	none	836 681 238	29 585 886	450 569 851	10.423		9.503	
	CHA	713 879 612 (14.7%)	29 585 886	450 569 851	9.635	1.08x	9.316	1.02x
	PTA	694 156 483 (17.0%)	29 585 886	450 569 851	9.386	1.11x	9.03	1.05x
jess	none	193 400 124	2 326 905	74 199 530	4.889		3.949	
	CHA	177 280 681 (8.3%)	2 326 905	74 197 591 (0.0%)	4.945	0.99x	3.962	1.00x
	PTA	141 340 271 (26.9%)	2 326 572 (0.0%)	74 188 965 (0.0%)	4.872	1.00x	4.002	0.99x
raytrace	none	278 990 954	1 359	70 558 731	4.38		2.735	
	CHA	217 369 769 (22.1%)	1 359	70 189 162 (0.5%)	3.93	1.11x	2.607	1.05x
	PTA	217 369 769 (22.1%)	1 359	70 125 938 (0.6%)	3.905	1.12x	2.615	1.05x
db	none	160 085 986	96 012	113 165 950	22.625		23.212	
	CHA	154 814 883 (3.3%)	96 012	113 165 950	22.605	1.00x	23.222	1.00x
	PTA	154 814 883 (3.3%)	96 012	113 165 950	22.471	1.01x	23.141	1.00x
javac	none	129 704 466	3 728 755	3 947 221	10.962		7.154	
	CHA	123 962 720 (4.4%)	3 726 381 (0.1%)	3 947 158 (0.0%)	11.138	0.98x	7.21	0.99x
	PTA	123 962 933 (4.4%)	3 726 306 (0.1%)	3 947 133 (0.0%)	11.142	0.98x	7.231	0.99x
mpegaudio	none	258 084 245	16 092 989	796 126 083	9.319		5.977	
	CHA	254 421 559 (1.4%)	16 075 411 (0.1%)	794 492 856 (0.2%)	8.41	1.11x	5.175	1.15x
	PTA	254 421 559 (1.4%)	16 075 411 (0.1%)	773 557 981 (2.8%)	7.932	1.17x	4.987	1.20x
mtrt	none	282 145 314	2 063	71 578 275	4.681		2.88	
	CHA	220 136 202 (22.0%)	2 063	71 124 467 (0.6%)	4.201	1.11x	2.788	1.03x
	PTA	220 136 202 (22.0%)	2 063	70 998 019 (0.8%)	4.208	1.11x	2.796	1.03x
jack	none	46 154 208	1 534 965	5 727 775	6.097		3.505	
	CHA	42 805 654 (7.3%)	1 530 924 (0.3%)	5 727 775	6.122	1.00x	3.47	1.01x
	PTA	42 805 654 (7.3%)	1 530 924 (0.3%)	5 727 775	6.101	1.00x	3.51	1.00x

operations, and improved performance in runtimes. Benchmarks with higher load densities benefited most from side-effect information. The results also show that points-to analysis improves side-effect information compared to only using CHA, but that the differences between points-to analysis variations are negligible.

5 Related Work

Early side-effect analyses for languages with pointers by Choi *et al.* [4] and Landi *et al.* [14] made use of may-alias analysis to distinguish reads and writes to locations known to be different. These analyses were mainly targeted at analysis of C, so the call graph was assumed to be mostly static. Therefore, in comparison with our work, in that setting, the information about pointers was most important, while the call graph was much easier to compute.

In contrast, Clausen's [6] side-effect analysis for Java was based on a call graph constructed with a CHA-like analysis, but it did not use any pointer information. This analysis computed read and write information for each field, ignoring which specific object contained the field read or written. In comparison with our work, Clausen's analysis is most similar to our CHA-based side-effect analysis. Clausen applies his analysis results in an ahead-of-time early Java bytecode optimizer to a similar set of optimizations as we do: dead code removal, loop invariant removal, constant propagation, and common subexpression elimination.

When evaluating the precision of points-to analyses, it is common to report the size of the points-to sets at field read and write instructions, as in [18, 25]. Rountev and Ryder [26] evaluate their points-to analysis for precompiled libraries in this way. Other points-to analysis work [19, 28, 13, 27] takes this evaluation one step further, by also computing read and write sets summarizing the effects of entire methods, rather than just individual statements, and propagating this information along the call graph. This is similar to the read and write set computation we mention in Section 2.3. In general, these studies conclude that differences in precision of the underlying analyses do have a significant effect on the static precision of side-effect information.

Chowdhury *et al.* [5] study the effect of alias analysis precision on the number of optimization opportunities for a range of scalar optimizations. However, they only measure the static number of optimizations performed (rather than their run-time effect), and their benchmarks are mostly pointer-free C programs, some translated directly from FORTRAN, so they find, unsurprisingly, that alias analysis precision has little effect.

Studies measuring the actual run-time impact of code optimized using side-effect information are surprisingly rare. Ghiya *et al.* [11, 12] measure the effectiveness of side-effect information on the run-time efficiency of code produced by an optimizing compiler for C. Diwan *et al.* [9] study redundant load elimination in Modula-3, using declared types to conservatively approximate aliasing relationships, and method read/write set summaries. The results of Diwan *et al.* on Modula-3 and Ghiya *et al.* on C are comparable to ours on Java. In particular, all three studies show that significant run-time improvements are possible, and that even simple, imprecise alias information enables many of the improvements. Razafimahefa [24] performs loop invariant code motion using side-effect information on Java in an ahead-of-time bytecode optimizer, and reports run-time speedups comparable with ours on an early-generation Java VM.

Pechtchanski and Sarkar [20] present a preliminary study of a framework which allows programmers to provide annotations indicating absence of side-effects. Like our side-effect information, these annotations are communicated to Jikes RVM in class file attributes and used to improve optimizations. Only limited, preliminary, empirical results of the effect of these annotations are provided, and verification of the correctness of the programmer-provided annotations has yet to be done.

In summary, existing work on other languages largely agrees with our findings on Java. Some side-effect information is useful for real run-time improvements from compiler optimizations. Although precision of the underlying analyses tends to have large effects on static counts of optimization opportunities, the effects on dynamic behaviour are much smaller; even simple analyses provide most of the improvement. Distinctions of our work from previous work are that we provide a study of run-time effects of side-effect information on Java, and that we show how to communicate analysis results from an off-line analyzer to a JIT.

6 Conclusion

In this study, we showed that side-effect analysis does improve performance in just-in-time (JIT) compilers, and that relatively simple analyses are sufficient for significant improvements. On level 1 optimizations, side-effect analyses had little impact on performance, except for one benchmark. On level 2 optimizations, however, our results showed an increase of up to 98% of static opportunities for load removal, a reduction of up to 27% of the dynamic fields reads, and execution time speedups ranging from

1.08x to 1.20x. As we expected, using side-effect analysis had the largest impact on the benchmarks with high load densities.

The feasibility of performing side-effect analysis inside the JIT is a topic for future research. The dynamic call graph construction presented in [23,22] is a first step in this work.

References

1. SPEC JVM98 benchmarks. `http://www.spec.org/osg/jvm98/`.
2. B. Alpern, C. R. Attanasio, J. J. Barton, M. G. Burke, P. Cheng, J.-D. Choi, A. Cocchi, S. J. Fink, D. Grove, M. Hind, S. F. Hummel, D. Lieber, V. Litvinov, M. F. Mergen, T. Ngo, J. R. Russell, V. Sarkar, M. J. Serrano, J. C. Shepherd, S. E. Smith, V. C. Sreedhar, H. Srinivasan, and J. Whaley. The Jalapeño virtual machine. *IBM Syst. J.*, 39(1):211–238, 2000.
3. B. Alpern, M. N. Wegman, and F. K. Zadeck. Detecting equality of variables in programs. In *Proceedings of POPL 1988*, pages 1–11, 1988.
4. J.-D. Choi, M. Burke, and P. Carini. Efficient flow-sensitive interprocedural computation of pointer-induced aliases and side effects. In *Proceedings of POPL 1993*, pages 232–245, 1993.
5. R. A. Chowdhury, P. Djeu, B. Cahoon, J. H. Burrill, and K. S. McKinley. The limits of alias analysis for scalar optimizations. In *CC 2004*, volume 2985 of *LNCS*, pages 24–38, 2004.
6. L. R. Clausen. A Java bytecode optimizer using side-effect analysis. *Concurrency: Practice and Experience*, 9(11):1031–1045, Nov. 1997.
7. C. Click. Global code motion/global value numbering. In *Proceedings of PLDI 1995*, pages 246–257, 1995.
8. J. Dean, D. Grove, and C. Chambers. Optimization of object-oriented programs using static class hierarchy analysis. In *ECOOP 95*, volume 952 of *LNCS*, pages 77–101, 1995.
9. A. Diwan, K. S. McKinley, and J. E. B. Moss. Type-based alias analysis. In *Proceedings of PLDI 1998*, pages 106–117, 1998.
10. S. J. Fink, K. Knobe, and V. Sarkar. Unified analysis of array and object references in strongly typed languages. In *Static Analysis Symposium*, pages 155–174, 2000.
11. R. Ghiya and L. J. Hendren. Putting pointer analysis to work. In *Proceedings of POPL 1998*, pages 121–133, 1998.
12. R. Ghiya, D. Lavery, and D. Sehr. On the importance of points-to analysis and other memory disambiguation methods for C programs. In *Proceedings of PLDI 2001*, pages 47–58, 2001.
13. M. Hind and A. Pioli. Which pointer analysis should I use? In *Proceedings of ISSTA 2000*, pages 113–123, 2000.
14. W. Landi, B. G. Ryder, and S. Zhang. Interprocedural modification side effect analysis with pointer aliasing. In *Proceedings of PLDI 1993*, pages 56–67, 1993.
15. O. Lhoták. Spark: A flexible points-to analysis framework for Java. Master's thesis, McGill University, Dec. 2002.
16. O. Lhoták and L. Hendren. Scaling Java points-to analysis using Spark. In *CC 2003*, volume 2622 of *LNCS*, pages 153–169, Warsaw, Poland, 2003.
17. T. Lindholm and F. Yellin. *The Java Virtual Machine Specification*. Addison-Wesley, Reading, MA, USA, second edition, 1999.
18. A. Milanova, A. Rountev, and B. G. Ryder. Parameterized object sensitivity for points-to and side-effect analyses for Java. In *Proceedings of ISSTA 2002*, pages 1–11, 2002.
19. G. Olivar. Fast points-to and side-effect analysis for the McCAT C compiler. M.Sc. project, McGill University, `http://citeseer.ist.psu.edu/350797.html`, Apr. 1997.

20. I. Pechtchanski and V. Sarkar. Immutability specification and its applications. In *Proceedings of the 2002 Joint ACM-ISCOPE Conference on Java Grande*, pages 202–211, 2002.
21. P. Pominville, F. Qian, R. Vallée-Rai, L. Hendren, and C. Verbrugge. A framework for optimizing Java using attributes. In *CC 2001*, volume 2027 of *LNCS*, pages 334–354, 2001.
22. F. Qian and L. Hendren. A study of type analysis for speculative method inlining in a JIT environment. In *CC 2005*, LNCS, Edinburgh, Scotland, April 2005. Springer.
23. F. Qian and L. J. Hendren. Towards dynamic interprocedural analysis in jvms. In *Virtual Machine Research and Technology Symposium*, pages 139–150, 2004.
24. C. Razafimahefa. A study of side-effect analyses for Java. Master's thesis, McGill University, Dec. 1999.
25. A. Rountev, A. Milanova, and B. G. Ryder. Points-to analysis for Java using annotated constraints. In *Proceedings of OOPSLA '01*, pages 43–55, 2001.
26. A. Rountev and B. G. Ryder. Points-to and side-effect analyses for programs built with precompiled libraries. In *CC 2001*, volume 2027 of *LNCS*, pages 20–36, 2001.
27. B. G. Ryder, W. A. Landi, P. A. Stocks, S. Zhang, and R. Altucher. A schema for interprocedural modification side-effect analysis with pointer aliasing. *ACM Transactions on Programming Languages and Systems*, 23(2):105–186, Mar. 2001.
28. P. A. Stocks, B. G. Ryder, W. A. Landi, and S. Zhang. Comparing flow and context sensitivity on the modification-side-effects problem. In *Proceedings of ISSTA 1998*, pages 21–31, 1998.
29. R. Vallée-Rai, E. Gagnon, L. J. Hendren, P. Lam, P. Pominville, and V. Sundaresan. Optimizing Java bytecode using the Soot framework: is it feasible? In *CC 2000*, volume 1781 of *LNCS*, pages 18–34, 2000.

Author Index

Lecture Notes in Computer Science

For information about Vols. 1–3342

please contact your bookseller or Springer

Vol. 3452: F. Baader, A. Voronkov (Eds.), Logic for Programming, Artificial Intelligence, and Reasoning. XI, 562 pages. 2005. (Subseries LNAI).

Vol. 3448: G.R. Raidl, J. Gottlieb (Eds.), Evolutionary Computation in Combinatorial Optimization. XI, 271 pages. 2005.

Vol. 3447: M. Keijzer, A. Tettamanzi, P. Collet, J.v. Hemert, M. Tomassini (Eds.), Genetic Programming. XIII, 382 pages. 2005.

Vol. 3443: R. Bodik (Ed.), Compiler Construction. XI, 305 pages. 2005.

Vol. 3442: M. Cerioli (Ed.), Fundamental Approaches to Software Engineering. XIII, 373 pages. 2005.

Vol. 3441: V. Sassone (Ed.), Foundations of Software Science and Computational Structures. XVIII, 521 pages. 2005.

Vol. 3440: N. Halbwachs, L.D. Zuck (Eds.), Tools and Algorithms for the Construction and Analysis of Systems. XVII, 588 pages. 2005.

Vol. 3436: B. Bouyssounouse, J. Sifakis (Eds.), Embedded Systems Design. XV, 492 pages. 2005.

Vol. 3434: L. Brun, M. Vento (Eds.), Graph-Based Representations in Pattern Recognition. XII, 384 pages. 2005.

Vol. 3433: S. Bhalla (Ed.), Databases in Networked Information Systems. VII, 319 pages. 2005.

Vol. 3432: M. Beigl, P. Lukowicz (Eds.), Systems Aspects in Organic and Pervasive Computing - ARCS 2005. X, 265 pages. 2005.

Vol. 3427: G. Kotsis, O. Spaniol, Wireless Systems and Mobility in Next Generation Internet. VIII, 249 pages. 2005.

Vol. 3423: J.L. Fiadeiro, P.D. Mosses, F. Orejas (Eds.), Recent Trends in Algebraic Development Techniques. VIII, 271 pages. 2005.

Vol. 3422: R.T. Mittermeir (Ed.), From Computer Literacy to Informatics Fundamentals. X, 203 pages. 2005.

Vol. 3421: P. Lorenz, P. Dini (Eds.), Networking - ICN 2005, Part II. XXXV, 1153 pages. 2005.

Vol. 3420: P. Lorenz, P. Dini (Eds.), Networking - ICN 2005, Part I. XXXV, 933 pages. 2005.

Vol. 3419: B. Faltings, A. Petcu, F. Fages, F. Rossi (Eds.), Constraint Satisfaction and Constraint Logic Programming. X, 217 pages. 2005. (Subseries LNAI).

Vol. 3418: U. Brandes, T. Erlebach (Eds.), Network Analysis. XII, 471 pages. 2005.

Vol. 3416: M. Böhlen, J. Gamper, W. Polasek, M.A. Wimmer (Eds.), E-Government: Towards Electronic Democracy. XIII, 311 pages. 2005. (Subseries LNAI).

Vol. 3415: P. Davidsson, B. Logan, K. Takadama (Eds.), Multi-Agent and Multi-Agent-Based Simulation. X, 265 pages. 2005. (Subseries LNAI).

Vol. 3414: M. Morari, L. Thiele (Eds.), Hybrid Systems: Computation and Control. XII, 684 pages. 2005.

Vol. 3412: X. Franch, D. Port (Eds.), COTS-Based Software Systems. XVI, 312 pages. 2005.

Vol. 3411: S.H. Myaeng, M. Zhou, K.-F. Wong, H.-J. Zhang (Eds.), Information Retrieval Technology. XIII, 337 pages. 2005.

Vol. 3410: C.A. Coello Coello, A. Hernández Aguirre, E. Zitzler (Eds.), Evolutionary Multi-Criterion Optimization. XVI, 912 pages. 2005.

Vol. 3409: N. Guelfi, G. Reggio, A. Romanovsky (Eds.), Scientific Engineering of Distributed Java Applications. X, 127 pages. 2005.

Vol. 3408: D.E. Losada, J.M. Fernández-Luna (Eds.), Advances in Information Retrieval. XVII, 572 pages. 2005.

Vol. 3407: Z. Liu, K. Araki (Eds.), Theoretical Aspects of Computing - ICTAC 2004. XIV, 562 pages. 2005.

Vol. 3406: A. Gelbukh (Ed.), Computational Linguistics and Intelligent Text Processing. XVII, 829 pages. 2005.

Vol. 3404: V. Diekert, B. Durand (Eds.), STACS 2005. XVI, 706 pages. 2005.

Vol. 3403: B. Ganter, R. Godin (Eds.), Formal Concept Analysis. XI, 419 pages. 2005. (Subseries LNAI).

Vol. 3401: Z. Li, L.G. Vulkov, J. Waśniewski (Eds.), Numerical Analysis and Its Applications. XIII, 630 pages. 2005.

Vol. 3399: Y. Zhang, K. Tanaka, J.X. Yu, S. Wang, M. Li (Eds.), Web Technologies Research and Development - APWeb 2005. XXII, 1082 pages. 2005.

Vol. 3398: D.-K. Baik (Ed.), Systems Modeling and Simulation: Theory and Applications. XIV, 733 pages. 2005. (Subseries LNAI).

Vol. 3397: T.G. Kim (Ed.), Artificial Intelligence and Simulation. XV, 711 pages. 2005. (Subseries LNAI).

Vol. 3396: R.M. van Eijk, M.-P. Huget, F. Dignum (Eds.), Agent Communication. X, 261 pages. 2005. (Subseries LNAI).

Vol. 3395: J. Grabowski, B. Nielsen (Eds.), Formal Approaches to Software Testing. X, 225 pages. 2005.

Vol. 3394: D. Kudenko, D. Kazakov, E. Alonso (Eds.), Adaptive Agents and Multi-Agent Systems III. VIII, 313 pages. 2005. (Subseries LNAI).

Vol. 3393: H.-J. Kreowski, U. Montanari, F. Orejas, G. Rozenberg, G. Taentzer (Eds.), Formal Methods in Software and Systems Modeling. XXVII, 413 pages. 2005.

Vol. 3391: C. Kim (Ed.), Information Networking. XVII, 936 pages. 2005.

Vol. 3390: R. Choren, A. Garcia, C. Lucena, A. Romanovsky (Eds.), Software Engineering for Multi-Agent Systems III. XII, 291 pages. 2005.

Vol. 3389: P. Van Roy (Ed.), Multiparadigm Programming in Mozart/OZ. XV, 329 pages. 2005.

Vol. 3388: J. Lagergren (Ed.), Comparative Genomics. VII, 133 pages. 2005. (Subseries LNBI).

Vol. 3387: J. Cardoso, A. Sheth (Eds.), Semantic Web Services and Web Process Composition. VIII, 147 pages. 2005.

Vol. 3386: S. Vaudenay (Ed.), Public Key Cryptography - PKC 2005. IX, 436 pages. 2005.

Vol. 3385: R. Cousot (Ed.), Verification, Model Checking, and Abstract Interpretation. XII, 483 pages. 2005.

Vol. 3383: J. Pach (Ed.), Graph Drawing. XII, 536 pages. 2005.

Vol. 3382: J. Odell, P. Giorgini, J.P. Müller (Eds.), Agent-Oriented Software Engineering V. X, 239 pages. 2005.

Vol. 3381: P. Vojtáš, M. Bieliková, B. Charron-Bost, O. Sýkora (Eds.), SOFSEM 2005: Theory and Practice of Computer Science. XV, 448 pages. 2005.

Vol. 3380: C. Priami, Transactions on Computational Systems Biology I. IX, 111 pages. 2005. (Subseries LNBI).

Vol. 3379: M. Hemmje, C. Niederee, T. Risse (Eds.), From Integrated Publication and Information Systems to Information and Knowledge Environments. XXIV, 321 pages. 2005.

Vol. 3378: J. Kilian (Ed.), Theory of Cryptography. XII, 621 pages. 2005.

Vol. 3377: B. Goethals, A. Siebes (Eds.), Knowledge Discovery in Inductive Databases. VII, 190 pages. 2005.

Vol. 3376: A. Menezes (Ed.), Topics in Cryptology – CT-RSA 2005. X, 385 pages. 2005.

Vol. 3375: M.A. Marsan, G. Bianchi, M. Listanti, M. Meo (Eds.), Quality of Service in Multiservice IP Networks. XIII, 656 pages. 2005.

Vol. 3374: D. Weyns, H.V.D. Parunak, F. Michel (Eds.), Environments for Multi-Agent Systems. X, 279 pages. 2005. (Subseries LNAI).

Vol. 3372: C. Bussler, V. Tannen, I. Fundulaki (Eds.), Semantic Web and Databases. X, 227 pages. 2005.

Vol. 3371: M.W. Barley, N. Kasabov (Eds.), Intelligent Agents and Multi-Agent Systems. X, 329 pages. 2005. (Subseries LNAI).

Vol. 3370: A. Konagaya, K. Satou (Eds.), Grid Computing in Life Science. X, 188 pages. 2005. (Subseries LNBI).

Vol. 3369: V.R. Benjamins, P. Casanovas, J. Breuker, A. Gangemi (Eds.), Law and the Semantic Web. XII, 249 pages. 2005. (Subseries LNAI).

Vol. 3368: L. Paletta, J.K. Tsotsos, E. Rome, G.W. Humphreys (Eds.), Attention and Performance in Computational Vision. VIII, 231 pages. 2005.

Vol. 3367: W.S. Ng, B.C. Ooi, A. Ouksel, C. Sartori (Eds.), Databases, Information Systems, and Peer-to-Peer Computing. X, 231 pages. 2005.

Vol. 3366: I. Rahwan, P. Moraitis, C. Reed (Eds.), Argumentation in Multi-Agent Systems. XII, 263 pages. 2005. (Subseries LNAI).

Vol. 3365: G. Mauri, G. Păun, M.J. Pérez-Jiménez, G. Rozenberg, A. Salomaa (Eds.), Membrane Computing. IX, 415 pages. 2005.

Vol. 3363: T. Eiter, L. Libkin (Eds.), Database Theory - ICDT 2005. XI, 413 pages. 2004.

Vol. 3362: G. Barthe, L. Burdy, M. Huisman, J.-L. Lanet, T. Muntean (Eds.), Construction and Analysis of Safe, Secure, and Interoperable Smart Devices. IX, 257 pages. 2005.

Vol. 3361: S. Bengio, H. Bourlard (Eds.), Machine Learning for Multimodal Interaction. XII, 362 pages. 2005.

Vol. 3360: S. Spaccapietra, E. Bertino, S. Jajodia, R. King, D. McLeod, M.E. Orlowska, L. Strous (Eds.), Journal on Data Semantics II. XI, 223 pages. 2005.

Vol. 3359: G. Grieser, Y. Tanaka (Eds.), Intuitive Human Interfaces for Organizing and Accessing Intellectual Assets. XIV, 257 pages. 2005. (Subseries LNAI).

Vol. 3358: J. Cao, L.T. Yang, M. Guo, F. Lau (Eds.), Parallel and Distributed Processing and Applications. XXIV, 1058 pages. 2004.

Vol. 3357: H. Handschuh, M.A. Hasan (Eds.), Selected Areas in Cryptography. XI, 354 pages. 2004.

Vol. 3356: G. Das, V.P. Gulati (Eds.), Intelligent Information Technology. XII, 428 pages. 2004.

Vol. 3355: R. Murray-Smith, R. Shorten (Eds.), Switching and Learning in Feedback Systems. X, 343 pages. 2005.

Vol. 3354: M. Margenstern (Ed.), Machines, Computations, and Universality. VIII, 329 pages. 2005.

Vol. 3353: J. Hromkovič, M. Nagl, B. Westfechtel (Eds.), Graph-Theoretic Concepts in Computer Science. XI, 404 pages. 2004.

Vol. 3352: C. Blundo, S. Cimato (Eds.), Security in Communication Networks. XI, 381 pages. 2005.

Vol. 3351: G. Persiano, R. Solis-Oba (Eds.), Approximation and Online Algorithms. VIII, 295 pages. 2005.

Vol. 3350: M. Hermenegildo, D. Cabeza (Eds.), Practical Aspects of Declarative Languages. VIII, 269 pages. 2005.

Vol. 3349: B.M. Chapman (Ed.), Shared Memory Parallel Programming with Open MP. X, 149 pages. 2005.

Vol. 3348: A. Canteaut, K. Viswanathan (Eds.), Progress in Cryptology - INDOCRYPT 2004. XIV, 431 pages. 2004.

Vol. 3347: R.K. Ghosh, H. Mohanty (Eds.), Distributed Computing and Internet Technology. XX, 472 pages. 2004.

Vol. 3346: R.H. Bordini, M. Dastani, J. Dix, A.E.F. Seghrouchni (Eds.), Programming Multi-Agent Systems. XIV, 249 pages. 2005. (Subseries LNAI).

Vol. 3345: Y. Cai (Ed.), Ambient Intelligence for Scientific Discovery. XII, 311 pages. 2005. (Subseries LNAI).

Vol. 3344: J. Malenfant, B.M. Østvold (Eds.), Object-Oriented Technology. ECOOP 2004 Workshop Reader. VIII, 215 pages. 2005.

Vol. 3343: C. Freksa, M. Knauff, B. Krieg-Brückner, B. Nebel, T. Barkowsky (Eds.), Spatial Cognition IV. Reasoning, Action, and Interaction. XIII, 519 pages. 2005. (Subseries LNAI).